American Traditions: Art from the Collections of Culver Alumni

BENTON · HA
PRENDERGA
SARGENT · W
REMINGTON
THIEBAUD ·
CASSATT · H
BIERSTADT
CHURCH · RU

AMERICAN TRADITIONS

ART FROM THE COLLECTIONS OF CULVER ALUMNI

Indianapolis Museum of Art
Eiteljorg Museum of American Indian and Western Art
Indianapolis Museum of Art – Columbus Gallery

in association with
The Culver Educational Foundation

American Traditions:
Art from the Collections of Culver Alumni
December 12, 1993 – March 6, 1994

Indianapolis Museum of Art
American Painting 1825 – 1945

Eiteljorg Museum of American Indian and Western Art
Western American Art 1822 – 1991

Indianapolis Museum of Art – Columbus Gallery
American Art 1953 – 1992

Library of Congress
Catalog Number 93-61168
ISBN 0-936260-59-9

This publication was organized at the
Indianapolis Museum of Art by
Jane Graham, Publications Manager.

Edited by Debra Edelstein
Medford, Massachusetts

Designed by
Richard Poulin Design Group Inc.
New York, New York
Typeset in Monotype Bembo
and Berthold Clarendon
Printed in the
United States of America by
Benham Press, Indianapolis, Indiana

© 1993
Indianapolis Museum of Art
1200 West 38th Street
Indianapolis, Indiana 46208.4196

Editor's Note: In this publication
the abbreviation *c.* indicates an
approximate date. Dimensions for
each work of art appear in the
sequence of height precedes width
precedes depth. The following
abbreviations have been adopted to
indicate the location of artists'
signatures or inscriptions:

ll – lower left
lc – lower center
lr – lower right
ul – upper left
ur – upper right
mr – middle right

A slash (/) indicates that the
signature or inscription carries over
to another line.

CONTENTS

K. S. "Bud" Adams, Jr.

James W. F. and Donna K. Brooks Collection

Collection of Paul and Fredrica Cassiday

The Culver Educational Foundation

The Dicke Collection, New Bremen, Ohio

Terry Huffington Dittman

Janet and Craig Duchossois

The Gund Collection of Western Art

Collection of Mr. and Mrs. Graham Gund

Ray J. Hillenbrand

Huffington Collection

Mrs. Edward Ingersoll

The R. C. Kemper Charitable Trust and Foundation and the
        Enid and Crosby Kemper Foundation

Phillip M. Knox

William I. Koch Collection

H. Ward Lay

Collection of Mr. and Mrs. Joseph T. Mendelson

Mr. and Mrs. Charles B. Moncrief

Mr. and Mrs. Richard W. Moncrief

Mr. and Mrs. W. A. Moncrief, Jr.

Private Collection, Mexico

Harry M. Rhett, Jr.

Spring Creek Art Foundation, Inc.

Mr. and Mrs. Jon R. Stuart

Dwight Sutherland

United Missouri Bank

The Warner Collection, Tuscaloosa, Alabama

Weil Brothers

Mr. and Mrs. Bucky Wharton

Whitney Museum of American Art

Collection of Mr. and Mrs. Frederic D. Wolfe

Anonymous Lenders

American Traditions: Art from the Collections of Culver Alumni raises a question. What bond do
these collectors, who have loaned such high-quality works of art to this exhibition, share
through Culver?

Preparation for "leadership and responsible citizenship in society" has
been the mission of Culver virtually since its inception one hundred years ago. This mission
has special significance in a democracy and is even more important today, given the stresses and
challenges we confront in our society. It is expressed in the statement of Mission and
Objectives that follows. The key elements were forged in Culver's early years, have guided it
successfully through its first century, and will remain the blueprint for its future.

Culver's broad offerings are rooted in the Classical Greek ideal of an
educated person. Academic preparation of the highest order is the preeminent objective of
the school, but Culver is also distinguished from most other schools by its emphasis on the
moral, spiritual, and physical development of its students. Character development, leadership,
personal honor and integrity, self-discipline, acceptance of responsibility, and appreciation
of diversity are the cornerstones of a Culver education. These aspects attract young men
and women from more than forty states and from fifteen to twenty countries to Culver's
regular program and to its unique summer program, attended by more than 1,200 young
people each year.

This all takes place on an exceptional 1,700-acre campus, with more
than thirty-five buildings, many with a castle's majesty, of Flemish and Gothic design in red
brick and limestone. The campus is situated on the northern shore of Indiana's Lake
Maxinkuckee, whose beauty and serenity have inspired Hoosier authors from James Whitcomb
Riley to Kurt Vonnegut, Jr.

The education works, as the accomplishments of its alumni testify.
The men and women who have loaned art to this exhibition are examples. That education
may also have influenced the type of art Culver alumni have and have not collected, as
Bret Waller and Michael Duty, the directors of the participating museums, have helped us
understand. A basic optimism, a belief that an individual can make a difference, and a spirit of
independence and discovery are all evident in the collections. We wish to thank all of our
Culver lenders for their willingness to support this exhibition. We appreciate that they have
disrupted their collections and, in some cases, given up pieces that are important in their
homes, especially at holiday time, when the home takes on a special focus.

The inspiration for this exhibition came from Jack Warner '36,
Tuscaloosa, Alabama, whose personal collection and that of the Gulf States Paper Company,
of which he was chairman, form an important part of the exhibition. He chaired the
organizing committee on which Jim Dicke '64, New Bremen, Ohio, and Jon Stuart '67,
Tulsa, Oklahoma, also served with distinction.

We would like to thank Bret Waller, director, and Ellen Lee, chief
curator, of the Indianapolis Museum of Art, and Michael Duty, executive director of the
Eiteljorg Museum of American Indian and Western Art. The professionalism, cooperation,

and warmth of these individuals and their staffs made this project to commemorate Culver's centennial a truly enjoyable experience.

James A. Henderson
President
Board of Trustees

Ralph N. Manuel
President
Culver Academies

The Culver Mission

Culver strives to prepare its students for leadership and responsible citizenship in society by developing and nurturing the whole individual—mind, character, spirit, and body.

Objectives

Culver is a unique college preparatory school with a diverse student population. Our preeminent objective is to foster intellectual growth through a demanding curriculum that prepares students for admission to and success in higher education and for a lifetime of intellectual curiosity and learning.

We believe leadership can be taught. Culver Military Academy is organized around our own distinctive military system of student leadership. Culver Girls Academy is modeled on a prefect system of leadership. Both are designed to provide our students with practical experience in leadership.

Character development is essential to our mission. We seek to have our students understand and uphold the values of self-discipline, personal responsibility, justice, respect for self and others, appreciation of diversity, and, above all, honor.

We are committed to the spiritual development of our students through personal reflection, individual counseling, small group experiences, and participation in religious services.

We believe physical fitness and extracurricular activities complement intellectual, spiritual, and character development. Our rich and varied athletic and extracurricular program is designed to present our students of all skill and experience levels with opportunities for individual growth and development of lifetime interests.

P R E F A C E

When Jim Henderson, president of the board of The Culver Educational Foundation, approached us with the idea for an exhibition of art from the collections of Culver alumni, we were, frankly, skeptical. Polite, of course, but skeptical. Both of us have seen enough university alumni exhibitions over the years to know that these usually turn out to be grab bags of the good, the bad, and the indifferent. Why, we asked ourselves, should we expect anything more from the graduates of a small college preparatory school—even one with so long and distinguished a history as Culver? We still have not found a completely satisfactory answer to the question of why it should be so, but as the evidence of the exhibition documented in these pages proves beyond all doubt, Culver can count among its alumni some of the most discriminating and devoted art collectors in this hemisphere. Their dedication to Culver, as evidenced by their willingness to part for a period of several months with the treasured works of art included in this exhibition, is equally remarkable.

The tripartite exhibition, which this catalogue accompanies, celebrates the centennial of Culver's founding. The exhibition is taking place simultaneously at three different Indiana venues: the Indianapolis Museum of Art (art before 1945), the Eiteljorg Museum of American Indian and Western Art (Western and American Indian art), and the Columbus Gallery of the Indianapolis Museum of Art (contemporary art), where it inaugurates a splendid new facility. Collaboration among these three organizations, together with The Culver Educational Foundation and the generous lenders listed elsewhere in the catalogue, has made the entire enterprise possible.

How and when the art collecting bug found its way into Culver's drinking water supply, Lake Maxinkuckee, remains a mystery beyond our ability to solve. The following observations, therefore, are offered with the more modest aim of stimulating the reader's own reflection on and enjoyment of the superb works of art brought together in our galleries for this unique occasion.

The exhibition is called *American Traditions*. We have used the plural advisedly—traditions, not tradition—because there are several interrelated themes that merit attention. In discussing them we will not restrict our attention to the succession of "isms" that forms the narrative backbone for most textbook histories of American art. Some of the most interesting aspects of collecting by Culver alumni have as much to do with social and cultural history as with the history of art. The introduction to this volume, which tells the story of the arts at Culver, offers a valuable insider's view of this phenomenon. As outsiders, we view the Culver phenomenon with fascination, but from a necessarily different, and we hope enlightening, perspective.

I must study politics and war that my sons may have liberty to study mathematics and philosophy. My sons ought to study mathematics and philosophy, geography, natural history and naval architecture, navigation, commerce, and agriculture, in order to give their children a right to study painting, poetry, music, architecture.

The evolutionary sequence posited in John Adams's letter to his wife, Abigail, written during this nation's struggle for independence, seems to have been internalized, compressed, and individually experienced by many of the Culver collectors we have met. Through some obscure alchemy, an education grounded in self-discipline and the study of the liberal arts has created in some of Culver's graduates a taste for art and the acumen to collect wisely. We have not conducted a scientific survey, but it is our strong impression that the great majority of Culver alumni who collect art tend to concentrate on the art of their own country. Some Culver collections have an admixture of European works, but most seem to be largely or exclusively comprised of paintings and sculpture by American artists. Hence, this exhibition's focus on American traditions.

The collecting interests of Culver alumni, however, are not evenly distributed across the broad field of American art. Certain schools and historical periods have attracted the attention of numerous Culver collectors, while others of comparable significance are less popular. We have found relatively few works, for example, by members of the so-called Ash Can School—early twentieth-century artists including John Sloan, George Bellows, George Luks, and William Glackens, who began their careers painting life in the tenements and teeming streets of America's burgeoning cities. Nor have we discovered many examples of Depression-era social realism, like Reginald Marsh's meticulously rendered depiction of unemployed men standing stoically in a bread line.

Culver alumni, to judge from the art they collect, are optimists. They favor paintings that celebrate the natural beauty of this vast land or the accomplishments and sometimes heroic exploits of its people. In the segment of the exhibition shown at the Indianapolis Museum of Art, devoted to art from before the Second World War, landscape holds the place of honor. More than a third of the sixty works in this section are representations of mountains, seas, lakes, woods, and prairies. These are mostly American scenes, though a few, like Arthur Wesley Dow's *A Field, Kerlaouen*, depict locations outside the United States. Thomas Cole's *Falls of Kaaterskill*, painted in 1826, is the earliest pure landscape in the exhibition, and one of the finest, capturing as it does not only the beauty of a wild and rugged landscape, but also the boundless optimism with which American artists of Cole's generation celebrated the wonders of their land. One of the most recent landscapes in this portion of the exhibition—if the admixture of narrative does not disqualify it from classification as a landscape—is Grant Wood's Depression-era rural scene called *Arbor Day*. Painted in 1932, its tidy Iowa buildings, well-kept fields, and clear blue skies give no hint of the tragedy then being played out in the Dust Bowl a few hundred miles to the west in Kansas and Oklahoma.

The Western frontier is a subject that Culver alumni find particularly appealing. In this, of course, their collections recapitulate an important aspect of the history of American art, which recorded the westward movement of settlers of European origin. From painters of the Hudson River School, like Cole and Frederic Church, who sought to develop a distinctively American vernacular with which to describe a distinctly American landscape, to Albert Bierstadt and Thomas Moran, who glorified the landscape of the far West, to George

Catlin, who early recorded the appearances and customs of the Plains Indians, to Frederic Remington and Charles Marion Russell, who, in the years when the Old West was dying, gave definitive visual form to its mythos, painters and paintings of the frontier hold a particular fascination for Culver collectors. Several, in fact, have chosen to specialize in Western subjects. If sculpture is included in the count, there probably are more works by Remington in Culver alumni collections than by any other single artist.

One can also discern across the spectrum of these collections a keen interest in the urbane world of New York and New England. This is especially evident in the landscapes of American impressionists like Frederick Childe Hassam, Willard Leroy Metcalf, John Henry Twachtman, and Theodore Robinson and in the elegant figural pieces by John Singer Sargent, Frederick Carl Frieseke, William Merritt Chase, and others from the decades just before and just after the turn of the century. The hypercivilized East of Henry James and the Wild West of Bret Harte are the opposite poles of the axis upon which the world of Culver collecting turns.

Early modernists—with the notable exception of Georgia O'Keeffe—are largely absent. Stuart Davis, the arch abstractionist, is not to be found, while Arthur Dove and Marsden Hartley (in his abstractionist phase) are rarely seen. On the other hand, their Regionalist contemporaries Thomas Hart Benton, Grant Wood, and John Steuart Curry are all represented by significant works. These three were in the vanguard of the "American Scene" movement that flourished briefly in the years just prior to the Second World War. Their determinedly American styles and subjects seem to hold for Culver alumni the same appeal that they had for the art critic Thomas Craven, whose portrait by Benton is included in the exhibition. Craven was both prophet and evangelist for a new, distinctively American art that he saw as a "revolt against European imitation" that would put an end "to our provincial servility."

Most of the Culver alumni collections we have been privileged to see concentrate on American painting from the middle of the nineteenth century to around the time of World War II, but several extend all the way to the present, and a few deal exclusively with contemporary art. We find it interesting to note that although at least one distinguished Culver collection focuses almost exclusively on nonrepresentational art, most of the collections that include contemporary art exhibit a decided preference for figuration, for art that deals with recognizable images, however distorted or abstracted. Works by contemporary figurative painters such as Janet Fish, Robert Cottingham, and Wayne Thiebaud are found more often than are the works of nonrepresentational artists like Josef Albers and Mark Rothko. Even so, the part of the exhibition focusing on art since 1945 contains a number of fine works by staunch abstractionists like Richard Diebenkorn and Linda Benglis.

We have noted, in this short essay, several qualities that can be found in most of the collections assembled by Culver alumni—at least those we have seen: a focus on American art; a taste for landscape, with a particular interest in scenes of the frontier and the American West; a countervailing fascination with the sophisticated portraiture and domesticated landscapes of the Northeast; a preference for figuration, even in contemporary art; a lack of interest either in early modernism or in contemporaneous social realism; and, finally, a delight in art that celebrates this country's natural beauty and the achievements of its people. Do these features add up to a Culver "look" or a Culver "style"? By no means! The lenders to this exhibition are individualists who chart their own courses. Each collection reflects the personal tastes of its owner or owners. There are far too many exceptions to our "rules" to make us want to claim for them anything more than a general applicability to the phenomenon we have discussed.

There is, however, one thing that more than any other characterizes the collecting of Culver alumni: a commitment to quality. This can be seen in the smallest collections from which we have drawn as well as the largest, in the most delicate watercolor sketch as well as the grandest canvas. The aesthetic merit of the works included in this exhibition is great enough to justify pride on the part of all Culver alumni, to provoke the covetousness of museum directors, and to stimulate both the admiration of the public and, we hope, the satisfaction of the collectors who have so generously shared their treasures with us.

Bret Waller
Director
Indianapolis Museum of Art

Michael W. Duty
Executive Director
Eiteljorg Museum of American Indian and Western Art

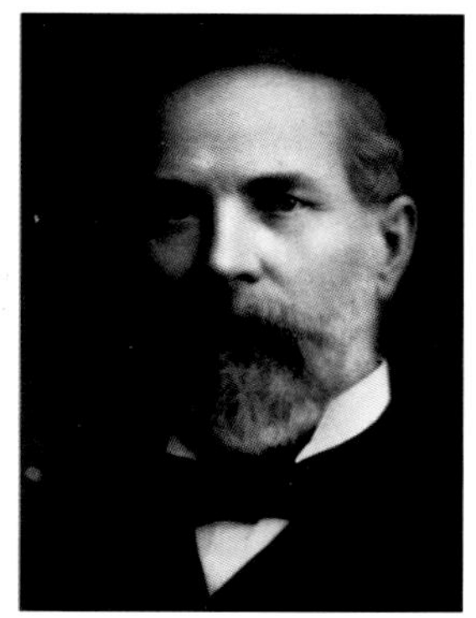

**Henry Harrison Culver
1840-1897**

*The founder of Culver Military
Academy used the camp
buildings of his financially
unsuccessful chautauqua to
build the school. The doors of
the Academy opened in
September 1894.*

Main Barrack

*The dedication of Main Barrack
in 1895 provided Culver
Military Academy with a three-
story brick, concrete, and steel
building. It contained sleeping
accommodations for ninety,
classrooms and mess hall on the
first floor, a chapel, infirmary,
and administrative offices. The
building at the right is the
tabernacle, which was converted
into a gymnasium. The white
structure was H. H. Culver's
boat house.*

I saw in my mind's eye where the school would have to be, and I began to prepare the ground for its location. It has been one of my castles in the air.
Henry Harrison Culver

Those were heady words for a fifty-four-year-old entrepreneur from St. Louis whose formal education totaled two years. Yet the century was the nineteenth—a golden time in America when there were no mountains too steep to climb, no obstacles the determined could not conquer.

Henry Harrison Culver, the founder of the Culver Military Academy, had started life on a hardscrabble farm in southern Ohio, and, at the age of fifteen, had "gone west" to Springfield, Illinois, where he sold cookstoves for a local hardware merchant. In the early 1870s he moved to St. Louis and, with two brothers, established the Wrought Iron Range Company, which manufactured a variety of cookstoves that were marketed across the Midwest.

A decade later, with the success of his business venture assured, Culver began to purchase land on the northeast shore of Lake Maxinkuckee in northern Indiana, and in 1886 he built a handsome seasonal residence there. It became a center for social activities, where members of the resort community and friends from Missouri were entertained throughout the summer months.

Always seeking new economic opportunities, Culver constructed a hotel and tabernacle in 1889 and developed about forty of his three hundred acres as a chautauqua, modeled on the educational institution founded by the Methodists in New York. While it drew substantial crowds, the chautauqua was a financial failure; and after two years of losses the operation was abandoned. With this as a dubious backdrop, Culver then decided to bring his "castle in the air" down to earth and start a school, utilizing the former camp buildings as the core of an evolving campus. The doors to Culver Military Academy opened in September 1894.

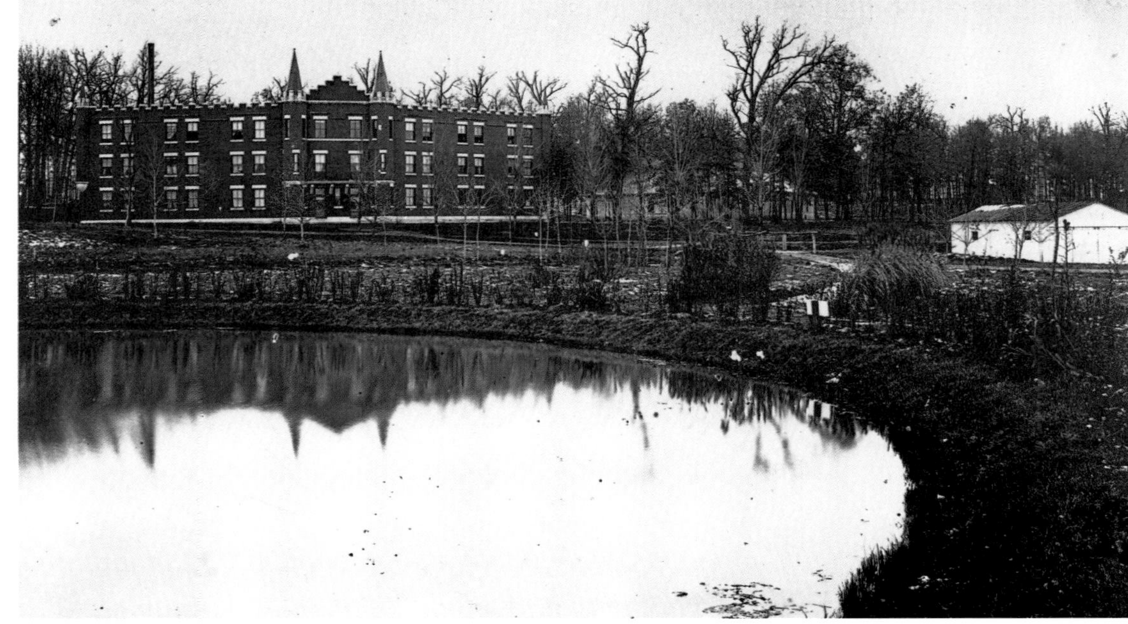

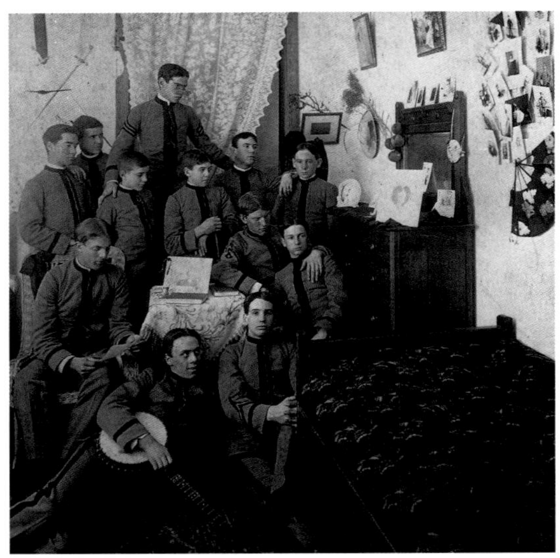

Cadet Room

The good old days of 1897 included this cadet room in Main Barrack, complete with lace curtains, dresser, mirror, postcard display, and several photographs. Early group photographs of cadets inevitably had someone holding a ukulele and mandolin.

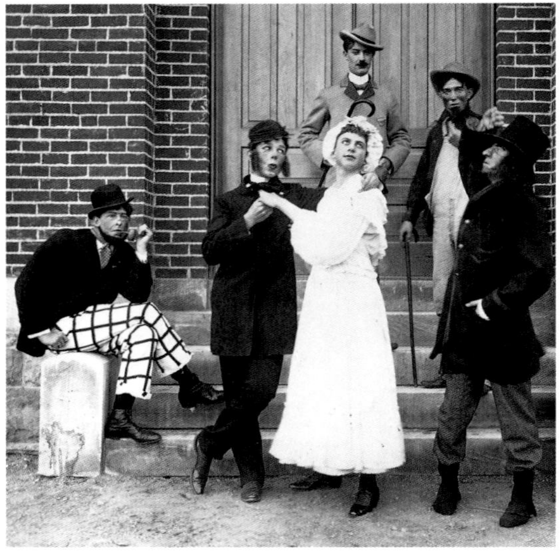

Theatricals 1900

Without the benefit of females, a creative theater director was able to present stage productions by coercing cadets into taking the female roles.

Initially, the struggle for success was fraught with problems in both administration and enrollment. In 1896, however, fire destroyed the Missouri Military Academy, and its head, Colonel Alexander Frederick Fleet, accepted Culver's invitation to move his student body and faculty to Indiana. This transfusion resulted in an amazing expansion, and by 1900 enrollment reached 260 boys, thus ensuring the Academy's financial viability.

After Culver's death at the age of fifty-seven in 1897, two of his sons, Edwin and Bertram, devoted themselves to realizing their father's dream. Edwin became intimately involved in the design and placement of the twenty-three buildings that comprised the pre-1925 campus. He worked closely with the great Norwegian landscape architect Jens Jensen and with St. Louis native Albert Knell, the Academy's architect from 1896 to 1924, to create the signature design of the campus, including the Americanized Tudor-Gothic buildings.

As the school grew, it underwent a rather remarkable metamorphosis. It became a military school that was not militaristic in philosophy. Few of its graduates embraced *combat de arms* as a profession, although its well-trained alumni stepped to the colors as citizen soldiers when the nation called. Nearly 3,500 served in the First World War and over 6,700 in the Second World War, Korea, and Vietnam. Instead, the education of the "whole boy," and since 1971 young women, became the linchpin of the school.

What has become *American Traditions: Art from the Collections of Culver Alumni* may have had its genesis in the discipline of a parade ground, but it was nurtured in the classroom and stemmed from an educational mission to produce leaders in business, industry, and for the nation. These objectives required attention not only to academic rigors, but also to the cultural aspects of gentlemanly behavior.

From the Academy's earliest days, music and theater played a vital part in both the entertainment and education of the students. Skits, plays, musicals, and declamation appeared on the weekly schedule and did much in the eras before film and television to stimulate the cultural imagination of the student body.

In the early 1920s the Academy hired a remarkable individual to teach public speaking and acting and to direct the theater program. Charles Mather, author of the acclaimed book *Behind the Footlights*, a discourse on acting, stagecraft, make-up, and lighting, had an extraordinary ability to spot talent and nurture it to maturity, which made him a highly visible person in American theater for nearly four decades. His proudest achievement was developing the talents of young thespians.

During a period of more than thirty-five years at the Academy, his successful students included director-producer Josh Logan '27, who received laurels for Broadway and Hollywood extravaganzas and a Pulitzer Prize for directing *South Pacific*; Edmund North '28, whose script for the movie *Patton* won an Academy Award; Ernest K. Gann '30, author of over twenty books, including *The High and the Mighty*, *Twilight of the Gods*, and the autobiography *Fate is the Hunter*—all of which were made into major motion pictures. Still in front of the footlights and the camera is Hal Holbrook '42, who continues to tread the

American Traditions: Art from the Collections of Culver Alumni

Legion Memorial Building

Familiar to all alumni, this building is a monument to the gallant men of the Academy who lost their lives in the Great War. Its cornerstone was laid in 1919. Labor difficulties delayed the completion until 1924, when it was dedicated on November 2. The great front entrance was modeled from the Hurst-Monceau Castle in Sussex, England, built in 1440.

In the Movies

The 1932 film Tom Brown of Culver *was made on the Academy campus and at Universal Studios in California. The technical advisor was Colonel Robert Rossow, commandant, left, and the director was William Wyler, right.*

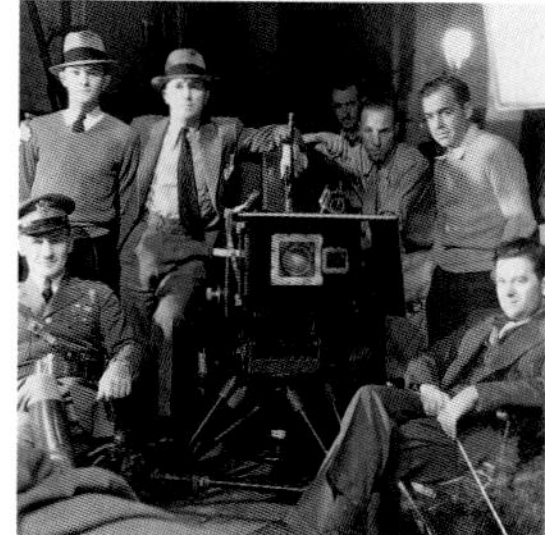

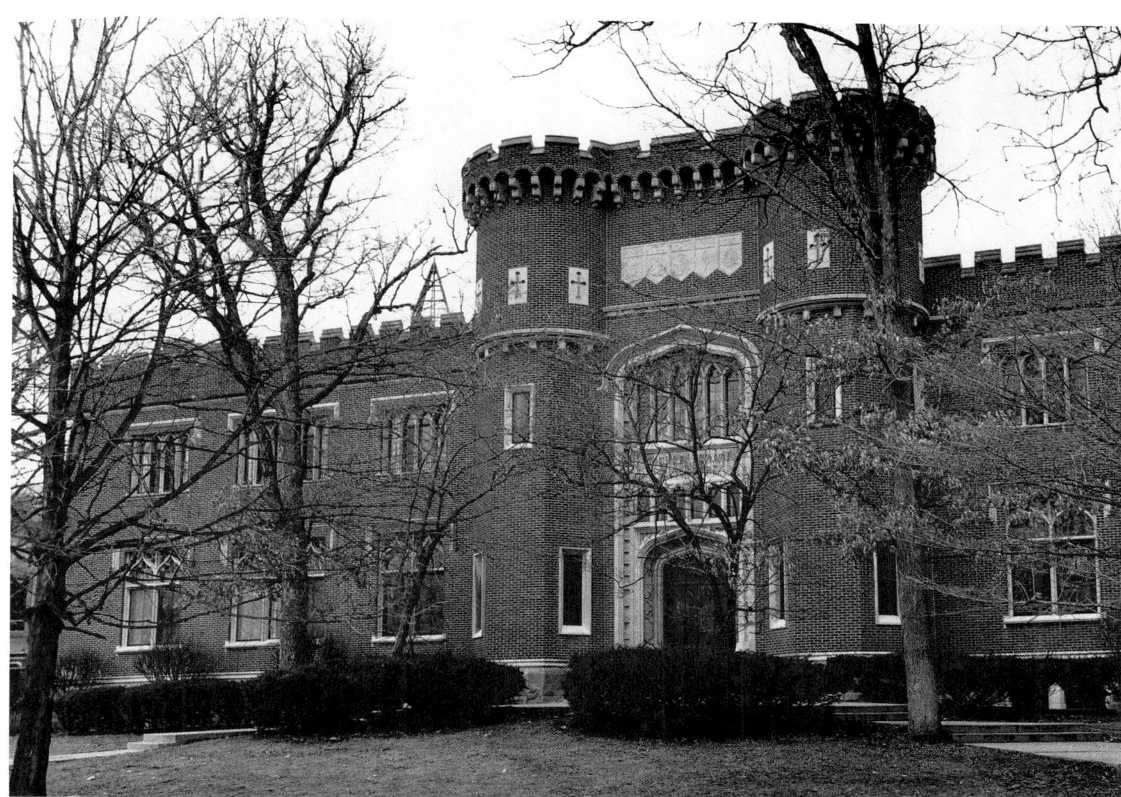

stage with his remarkable one-man presentation *Mark Twain Tonight*, who performs regularly in the television series *Evening Shade*, and whose most recent film role was in *The Firm*.

More than anyone, however, it was the Academy's fourth superintendent, General Leigh R. Gignilliat, who created the environment that enabled music and the fine arts to thrive within an institution built on a military framework. He recruited for the Culver faculty individuals who brought great diversity and scholarship to the institution. Five Rhodes Scholars, master teachers from Czarist Russia, French and Spanish scholars, and graduates of Cambridge and Oxford joined their faculty colleagues in expanding the educational horizons of the student body.

In 1925 General Gignilliat initiated the first major art effort on the campus. He commissioned a young Indiana artist, Hugh Poe, to prepare from photographs over sixty pastels of Culver men who had fallen in World War I. The resulting portraits were on display until the 1950s in the Legion Memorial Building, the turreted building patterned after the Hurst-Monceau Castle in England, whose magnificent lounges provide a perfect setting for exhibitions.

The following year the Academy became a major participant in the newly formed Hoosier Salon, a group of art aficionados dedicated to promoting Indiana artists. With the blessing of the Academy's board of trustees, Gignilliat authorized a substantial prize for the best Hoosier artist under the age of twenty-six. As the salon's reputation grew, particularly as a result of an annual show of about 150 works at the art department of Chicago's Marshall Fields store, Culver's place in the cultural milieu became more apparent.

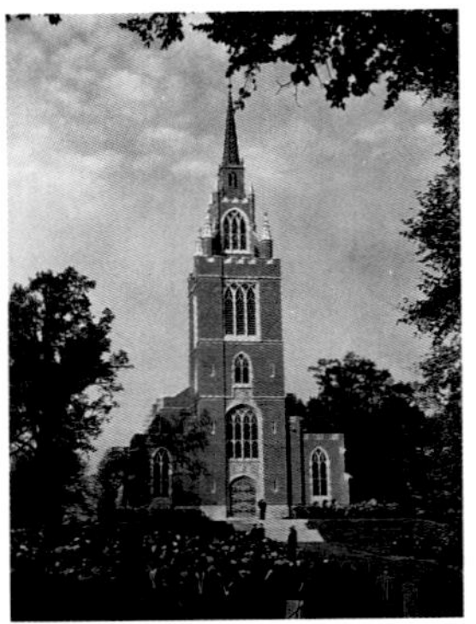

Memorial Chapel

Shortly after World War II, alumni expressed a wish to commemorate the more than 6,500 alumni who had served in the conflict. Architect Jens Frederick Larson was selected to prepare a design, and construction began in April 1950. On October 21, 1951, the Memorial Chapel was formally dedicated.

**Culver Academy Campus
1968**

Equally significant for the students was the Academy's affiliation with the American Federation of Arts. Throughout the 1920s and 1930s the Academy was a regular venue for the AFA's traveling exhibitions, and each year this organization brought upward of fifty paintings to the campus for a two-week exhibit. Through these exhibitions, as well as classes and individual tutoring, Culver students were able to gain a greater understanding of art and its place in our culture. They were also introduced to the world of collecting, since many of the works were available to the buying public, with delivery at the conclusion of the exhibition.

These shows spurred a growing interest in art among the students. The class of 1928, for instance, commissioned Robert Grafton to paint four murals in the dining hall, each focusing on a major event in Indiana history. This marked the first of many class gifts that were to recognize the arts as an essential element of the visual identity of the campus.

Sculpture found a special place along the Academy walkways. Reproductions of heroic bronzes such as Cyrus Dallin's *Appeal to the Great Spirit* and *The Scout*, the anonymous *Roman Gladiator*, and more contemporary pieces are now a cherished part of the campus grounds.

By 1938 paintings had become a major element in the lives of Culver cadets. The graduating class of that year presented the Academy with five prize-winning paintings from the fourteenth Hoosier Salon exhibition. Two years later the Academy dedicated a new building devoted to music and the arts, hired a full-time artist-in-residence, and expanded its cultural offerings.

The opening of this new facility provided the first permanent home to

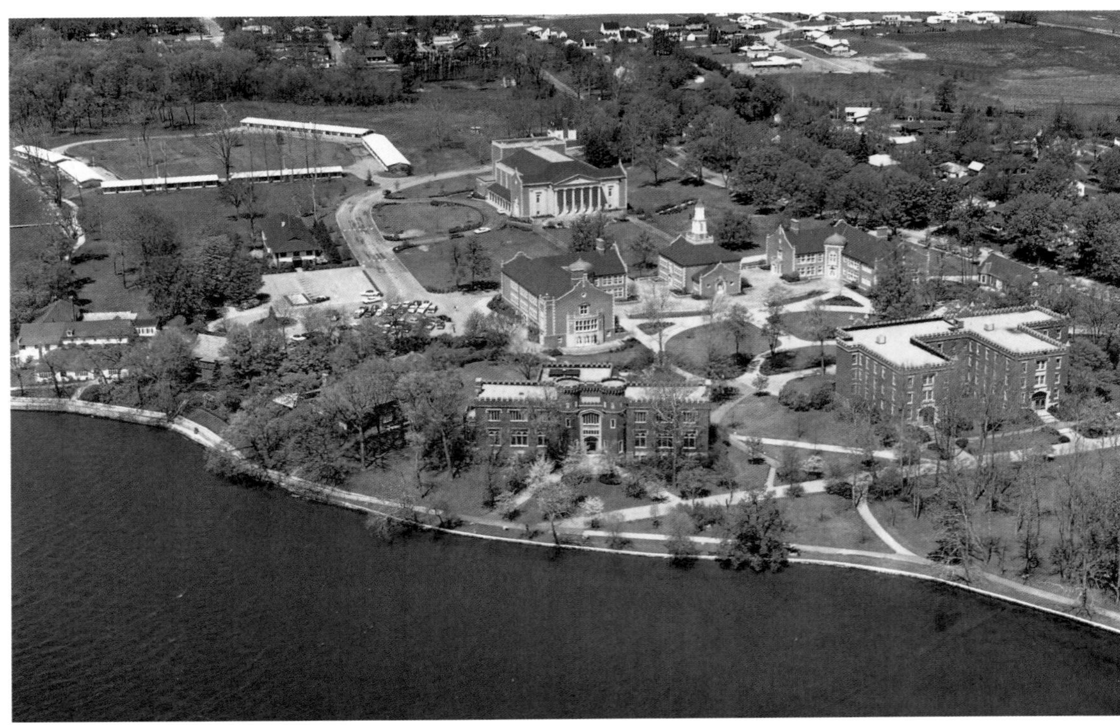

American Traditions: Art from the Collections of Culver Alumni

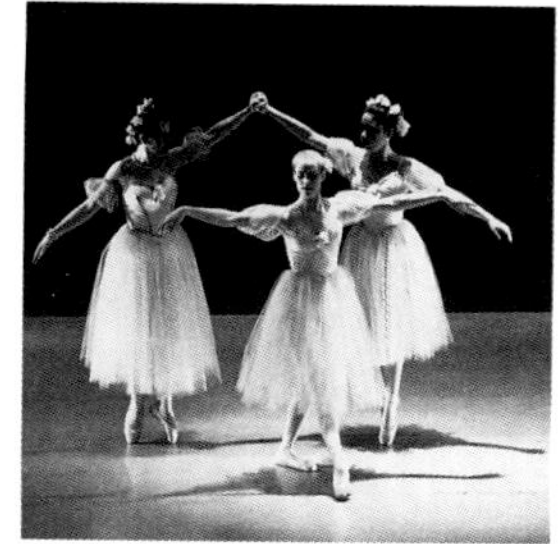

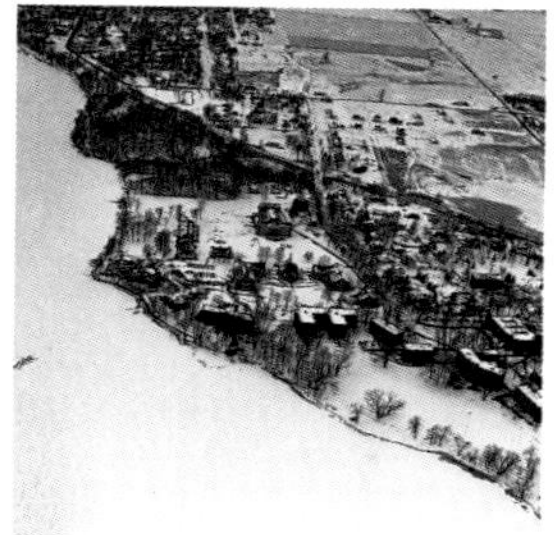

Ballet
*The arts are a major part of the
Culver Girls Academy
program. Modern dance and
ballet performances grace the
stage of Eppley Auditorium
during the fall and spring.*

Winter Aerial, 1959

Academy musicians and artists. A large, skylighted studio was complemented by an exhibition gallery with over one hundred feet of hanging space. Courses were offered by the artist-in-residence, Warner Williams, to meet particular interests. Cadets who planned to enter the medical profession studied anatomy; those interested in advertising, publishing, or printing were offered courses in graphics, layout, lettering, and illustration; while industrial design, pigment chemistry, and ceramics were taught to students who showed a more mechanical interest in art.

In 1959 a major gift from Eugene C. Eppley, class of 1901, made possible a splendid auditorium; and theater found a home on its fully equipped stage. Rehearsal studios, dressing rooms, and an art gallery provided a testament to the performing and visual arts and their place in the life of the Academy community.

With this heritage, it is hardly surprising that Culver alumni have decided to mark the Academy's centennial by contributing to an art exhibition celebrating the theme American Traditions. From their remarkable collections comes a tribute to Culver and its place as a leader in secondary education.

Robert B. D. Hartman
Centennial Historian and Archivist

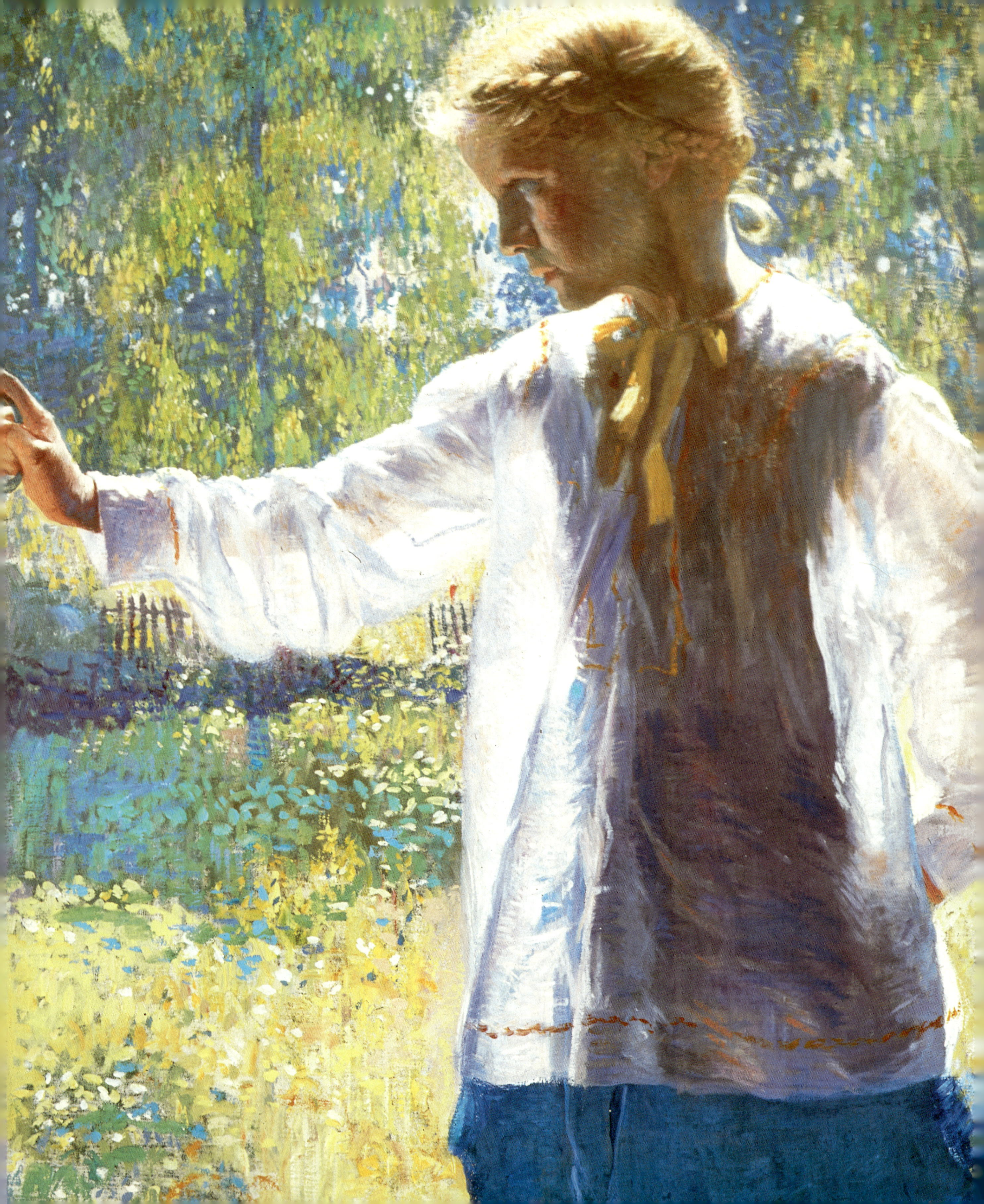

AMERICAN PAINTING
1825 - 1945

INDIANAPOLIS MUSEUM OF ART

American Traditions: Art from the Collections of Culver Alumni

Thomas Cole
1801–1848

Falls of Kaaterskill
1826
oil on canvas
43 x 36 inches
signed and dated lr:
T. Cole 1826
The Warner Collection
Tuscaloosa, Alabama

22

Born in Lancashire, England, Thomas Cole was the first painter to bind his reputation to the American landscape. Cole came to America with his family in 1818 and studied at the Pennsylvania Academy of the Fine Arts. In 1825 he moved to New York City, where he was one of the founding members of the National Academy of Design. During the same year Cole had his first exhibition of landscapes in New York. This occasion is frequently cited as the beginning of the national landscape style that became known as the Hudson River School. Cole's landscapes are minutely detailed, idealized interpretations of what he saw on his sketching trips through the region of the Hudson River and the Catskill Mountains. His reputation also rests upon moralizing landscape scenes inspired by his sojourns in Europe.

Falls of Kaaterskill was sketched on the spot in the Catskills and finished in Cole's studio. The final version is a carefully composed, meticulously executed scene intended to display what Cole called "the most lovely and perfect parts of Nature." This landscape exhibits Cole's predilection for autumn colors and dramatic lighting. The twisted, broken trees and panoramic view are hallmarks of Hudson River School romanticism. Also typical is the dwarfed figure of an Indian, which suggests that man is only a temporary inhabitant of the land and subordinate to nature.

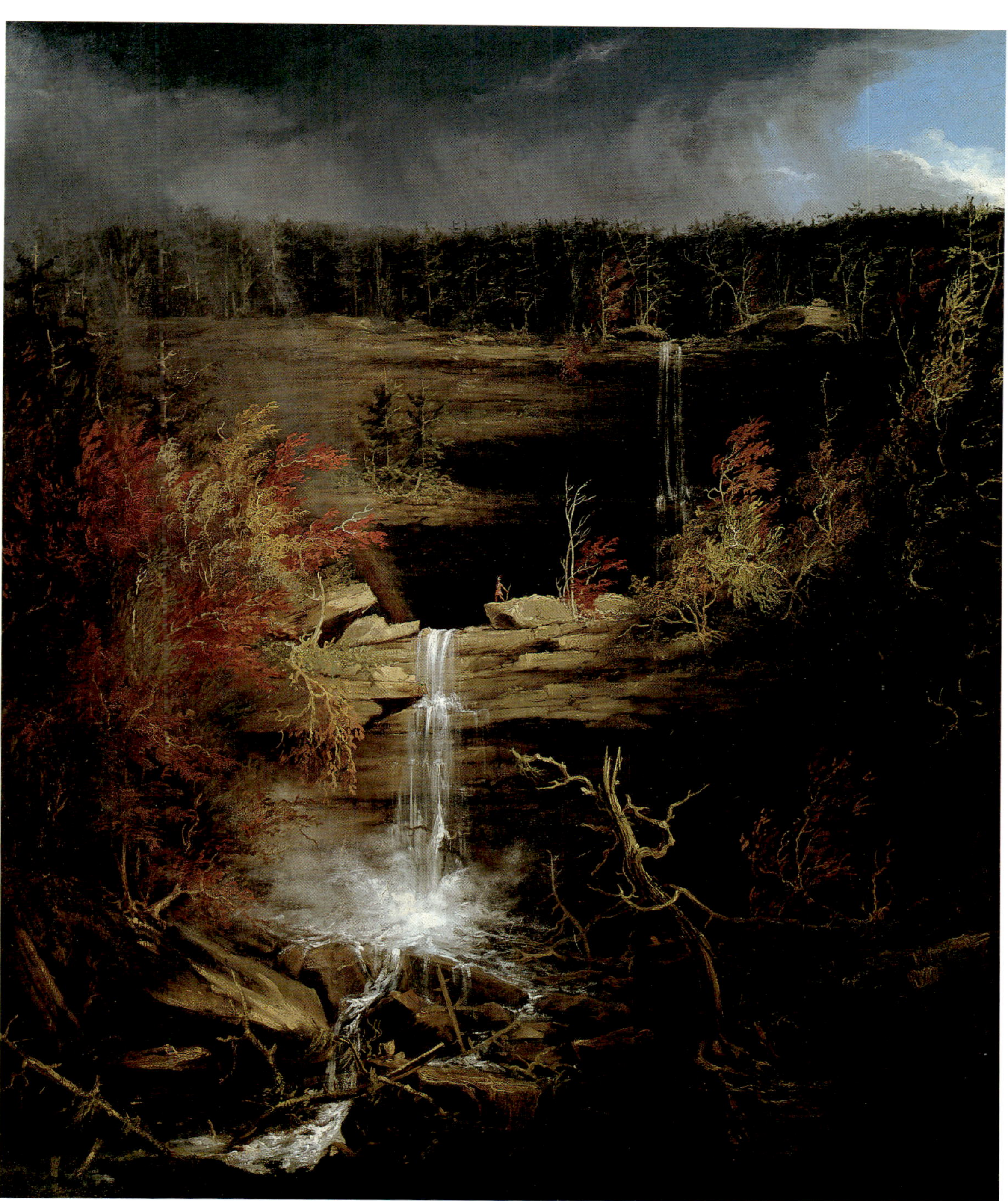

James Peale
1749–1831

Arrangement of Grapes
1829
oil on canvas
20 x 26 3/4 inches
The Warner Collection
Tuscaloosa, Alabama

24

James Peale was a prominent member of the talented Peale family of artists who settled in Philadelphia. Five of his seven children and several nieces and nephews became painters. Under the influence of his brother Charles Willson Peale, he became a professional painter of miniatures and still lifes beginning in 1782. As Peale grew older and his eyesight worsened, he gave up painting miniatures and focused exclusively on still-life painting. During the 1820s he devoted almost all his time to this genre.

Peale's favorite still-life topic was grapes. This composition shows the artist's fondness for exhibiting the different varieties of grapes in overflowing baskets. The small, juicy fruit, with its range of tones and hues, offers the still-life painter numerous choices of color schemes. The shallow background, plain wooden table, and contrasting light all accentuate the richness of the fruit. The curled leaves that rest on the edge of the table and the numerous age spots on the grapes reflect Peale's interest in the transience of life. Like the painters of seventeenth-century Holland, Peale used familiar still-life elements as reminders of the irrevocable passage of time.

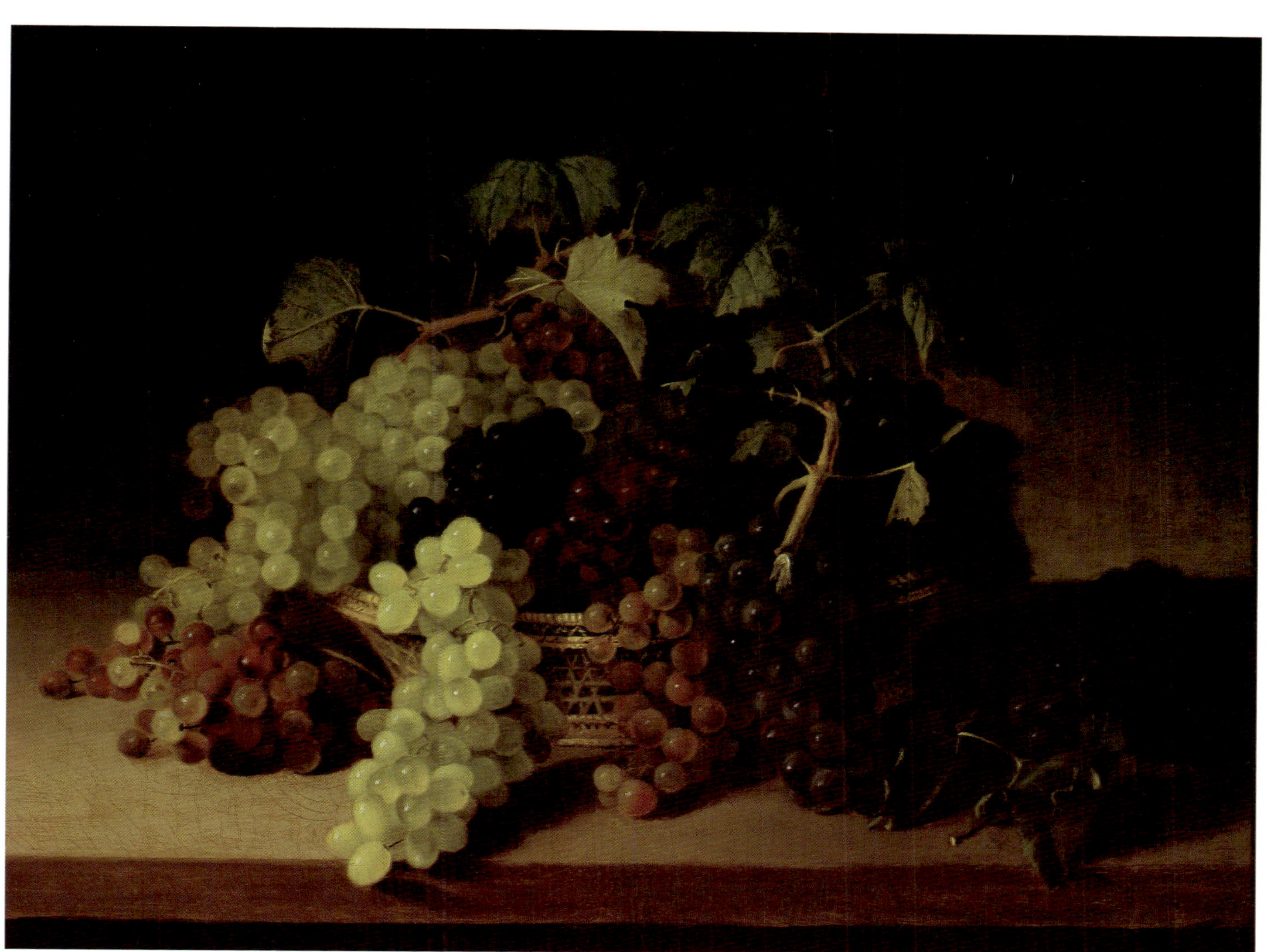

Edward Hicks
1780-1849

The Peaceable Kingdom
c. 1833
oil on canvas
17 1/2 x 23 1/2 inches
The Warner Collection
Tuscaloosa, Alabama

Edward Hicks was born in what is now Langhorne, Pennsylvania. A self-taught artist, he was a coach and sign painter before becoming a Quaker preacher. Hicks also painted historical and religious scenes that have established him as one of America's most important folk artists. His favorite subject was *The Peaceable Kingdom*. He executed more than one hundred versions of this theme, which was taken from chapter eleven of the Book of Isaiah. Hicks based these works on an engraved illustration of a painting by English academician Richard Westall and an English engraving after *William Penn's Treaty with the Indians* by Anglo-American history painter Benjamin West.

In *The Peaceable Kingdom* Hicks is both artist and preacher. The painting illustrates Isaiah's prophecy: "The wolf also shall dwell with the lamb, and the leopard shall lie down with the kid; and the calf and the young lion and the fatling together; and a little child shall lead them." The kingdom depicted is not of this world, but is a place where love and kindness reign under the triumphant rule of God. By including in the background William Penn signing his treaty with the Indians, Hicks reinforces the biblical promise of peace and the belief that America was the promised land. *The Peaceable Kingdom* is painted with a naive charm typical of folk artists. Hicks has chosen stylized forms with minimal modeling and has emphasized frontal views. The animals are not in standard scale but vary in size according to their importance within the scene. Hicks wrote in his diary about his art: "I have nothing to depend on but the mercy and forgiveness of God, for I have no works of righteousness of my own. I am nothing but a poor old worthless insignificant painter."

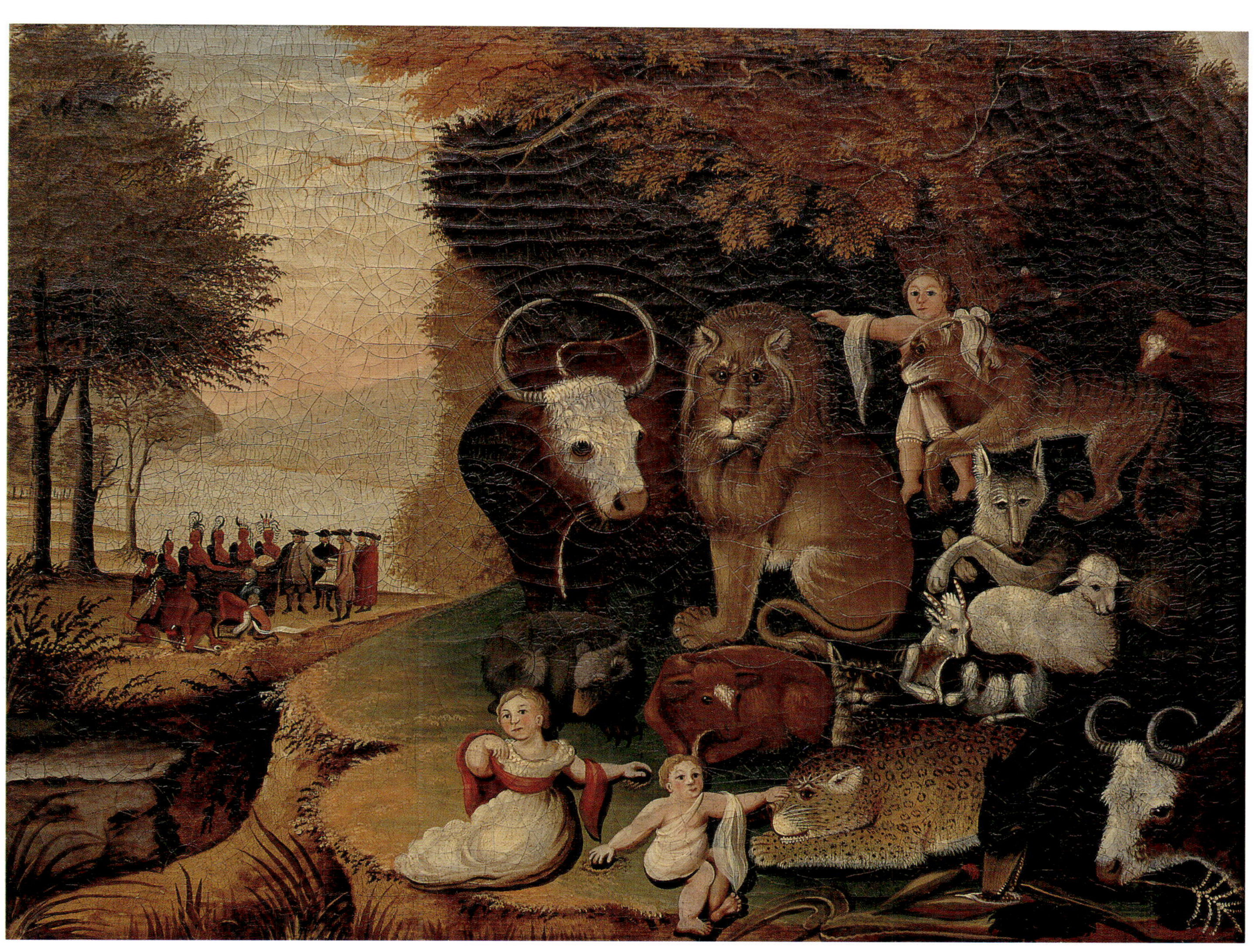

Frederic E. Church
1826-1900

Above the Clouds at Sunrise
1849
oil on canvas
27 x 40 inches
signed and dated lr:
F.E. CHURCH/1849
The Warner Collection
Tuscaloosa, Alabama

Frederic Edwin Church was born to a wealthy family in Hartford, Connecticut. In 1844 he became a pupil of Thomas Cole, and the following year, at the age of nineteen, he showed his work at the National Academy of Design in New York City. His style reflects the Hudson River School tradition, but as one of America's most widely traveled artists, Church favored distant lands and exotic places. His trips to Colombia, Ecuador and its Andes Mountains, the Arctic, Jamaica and the tropics, the Mediterranean, and North Africa produced breathtaking landscapes that emphasize the dramatic aspects of nature. Many of Church's canvases are massive panoramas intended to engulf the viewer in the marvelous splendor of nature.

Before Church ventured to exotic lands for his subject matter, he looked at the American landscape and found a multitude of magnificent views. *Above the Clouds at Sunrise*, with its pink clouds and dramatic light, is an early example of Church's celestial landscapes, devoid of humanity but filled with the spirit of creation. Though the painting appears to be an imagined scene, it is actually a specific place viewed from the Catskill Mountain House, a prominent hotel in the area. The artist captures the form, color, and texture of the rocks and trees, and encloses them in a swirling mist from which a dazzling sun emerges. The sky's striking color and the illusion of atmosphere are features for which Church is best known. In spite of the romantic appearance of this painting, Church believed that art should mirror nature and that the artist should never allow his personality or his emotions to intrude on the landscape.

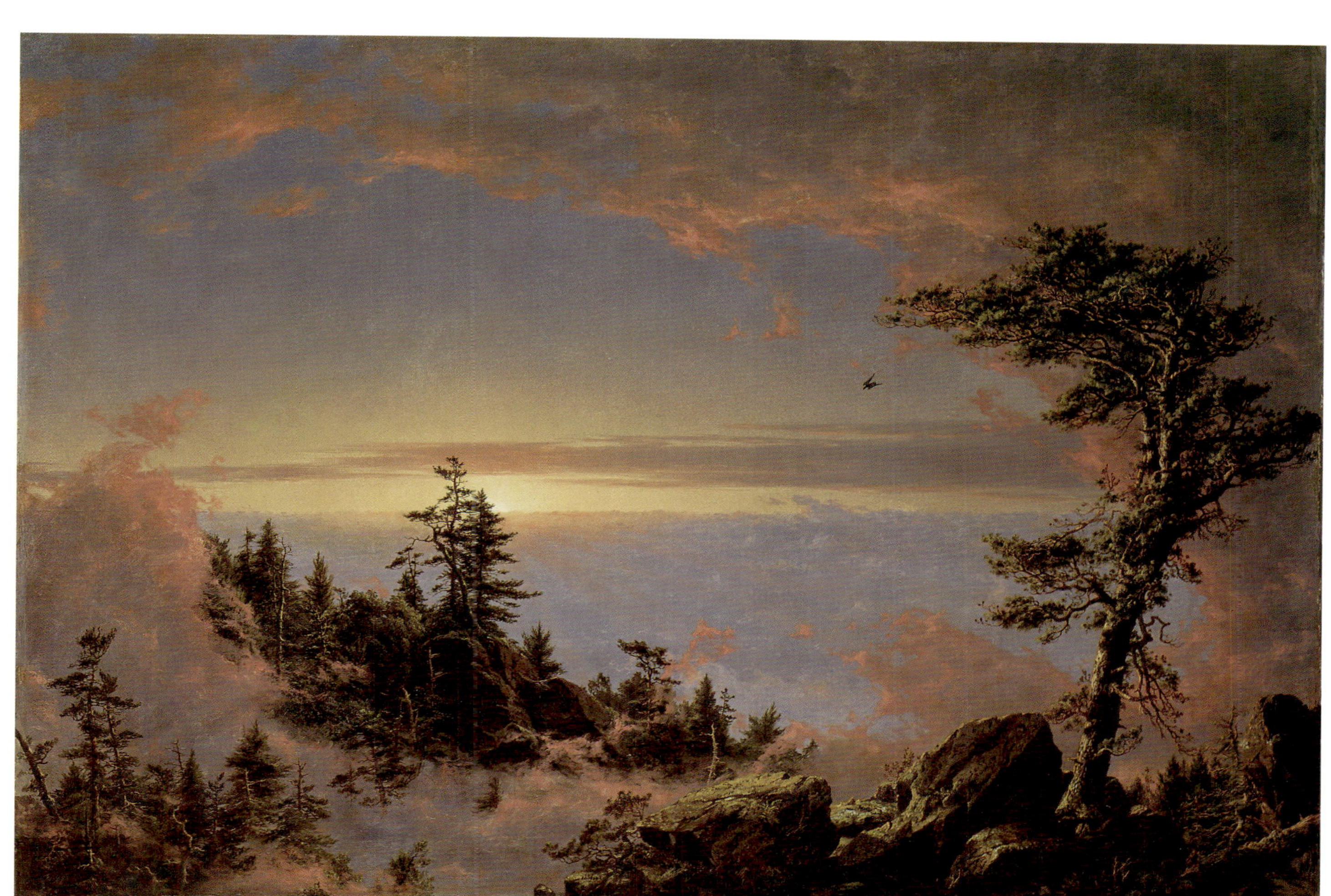

Progress
1853
oil on canvas
48 x 71 15/16 inches
signed and dated ll:
A.B. Durand 1853
The Warner Collection
Tuscaloosa, Alabama

Asher B. Durand's chief contribution to American landscape painting is his emphasis on sketching outdoors. He was born in Jefferson Village (now Maplewood), New Jersey, and was apprenticed to an engraver in 1812. Although he developed a reputation as an outstanding printmaker, Durand turned to painting in the 1830s. After Thomas Cole's death in 1848, Durand became the leader of the Hudson River School. His serene and pastoral scenes provide a distinct contrast with Cole's dramatic landscapes. In 1855 Durand wrote for *The Crayon* magazine a series of nine "Letters on Landscape Painting" that articulated the philosophy of Hudson River landscape painting.

 Progress is a glorious panoramic view of man and nature, ripe with symbolism. Durand divides his canvas between the untouched land inhabited by Native Americans, who have learned to live in harmony with nature, and the white settlers, who have cut down trees and built homes in what was once a forest. He suggests that both groups have a place on the land, but underscores the topographical changes wrought by the new inhabitants in their westward "progress" across the American landscape.

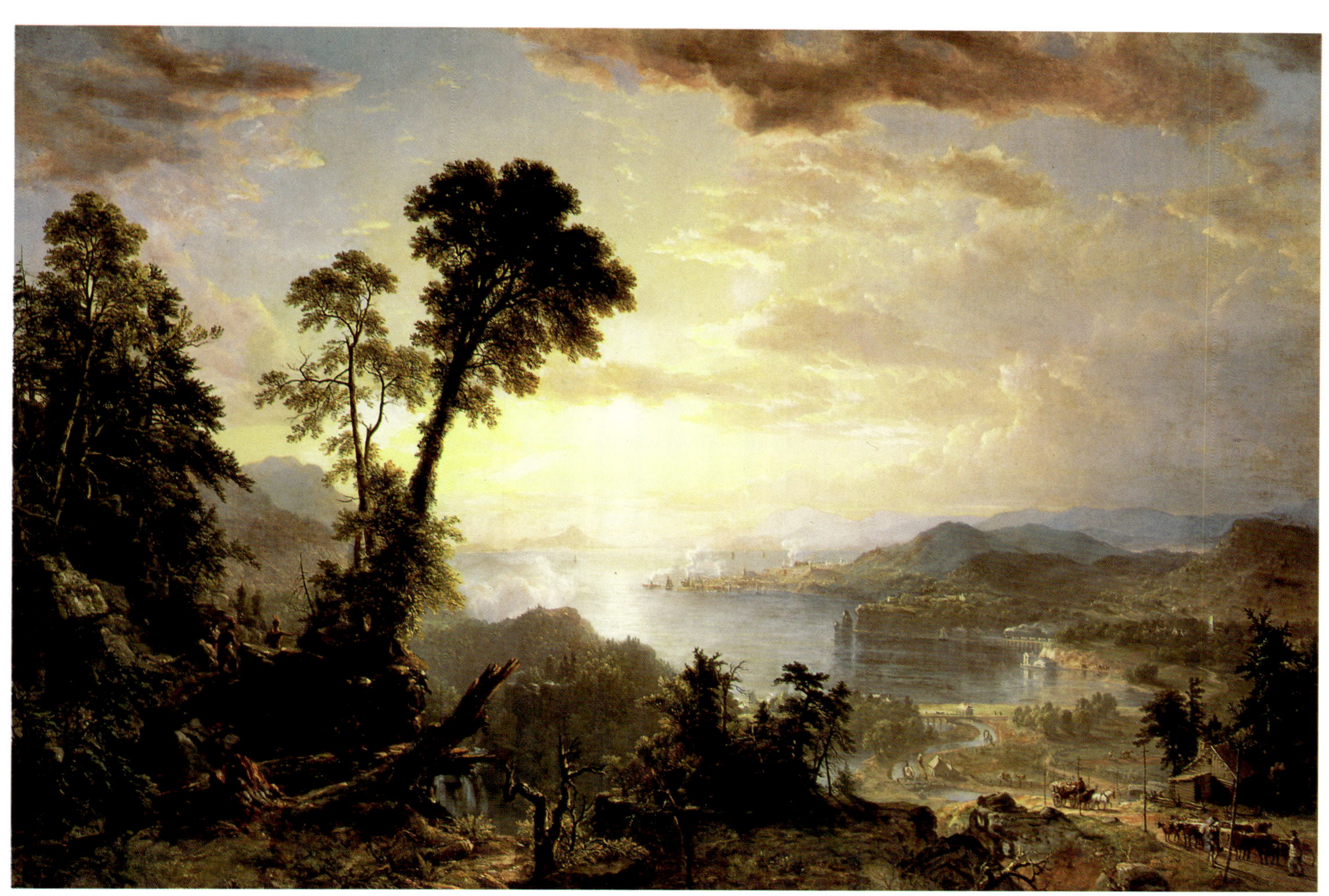

Sanford R. Gifford
1823-1880

Morning in the Adirondacks
1854
oil on canvas
40 7/8 x 36 inches (oval)
signed lc: S. R. Gifford

Shawangunk Mountains
1854
oil on canvas
40 7/8 x 36 inches (oval)
signed lc: S. R. Gifford
The Warner Collection
Tuscaloosa, Alabama

Sanford Gifford was raised in Hudson, New York, and sketched in the Adirondack, Shawangunk, and Catskill mountains until traveling to Europe for study in 1855. His admiration for Thomas Cole was an important factor in his decision to become a landscape painter; Gifford, however, eschewed Cole's allegorical, historical, and literary references, which he felt interfered with a true conception of the American landscape. With their explorations of light and atmosphere, Gifford's canvases belong to America's luminist painting tradition.

    Morning in the Adirondacks was painted just before Gifford's two-year sojourn in Europe. The artist maintains a delicate balance between his desire to show the landscape's details and his interest in atmospheric effects and the play of light. The mountains are enveloped in a heavy early-morning haze, and the landscape is suffused with the misty glow of sunrise. The gnarled tree stump in the foreground is a standard motif of Hudson River School compositions. Also typical is the human presence as suggested by the house and boat.

    A companion piece, *Shawangunk Mountains*, shares the same oval format, unusual for landscape subjects. In this canvas light reflects off the autumn foliage, softly illuminating the mountains and valley. Within the vast landscape stands a small figure. Holding a shovel, he appears to be a symbol of man's power to cultivate and alter the land. Such references to the impact of humanity on nature appeared in Gifford's paintings throughout his career.

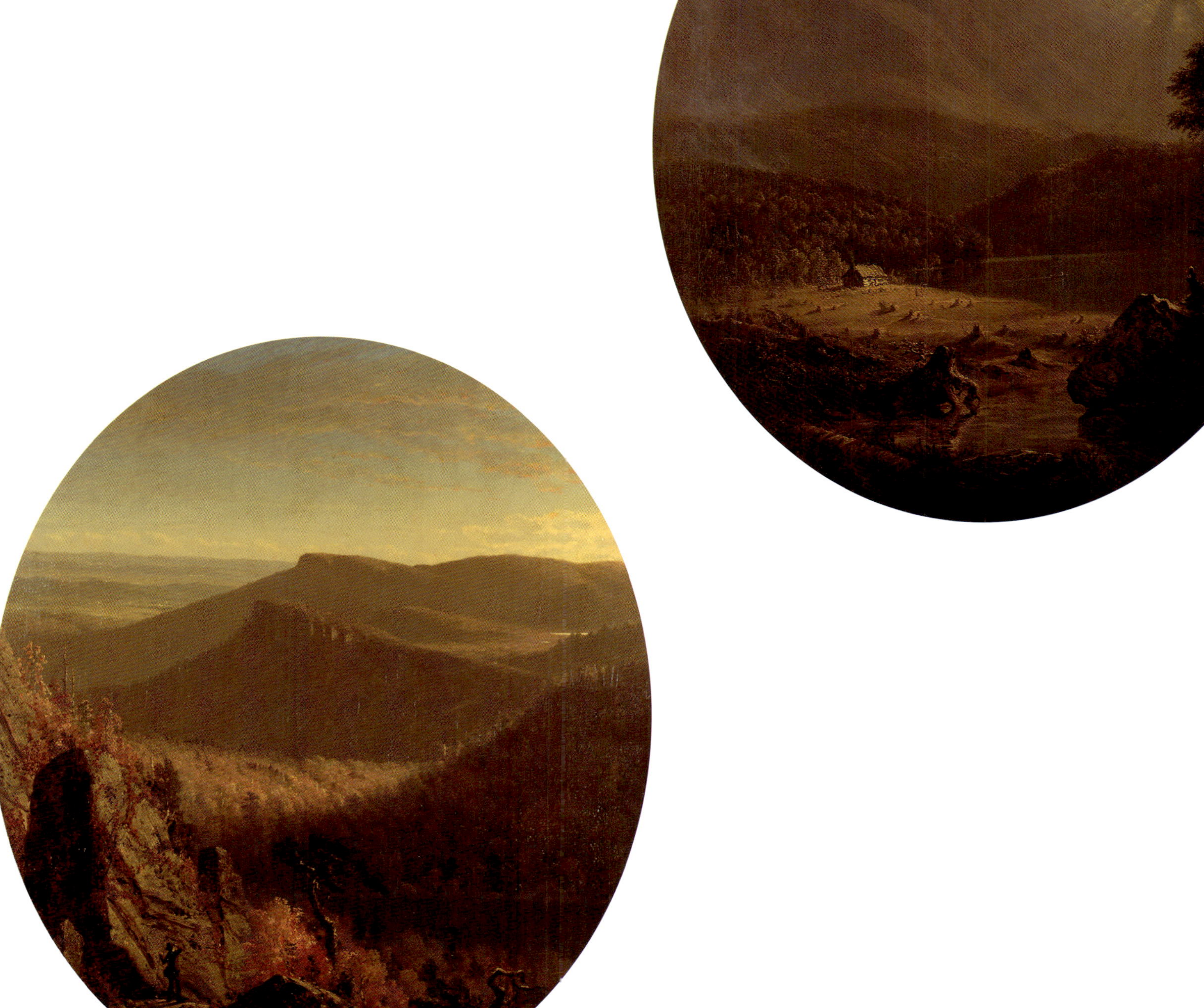

John F. Kensett
1816-1872

Lake George
1858
oil on canvas
24 1/8 x 36 1/4 inches
signed with monogram and
dated lr: JF.K. 58
The Warner Collection
Tuscaloosa, Alabama

34

John Frederick Kensett is best known for his luminous views of the scenery of New York and New England. He was born in Cheshire, Connecticut, and learned to draw from his father, who was an expert engraver. Kensett sailed for Europe in 1840, where for seven years he toured and studied. He returned to America a respected artist and became one of the most popular painters of his era. Kensett was a leading member of the second generation of the Hudson River School; his landscapes feature rugged terrain, twisted trees, and picturesque settings in the manner of Thomas Cole. In the 1850s Kensett's style began to reflect a calmer view of the landscape, with barely perceptible brush strokes and a concentration on the effects of light.

During the summer months Kensett abandoned his New York City studio for waterside resorts such as Lake George in the Adirondacks of New York. *Lake George*, with its radiant light, calm water, low horizon, and precise brushwork, exemplifies the artist's early luminist style. A soft glow, created by Kensett's delicate colors and the autumn mist, permeates the idyllic setting. The tranquility is broken only by a canoe and its occupants, who are almost hidden by the island. This peaceful landscape was painted in the shadow of the unrest that would lead to the Civil War, and it offers a reassuring image of the enduring aspects of nature.

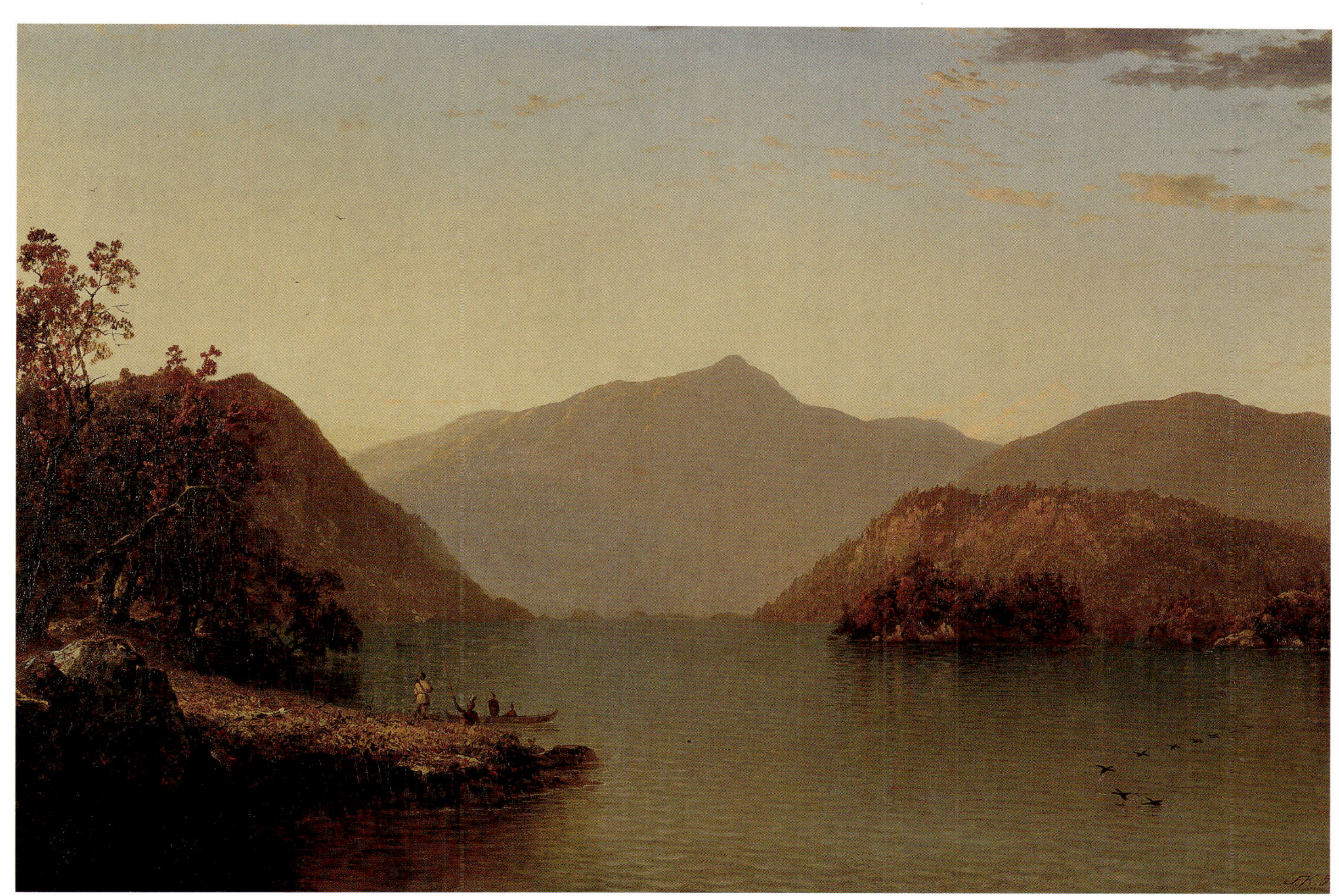

Severin Roesen
c. 1815–1872

Abundance of Fruit
c. 1860
oil on canvas
30 x 50 1/4 inches
signed lr: Roesen
The Warner Collection
Tuscaloosa, Alabama

Severin Roesen is a key figure in the history of American still-life painting, but details of his life have remained obscure. It is believed that he was born in the German Rhineland and emigrated to New York City in 1848, eventually settling in Williamsport, Pennsylvania, by 1862. Nothing is known of Roesen's life or work after 1872, when he disappeared from the Williamsport scene. His large, complex arrangements of fruits and flowers survive in surprising numbers, considering the lack of documentation on his career. These depictions of nature's bounty reflect the optimistic outlook of the Victorian era.

The elaborately composed *Abundance of Fruit* overflows with cascading tiers of grapes, pears, peaches, and watermelon that are barely contained by the compotes, baskets, and marble table. This spectacle of the benevolence of nature is set against a dramatically lit sky, perhaps a reference to God as the source of all abundant harvests. Roesen renders every fruit with meticulous detail and every object with a microscopic precision. Over four hundred such canvases by Roesen have come to light. These paintings probably served as the focal point of numerous Victorian dining rooms, each one attesting to nature's succulent bounty and the blessings bestowed upon the family.

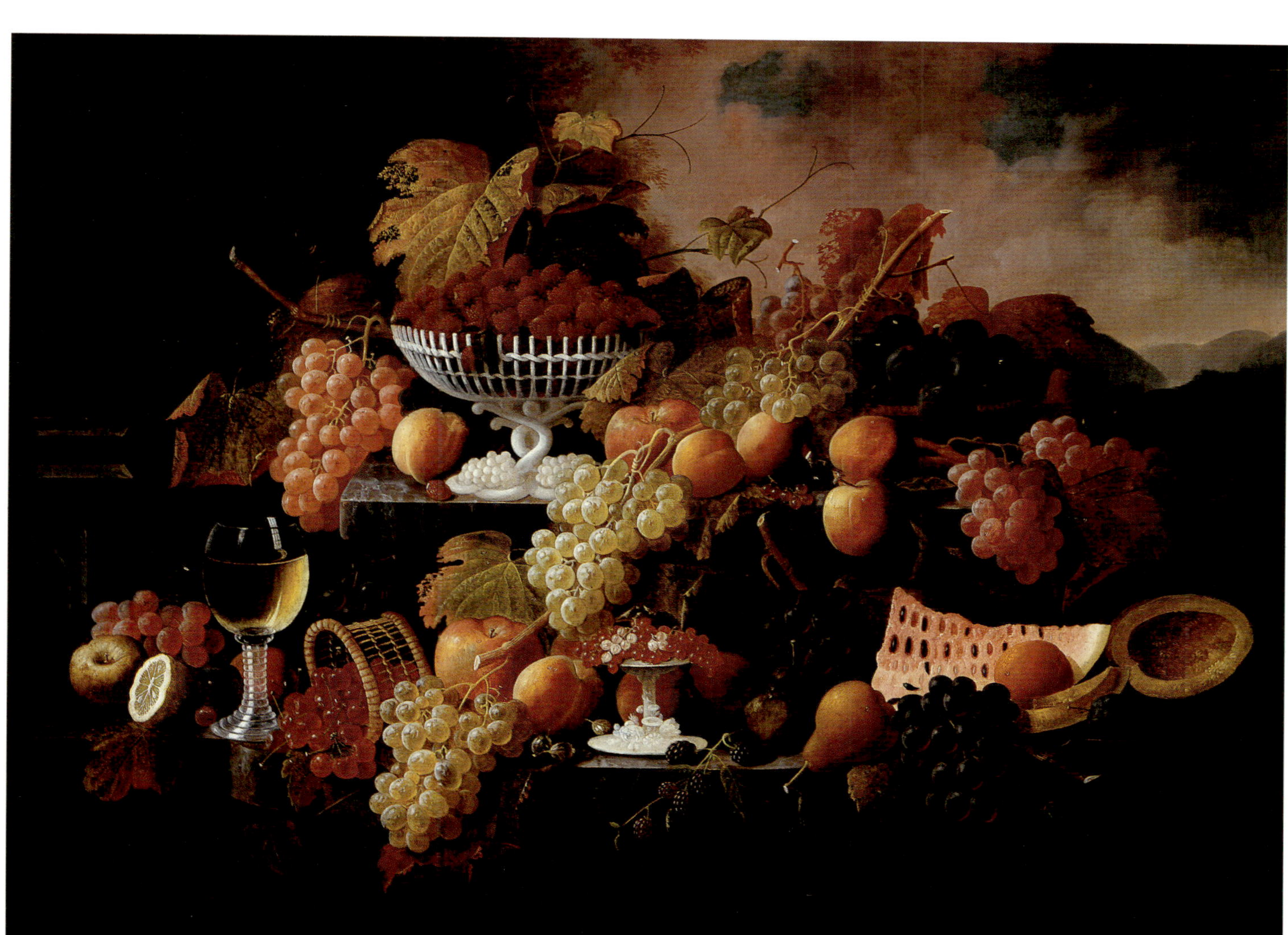

James Buttersworth
1817–1894

Racing Yacht off the Needles
c. 1860
oil on canvas
21 1/8 x 32 inches
signed lr: J. E. Buttersworth
William I. Koch Collection

James Buttersworth was born in England and trained by a family member in the tradition of English marine painting. He came to America around 1845 and set up a studio in West Hoboken, New Jersey. With an active maritime economy, mid-nineteenth-century America had a healthy interest in marine paintings. Buttersworth was soon instrumental in creating the popular image of the clipper ship as master of the sea. He also developed a reputation for painting scenes of yachting races that emphasized the diagonals of the ships' sails, low horizons, dark skies, and threatening seas. When steam engines replaced sails, the artist quickly incorporated this new technology into his paintings. That willingness to reflect the changes in shipbuilding ensured Buttersworth's continuous popularity. In the 1850s he worked for Nathaniel Currier, and several of his paintings were made into prints by Currier and Ives.

Racing Yacht off the Needles is typical of Buttersworth's precisely rendered yachting scenes. He creates strong diagonals with sails that are stretched to their capacity by the wind. The ominous sky and rough sea add drama as the ship appears to rush toward its destination ahead of the impending storm. The transitory effects of light and air along with contrasts of darks and lights help create the mood. By painting ships in action rather than formal portraits of vessels, Buttersworth was able to concentrate on the same subject while still maintaining a sense of freshness and vibrancy.

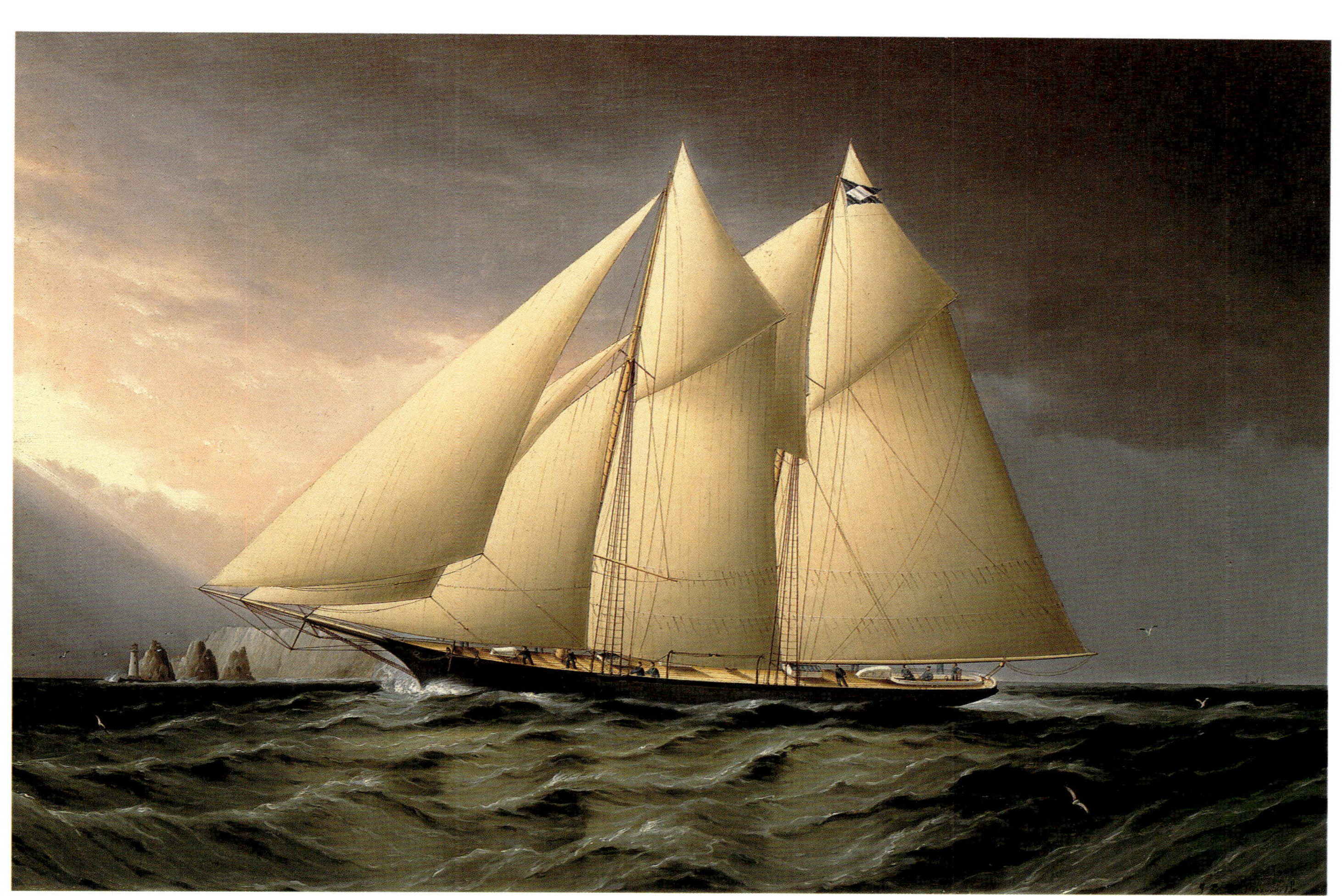

William Sidney Mount
1807-1868

Any Fish Today?
1857
oil on canvas
21 1/4 x 16 1/4 inches
signed and dated lr:
W*m* S. Mount/1857.
The Warner Collection
Tuscaloosa, Alabama

40

During the early nineteenth century, when the Hudson River School began to dominate American landscape painting, William Sidney Mount developed a parallel approach to genre painting that reflected the same optimism, fidelity to nature, and idealism. Mount was born in Setauket, Long Island, and spent most of his life in the region. As a young man he was apprenticed to his brother, a sign and ornamental painter. Not wanting to be overly influenced by European traditions, Mount never went abroad. He did, however, study original paintings by older masters during his trips to New York City and was particularly influenced by seventeenth-century Dutch art. Mount glorified the achievements of the common man as he painted the life and people of his native Long Island with humor and sensitivity.

Any Fish Today? reflects the thoughtful, quiet mood of Mount's late style. The artist uses sunlight to emphasize the well-dressed country boy with his bountiful catch. The young salesman looks straight ahead, confronting the unseen occupant of the house and inviting the viewer into the scene. The carpeted interior, with its elegant caned chair, indicates the family is comfortable, while the inclusion of the book suggests they are also well educated. The gun and hatchet are reminders that their prosperity derives from hard work and nature. Mount celebrates the feelings of abundance and well-being that were prevalent in the years preceding the Civil War.

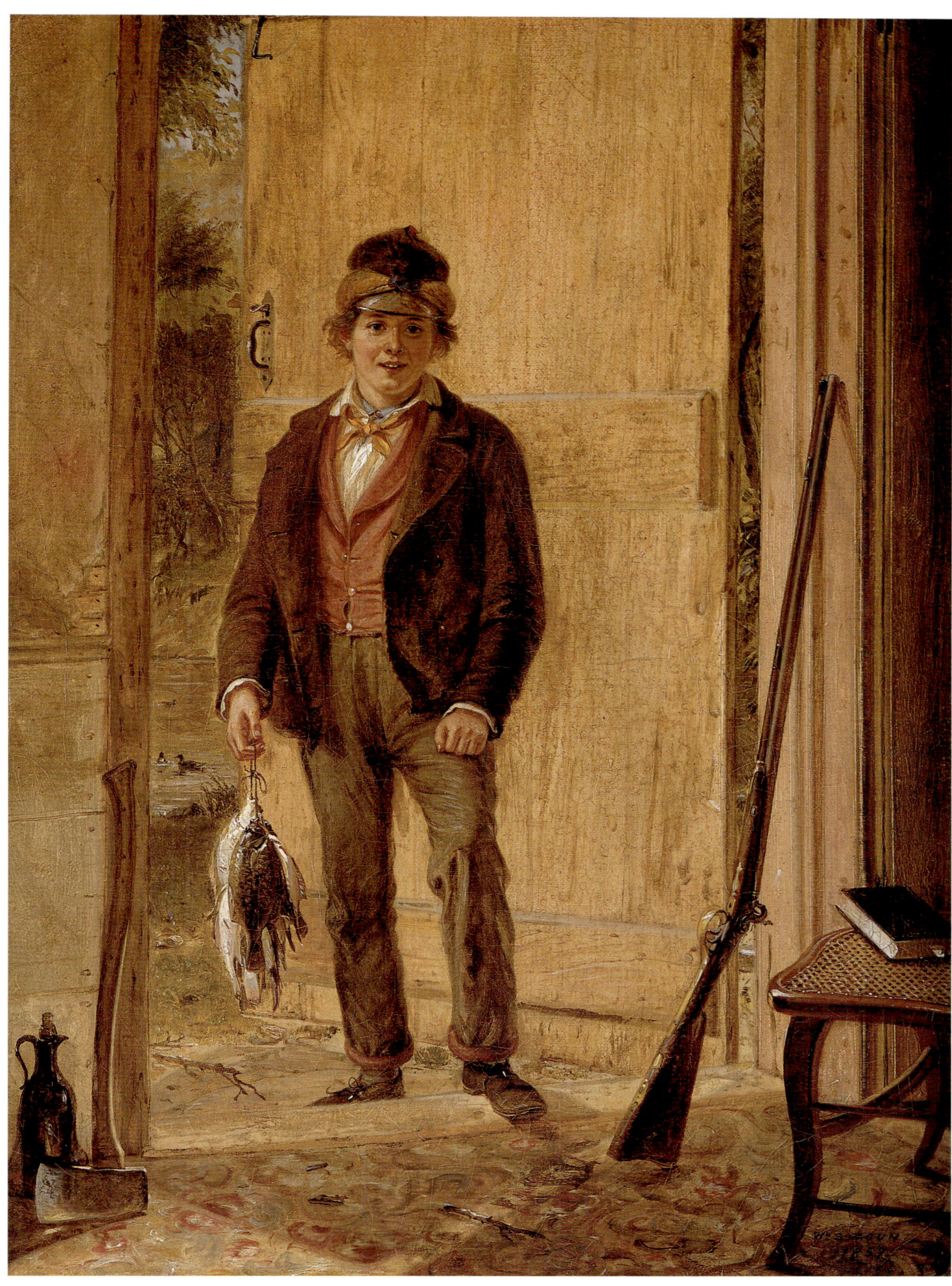

John George Brown
1831-1913

On Guard

oil on canvas
25 1/2 x 20 1/8 inches
inscribed and signed lr:
copyright/J.G.Brown N.A.
Anonymous

42

During the Victorian era, a keen interest in the behavior of children led to a dramatic increase in paintings with youthful subject matter. Artists such as William Sidney Mount, Winslow Homer, and John George Brown created scenes of America's children at work and play. Brown was born in Durham, England, and received his early art training in England and Scotland. Around 1855 he settled in Brooklyn, New York, where he worked as a glassblower and continued his studies at the National Academy of Design. When he first began to paint genre subjects in 1860, Brown placed his figures in a landscape setting. In 1880 he turned to urban genre scenes of newsboys, street urchins, and other spirited youths. Brown's paintings were reproduced by the thousands, making him one of the richest and most celebrated genre painters at the turn of the century.

In *On Guard* a boy hides in the corner of a building whose only architectural element is the cropped window. With a pet dog at his feet and an armful of snowballs, the child stands ready to surprise his opponents. He leans against the smooth surface of the wall, which is bathed in a strong, clear light that emphasizes the tense situation. Brown is noted for his focus on the figures in his paintings, which he achieves by eliminating any extraneous detail that would detract from the subject. Although Brown often depicted working children, his street juveniles are never sad, hungry, or sick. The picturesque quality of these paintings appealed to contemporary collectors, which assured Brown continued patronage throughout his life.

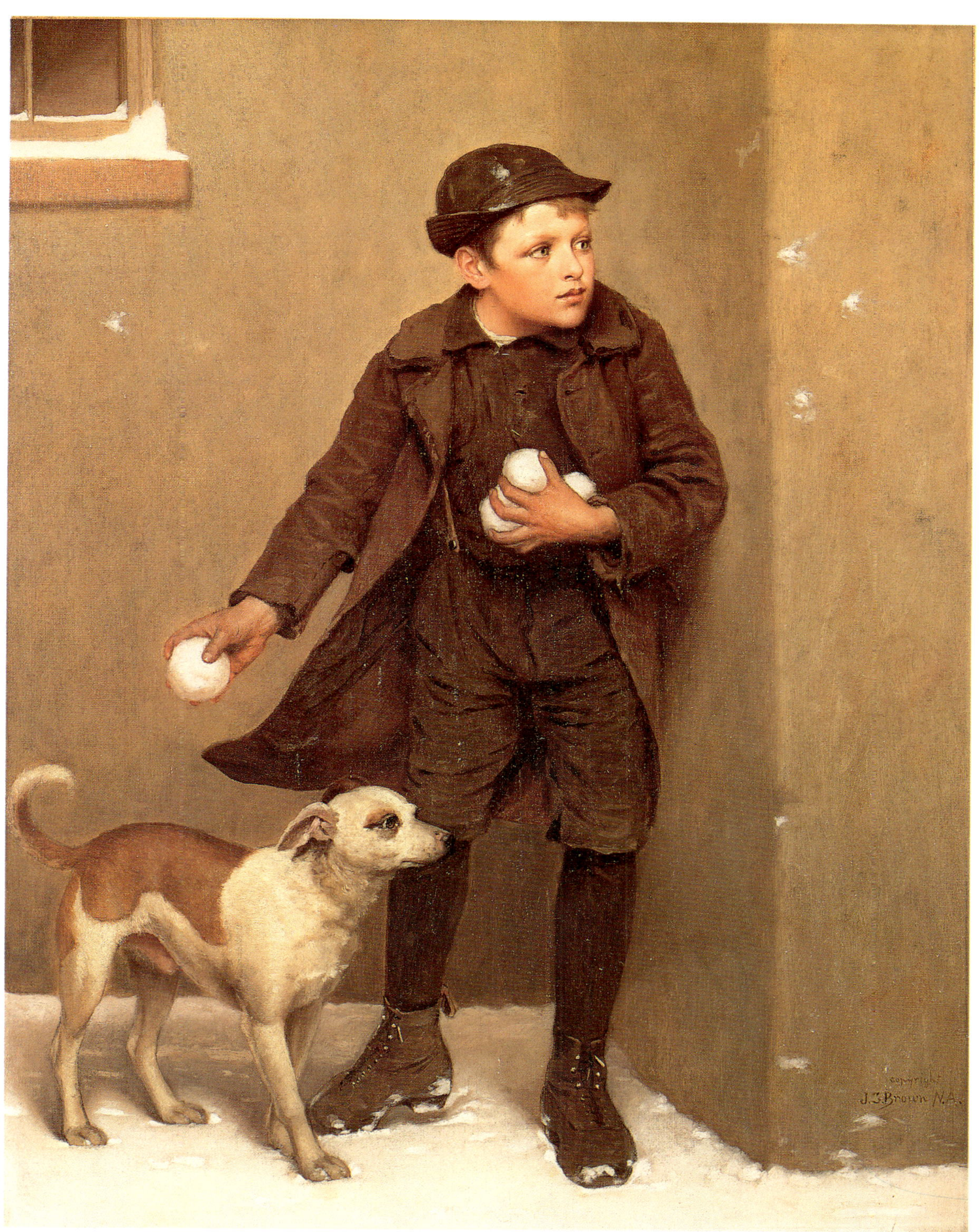

William Aiken Walker
1838-1921

Wheat Threshing
oil on canvas
12 1/2 x 25 1/2 inches
signed ll: WAWalker
Harry M. Rhett, Jr.

44

William Aiken Walker drew upon the life and landscape of his environment to create his numerous views of the rural South after the Civil War. He was born in Charleston, South Carolina, and by the age of twelve was already painting African-American subjects. Although his career was flourishing, he enlisted in the Confederate Army in 1861; he was wounded in action and discharged the same year. In 1865 he moved to Baltimore and began traveling through southern communities painting black farm workers and their families. During the 1880s Currier and Ives made lithographs of several of Walker's paintings. Walker continued to record his native South until the early 1900s.

In *Wheat Threshing* laborers are loading wheat into a threshing device that removes the grain from the stalks. The artist concentrates on the action around the machine, creating an interesting off-center composition. The friezelike construction is typical of Walker, who routinely spreads the figures frontally across the picture plane. A distant viewpoint emphasizes the vastness of the farm, which contrasts with the small figures of the men. The painting's accurate detail and clear, sharp focus are probably the result of Walker's use of a camera during his travels.

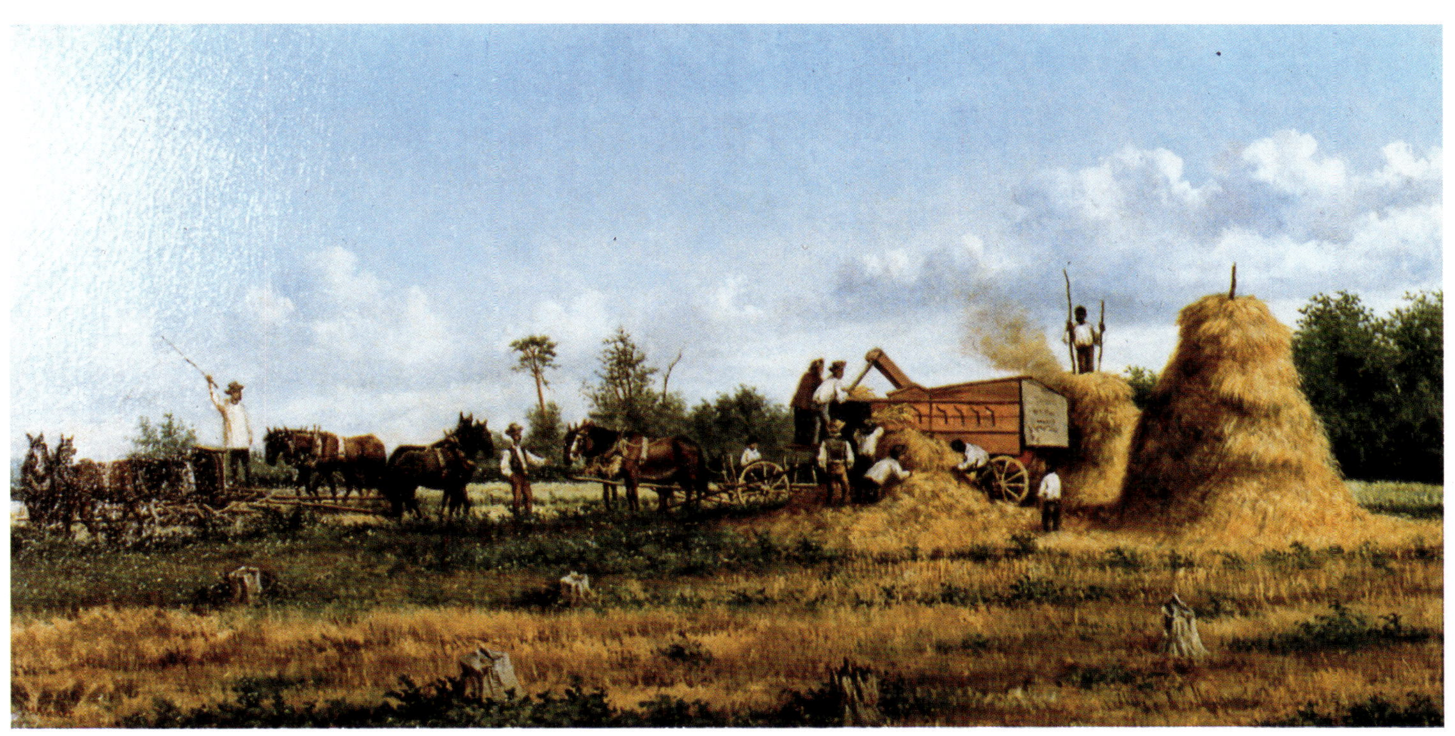

Martin Johnson Heade
1819-1904

*Two Hummingbirds
by an Orchid*
1873 or 1875
oil on canvas
15 1/2 x 20 inches
signed and dated lr:
MJ Heade 1873 [or] 75
The Warner Collection
Tuscaloosa, Alabama

46

Martin Johnson Heade was born in Lumberville, Pennsylvania, and received his initial art training from Edward Hicks, a folk artist, and Thomas Hicks, a portraitist. Heade's fascination with painting hummingbirds derives from his trip to Brazil in 1863–64, the first of three stays in South America. On a visit to Jamaica in 1870, he was struck by the beauty of the orchid. Heade completed his first painting combining the hummingbird and orchid in 1871 and continued to paint this subject until his death.

Heade's paintings of flowers and birds were derived from direct observation and from his study of scientific sources. *Two Hummingbirds by an Orchid* is an early example of the artist's signature compositions. As here, he often suggests the fecundity of nature by combining the male and female hummingbird with the orchid in a lush tropical setting. Their juxtaposition also establishes a sense of scale for the tiny birds, which are poised in the foreground of a vast landscape. The vivid pink of the flower, which is repeated in the hummingbird's throat, creates a strong contrast with the hazy atmosphere in the distance. The orchid's elegant contours and undulating tendrils form a dynamic, rhythmic pattern that animates the composition. While Heade was also an accomplished landscape painter, this exotic choice of flora and fauna was his unique contribution to American art.

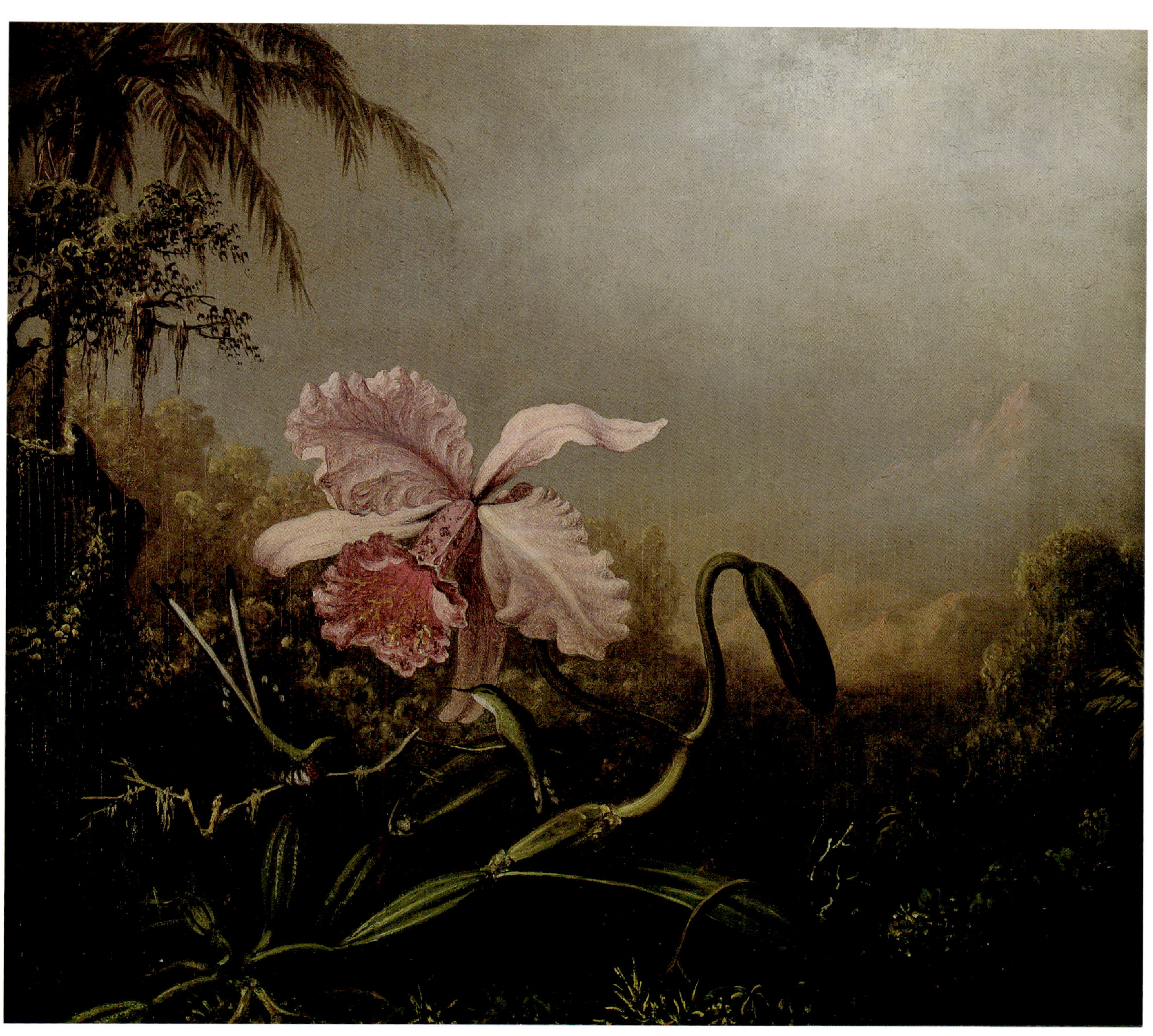

Albert Bierstadt
1830-1902

Seal Rock, Farallon Islands
1871–72
oil on canvas
37 x 58 inches
signed lr: ABierstadt
The Warner Collection
Tuscaloosa, Alabama

In 1832 Albert Bierstadt emigrated with his family from Germany to New Bedford, Massachusetts. His interest in art led him back to Germany in 1853, where he studied at the Düsseldorf Art Academy. He returned to the United States in 1857 and made his first trip west two years later. Bierstadt was struck by the vastness and beauty of the American frontier and eventually made it the dominant theme of his paintings. Both he and Frederic Church painted what are often called "epic" landscapes because of their panoramic views, large format, spectacular effects, and emphasis on the grandeur of the landscape.

In July 1871 Bierstadt began a two-year stay in California. In April of the following year he journeyed by boat to the Farallon Islands, just off San Francisco Bay. There he sketched extensively, gathering material for several oil paintings later completed in his studio. *Seal Rock* was one of the many areas of the island Bierstadt captured in his drawings. The wild and beautiful rock formations are inhabited by thousands of sea lions and sea birds. The drama of the ocean crashing against the cliffs is enhanced by the use of backlighting, which frames the giant waves and the massive rocks. The fierce waves lashing the rocks barely disturb the seals who have made this turbulent environment their home. Bierstadt's interpretation of the scene provides an awe-inspiring view of the beauty and power of nature.

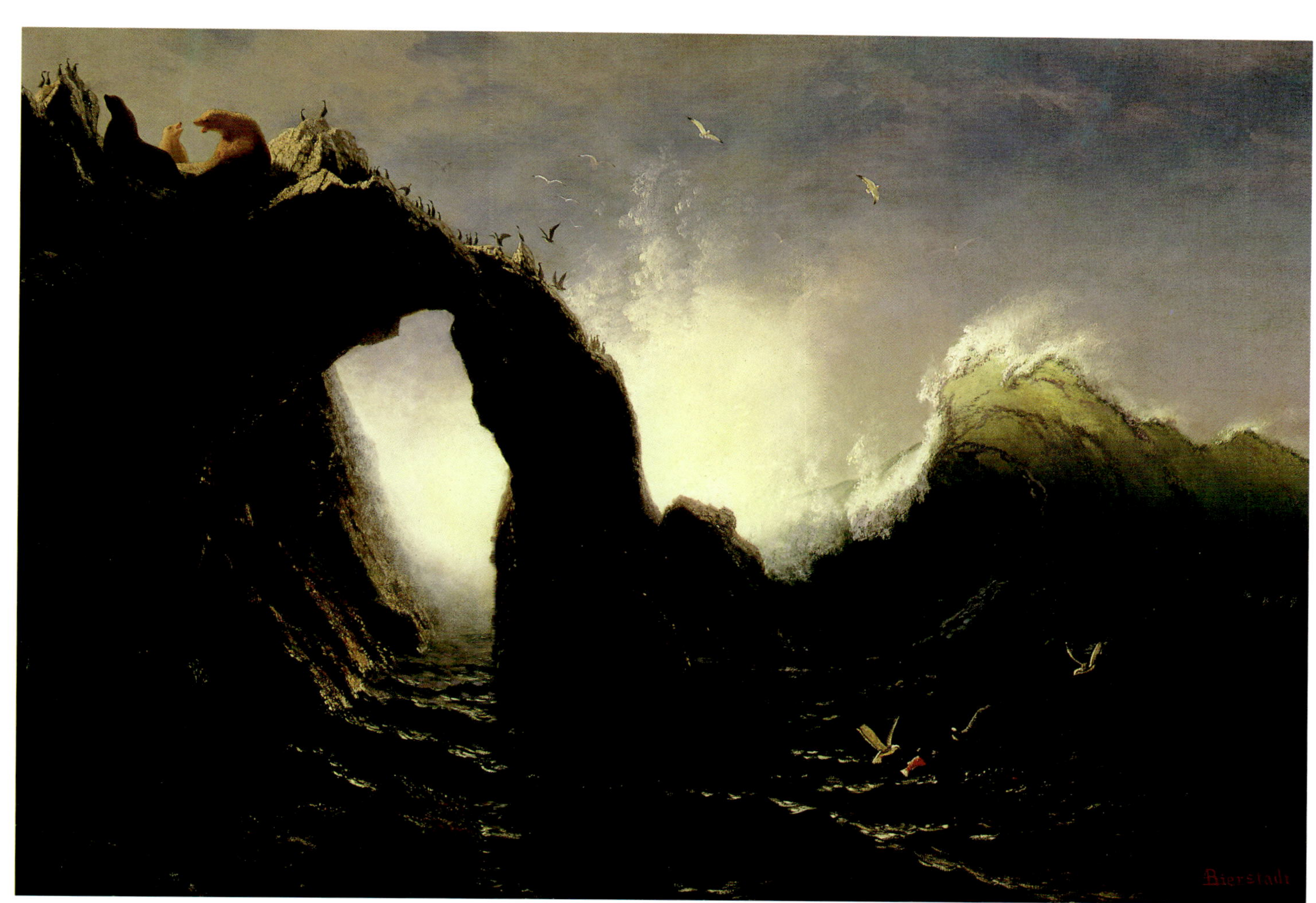

William Bradford
1823-1892

Muir Glacier
oil on canvas
39 1/4 x 69 inches
The Warner Collection
Tuscaloosa, Alabama

William Bradford was raised a Quaker in the fishing town of Fairhaven, Massachusetts. During the mid-1850s he shared a studio with the Dutch marine painter Albert Van Beest, whose paintings with low horizons and thick atmosphere influenced Bradford's art. The meticulously detailed compositions of the American marine painter Fitz Hugh Lane, who was just a generation older, also proved influential. Bradford's fascination with the distant North Pole led him to make a series of long summer trips to the Arctic in the 1860s. The artist became famous not only for his paintings of the region, but also for his superb photography. His travels resulted in a large folio of over a hundred photographs published in 1873 under the title *The Arctic Regions*. These photographs also served as an unlimited source of motifs for the Arctic paintings that remain the cornerstone of Bradford's reputation.

One of Bradford's favorite themes was the Arctic's unusual ice formations. Muir Glacier was named for the naturalist and conservationist John Muir, who documented it in 1879. In this broad canvas, Bradford captures the polar landscape and contrasts its immense scale with the small ship that stands in isolation against this spectacle of nature. The surreal character of the landscape is created by the dramatically intense pink light that surrounds the stark, white glacier. The keen sense of color and attention to detail produce a haunting depiction of nature's icy Arctic realm. Bradford's approach to the timeless and cosmic character of this remote region links him to Hudson River School painters such as Frederic Church and Albert Bierstadt, whose paintings of exotic places are suffused with a spiritual quality.

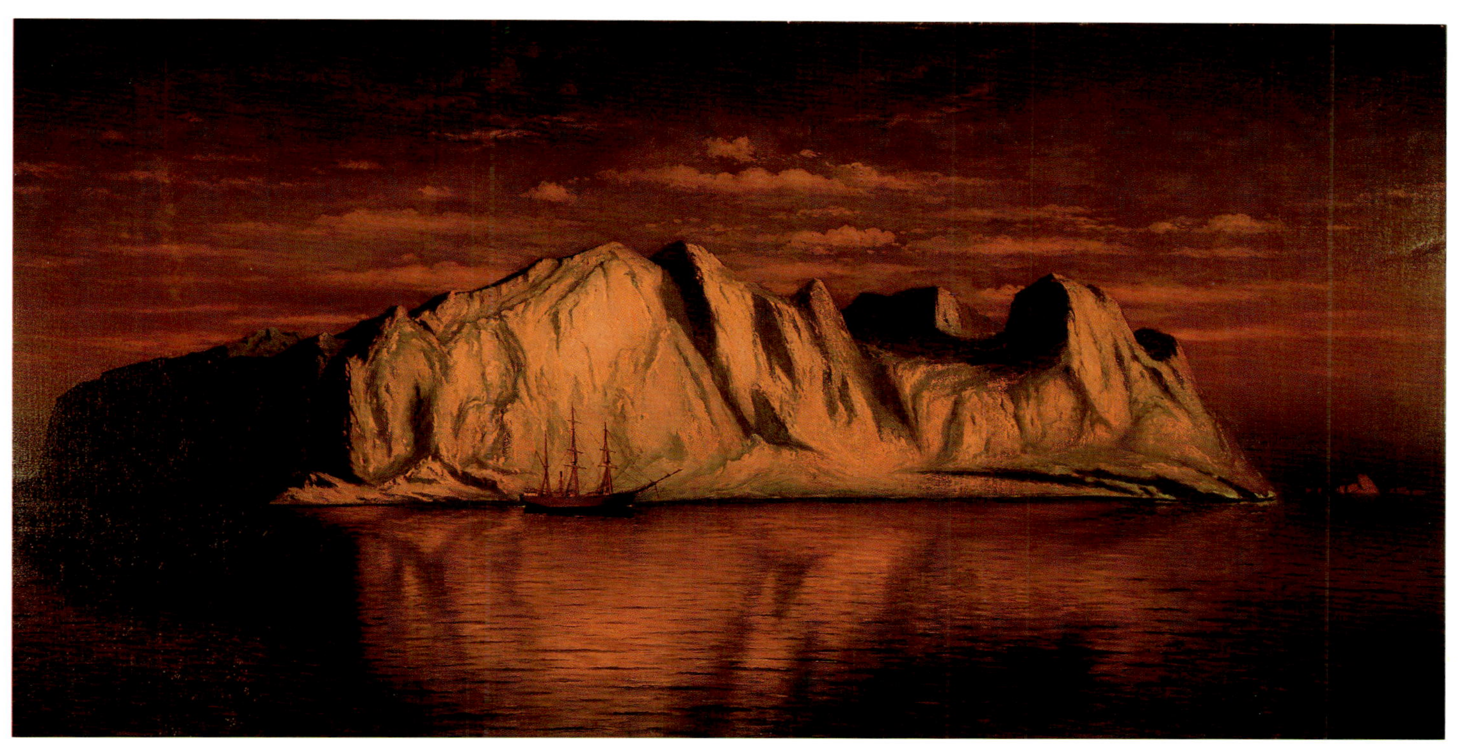

William T. Richards
1833-1905

Mackerel Cove,
Jamestown, Rhode Island
1894
oil on canvas
26 1/4 x 47 inches
signed and dated ll:
Wm T. Richards, 94
The Warner Collection
Tuscaloosa, Alabama

52

As a young artist, William Trost Richards took sketching trips in the area around his native Philadelphia and, like landscape painters of the preceding generations, also worked along the Hudson River. Richards left for Europe in 1855 and visited Paris, Switzerland, Italy, and Germany. He came under the influence of British critic John Ruskin, who believed there is a moral necessity for the artist to accurately represent nature. In 1863 Richards joined the Association for the Advancement of Truth in Art, whose members became known as the American Pre-Raphaelites. The group advocated plein-air painting with an emphasis on meticulous natural detail. This movement was based on the work of the English Pre-Raphaelites, who drew their inspiration from the straightforwardness of medieval art. Around 1867 Richards developed a preference for coastal scenes, which he rendered with icy precision.

In the 1870s Richards began spending his summers in Newport, Rhode Island, and painted the surrounding area, which included Jamestown. He moved permanently to Newport in 1890. *Mackerel Cove, Jamestown, Rhode Island* exhibits both the Pre-Raphaelite concern for precise natural detail and an attention to light and atmosphere that links Richards with America's luminist painters. This serene landscape with its deep space exhibits the artist's preoccupation with the effects of sunlight reflecting off land, sea, and sky.

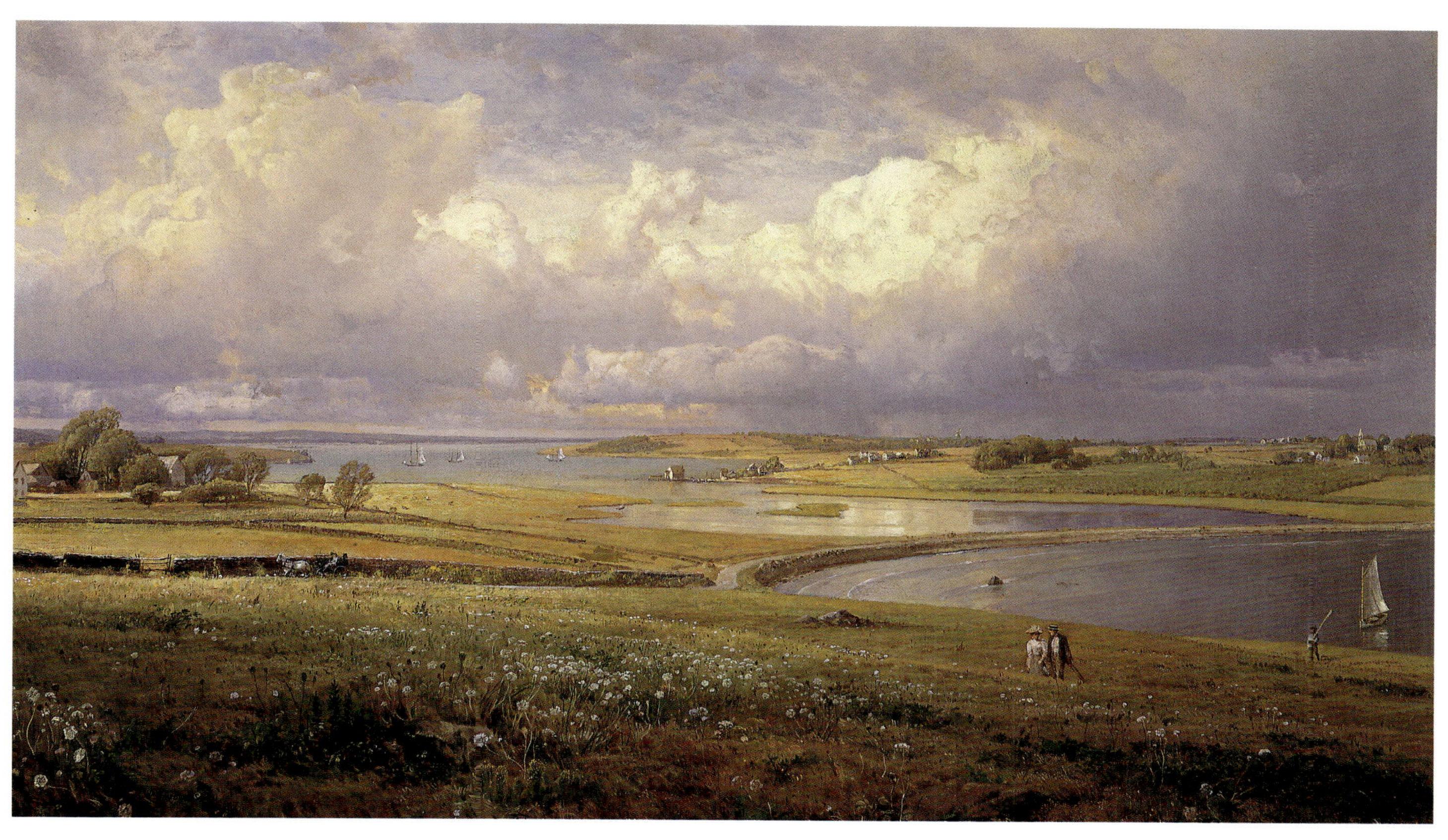

54

With their meticulous construction and close attention to the effects of glowing sunlight, Alfred Thompson Bricher's marine paintings link him to the later phase of America's luminist tradition. Born in Portsmouth, New Hampshire, Bricher was largely self-taught. He moved to New York City in 1868, where he kept a studio until his death in 1908. Bricher enjoyed a long and prolific career, producing and exhibiting oils and watercolors devoted to images of the sea. Most of his subjects came from summer sketching trips up and down the North Atlantic coast. Bricher's sun-filled, harmonious coastal scenes emphasize rocks, sky, and gently rolling surf in a precise manner that exhibits an underlying sense of geometry.

Bricher made his first trip to Grand Manan Island, New Brunswick, Canada, around 1874. He painted many scenes of the island, several of which depict Hetherington's Cove. The artist captures the rugged coast of the area in a shimmering light that penetrates the thick clouds, giving the sea a translucent appearance under the clear, sharp horizon. There is a sense of isolation in these panoramic views of the endless coastline, but in Bricher's paintings nature is not threatening. His tranquil rendering of sea, sun, and shore offers a straightforward view of nature's majesty and perfection.

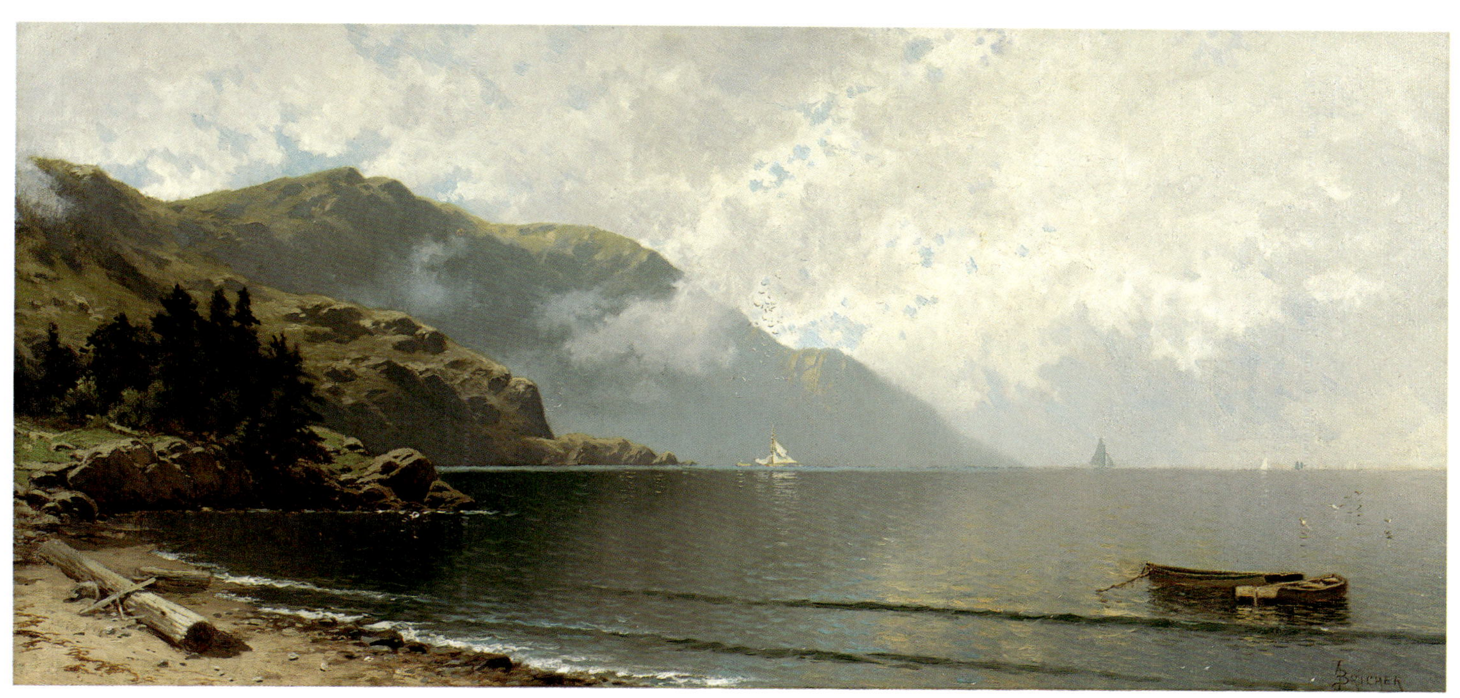

Winslow Homer
1836-1910

Three Boys in a Dory
1873
oil on panel
5 3/4 x 9 3/4 inches
signed and dated ll:
WINSLOW HOMER 1873
inscribed lr: Gloucester
William I. Koch Collection

Through his oil paintings, watercolors, and graphics, Winslow Homer defined the life and landscape of America in the latter part of the nineteenth century. Homer, who was born in Boston, Massachusetts, began his career as an illustrator for *Harper's Weekly* around 1857 and moved to New York City in 1859. The clear, precise manner in which he recorded the Civil War for *Harper's* and his adherence to factual representation would emerge as factors in his later painting style. After the war, Homer turned his attention to country life in America. His approach to nature was straightforward and unsentimental but still possessed a poetic quality.

During the 1860s and 1870s Homer summered in New England and upstate New York, and children became an important part of his imagery. *Three Boys in a Dory* was painted in Gloucester, Massachusetts, in the summer of 1873. During this period, Homer used the sea as a backdrop for views of children sailing, fishing, and sleeping in the sun, and as a means to express his concern for light, color, and reflections. The influence of Japanese prints is discernible in the flat color patterns, the elimination of unnecessary detail, and the off-center placement of the figures. Homer's Gloucester paintings, popular for their storytelling as well as their deft construction, pair the artist's love of outdoor subjects with his fondness for themes of children at play.

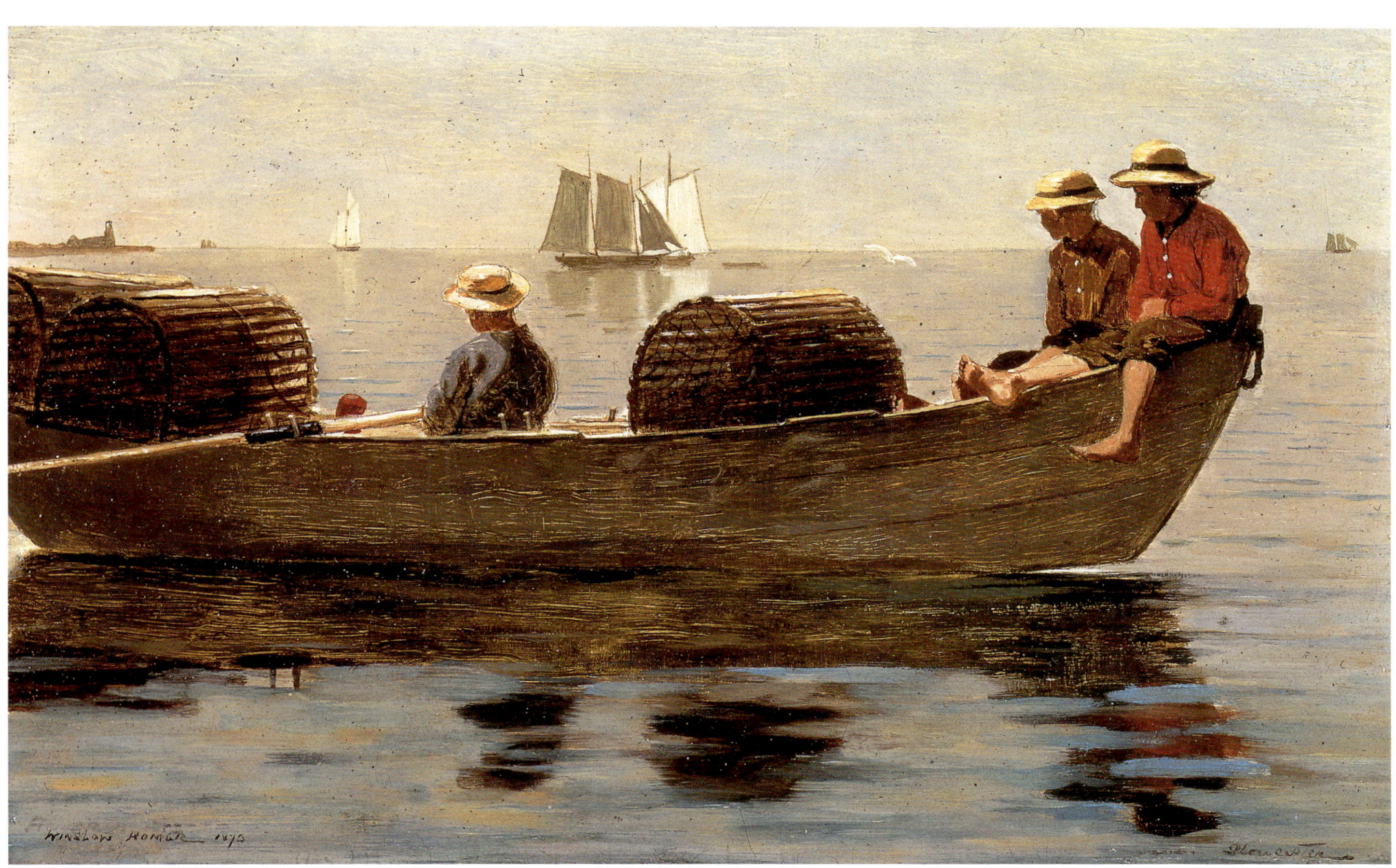

Winslow Homer
1836-1910

Down the Cliff
1883
watercolor, gouache, and
pencil on paper
14 x 19 7/8 inches
signed and dated ll:
Winslow Homer 1883
Weil Brothers

Homer began to paint the robust men and women whose livelihood depended on the sea during his trip to England in the spring of 1881. He spent two seasons near the fishing port of Tynemouth on the North Sea before returning to America in November 1882. The following year he built a studio at Prout's Neck, Maine, where he lived a solitary existence near the ocean. Except for occasional visits to New York City and Boston, Homer remained in Prout's Neck until his death. The power of the sea, the ruggedness of the land, and the sturdy fisherfolk became the subjects of his watercolors.

 Down the Cliff was painted a year after Homer's return from Tynemouth. Its subject is a fisherwoman, probably taken from sketches made in England. The gray sky and subdued colors of this work are typical of the somber tonalities Homer used in his sea paintings. Despite the dark palette, Homer achieved a richness and depth by using a wide variety of grays. Also characteristic of this period is his emphasis on wind and atmosphere. The woman stands on the steep cliff under a foreboding sky, her skirt blowing in the breeze, waiting for the return of the fishing ships.

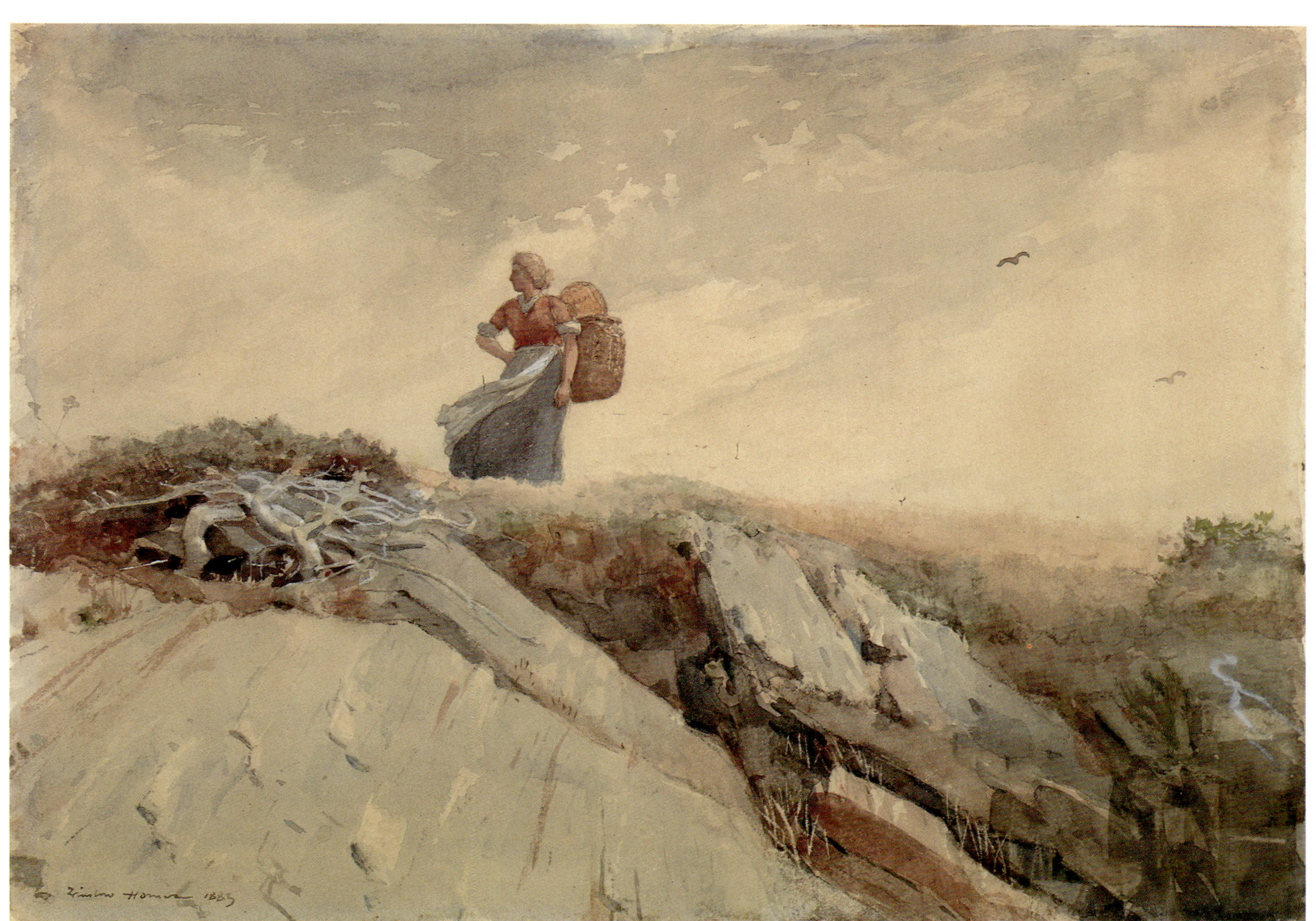

George Inness
1825-1894

Mount Washington,
Conway, New Hampshire
1875
oil on canvas
24 x 38 inches
signed and dated lr:
G. Inness 1875
The Warner Collection
Tuscaloosa, Alabama

60

Early in his career George Inness struggled between the prevailing aesthetic of the precisely detailed Hudson River School landscapes and his own desire to paint a more subjective view of nature. Inness was born near Newburgh, New York. Except for a two-year apprenticeship as an engraver and some brief instruction in painting, most of his early education consisted of studying prints of paintings by the French classicist Claude Lorrain and seventeenth-century Dutch landscape painters. During his many trips to Europe, Inness came under the influence of the French Barbizon School artists, whose broadly painted landscapes and romanticized views of nature promised him the freedom of expression he had been seeking.

In this mid-career landscape, a single figure sits in an open field against a panoramic view of the New Hampshire mountains. Reminiscent of the Barbizon painters' lyrical approach to the landscape, *Mount Washington, Conway, New Hampshire* displays Inness's loose brushwork and emphasis on atmospheric effects. The lower half of the canvas has alternating bands of shadow and radiant sunlight, while the crest of the mountains is bathed in a cool, luminous mist. Inness's landscapes were not a literal transcription of nature but his own personal interpretation of the scene. His chief goal was the creation of an emotional response to the landscape that evoked religious and spiritual associations.

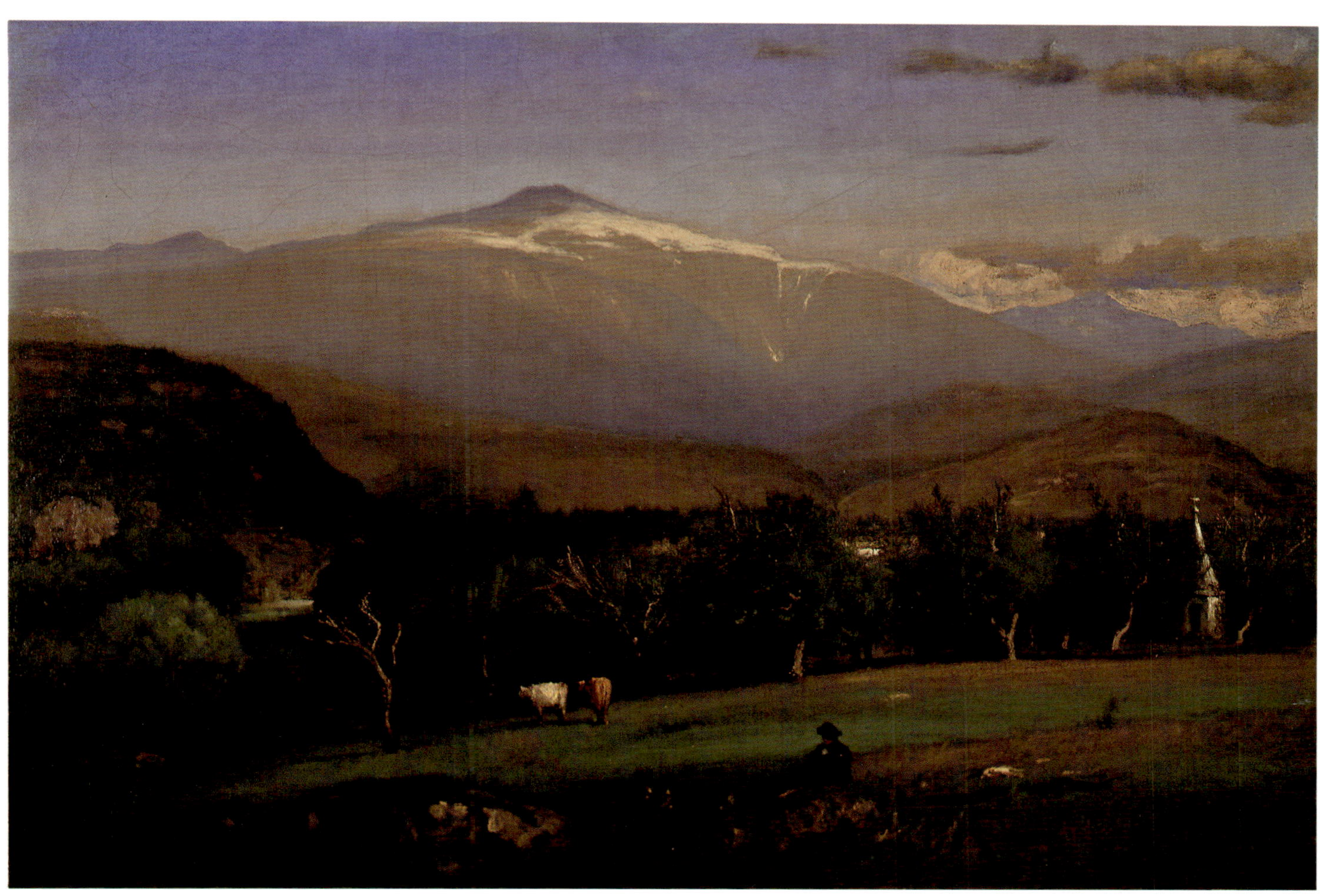

George Inness
1825-1894

Apple Orchard, Spring Showers
1883
oil on canvas
22 x 36 inches
signed and dated lr:
G. Inness 1883
The Warner Collection
Tuscaloosa, Alabama

In 1863 Inness was introduced to the teachings of Emanuel Swedenborg, a Scandinavian theologian who believed that all things on earth correspond to a parallel realm of the spirit. Beginning about 1874 Inness tried to express the spiritual side of nature in his poetic landscapes. Simplified compositions and tranquil moods dominate these paintings. In an attempt to suggest rather than define nature, Inness suppresses detail, concentrates on atmospheric effects, and thus gives his forms an evanescent quality.

The thick atmospheric haze that envelops the landscape in *Apple Orchard, Spring Showers* allows Inness to focus on its immaterial qualities. The forms are indistinct, which suggests that they are heavenly manifestations rather than topographical descriptions. A solitary figure in the foreground is only vaguely defined amidst the grass and sky, which appear as veils of color. The faintly delineated white blossoms of the trees are set against an eerie green sky, like billowing clouds on a mystical horizon. Inness's contemplative mood and the intangible quality of the landscape invite the viewer to experience the spiritual instead of the literal character of nature.

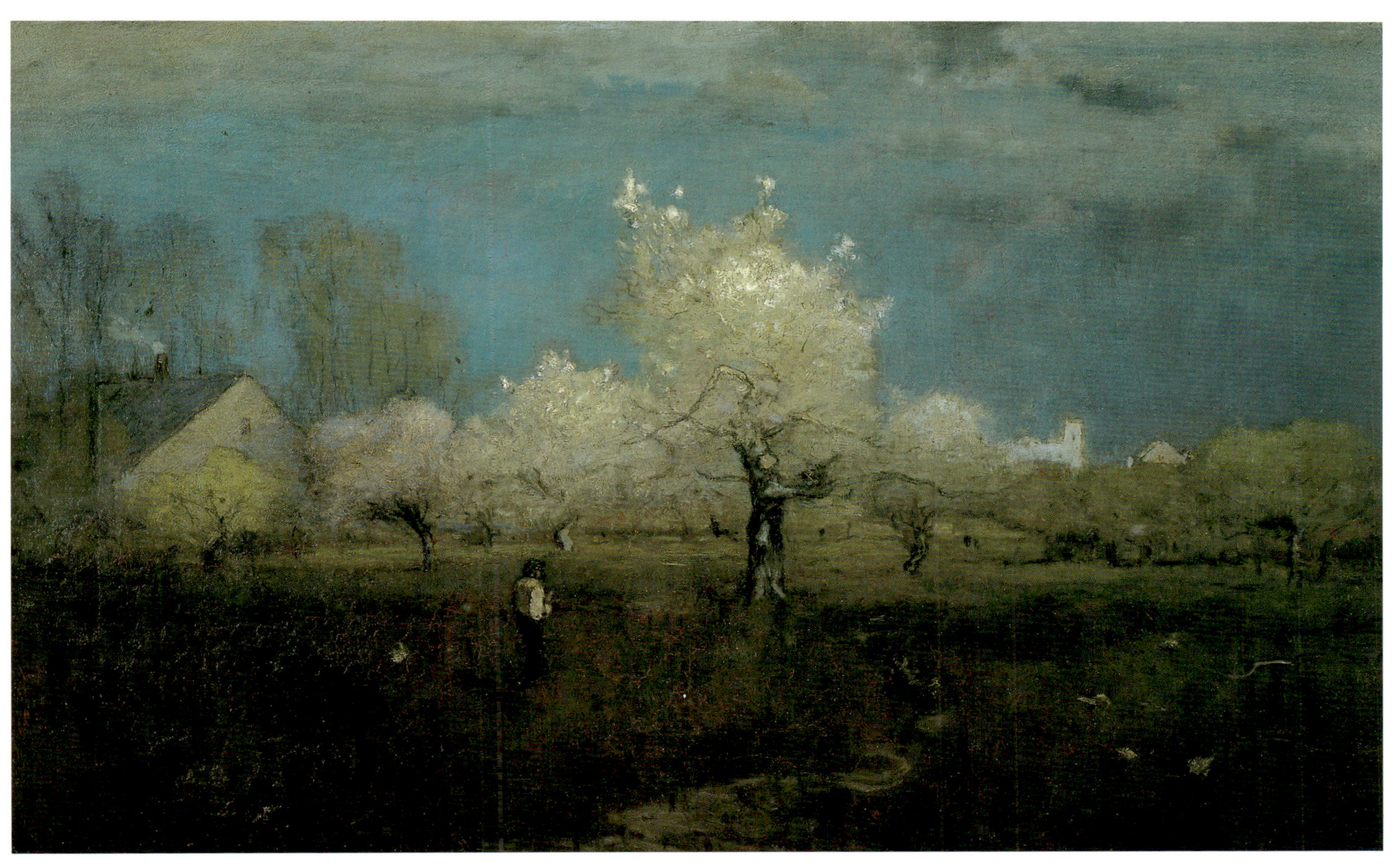

Frank Duveneck
1848-1919

Miss Blood
1880
oil on canvas
48 x 28 inches
signed ul: FD.
inscribed and dated ur:
Venice 1880.
The Warner Collection
Tuscaloosa, Alabama

Frank Duveneck was trained under Wilhelm von Diez in the realist tradition of the Royal Academy of Munich, where he was introduced to the bravura brush strokes and dark tonalities of the Munich School. A successful exhibition at the Boston Art Club in 1875 helped launch his career. When he returned to Munich in 1876 he brought with him a small entourage of fellow painters and began to teach painting to a steady stream of American students, who became known as the "Duveneck boys." In 1879 he moved his classes to Italy, where he spent the winter in Florence and the summer in Venice. After the death of his wife in 1888, Duveneck returned to America. He continued teaching and painting in Cincinnati, across the Ohio River from his birthplace in Covington, Kentucky.

Duveneck befriended the young English beauty Gertrude Elizabeth Blood in Venice in 1880. It was Miss Blood (later Lady Colin Campbell) who sent his etchings to an 1881 London exhibition where they were mistaken for J. A. M. Whistler's, igniting a great controversy. This likeness, painted when Duveneck was entering his most successful period as a portraitist, clearly shows his realist style. The uniformly lit figure stands out against a dark, undefined background. Her bracelet, ring, and fan are precisely rendered, as are the fabric and lace of her dress. Although Duveneck never completely abandoned the Munich style, this portrait exhibits a change from his earlier rapid brush strokes to a smoother, more specific rendering of form.

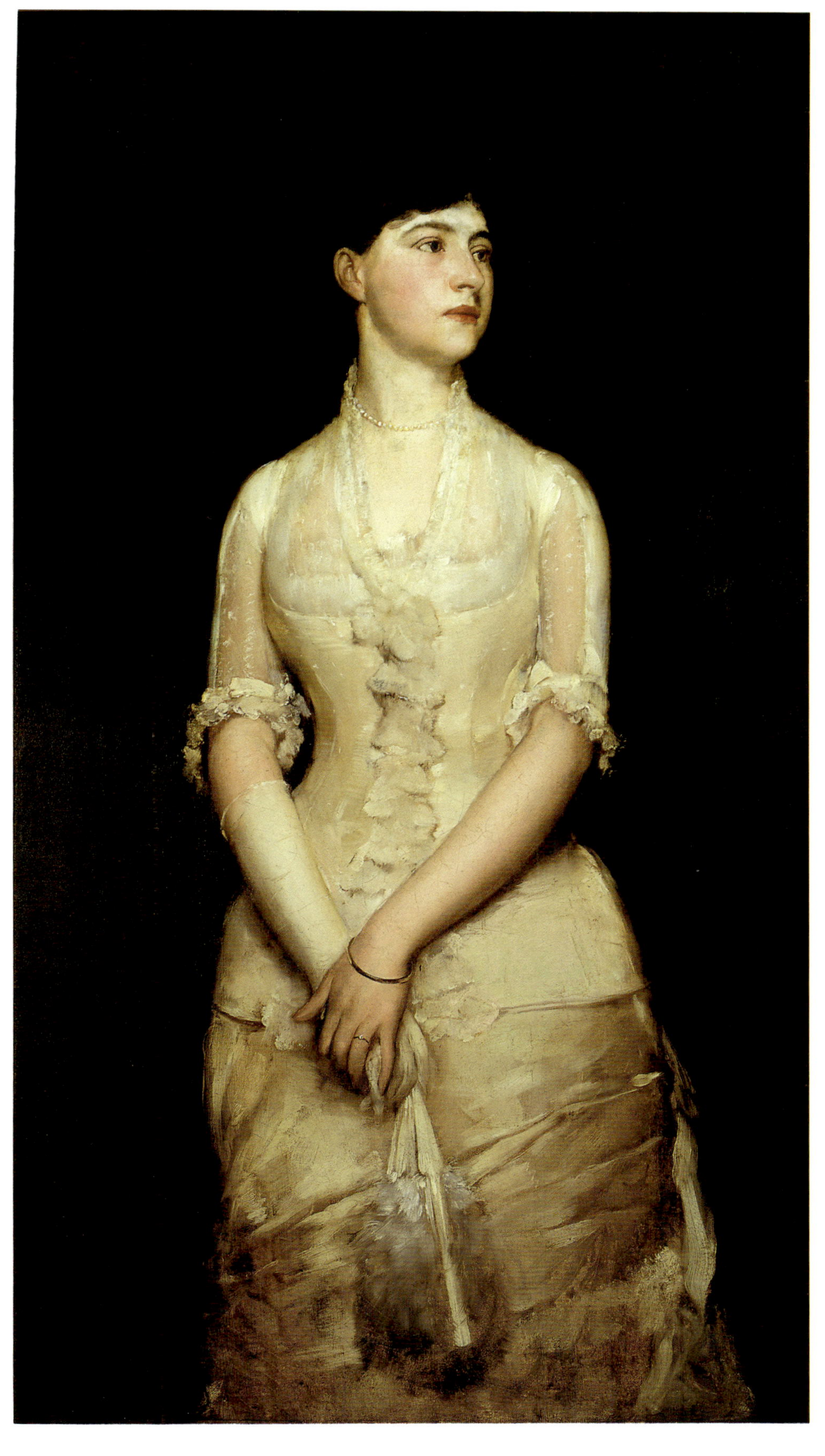

Woman in an Interior
1895
oil on canvas
36 x 26 inches
signed ll: JL Stewart
The Dicke Collection
New Bremen, Ohio

Julius Stewart was the son of a wealthy sugar plantation owner who was also an art collector. He was influenced by the Spanish academic painters in his father's collection as well as by the French academician Jean-Léon Gérôme. Stewart was born in Philadelphia, but after the age of ten lived virtually his entire life in Paris, where he became known as "The Parisian from Philadelphia." Stewart belonged to French high society, which he depicted with meticulous and sumptuous detail in a style combining portraiture and fashionable genre. His technique and subject matter resemble those of the French painter James Tissot, an artist he greatly admired. Stewart became famous for his paintings of celebrities, such as the actresses Lillie Langtry and Sarah Bernhardt. During the last quarter of the nineteenth century he was a frequent exhibitor in both Europe and America. His elegant figural pieces won him particular acclaim in Paris during the 1880s.

Woman in an Interior displays Stewart's talent for depicting fashionable women posed in intimate settings. During the 1890s Stewart was also painting conversation pieces, large compositions of balls and weddings, and nudes in the manner of Gérôme. In all these works, the artist's focus is beautiful women. The composition of *Woman in an Interior* is a subtle interplay of diagonals and rectilinear shapes. While Stewart adheres to academic principles, he also acknowledges the popularity of impressionism in his looser handling of the paintings in the background. The relaxed pose, subdued atmosphere, and warm tonality contribute to an overall impression of the sitter's sophistication and approachability. While the name of this elegant model has not been identified, her image is typical of the works that established Stewart as one of Paris's most successful portraitists.

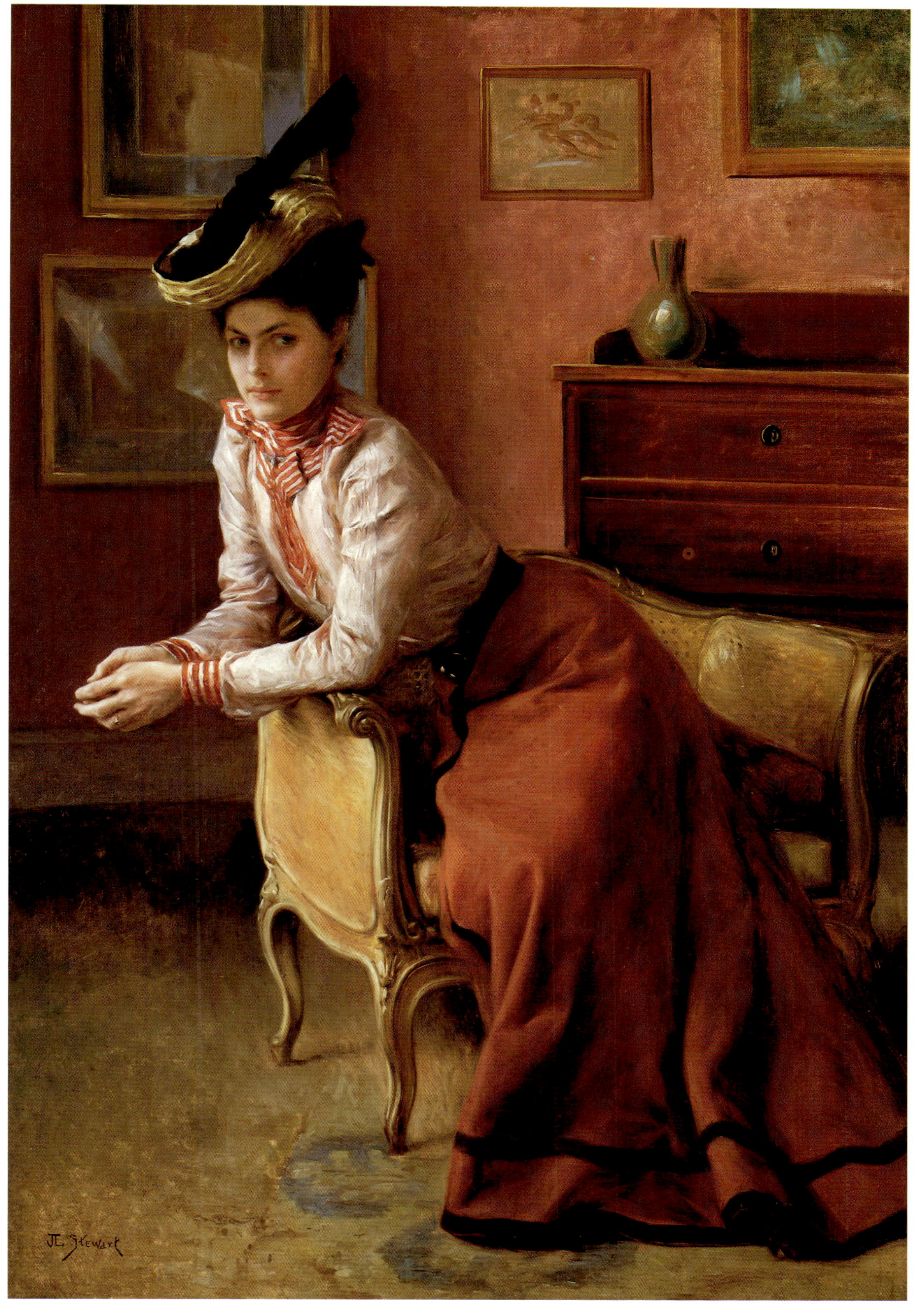

John Frederick Peto
1854–1907

Still Life with Oranges and Banana
1880
oil on wood panel
5 x 10 inches
The Warner Collection
Tuscaloosa, Alabama

Although he is now recognized as one of America's most important still-life painters of the nineteenth century, John Frederick Peto spent much of his life in relative obscurity. He was born in Philadelphia and studied briefly at the Pennsylvania Academy of the Fine Arts. He became acquainted with the Philadelphia artist William Harnett, whose fame as a still-life painter was well established. Both men painted in the *trompe-l'oeil* or "deceive the eye" style, which creates the illusion that the painted object is real. Shortly after Peto's death, Harnett's name was added to several of his works. Although Peto's still-lifes have a luminous quality and an intimacy that are not found in Harnett's paintings, their styles are sufficiently similar that the false signatures were not discovered until 1949.

One of Peto's preferred still-life formats is the tabletop composition. In *Still Life with Oranges and Banana* he focuses on three pieces of fruit resting on a table. The orange peel and the banana are positioned so that they appear to extend into the viewer's space. The illusion derives from a meticulous rendering of the fruit against a dark background and the use of a bright light to bring the objects into prominence. The fruit is literally bursting with flavor and tempting to touch. This play on various sensory perceptions is an important aspect of *trompe-l'oeil* still-life painting.

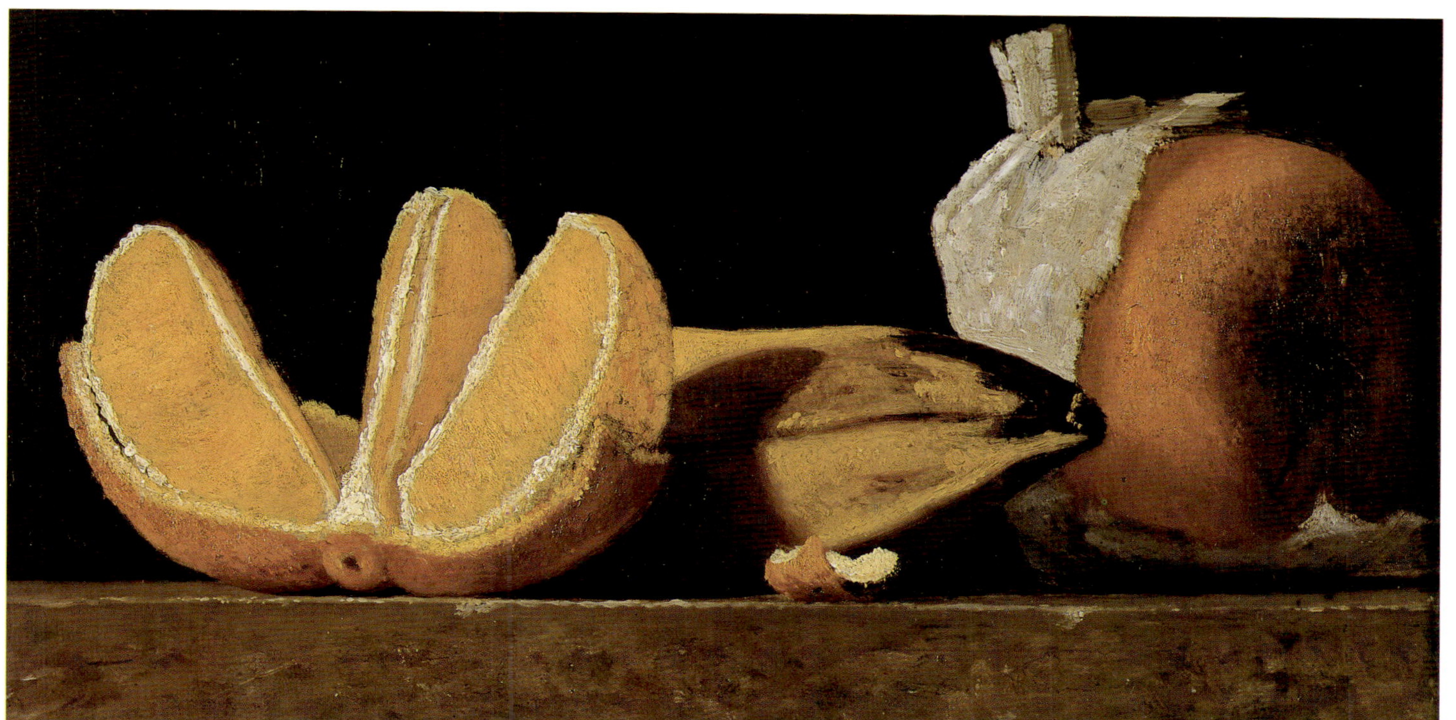

Abbott H. Thayer
1849-1921

Water Lilies
c. 1886
oil on canvas
13 x 16 inches
signed ul: A. H. Thayer
The Dicke Collection
New Bremen, Ohio

Although Abbott Handerson Thayer is best known for his idealized images of young women, he was also an ardent student of nature who painted landscape and still-life subjects. Thayer was born in Boston and studied at the Brooklyn Art School and the National Academy of Design. He went to Paris in 1875 and became a pupil of Jean-Léon Gérôme at the Ecole des Beaux-Arts. In 1879 he returned to New York, where he divided his time between the city and the Hudson River area. Thayer settled in Dublin, New Hampshire, in 1901, where he turned increasingly to the painting of landscapes that exhibit an impressionist influence.

Thayer spent the summer of 1886 in South Woodstock, Connecticut, working with two friends. He obtained a flat-bottomed boat, which the trio used as a floating studio. *Water Lilies* is certainly the result of one of their excursions. Emerging from the surface of their watery garden are several lilies in various stages of flowering. Unlike the luminous, shimmering settings of Claude Monet's water lilies, which they predate, Thayer's blossoms are set in a dark, flat background that produces an impenetrable space. He uses contrast and dramatic lighting to enhance the prominence and luminosity of the white petals. With thick strokes of impasto, Thayer also distinguishes their soft, delicate texture from the glossy surfaces of the floating leaves. While nature may have been Thayer's immediate inspiration, his still-life subjects were also influenced by the widely admired floral works of American artist John La Farge. Thayer's feeling for nature—and design—enables him to endow an intimate composition with a monumental scale.

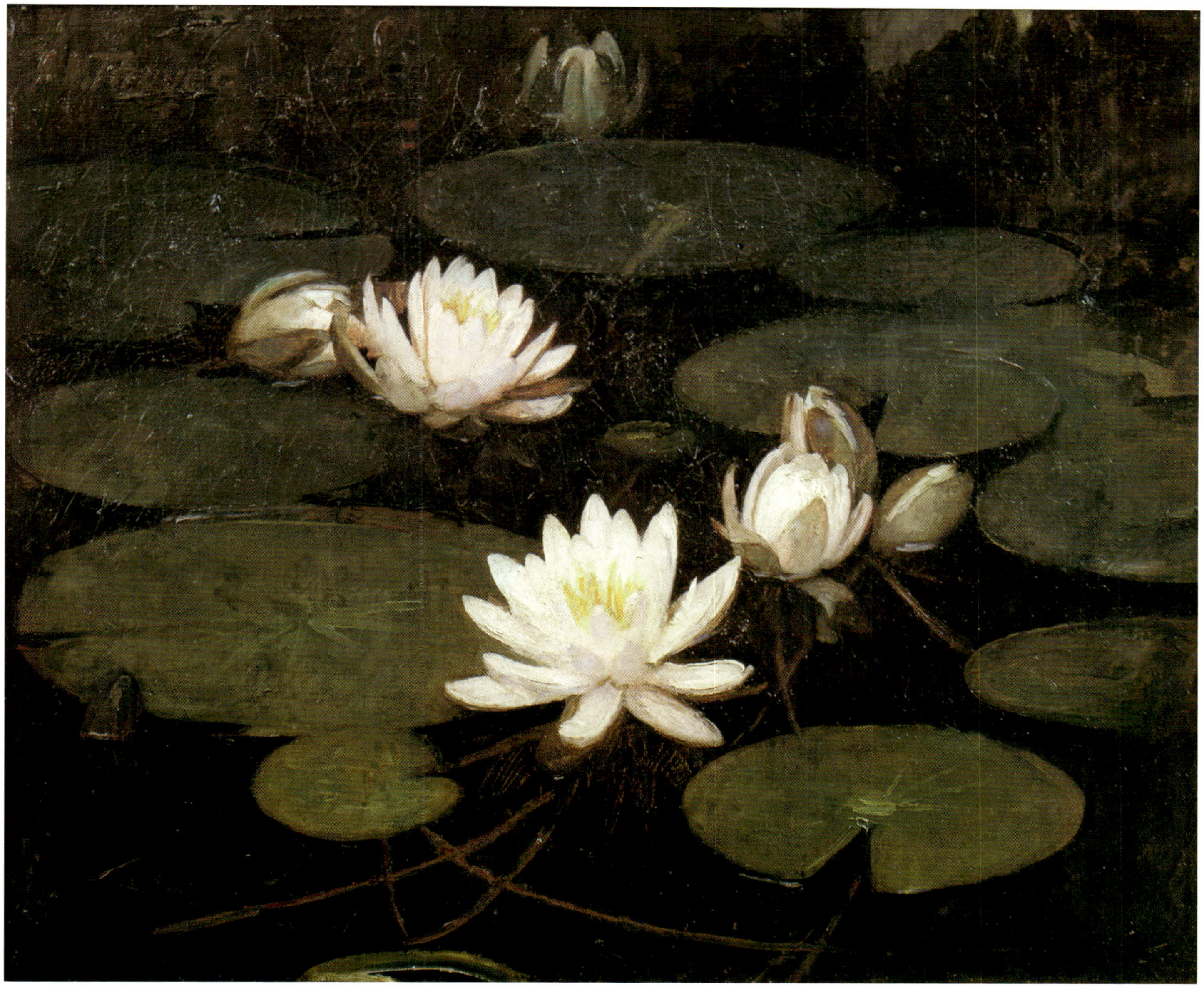

A Field, Kerlaouen
1885
oil on canvas
32 x 53 inches
signed ll: Arthur W. Dow
The Dicke Collection
New Bremen, Ohio

Arthur Wesley Dow exerted a major influence on American art through his teaching and writing. He was born in Ipswich, Massachusetts, and studied art in Boston and at the Académie Julian in Paris. There Dow was influenced by the classicism of Puvis de Chavannes and the subdued colors of the French Barbizon painters. He returned to Ipswich in 1889, and moved to New York City in 1895 to teach at Pratt Institute. His art manual *Composition* (1899) popularized Japanese design principles and color theory. In 1903 he became head of the art education department at Columbia University Teachers College. Among Dow's students were Max Weber and Georgia O'Keeffe—both early exponents of the modernist tradition.

Dow arrived in Paris in 1884 and began painting in Brittany, France's rugged western province, in May 1885. The titles of his Brittany landscapes often bear the names of specific painting sites, such as *A Field, Kerlaouen*. Dow preferred to paint in the diffuse light of overcast Breton days, when the atmosphere was misty. Although he uses divided color and brushwork in his field of wildflowers, the results are tonal rather than impressionist. The emphasis is on atmospheric conditions and a desire to maintain the integrity of the landscape. The composition's high horizon line and asymmetrical placement of trees suggest that Dow was already employing elements of Japanese design that would appear in his art manual *Composition* at the end of the century.

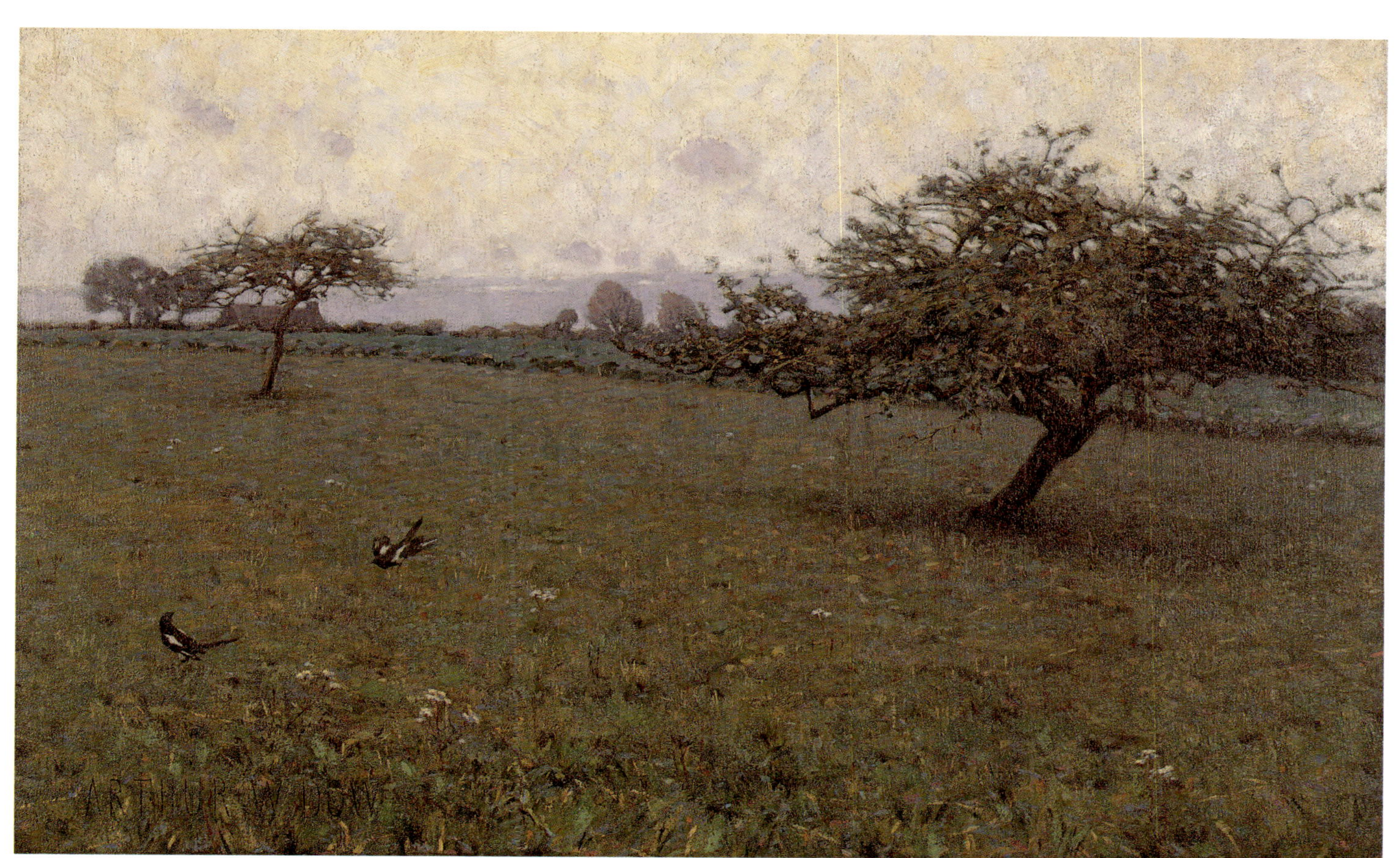
ARTHUR W. DOW

Moonlight and Sea
oil on canvas
32 1/4 x 34 1/4 inches
signed lr: Emil Carlsen
The Dicke Collection
New Bremen, Ohio

74

Before moving to Chicago in 1872, Emil Carlsen studied architecture in his native Denmark. Within a few years of his arrival, he had turned his talents as a draftsman into a career as a painter and teacher. Carlsen's early success was based on his still-life paintings, which emphasize pure form and rich textural distinctions. From 1885 to 1887 he lived in Paris, where he studied the still lifes of the eighteenth-century French painter Jean Baptiste Chardin and executed still lifes on commission. While Carlsen had long been devoted to images of the sea, he did not concentrate on marine and landscape painting until the late 1880s. His large, often square compositions display his preference for subdued color harmonies and decorative effects rather than naturalistic details. In his marine paintings, Carlsen directed his technical prowess to lyrical explorations in mood and spirituality.

One of Carlsen's most poetic canvases is *Moonlight and Sea.* Clouds glowing with subtle reflections of blue, rose, and yellow billow from the low horizon and compress the sea to the bottom of the composition. Carlsen sometimes painted religious subjects in similar seascape settings, but *Moonlight and Sea* exudes a less explicit spirituality. With its expansive sky and luminous moonlight, Carlsen's painting breathes a sense of the infinite.

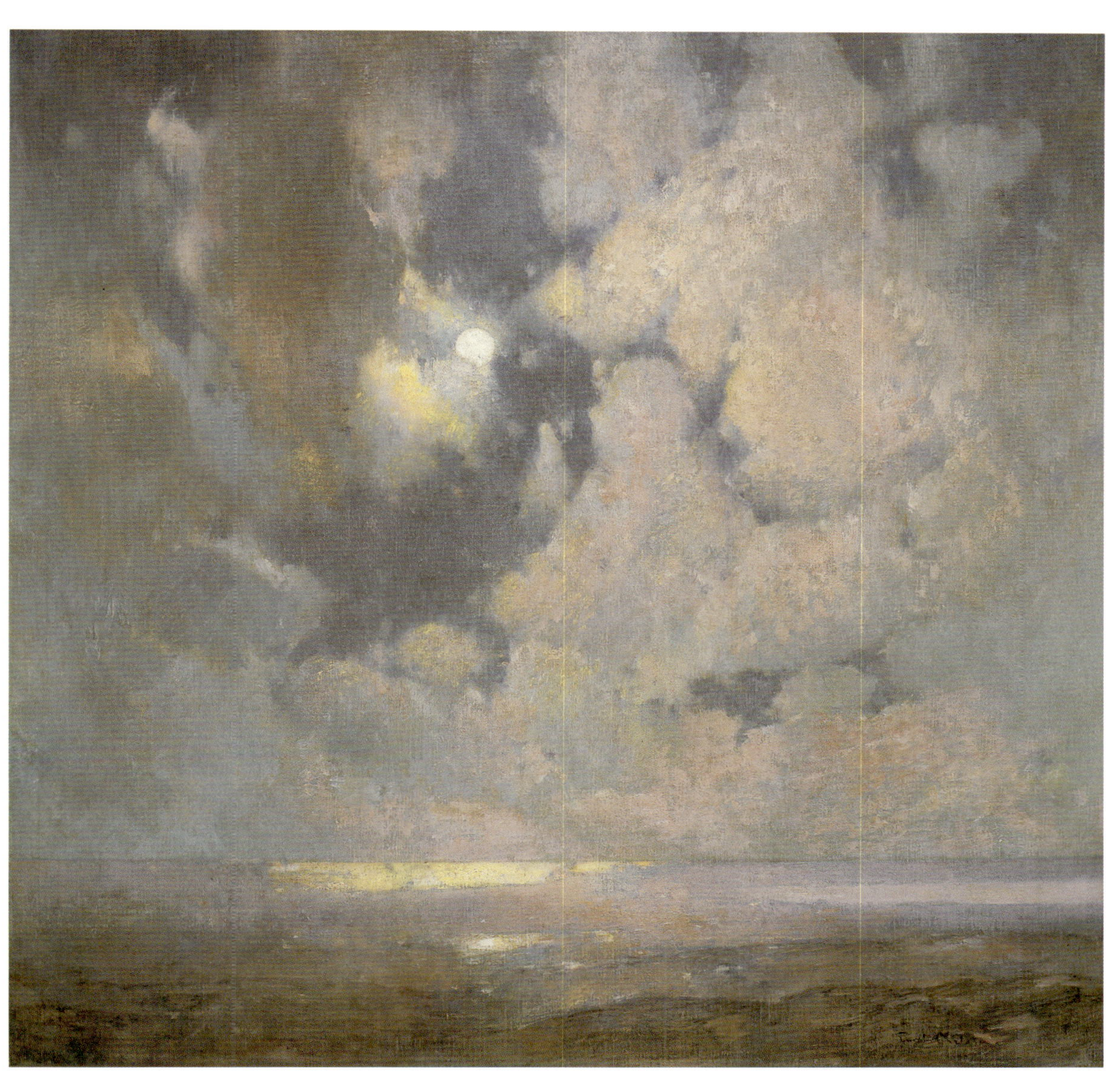

Young Girl
on an Ocean Steamer
c. 1884
pastel on paper
29 x 24 inches
signed mr: W.M. Chase
and stamped P.P.
The Warner Collection
Tuscaloosa, Alabama

76

Born in 1849 in Nineveh, Indiana, William Merritt Chase grew up in Indianapolis. He studied at the National Academy of Design in New York City before embarking for Munich, where he attended the Royal Academy. Chase also visited Venice with fellow Munich students Frank Duveneck and John H. Twachtman. Upon returning to New York City in 1878, he took a position as one of the first teachers at the new Art Students League. The outgoing, dynamic artist, who conducted classes at the Brooklyn Art Association, Pennsylvania Academy of the Fine Arts, and two schools he founded himself, became one of America's most influential teachers. His open manner attracted students with diverse sensibilities, and among them were future modernists such as Charles Demuth, Charles Sheeler, and Georgia O'Keeffe. As a mature painter, Chase was a versatile virtuoso, capable of expressing himself as a realist, an impressionist, or an exponent of the dark manner and vigorous brush strokes of the Munich School.

Chase's numerous voyages to Europe no doubt provided the inspiration for *Young Girl on an Ocean Steamer*. It presents a young lady in Victorian attire enduring the tedium of a long trip. The composition demonstrates Chase's finesse in working with pastels. The picture is stamped P.P., indicating that the artist was a member of the Society of Painters in Pastel. Chase was adept at using the medium to create luminous effects or to suggest a rich variety of surfaces. The contrasting textures of the tablecloth, carpet, and girl's dress are enhanced by a subtle illumination that is typical of Chase's use of pastel. Brilliant highlights and deep shadows, along with the strong contrasts of white and black, reflect Chase's admiration for the French artist Edouard Manet.

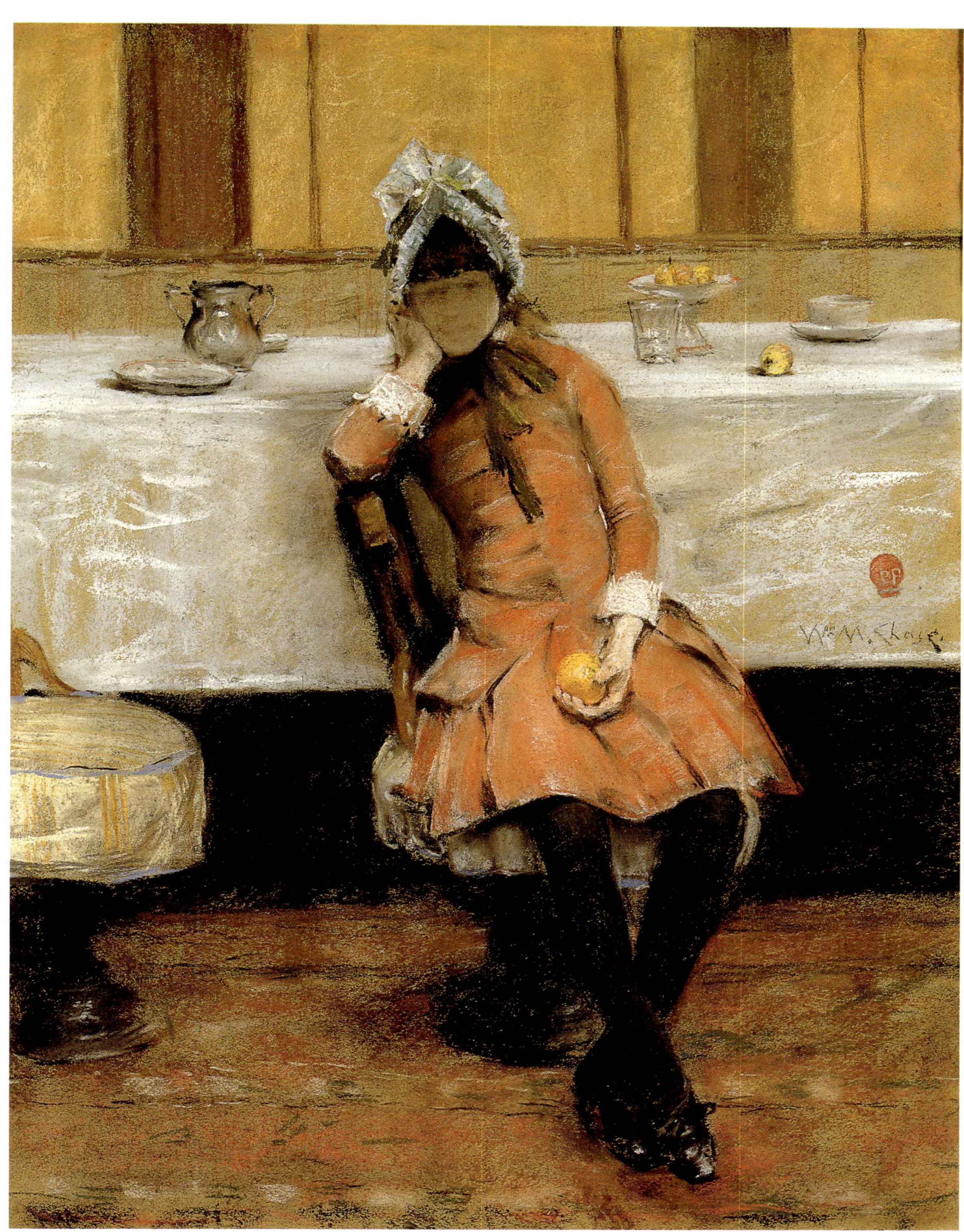

William Merritt Chase
1849-1916

Pot Hunter
c. 1895
pastel on paper
22 x 39 inches
signed lr: Wm M. Chase
The Warner Collection
Tuscaloosa, Alabama

In 1891 Chase began spending his summers at Shinnecock Hills, Long Island. There he established a summer school in which he taught the principles of *plein-air* painting, the basis of the impressionist landscape style. *Pot Hunter* is one of a series of outdoor subjects devoted to the lone hunter in search of food. The title refers to a person who hunts for need rather than for sport. The dominant landscape and solitary figure recall Hudson River School paintings, which emphasize man's dependence on nature. Chase's view, however, captures a scene from everyday life in the simple, straightforward manner that characterized his approach to art.

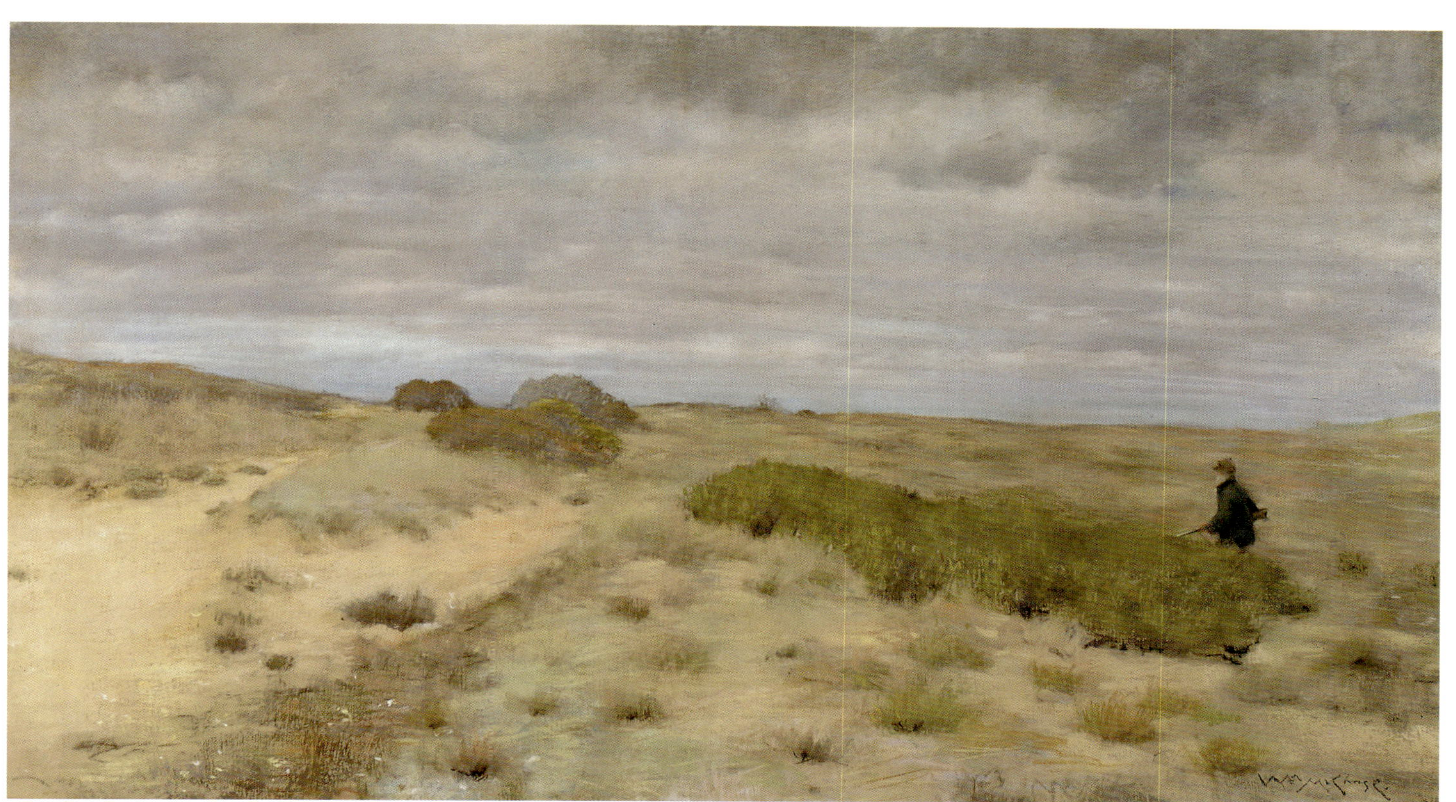

William Merritt Chase
1849-1916

Portrait of the Artist's Daughter
c. 1897
oil on canvas
35 1/2 x 25 1/2 inches
inscribed and signed lr:
To my friend Clinedinst/
Wm M. Chase
The Warner Collection
Tuscaloosa, Alabama

Chase was the father of eight children, many of whom are the subjects of his portraits and domestic scenes. His daughter Dorothy was one of his most frequent models. In *Portrait of the Artist's Daughter* he captures her playfulness with refreshing spontaneity. The informal pose, dark background, and deep perspective are hallmarks of Chase's portrait style. In an otherwise empty room, Dorothy stands next to a screen, a rigid element that serves as a foil for her engaging stance. Here as in other paintings, the oriental screen hints at Chase's debt to Japanese art. The somber setting is reminiscent of the portraits of James Abbott McNeill Whistler, while the facile brushwork suggests the influence of John Singer Sargent.

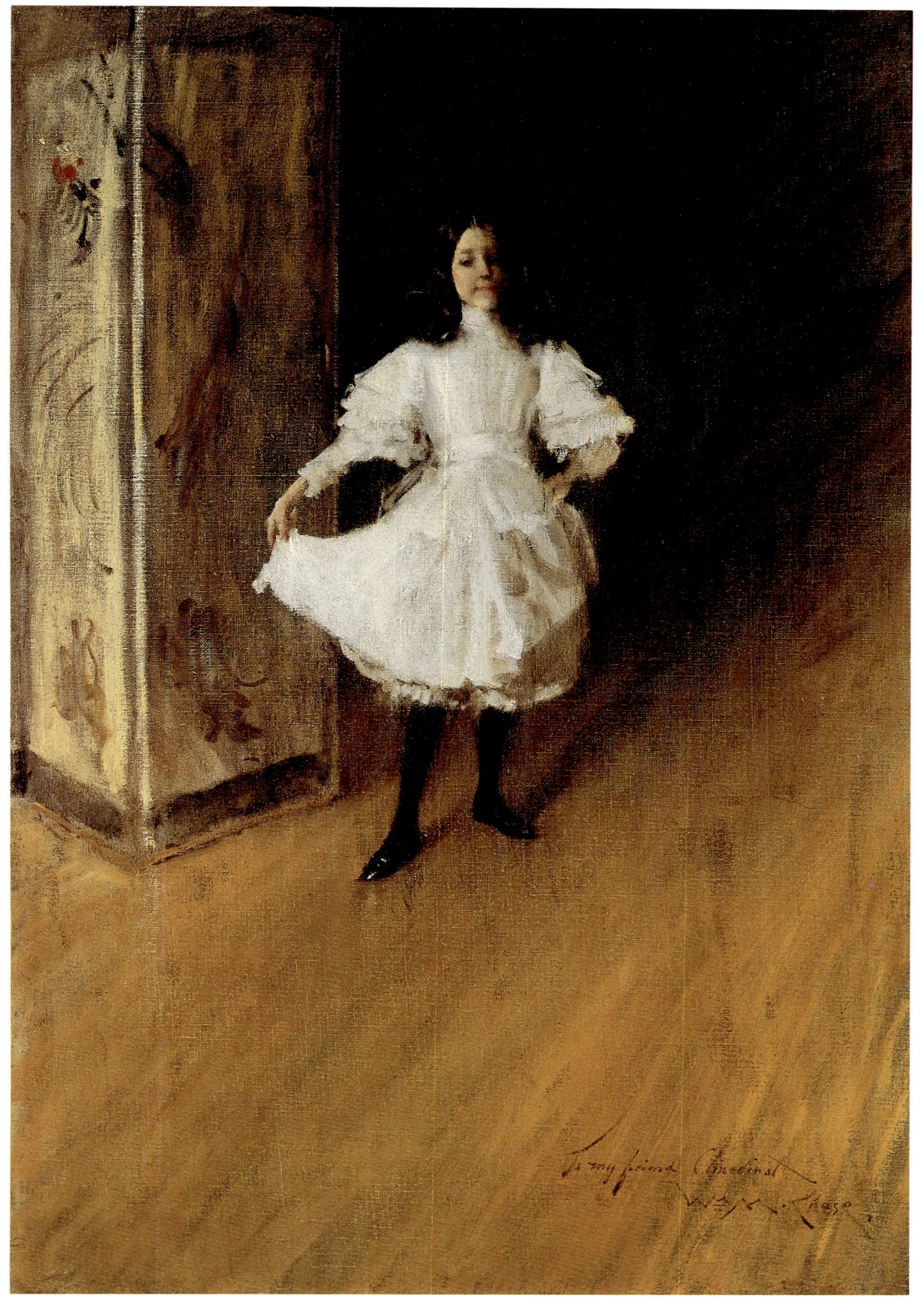

Capri

1878

oil on canvas

20 x 25 inches

inscribed and signed ll:

To my friend Fanny/

John S. Sargent

inscribed and dated lr:

Capri 1878

The Warner Collection

Tuscaloosa, Alabama

82

John Singer Sargent was born in Florence, Italy, to affluent American parents. His mother, an amateur painter, encouraged her son's artistic tendencies. At the age of twelve Sargent began his studies in Rome, after which he attended the Accademia delle Belle Arti in Florence. In 1874 he enrolled in the Ecole des Beaux-Arts in Paris and sought instruction at the atelier of Emile Carolus-Duran, whose animated brush strokes were an important influence on his style. In Paris Sargent was also exposed to the art of the French impressionists, who were just beginning to exhibit their work. On trips to Holland, Belgium, and Spain, he studied the paintings of Diego Velázquez and Frans Hals. In 1880, during a stay in Venice with his family, he met J. A. M. Whistler. When Sargent's *Madame X (Portrait of Madame Pierre Gautreau)* was exhibited in the 1884 Paris salon, the sitter's unconventional pose and costume caused a scandal. Sargent felt compelled to leave Paris, and in 1886 he settled in London.

In the summer of 1878 Sargent traveled to the Mediterranean island of Capri. He found lodging at the Marina Hotel and organized a festive party for several European painters also staying on the island. *Capri*, a scene from this rooftop party, shows the artist's model Rosina dancing the tarantella to the sound of a tambourine played by the seated figure. This theme recurs in Sargent's famous painting of a Spanish dance, *El Jaleo*, 1882. The rapid brushwork in the women's costumes is reminiscent of Hals and Velázquez. These animated figures stand out against the more broadly painted white building. The unusually cropped composition and the spontaneity of Sargent's treatment suggest his affinities with impressionism, but his palette of subtly modulated light and dark tones takes *Capri* far from the French aesthetic.

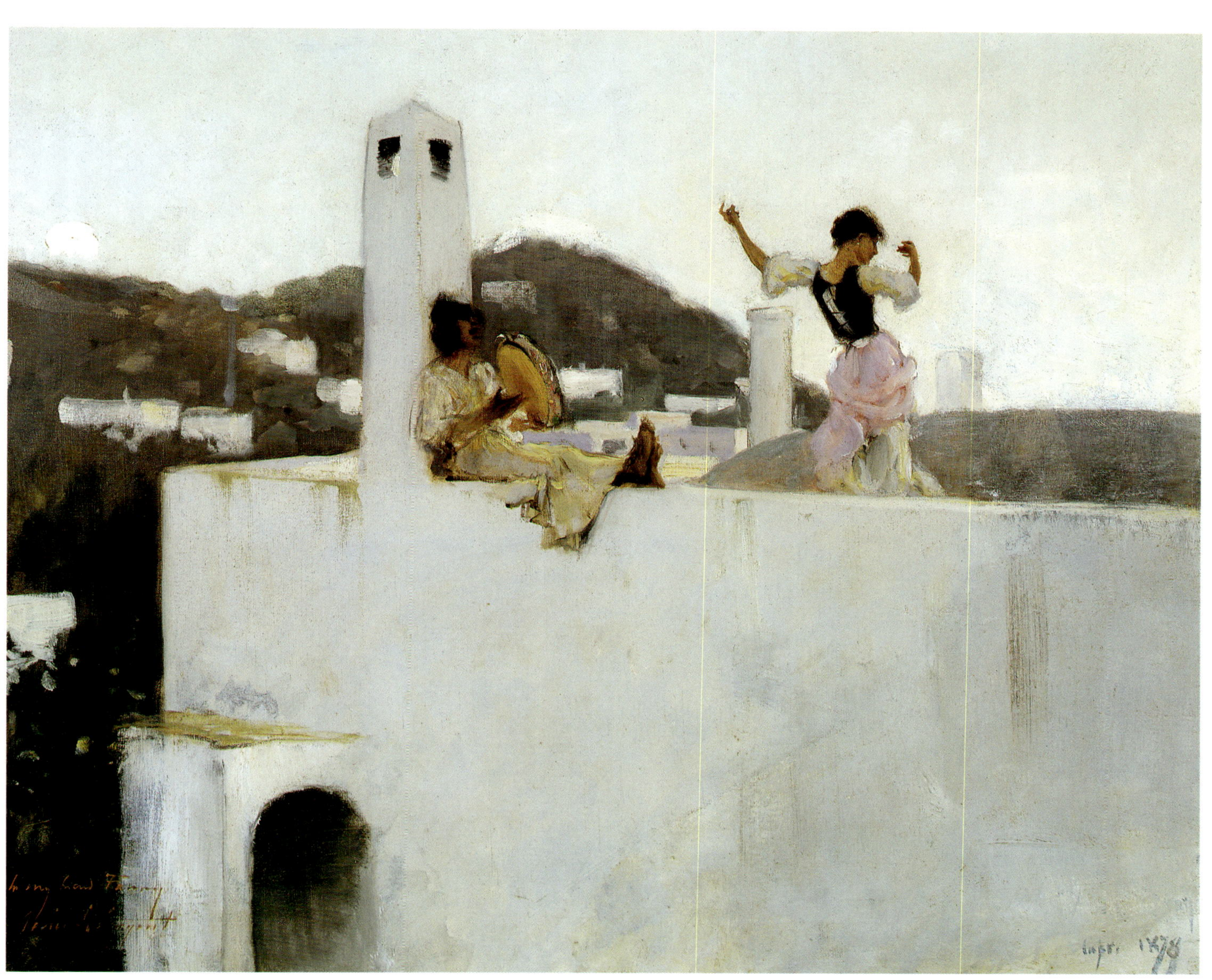

John Singer Sargent
1856-1925

*Portrait of a Young Boy
—Gordon Fairchild*
1890
oil on canvas
62 x 36 inches
inscribed and signed ur:
To Mrs. Fairchild
John Singer Sargent
Huffington Collection

84

Sargent, one of the finest portraitists of his era, drew his subjects from the elite of international society, painting fashionable women in elegant gowns, rich industrialists, and their children. By the early twentieth century Sargent had painted hundreds of portraits and had earned fame, fortune, and honors. His style reflects the teaching of Emile Carolus-Duran in its bravura brush strokes and mastery of tones. Although Sargent was influenced by impressionism, he never fully abandoned the use of dark tonalities in his formal portraits.

The free, spontaneous style that made Sargent famous is evident in *Portrait of a Young Boy—Gordon Fairchild*. The boy was the son of Charles and Elizabeth Fairchild of Boston, who were lifelong friends of the artist. Gordon is presented as a somber figure: he is dressed in black and sits with eyes downcast, lost in private thoughts. Only the boy's white collar and the white guinea pig in his lap ease the severity of his dark attire. Sargent's rapid, dexterous brush strokes on this thinly painted canvas are particularly noticeable in the clothes and background. The large, patterned red pillow that cushions the boy's head provides some relief from the painting's somber tonality. Gordon appears to be encircled by the oversized chair in which he sits, as if it were a substitute for his mother's arms.

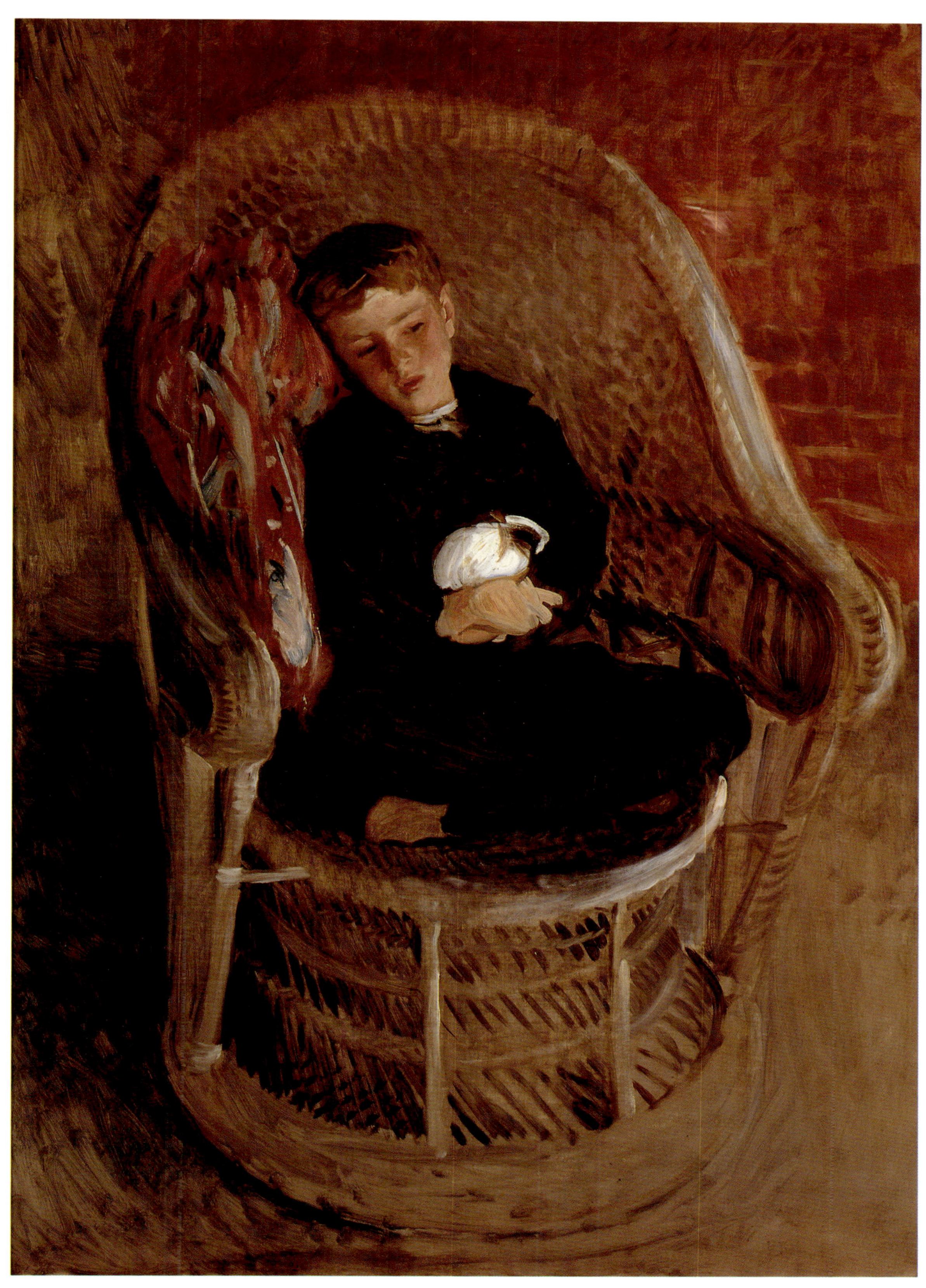

Childe Hassam
1859-1935

The Lighthouse
1886
watercolor on paper
19 x 12 inches
signed and dated ll:
Childe/Hassam/86
Terry Huffington Dittman

86

Childe Hassam is one of America's most renowned impressionist painters. He was born in Dorchester, Massachusetts, to a prominent family who named him Frederick, which he dropped in favor of his middle name early in his career. By the time he was seventeen, Hassam had decided to become an artist, and he began working as a free-lance illustrator while attending evening classes at the Boston Art Club. In 1886, just before his departure for three years of work and study in Paris, Hassam visited the Isles of Shoals, a group of nine small islands about ten miles off the Maine-New Hampshire coast.

During his stay on the Isles of Shoals, Hassam painted a series of about a half dozen watercolors of the White Island Light. This lighthouse, built in 1865, was the most famous structure at the Shoals and a major summer tourist attraction. The picturesque landmark is the subject of many photographs and of paintings by artists such as Alfred Thompson Bricher. In his rendering, Hassam focuses on the tower and its unusual covered walkway. Painted from close range, the image is based on soft tonalities applied in even brush strokes. The billowing clouds act as a backdrop to the emphatic vertical of the tower. Hassam eliminated all nonessential details with the intention of endowing the lighthouse with a powerful presence. This stark depiction of a familiar subject was an attempt by Hassam to find something new in commonplace images.

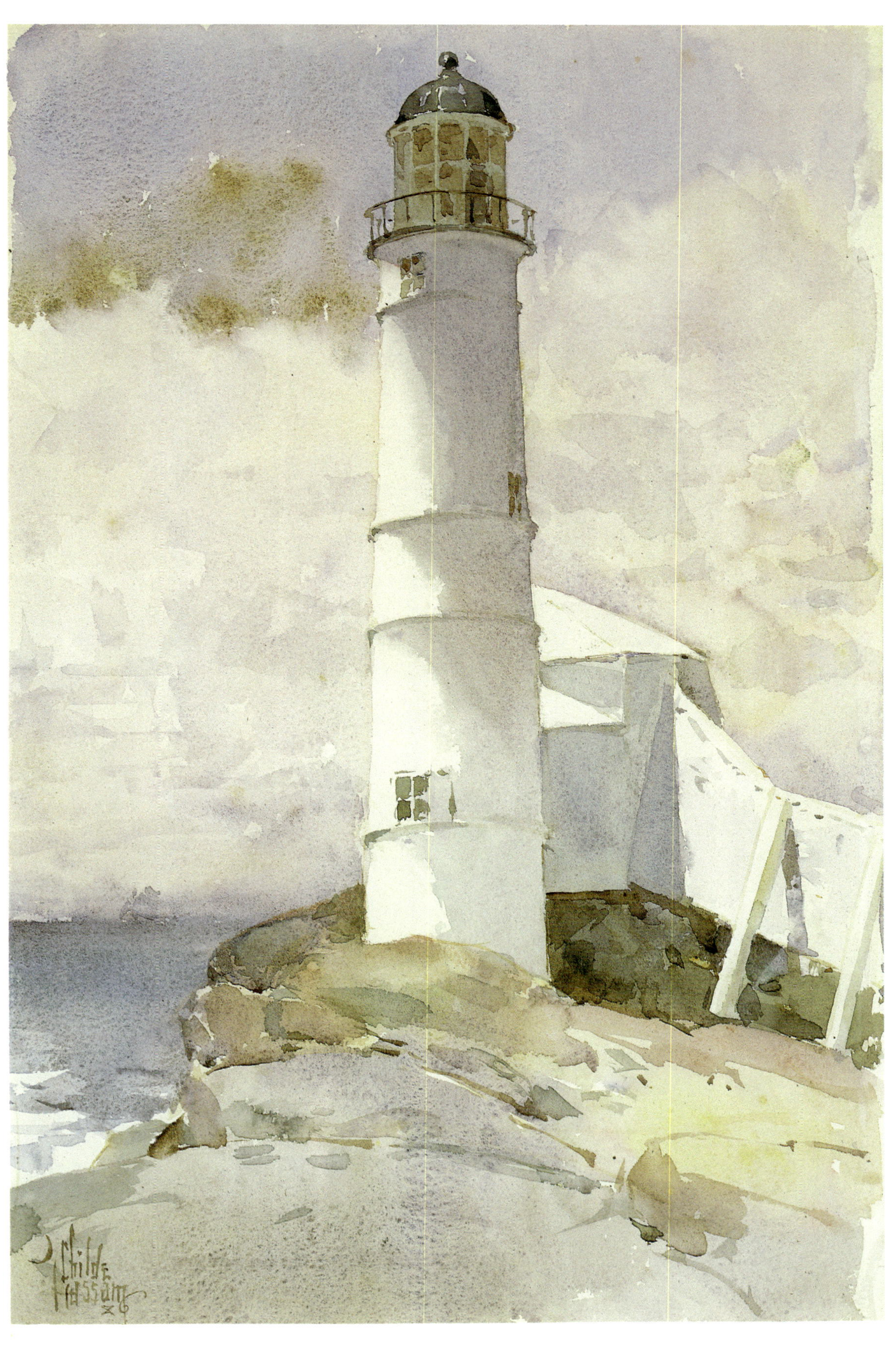

Childe Hassam
1859-1935

Ten Pound Island
1896
oil on canvas
32 1/4 x 32 1/4 inches
signed and dated lr:
Childe Hassam/1896
The Warner Collection
Tuscaloosa, Alabama

The small port of Gloucester, Massachusetts, with its light-filled atmosphere and coastal setting, has inspired numerous painters, including Childe Hassam, Winslow Homer, and John Twachtman. Hassam first painted in the vicinity of Gloucester during a summer trip to the New England coast in 1890, shortly after his return from Europe. He included the area in his summer sojourns until well beyond the turn of the century.

During the hot summer months, when the sun shines brightly over the Gloucester landscape, women used to spend their leisure hours on the porch, protected by the cool shade of the roof. This painting shows the artist's wife and her sister relaxing on the veranda. In the middle distance is Ten Pound Island. The only structure on this uninhabited island is the green building, which functions as a lighthouse. Hassam's broken strokes of bright color give this quiet setting a striking vibrancy and suggest the example of the French impressionists, which Hassam saw first hand during his stay in Paris. The rapid brushwork and abruptly cropped chair add spontaneity to the scene. Through its diagonal placement in front of the two figures, the empty rocking chair leads the viewer into the picture space. A book and fan on the seat of this chair indicate that someone has recently left the group. This sense of catching a fleeting moment in time was one of Hassam's principal objectives—and one he shared with the French impressionists.

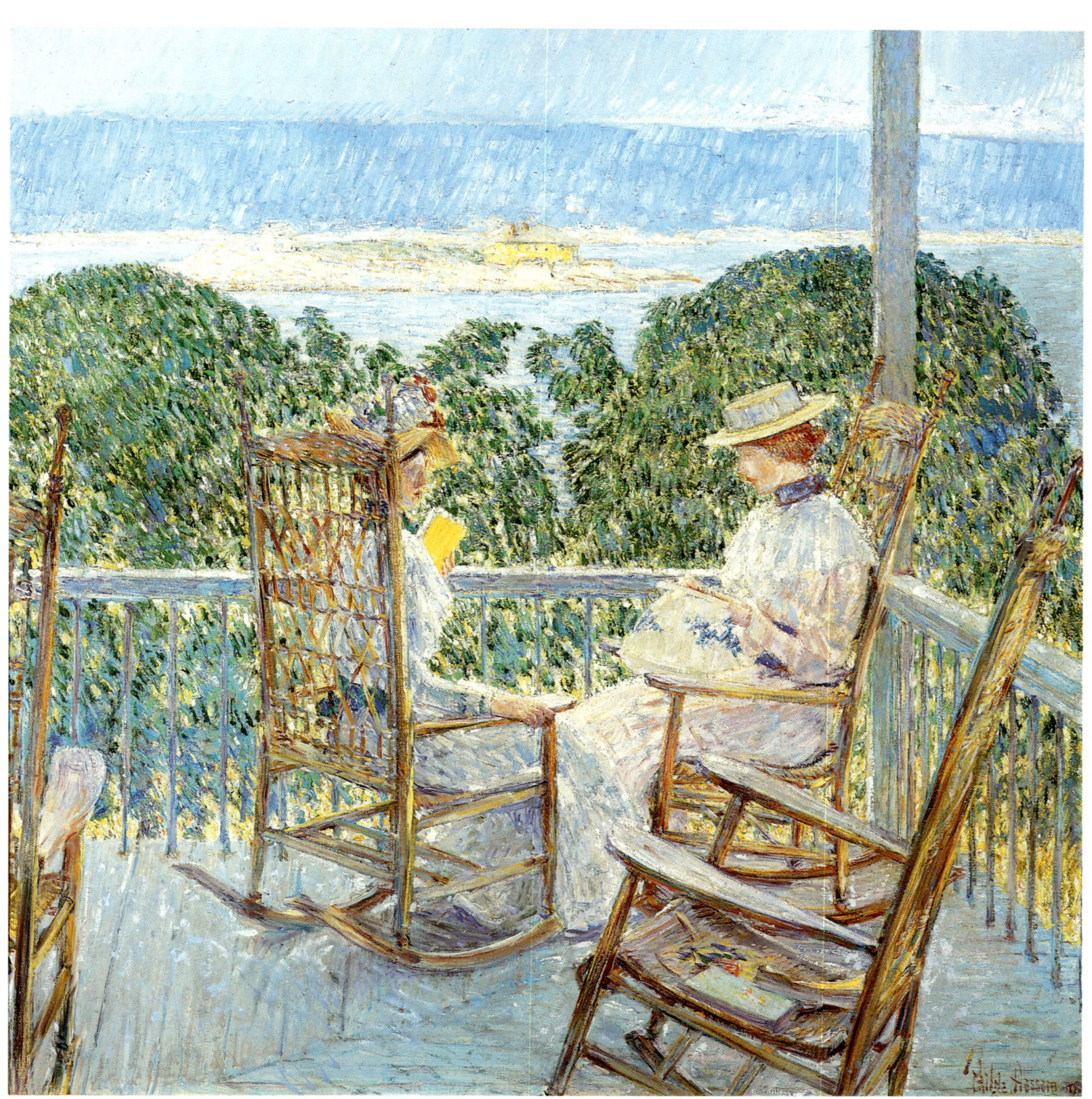

Childe Hassam
1859-1935

Lyman's Ledge—Appledore
1901
oil on canvas
25 x 30 inches
signed and dated lr:
Childe Hassam 1901
The Dicke Collection
New Bremen, Ohio

When Childe Hassam returned to America after three years in Paris, he established a studio in the heart of New York City and spent the summer months painting out-of-doors along the Atlantic seaboard. Over the course of two decades, Hassam painted the rocky shores of Appledore, one of the nine small islands that comprise the Isles of Shoals. His Appledore land- and seascapes evoke the spirit of Claude Monet's coastal scenes of the mid-1880s. Indeed, of the artists who formed the Ten American Painters, which included America's most devoted impressionists, Hassam was most inspired by his French counterparts.

Lyman's Ledge—Appledore exhibits the high horizon, enclosed space, and broken brushwork typical of Hassam's Isles of Shoals paintings. The interplay of broad brush strokes and short touches of vibrant color in the foreground contrasts with the more even texture of the sky. Extensive areas of white create a sensation of intense sunlight reflecting off the rocks. Although Hassam utilizes the palette and technique of the French impressionists, he also exemplifies the tendency to maintain the solidity of form that characterizes the American brand of impressionism. In this composition, the rocky structure of Lyman's Ledge retains its power and volume.

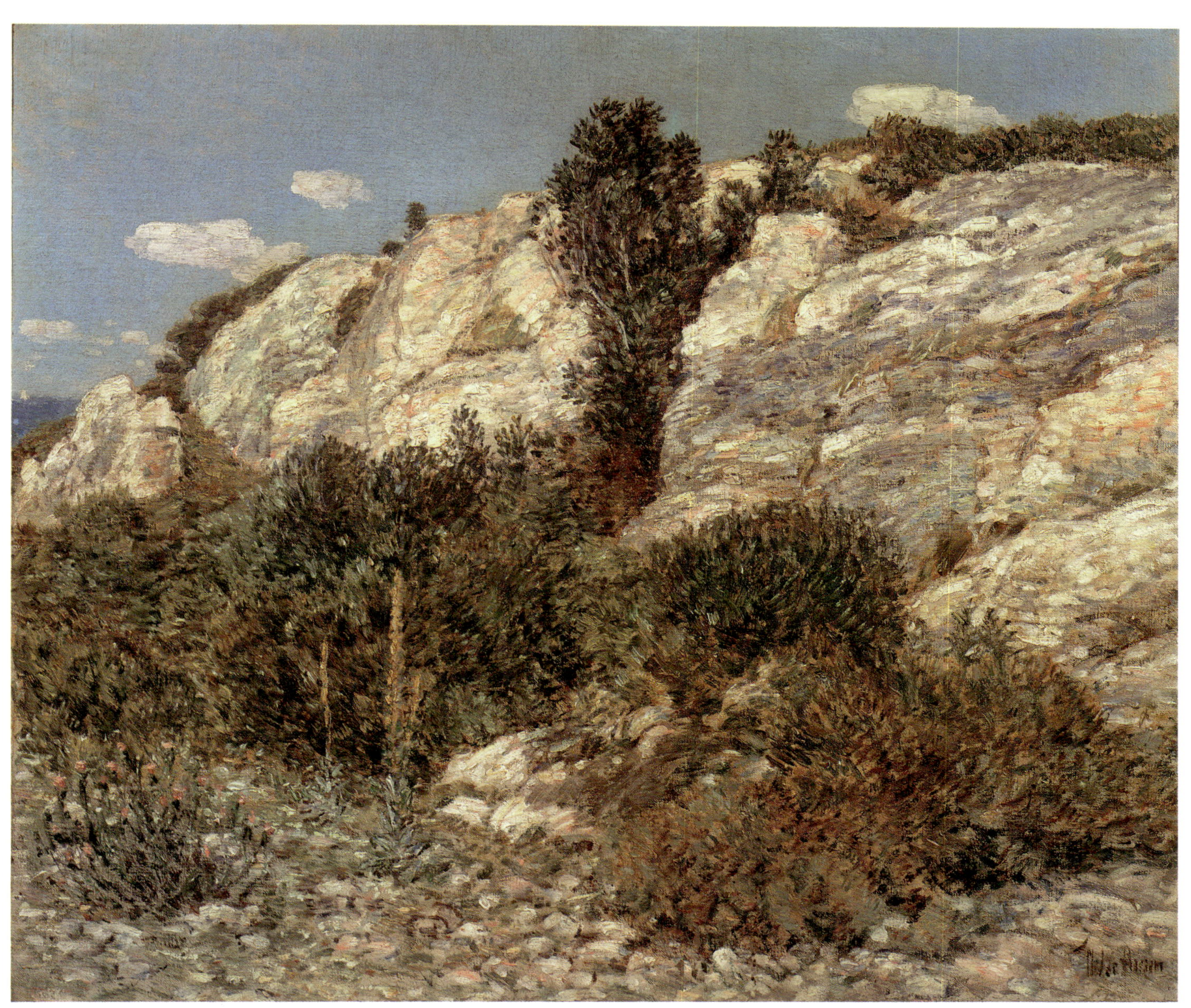

92

John Henry Twachtman was one of the founding members of the Ten American Painters, a stylistically diverse group usually identified with American impressionism. Born in Cincinnati, Ohio, he studied at the Cincinnati Art Academy under Frank Duveneck. In 1875 he accompanied Duveneck to Germany for two years of study at the Munich Academy. Twachtman's Munich training was tempered by a stay in Paris from 1883 to 1886, where he continued his studies at the Académie Julian under Jules Lefebvre and Gustave Boulanger and absorbed the tenets of French impressionism and Japanese prints. Upon his return from France in 1886, he and his family settled in Connecticut. Twachtman is best known for his delicate handling of paint and subtle harmonies. While the freedom of brushwork and vibrant palette of his late works often linked Twachtman to impressionism, he was less interested than the impressionists in recording his perceptions of a particular scene or moment. Twachtman focused instead on the expressive and poetic aspects of his subjects, often presenting them through a hazy atmospheric veil.

Snowbound Stream reveals Twachtman's romantic and contemplative attitude toward nature. The delicately painted landscape, with its soft contours, subtle modulations of color, and simplicity of form, is an essay in serenity. Twachtman avoided the dramatic side of nature, preferring instead to record the change of seasons with a gentle touch. The square format of *Snowbound Stream* gives this ethereal composition a sense of stability and permanence. Twachtman's fondness for winter scenes was poetically expressed in a letter to his colleague Alden Weir: "We must have snow and lots of it. Never is nature more lively than when it is snowing. Everything is so quiet and the whole earth seems wrapped in a mantle. That feeling of quiet and all nature is hushed to silence."

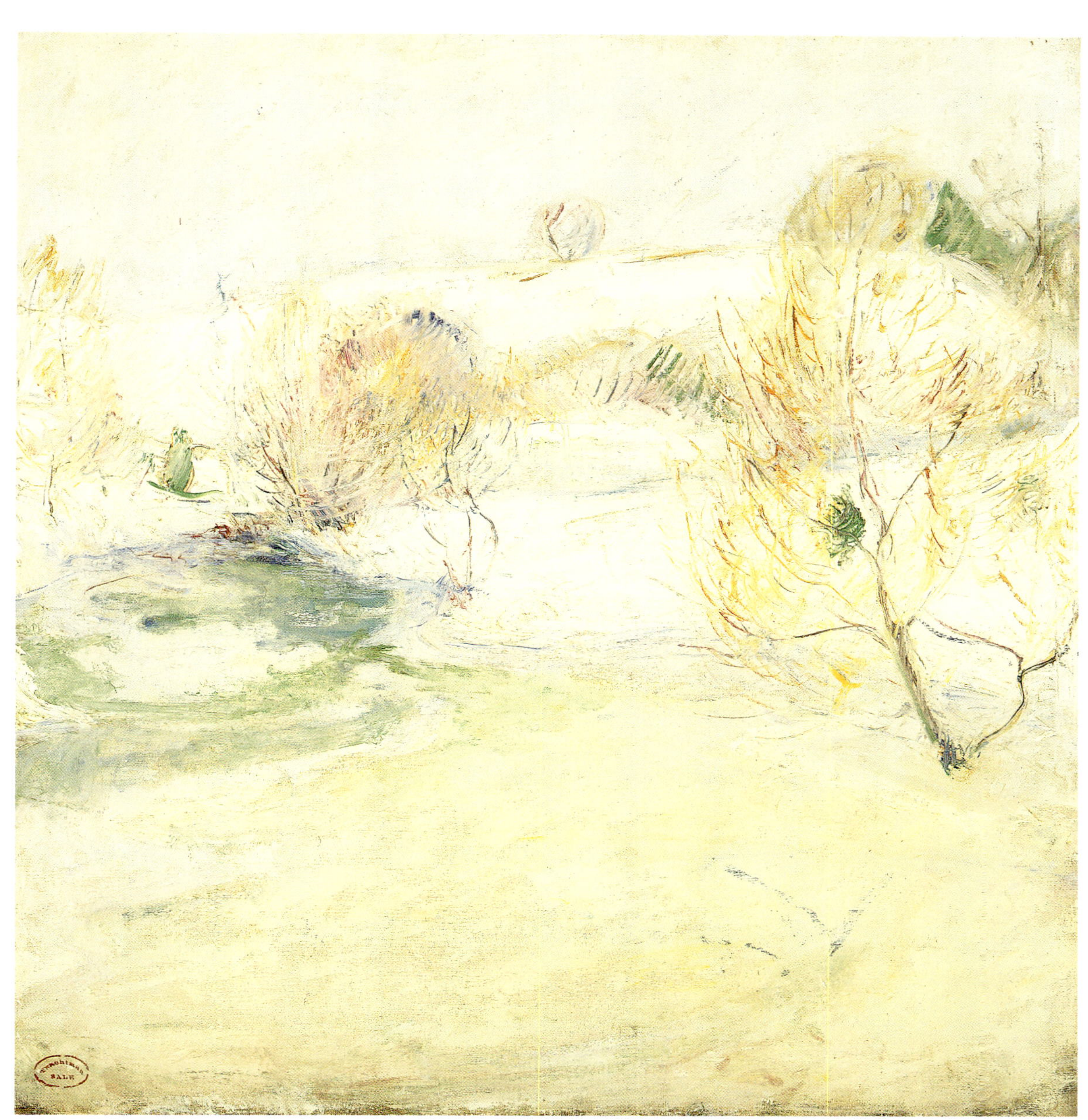

Theodore Robinson
1852–1896

The Farmer's Daughter
c. 1890
oil on canvas
25 1/2 x 21 1/2 inches
The Warner Collection
Tuscaloosa, Alabama

As a teacher and exponent of the style, Theodore Robinson introduced American art students to the principles of impressionism. He was born in Irasburg, Vermont, and at the age of three moved with his family to Wisconsin. He studied at the Art Institute of Chicago School of Art and at the National Academy of Design in New York City before leaving in 1876 for further training in Paris with Emile Carolus-Duran and Jean-Léon Gérôme. He returned to New York around 1879. By the fall of 1887 Robinson was in France again, spending time at Giverny, where he developed a close relationship with Claude Monet. He visited Giverny each year until he returned to America permanently in 1892. Although influenced by Monet, Robinson did not slavishly copy his technique. Impressionism clearly lightened his palette, but Robinson sustained his own emphasis on compositional structure and geometry. He also did not fully subscribe to the impressionist practice of outdoor painting, often preferring to work in his studio from photographs and sketches.

The Farmer's Daughter exemplifies Robinson's outdoor figural subjects. Despite the painting's title, the canvas is dominated by the architecture of its setting. Typical of the artist's interest in structural integrity, he clearly delineates the forms of the facade and porch. Depth is created by the diagonal position of the steps, open window, and recessed doorway. Across this compositional framework Robinson washes his broad, deft brush strokes and subdued colors. The work is so thinly painted that the canvas is visible in some areas and the outline of a step can be seen through the girl's blue dress. The result is a blend of careful construction and airy spontaneity, as Robinson achieves a delicate balance between traditional realism and impressionism.

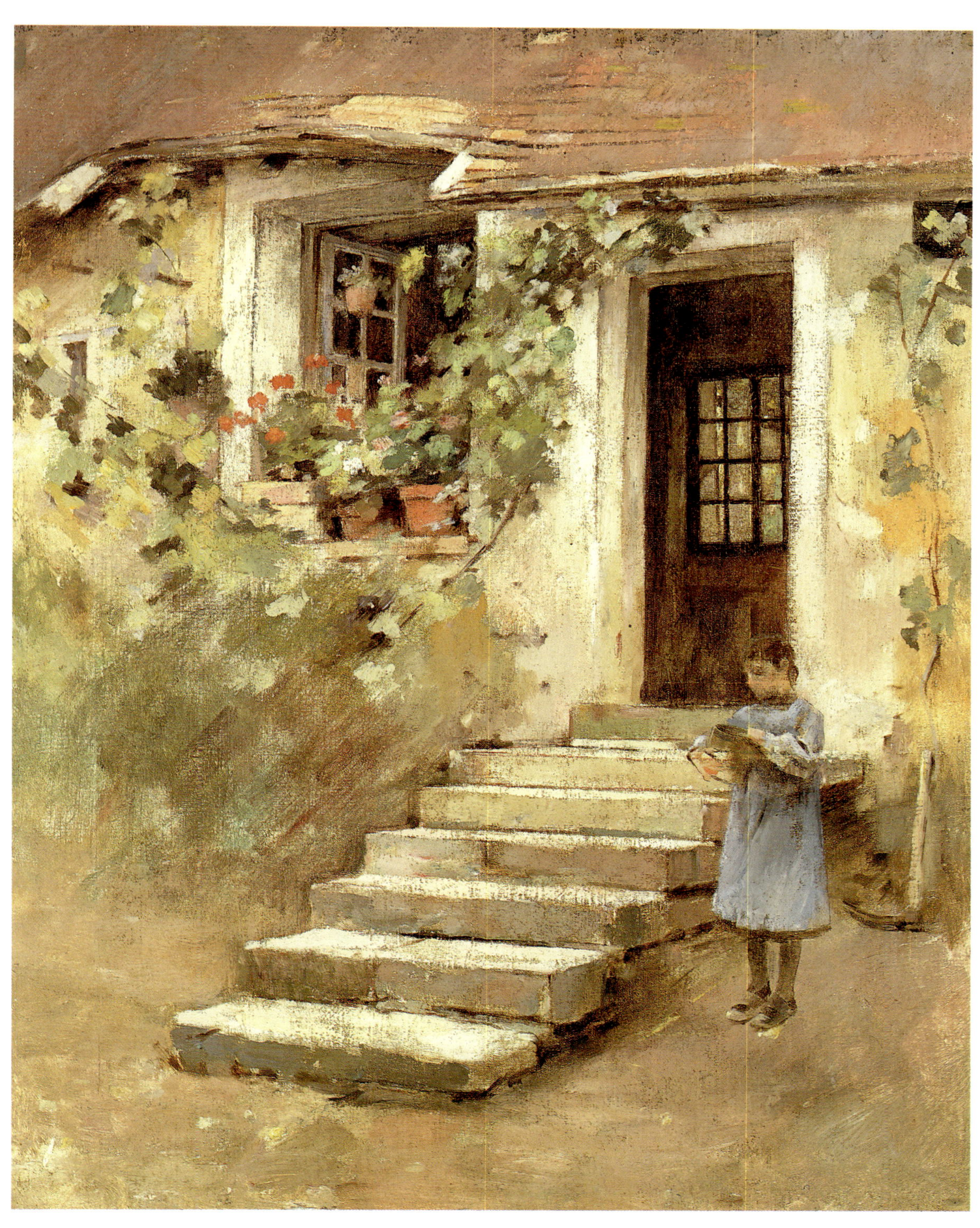

Willard Leroy Metcalf
1858-1925

Ebb Tide
1895
oil on canvas
13 x 16 inches
signed ll: W.L. Metcalf
The Dicke Collection
New Bremen, Ohio

Willard Leroy Metcalf was born in Lowell, Massachusetts, and began his studies under the landscape painter George Loring Brown. Two years later he was awarded a full scholarship to the School of the Museum of Fine Arts in Boston. In 1883, when Metcalf decided to pursue his studies in Paris, Europe was feeling the impact of impressionism, but his study with Gustave Boulanger and Jules Lefebvre at the Académie Julian was grounded in academic tradition. Summer travel to various art colonies provided the opportunity for landscape sketching outdoors. After five years abroad, Metcalf returned home, eventually settling in New York City. He developed a friendship with Childe Hassam and joined the circle that included America's most prominent impressionists. This association resulted in the formation of the group known as the Ten American Painters, which began exhibiting in 1898.

Ebb Tide, painted at Gloucester during Metcalf's first summer visit to the picturesque harbor town, was included in the 1901 exhibition of The Ten. His Gloucester compositions show Metcalf's first use of broken color. *Ebb Tide* is an expansive glimpse of the ocean that hints at a Japanese influence. The high horizon line and broad sweep of the sea contribute to the composition's flattened perspective. Changing patterns of color, light, and brushwork create the sensation of rippling waves and suggest Metcalf's affinity for impressionist practices. Only the foreground rocks and narrow strip of land keep the canvas from becoming an abstract composition of pulsating light and color.

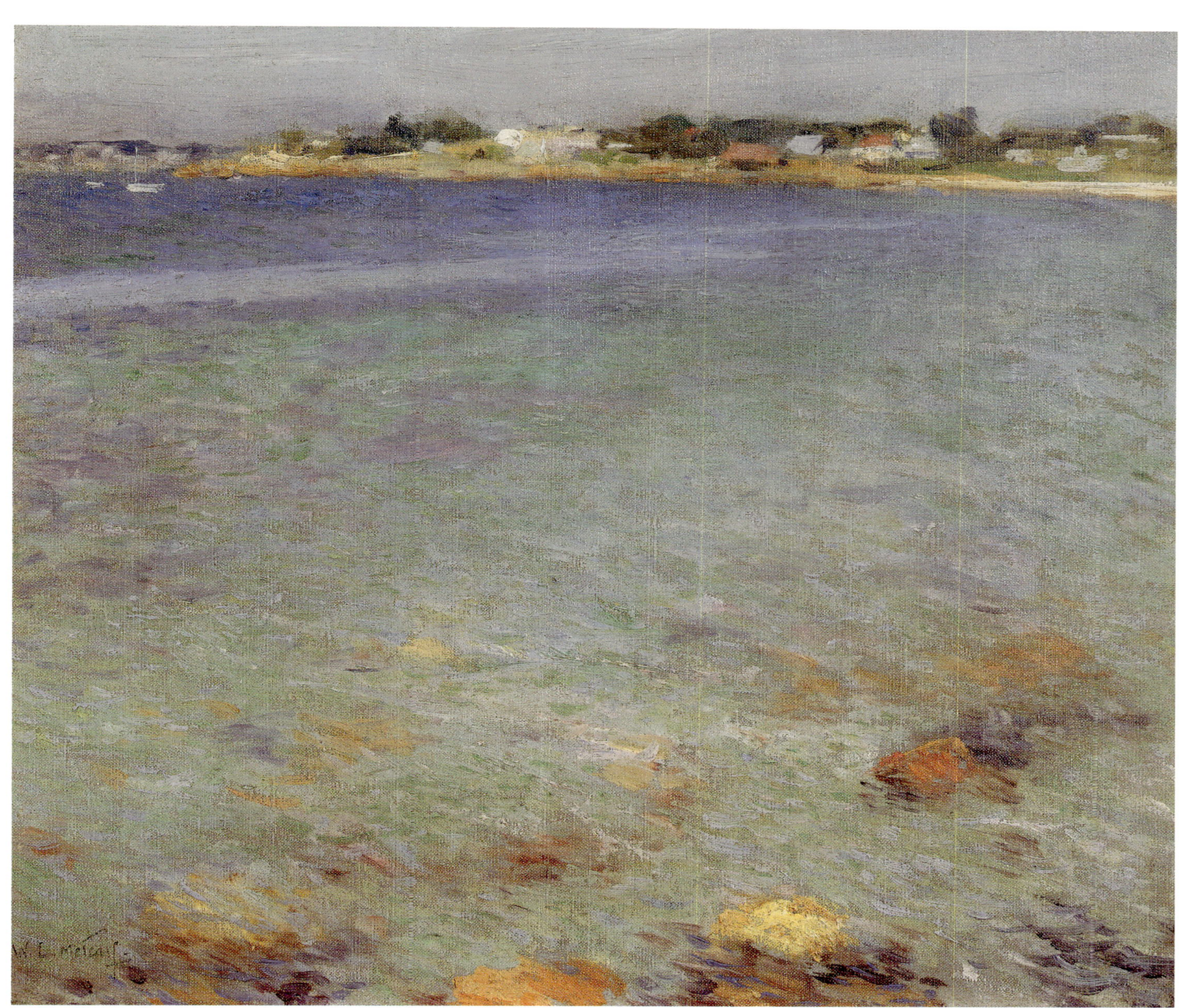

Mary Cassatt
1845-1926

*Denise and Her Child Holding
a Hand Mirror*
c. 1905
oil on canvas
39 1/2 x 29 inches
signed lr: Mary Cassatt
The Warner Collection
Tuscaloosa, Alabama

Mary Cassatt is one of America's most famous women artists, despite spending most of her career in Europe. She was born of affluent parents near Pittsburgh, Pennsylvania, and first traveled to France and Germany with them at the age of six. They remained in Europe for seven years, returning to Philadelphia in 1858. She attended the Pennsylvania Academy of the Fine Arts from 1861 to 1865 and then left for Europe, where she eventually settled in Paris. Cassatt was closely associated with Edgar Degas and was the only American to exhibit with the French impressionists, contributing paintings to their exhibitions of 1879, 1880, 1881, and 1886.

Although Cassatt never married, she used her art to express her feelings about motherhood and family. *Denise and Her Child Holding a Hand Mirror* is characteristic of her style and her sensitive approach. There is a sense of intimacy, warmth, and tenderness in the way the mother's arm embraces the child's shoulder and in her gentle support of the hand mirror that the child eagerly clasps with both hands. The mirror is a favorite device in Cassatt's paintings and is used in this instance not only to create a perception of depth, but also to form an unusual angular composition using the chair and its reflections. The design, flat planes of color, and elevated viewpoint of the composition show the influence of Japanese prints, which Cassatt had studied intensely during the early 1890s.

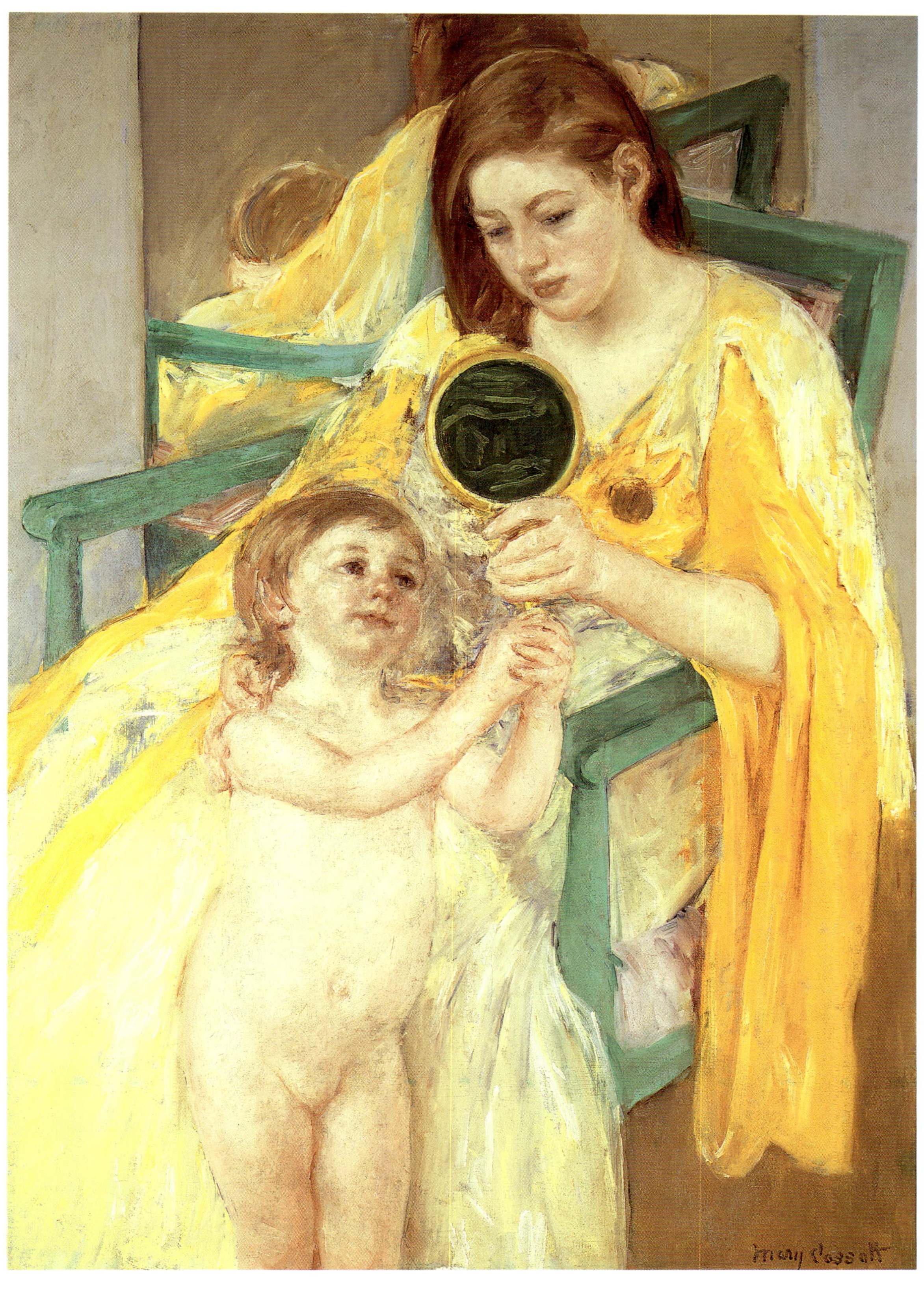

Frederick Frieseke
1874-1939

The Green Parasol
oil on canvas
31 3/4 x 32 inches
signed lr: F. C. Frieseke
The Warner Collection
Tuscaloosa, Alabama

Frederick Frieseke spent most of his life in France painting figures of women in lush, patterned interiors and sunlit gardens. Born in Owasso, Michigan, he studied at the Art Institute of Chicago School of Art and the Art Students League in New York City. Frieseke left for Paris in 1898 to continue his studies at the Académie Julian. After completing his art education, he found immediate success in the form of lucrative commissions and acceptance at the Paris salons. His work was also shown annually at the National Academy of Design. By 1900 Frieseke, a leading member of the second generation of American impressionist painters, lived and worked near Claude Monet's residence in Giverny. He came under the influence of Monet's rich impressionist palette, but it was Pierre Auguste Renoir's figure paintings that inspired his subject matter.

The Green Parasol appears to be set in Frieseke's Giverny garden, where the brilliantly colored flowers were carefully tended by the artist's wife. As Frieseke acknowledged: "I know nothing about the different kinds of gardens, nor do I ever make studies of flowers. My one idea is to reproduce flowers in sunlight. . . to produce the effect of vibration, completing as I go." The parasol is a recurrent element in Frieseke's paintings, offsetting his vivid patterns of flowers and foliage. In this composition, the figure and her parasol afford the artist an opportunity to experiment with the flickering effects of sunlight. *The Green Parasol* also shows Frieseke's interest in the exploration of color; here the intense violets, whites, and greens become virtual abstractions. Despite the emphasis on color and light, however, Frieseke's paintings retain a sure sense of mass and weight.

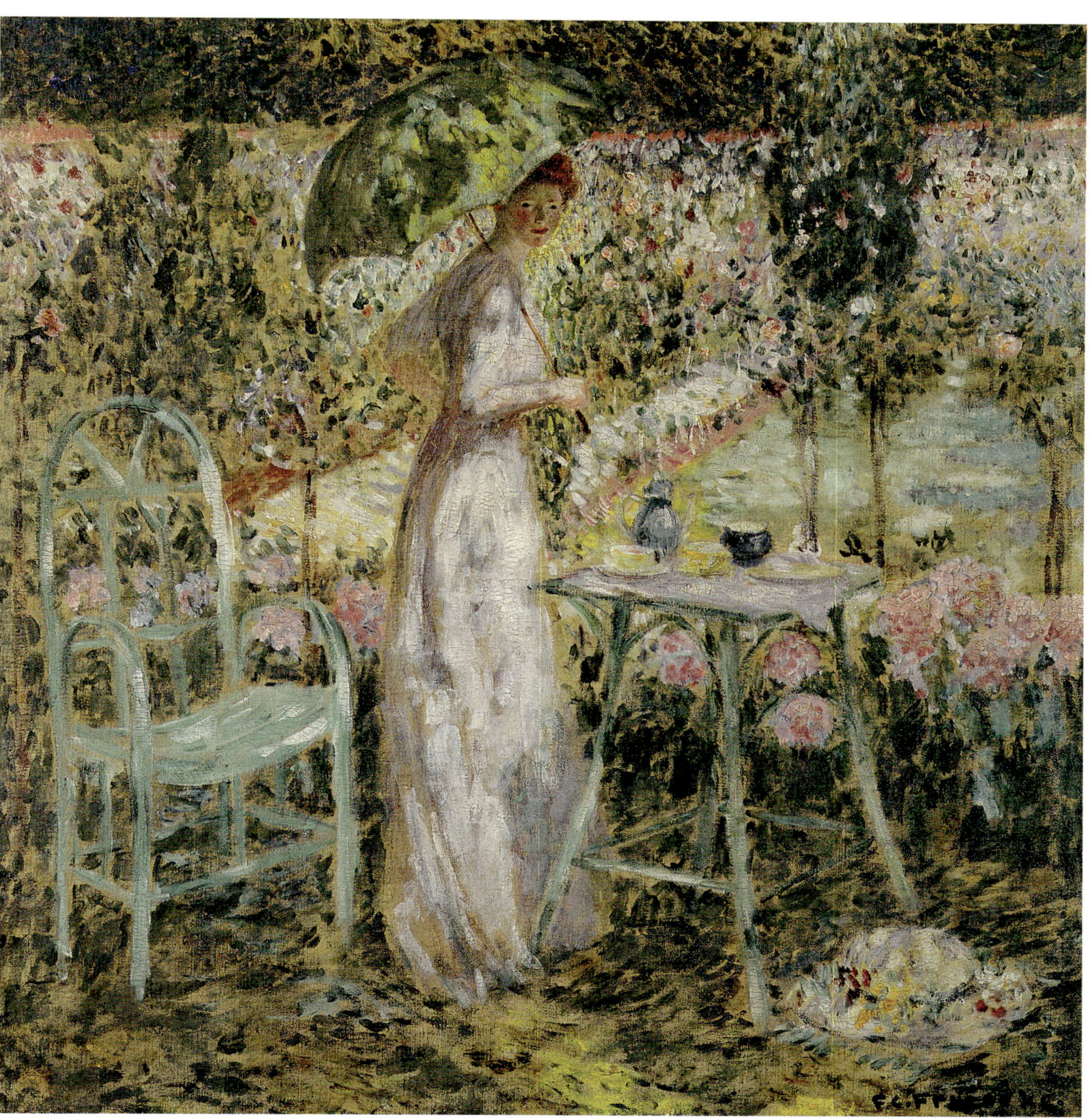

Thomas W. Dewing
1851–1939

Jessica
c. 1905
oil on panel
20 x 15 1/4 inches
signed lr: T. W. Dewing
The Warner Collection
Tuscaloosa, Alabama

102

Bostonian Thomas Wilmer Dewing was apprenticed to a lithographer while still in his teens. In 1876 he went to Paris for two years of study at the Académie Julian under Gustave Boulanger and Jules Lefebvre. Dewing is best known for his paintings of female figures, who are usually shown wandering through fields, or sitting, isolated and introspective, within an interior. Although Dewing was a member of the Ten American Painters, a group that included America's foremost impressionists, he was less interested than they in the exploration of natural light effects. Instead he was more concerned with the study of moods and the orchestration of slight tonal variations. His paintings are related to Whistler's chromatic and tonal arrangements and their associations with music.

    Jessica typifies the mood Dewing achieved in many of his solitary figural subjects. While the subdued color and loose brushwork suggest tranquility, the woman's presence seems charged with intensity. She sits somewhat stiffly posed in an undefined setting, and appears deep in thought and strangely detached from her surroundings. Dewing told one of his most important patrons, Charles Lang Freer, that he felt his paintings were "above the heads of the public. . . [they] belong to the poetic & imaginative world where a few choice spirits live."

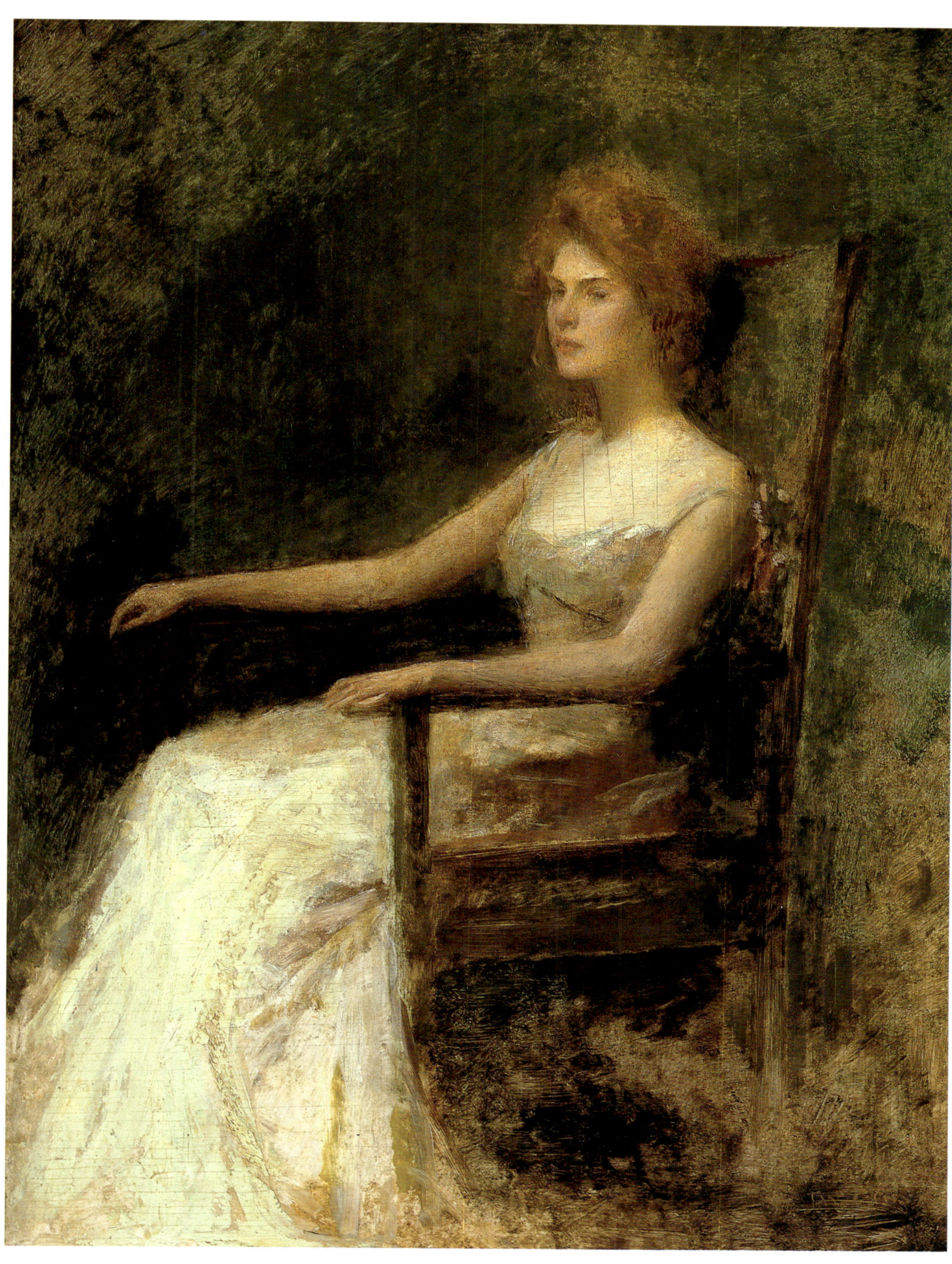

Edward H. Potthast
1857-1927

Children Playing at the Beach
(At the Beach)
oil on board
30 x 40 inches
signed lr: E Potthast
The Warner Collection
Tuscaloosa, Alabama

Edward Potthast began his career as a lithographer in his hometown of Cincinnati in 1879. He studied at the McMicken School of Design and at the Art Academy of Cincinnati. Following the practice of many Cincinnati artists of German heritage, Potthast went to Munich to study in 1882. On a second trip to Europe around 1887, his destination was Paris, where he was introduced to French impressionism. In 1896 Potthast moved to New York City, which remained his home for the rest of his life. He worked as an illustrator for *Harper's*, *Scribner's*, and *Century* magazines before supporting himself as a painter. While Potthast also created views of Central Park and the Rocky Mountains, it is the sun-drenched New York beach scenes, painted mostly after 1910, upon which his reputation rests.

Potthast's mature style—a combination of the bravura brushwork of the Munich School and the vivid color and light associated with impressionism — is ideally suited to his lively outdoor subjects. These elements reach one of Potthast's most successful resolutions in *Children Playing at the Beach*. With broad, vigorous strokes he summons a spontaneity that endows the scene with vitality. His brilliant palette, with healthy doses of white pigment, provides the luminous raw material for recording the summer sunlight. While Potthast's inspiration may have been the reflection of light on sand and water, he still gives prominence to the children wading on the shore. The four figures, presented in a scale larger than Potthast's standard treatment, are further accentuated by the high horizon line. Their carefully crafted placement, in a continuous rhythm of forms, belies Potthast's seemingly casual scenario.

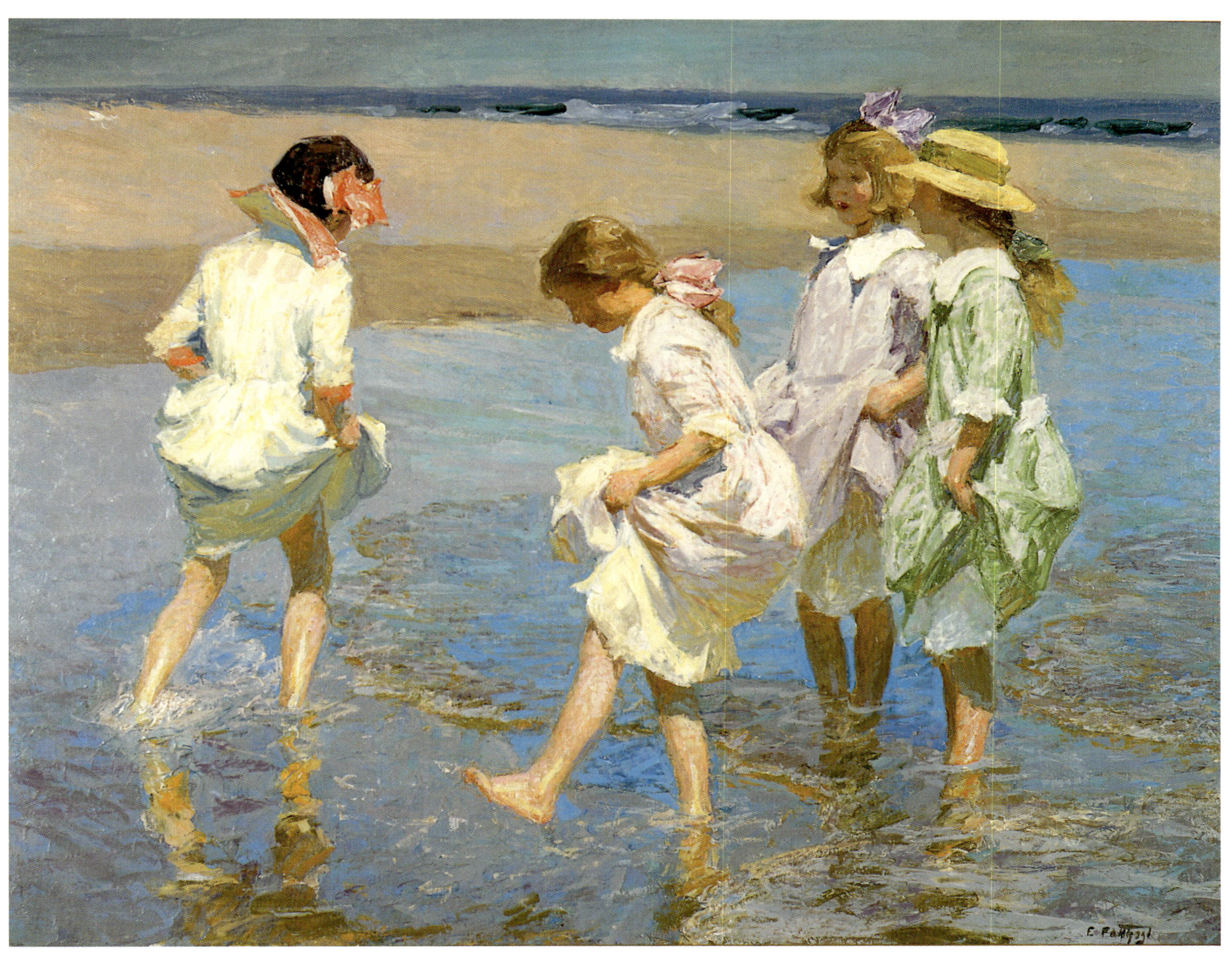

Daniel Garber
1880-1958

Tanis
1915
oil on canvas
60 x 46 1/2 inches
signed ll: Daniel Garber
The Warner Collection
Tuscaloosa, Alabama

Daniel Garber was born in North Manchester, Indiana, and received his early training from Frank Duveneck in Cincinnati. He also studied at the Pennsylvania Academy of the Fine Arts under Thomas Anschutz, a pupil of Thomas Eakins. Garber joined the faculty of the Pennsylvania Academy and maintained a summer studio near New Hope, the home of the Pennsylvania impressionists. Because of his individual use of color and light, Garber was considered one of the most original of this group of artists. Garber painted landscapes as well as figures and often incorporated bright sunlight, vivid colors, and decorative designs into his depictions of the quarries and fields near his home in Bucks County.

Tanis, a painting of the artist's daughter, exemplifies both his figure studies and his decorative landscapes. The painting was awarded the Second Altman Prize by the National Academy of Design. Its rich, vibrant colors convey the sensation of a landscape glowing in the warm sun. Garber creates a strong contrast between sunlight and shadow by backlighting the figure. With this skillful manipulation of color and light, he surrounds the girl in an iridescent radiance without sacrificing the solidity of her form. The desire to maintain structure and volume is one of the hallmarks of American impressionism.

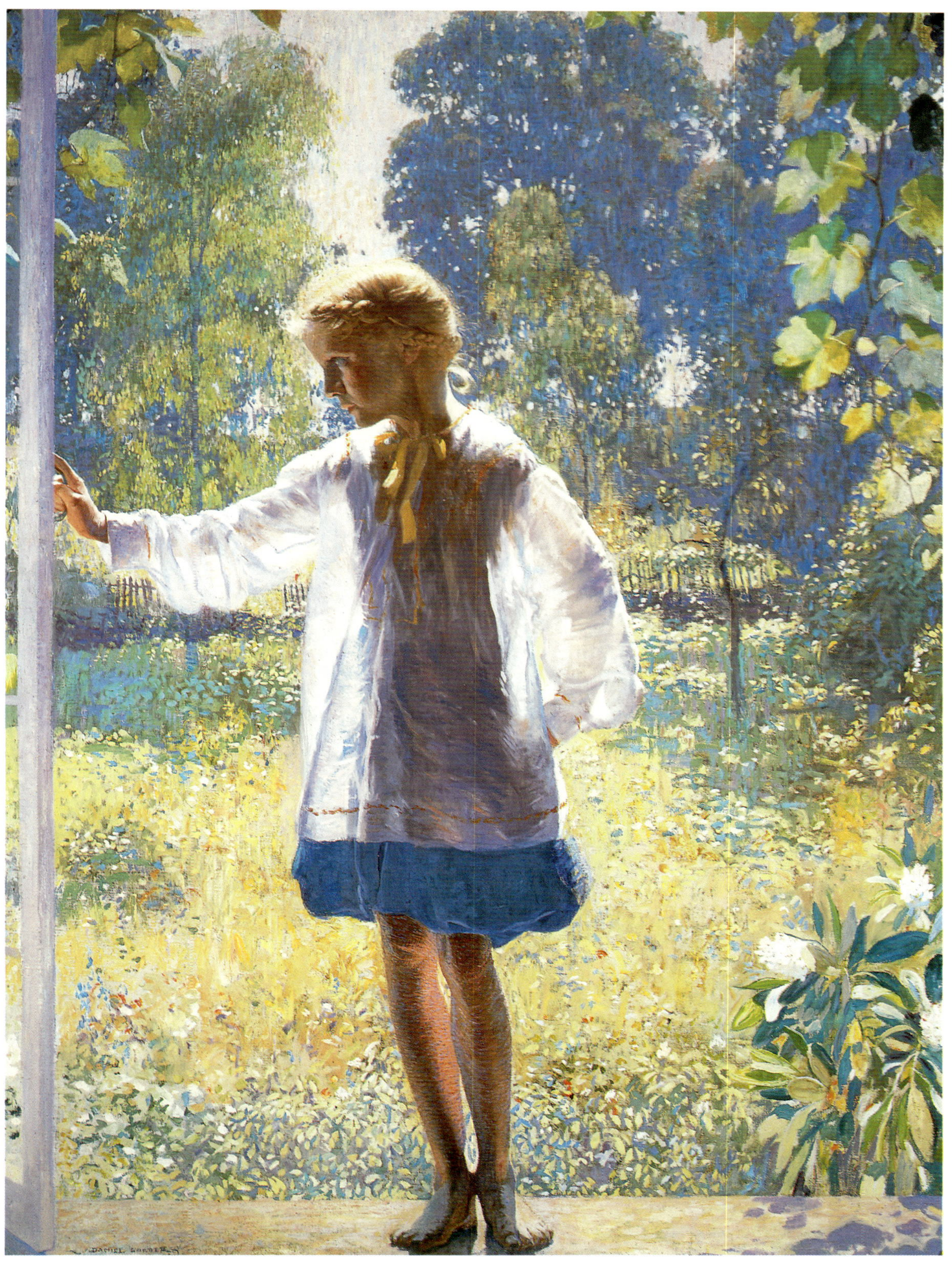

Frederic Remington
1861-1909

Evening on a Canadian Lake
1905
oil on canvas
27 1/4 x 40 inches
signed ur:
Frederic Remington
William I. Koch Collection

Frederic Sackrider Remington's paintings, drawings, and bronzes are synonymous with images of the Old West. Born in Canton, New York, to a wealthy publishing family, Remington began his art training at the Yale University School of Art. Though his work was exhibited at the National Academy of Design and in New York galleries, he continued illustrating for books and magazines and was a war correspondent in the Spanish-American War. His more than two thousand works of art gave Easterners their primary conception of the cowboys, Indians, ranchers, and marshals who populated America's untamed western frontier.

Despite Remington's reputation as an artist of the American West, several of his important paintings are not Western scenes. In 1900 he purchased an island called Ingleneuk in the St. Lawrence River. The many hours that he spent in his canoe sketching the evening sunsets resulted in numerous completed paintings that were chosen for exhibitions and were used as illustrations for *Collier's Weekly* magazine. *Evening on a Canadian Lake* appeared in color in *Collier's Weekly* on March 18, 1905, and earned the artist $1,000 for the reproduction rights. The canvas reflects Remington's poetic side and his interest in the serenity derived from communion with nature. The evening shadows encase the landscape in a thick, black veil. At the edge of the encroaching darkness a canoe barely disturbs the tranquil lake. The vessel and its cargo, mirrored in the surface of the limpid water, catch the fading rays of the sunlight and underscore Remington's dramatic division between the murky shore and the luminous blue foreground. This peaceful reverie contrasts with Remington's turbulent illustrations of the American West.

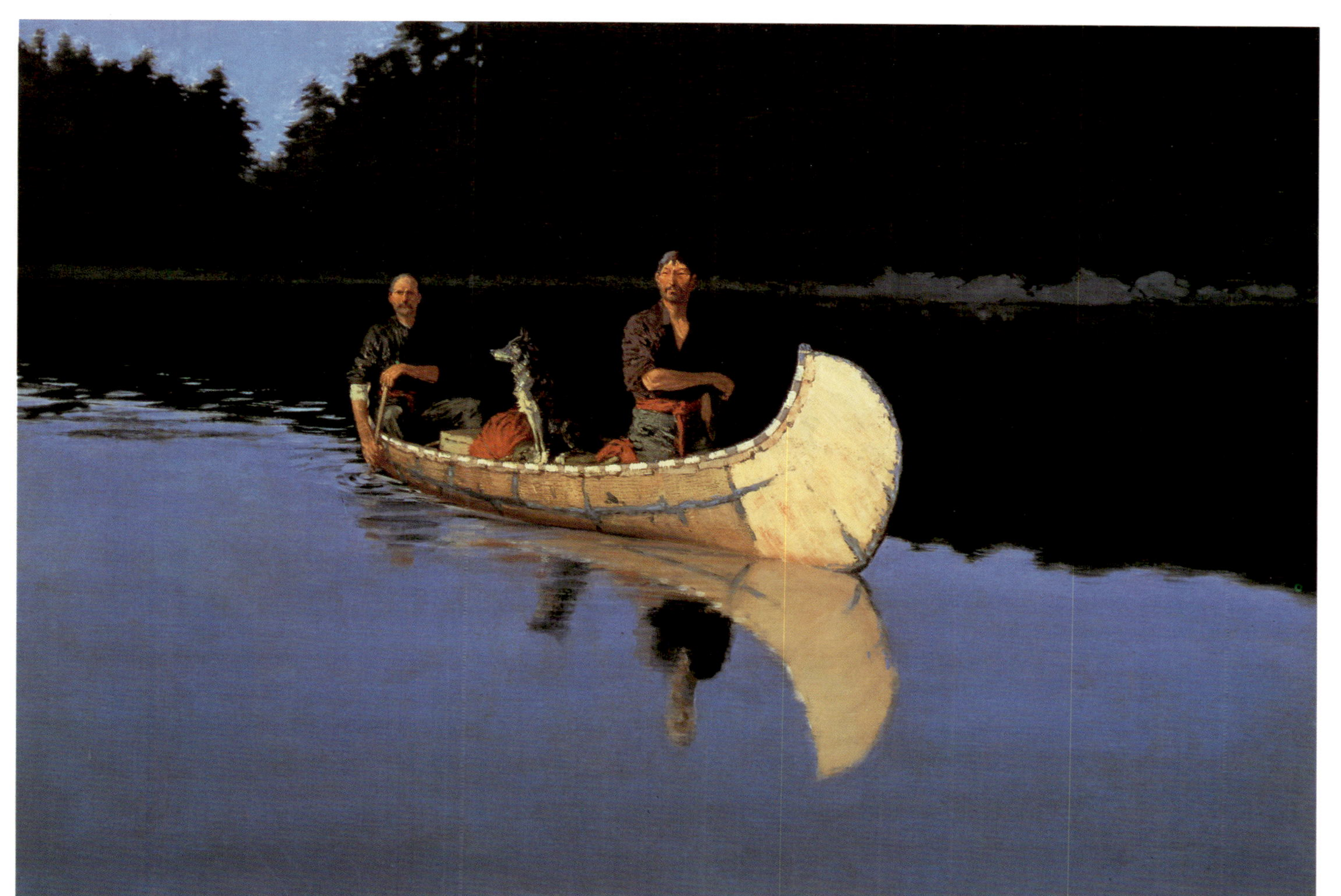

**Maurice Prendergast
1859-1924**

*The Bartol Church,
West Church, Boston*
1909
watercolor on paper
21 x 14 3/4 inches
signed ll:
Maurice B. Prendergast
Weil Brothers

Maurice Prendergast loved to watch people, especially in parks, at the beach, and on the crowded streets of Boston. He was born in St. John's, Newfoundland, and grew up in Boston. In 1891 he began a three-year stay in France, where he studied at the Académie Julian and met members of the avant-garde coterie known as the Nabis. This group of artists, which included Edouard Vuillard and Pierre Bonnard, influenced the patterned surfaces, simplified forms, bold colors, and flat shapes that characterize Prendergast's work. After returning to Boston in 1895, Prendergast created watercolors and oils whose energy and freedom of handling make him unique among American artists. He was also a member of The Eight and participated in their historic 1908 exhibition at the Macbeth Gallery in New York City.

From the beginning of his career, Prendergast painted people enjoying the innocent pleasures of life. Here he shows a group of people on a leisurely outing in front of the Bartol Church, West Church, Boston, named in honor of Cyrus Bartol, who had been a pastor of West Church for thirty-five years. This watercolor demonstrates Prendergast's easy control of the medium. The flattened areas of color form an animated, decorative pattern; and the church itself is almost completely covered by the flickering design of light and color created by the trees encircling the structure. Indistinctly painted figures are simply decorative objects in the overall surface pattern of the composition. The energy and movement of the people are conveyed through the carefully placed daubs of pigment. Prendergast's paintings are tapestries of human activity, uniquely suited to his depictions of the festive side of life.

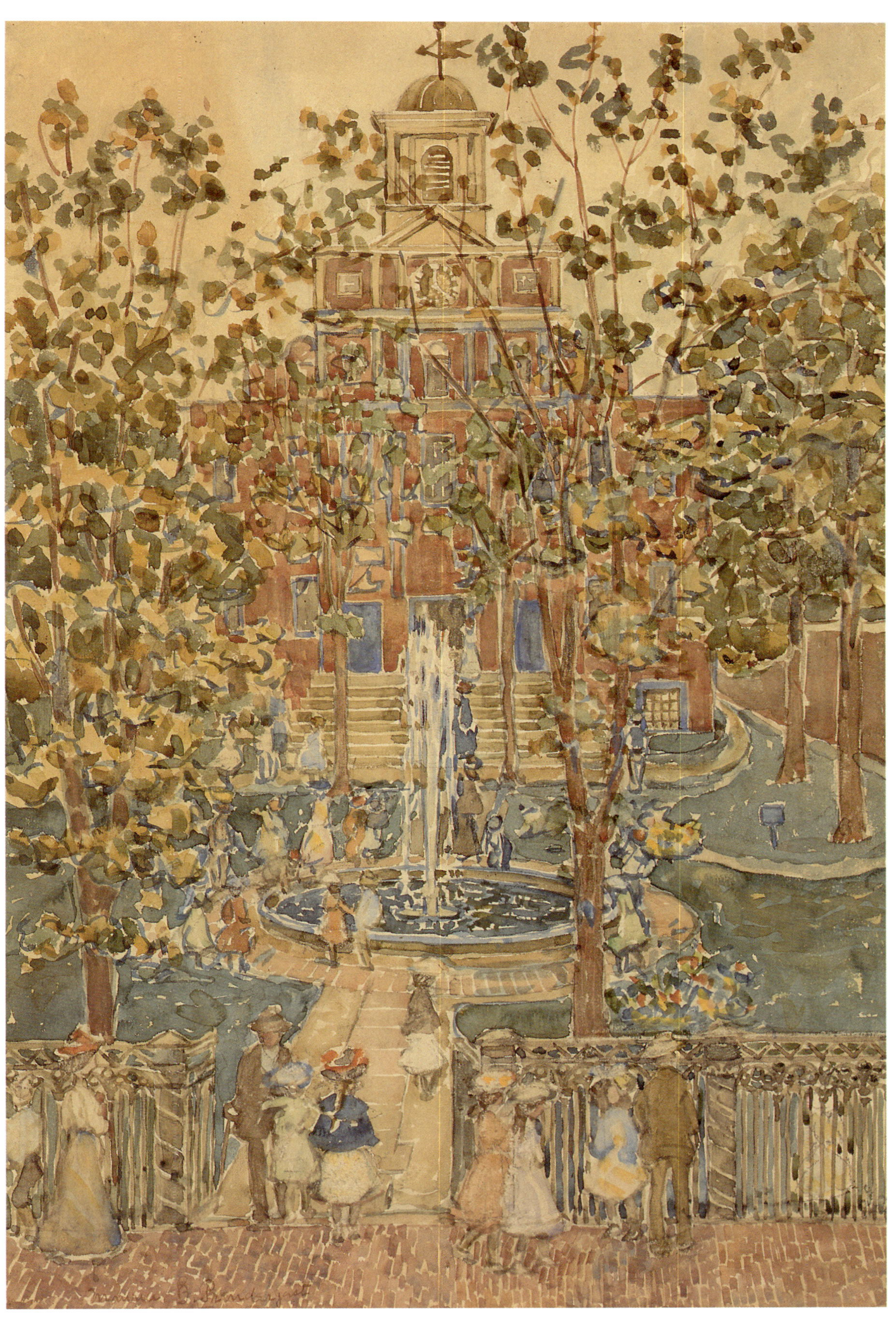

Robert Henri
1865-1929

Marjorie in a Yellow Shawl
1909
oil on canvas
77 x 38 inches
signed ll: Robert Henri
The Warner Collection
Tuscaloosa, Alabama

Robert Henri was the leader of a group of realists known as The Eight. His gritty urban subjects, drawn from the ordinary activities of everyday life, reflect his commitment to the artist's right to freedom of expression. Born Robert Henry Cozad in Cincinnati, Henri changed his name in 1883 because his father was involved in a murder. He studied at the Pennsylvania Academy of the Fine Arts and in Paris at the Académie Julian and the Ecole des Beaux-Arts. After his return to America, Henri settled in New York City and became an influential teacher who encouraged his students to fight against academic constraints and tradition. He helped organize the 1908 landmark show of The Eight at Macbeth Gallery, which challenged the National Academy of Design's stranglehold on the exhibition of American art. Inspired by the baroque portraits of the Spanish painter Diego Velázquez and the Dutch artist Frans Hals, Henri increasingly concentrated on figure studies and portraits after 1910.

The spirited brush strokes and subdued tonality of *Marjorie in a Yellow Shawl* are derived from Henri's study of Velázquez and Hals. The model was a redheaded Irish woman named Marjorie Organ, who had become the artist's second wife in 1908. Henri focused on his model's face, using only a few vigorous strokes to suggest her slender form. He enlivened the full-length portrait with touches of red that echo her hair and a bright yellow shawl that accentuates her long neck. Henri habitually avoided furniture, flowers, or carpets in his portraits, believing that compositional devices interfere with the viewer's perception of the subject. Marjorie's direct gaze, unassuming pose, and modest dress capture the essence of life without the artificiality that dominates academic portraits.

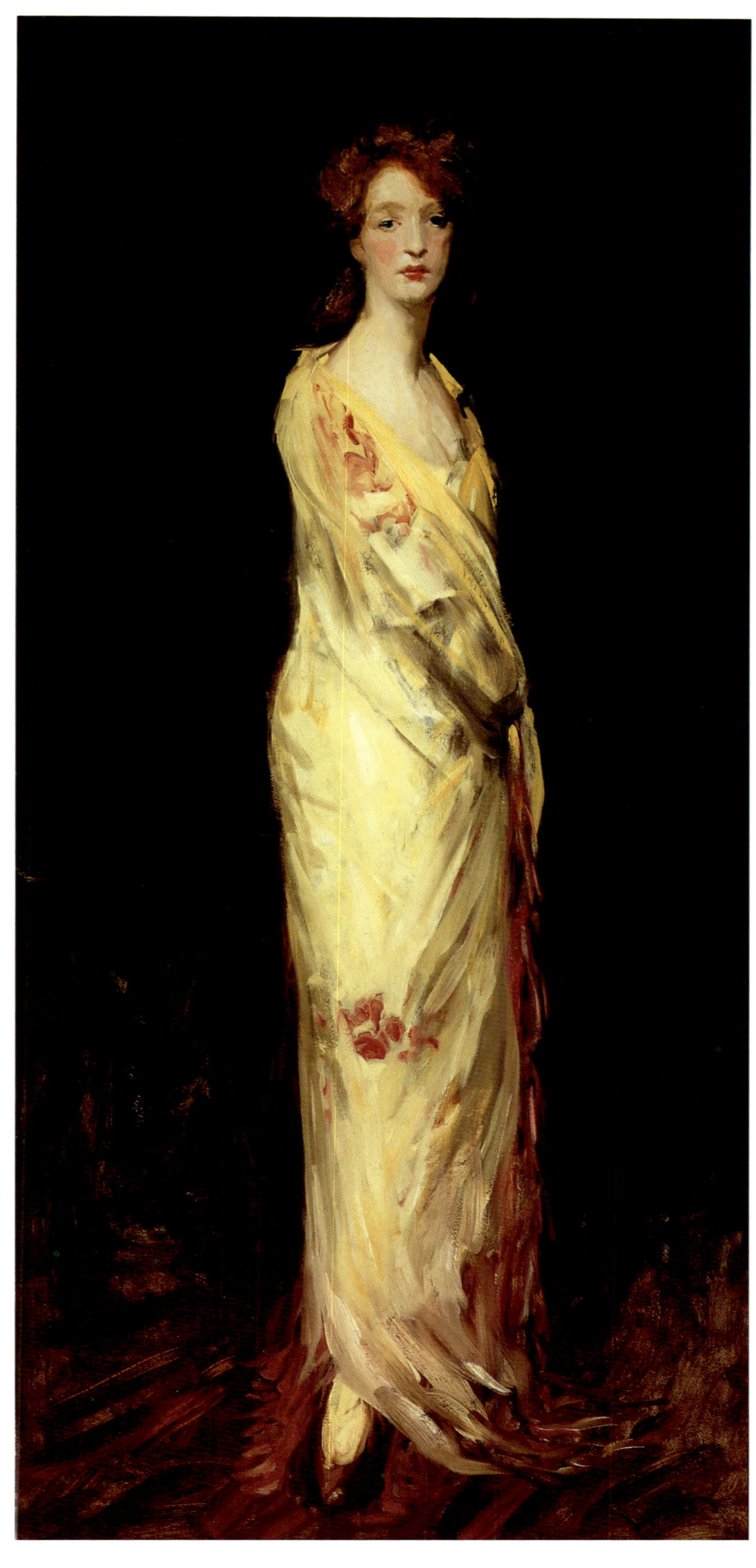

Walt Kuhn
1877–1949

Sybil
1932
oil on canvas
68 x 33 inches
signed and dated lr:
Walt Kuhn/1932
Janet and Craig Duchossois

Walt Kuhn was thirty years into his career before he concentrated on the circus performers for which he is best known. He was born in Brooklyn, New York, and studied at the Académie Colarossi in Paris and the Royal Academy in Munich. His first artistic venture was as a cartoonist, and he later designed sets and costumes for stage performances. In 1912 he became the executive secretary for the New York City Armory Show and traveled to Europe with the director, Arthur B. Davies, to select the art that would create an uproar when it was presented in America in 1913. For almost twenty years following the show, Kuhn advised wealthy art patrons on the purchase of French art.

In 1925 Kuhn began to look to the circus and theater for subjects. Following the tradition of Antoine Watteau, Honoré Daumier, Edgar Degas, and Henri de Toulouse-Lautrec, he painted acrobats, clowns, and showgirls. Kuhn's work is based in the realist tradition, but he incorporated modernist concepts such as brilliant Fauve colors and powerful imagery from German expressionism. His models were actual performers, who often chose their own costumes and poses. Sybil, a carnival performer in splendid attire, is covered with makeup so that she seems to be wearing a mask. Kuhn outlined her form in black and contrasted her pale white skin with the striking red and green of the costume. Sybil appears strong, sturdy, and in command, a monument to the pride and stoicism of these performers. The composition, with its strident colors, dark background, and poignant figure, sounds a discordant note on the human condition.

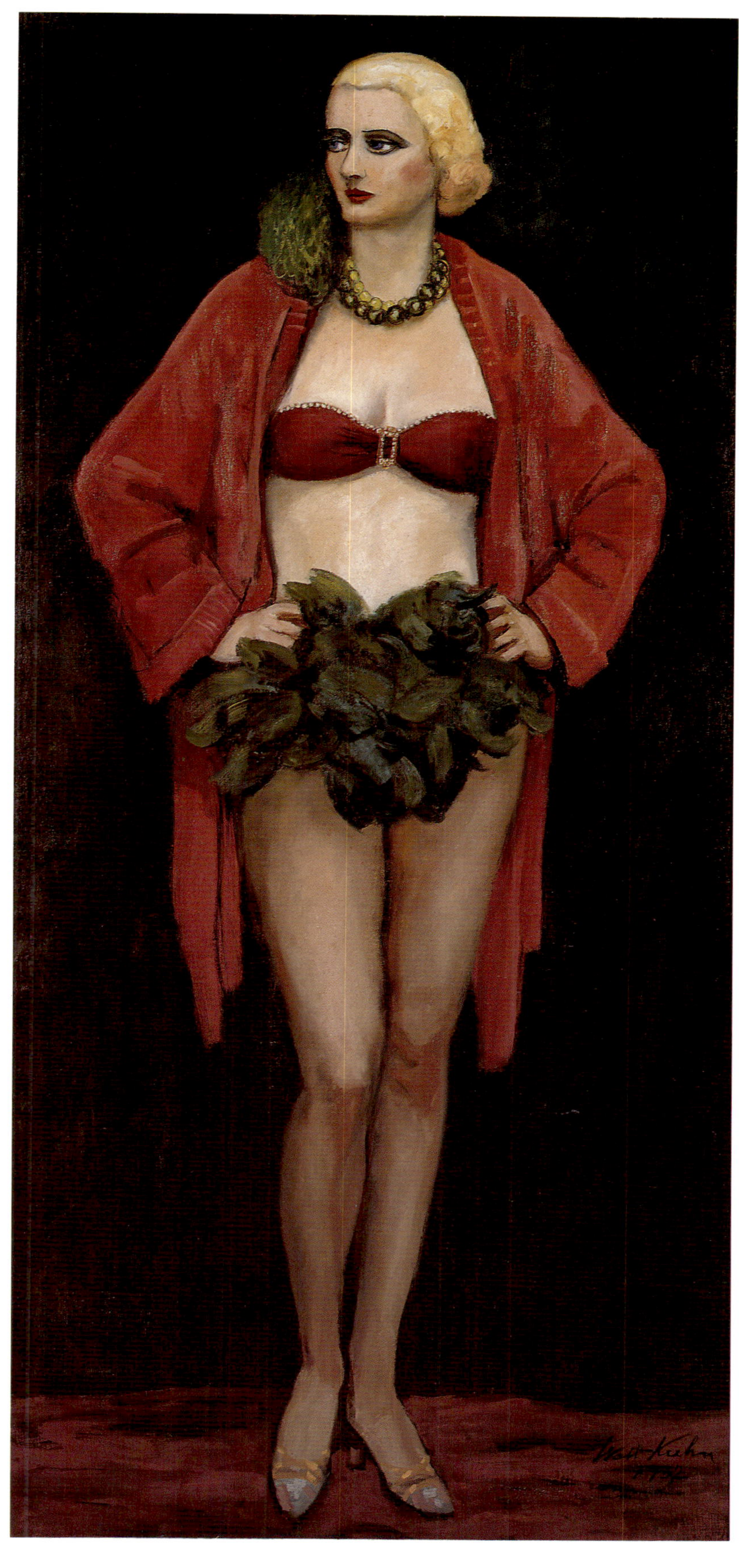

Oscar F. Bluemner
1867-1938

Red Port in Winter
c. 1922
oil on panel
15 x 20 inches
signed lr: OBLÜMNER
The Warner Collection
Tuscaloosa, Alabama

When Oscar Bluemner arrived in the United States from his native Germany in 1892, he was an architect seeking commissions at the World's Columbian Exposition in Chicago. He had studied painting and architecture at the Academy of Fine Arts in Berlin and had earned a royal medal for an architectural painting. In 1900 his beaux-arts design won the competition for the county courthouse in the Bronx area of New York City, but a disagreement with his partner led him to abandon architecture for a career in painting. Bluemner exhibited five brightly colored landscapes in the 1913 Armory Show in New York City, which influenced many American artists through its rich display of avant-garde European and American art. In 1915 Alfred Stieglitz, who was a strong supporter of America's early modern artists, gave Bluemner a one-man show at his 291 Gallery.

Red Port in Winter presents key elements of Bluemner's style, including an overall dominance of bright red hues, blocklike forms outlined in black, and shallow space. His fondness for striking contrasts is evident in the white snow against the red structures and in the curves of the bare trees and bridge, which oppose the rigid angularity of the buildings. The vivid colors are applied in a variety of tonal gradations, creating a rhythmic display of reds and browns. For Bluemner, colors join with shapes to create meaning: "Every color has a specific effect on our feelings. I give to such a color-effect a corresponding shape in analogy with nature. A color and shape produces [sic] an emotion." Bluemner's treatment of form has its closest antecedents in the early cubism of Georges Braque and Pablo Picasso, while his vibrant colors suggest the palette of the German expressionists. With their crisp edges and simplified shapes, Bluemner's works also relate to the industrial subjects painted during the same era by America's precisionist artists.

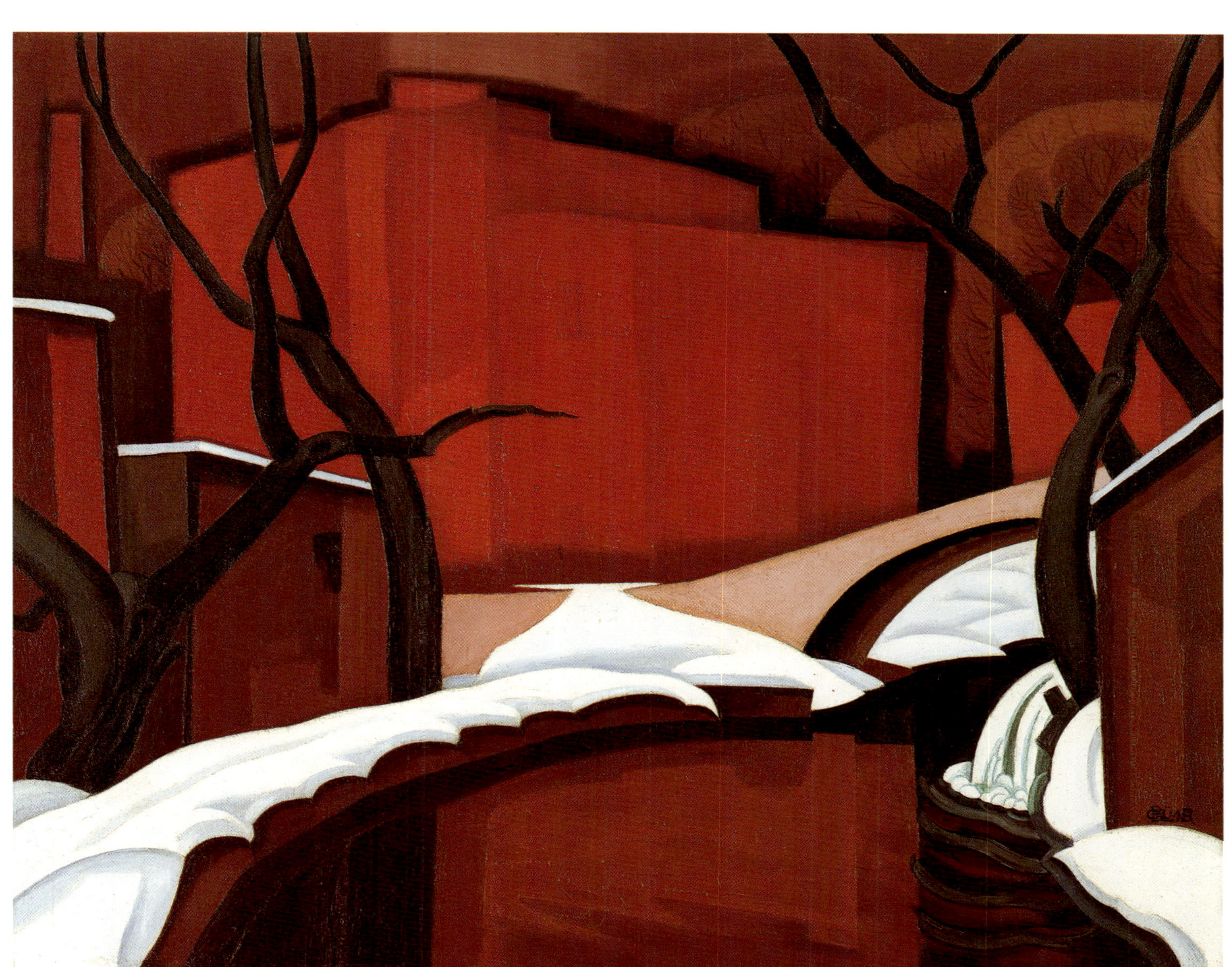

Thomas Hart Benton was the leading voice among a group of artists known as Regionalists, yet his path to this realist style took some unusual turns. Born in Neosho, Missouri, Benton studied at the Corcoran School of Art in Washington, D. C., and the Art Institute of Chicago School of Art before traveling to Paris in 1908. While abroad, he came under the influence of French modernism. Benton returned to Neosho in 1911 and moved to New York City shortly thereafter. For almost twenty years, he experimented with modernist styles, including pointillism, cubism, and synchromism. As Benton stated, "I wallowed in every cockeyed 'ism' that came along."

Within a month of his arrival in New York City, Benton met Thomas Craven. The two became close friends and joined the navy together in 1918. At the end of his tour of duty, Craven began writing for *The Dial*, a magazine that published articles and criticism by the best writers of the time. As a prime exponent of French modernism, Craven encouraged Benton's modernist inclination. Ironically, Craven later became a champion of the Regionalists and wrote articles against modernism and in favor of what he saw as a native American school whose leader was Benton.

In this portrait, the artist shows his friend typing a review for *The Dial*. The painting exhibits a cubist influence in its shallow space, simplification of form, and shifting perspective. Benton's attempt to merge the figure with the environment, however, is more realist than cubist in effect. The handling of the tablecloth and the arrangement of the forms on the table are reminiscent of Paul Cézanne. There is also a hint of the elongated, rhythmic distortions of the human figure that would characterize Benton's mature work.

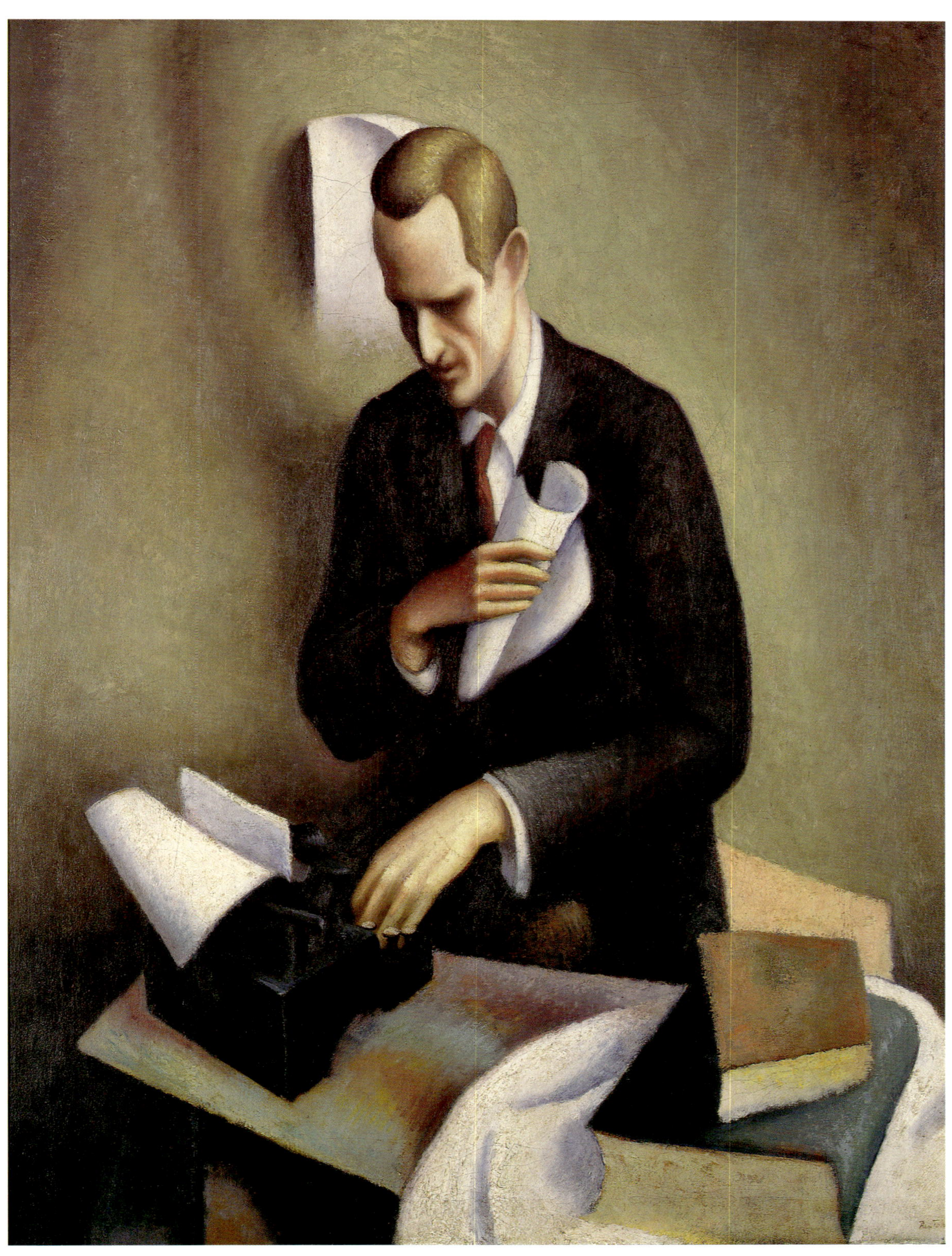

Thomas Hart Benton
1889-1975

Night Firing of Tobacco
1943
oil and tempera on canvas
mounted on panel
20 x 31 inches
signed lr: Benton
United Missouri Bank

Despite his early modernist tendencies, Benton became one of the harshest and most outspoken critics of the abstractionists. In 1935 he left New York City, where he had become increasingly embroiled in controversy over nonrepresentational art, and moved permanently to Kansas City. His Midwestern paintings portray the character of the people and their land, activities, and lifestyle. They reflect his desire to enable the average person to identify with his art and immediately understand its content.

During the war years Benton alternated between paintings that commented on the brutality of war and the rural subjects with which he was most comfortable. *Night Firing of Tobacco* was part of a series of paintings for the American Tobacco Company. Benton shows a worker preparing to fire the furnace used for curing tobacco, which was kept running day and night. The large diagonal tool helps to focus the viewer on the small figure performing his task. The undulating contours of the landscape, the soft curves of the clouds, and the contrasting rigidity of the structures are the hallmarks of Benton's style. The glow of the fire is reflected on the foreground grain shoots, bathing the scene in a tranquil atmosphere that belies the perils of the escalating war abroad.

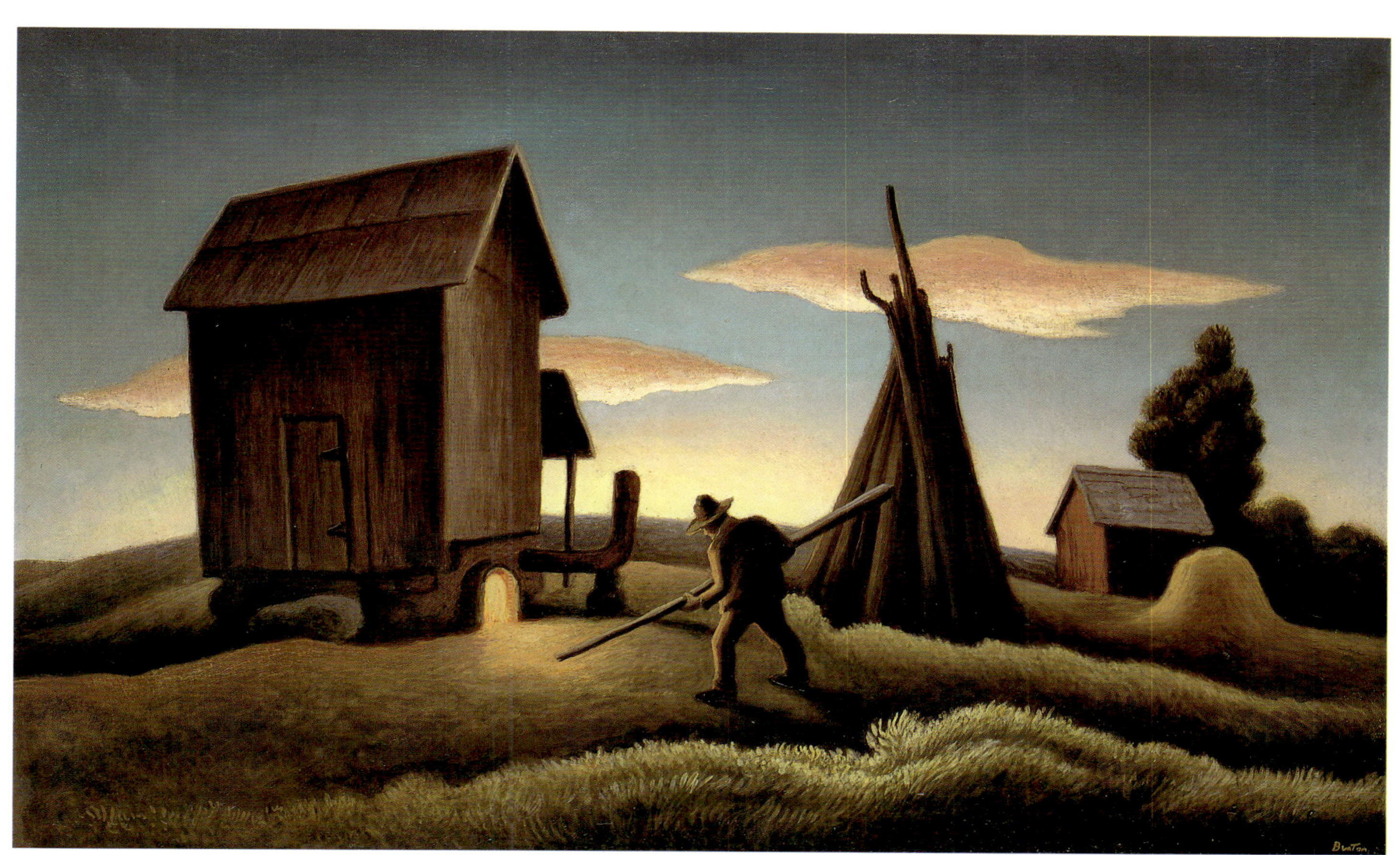

Thomas Hart Benton
1889-1975

Swing Your Partner
1945
watercolor on paper
23 1/2 x 32 1/2 inches
signed and dated lr:
Benton '45
Weil Brothers

Swing Your Partner was painted near the end of the Second World War, when the nation was focused on international affairs rather than the local issues that Benton depicted. In this watercolor he tries to capture the festive side of a vanishing lifestyle. Benton's rhythmic drawing is uniquely suited to the depiction of a rollicking party. The addition of glaring lights and harsh, contrasting colors gives the scene a raucous atmosphere. Benton's interest in watercolor began at Norfolk Naval Base, where he sketched in this medium during off-duty hours. He developed a rapid sketching technique that contributes to the animated quality of this watercolor. Benton summed up his contribution to American art when he said: "I have come to something that is in the image of America and the American people of my time. . . My American image is made up of what I have come across, of what was 'there' in the time of my experiences—no more, no less."

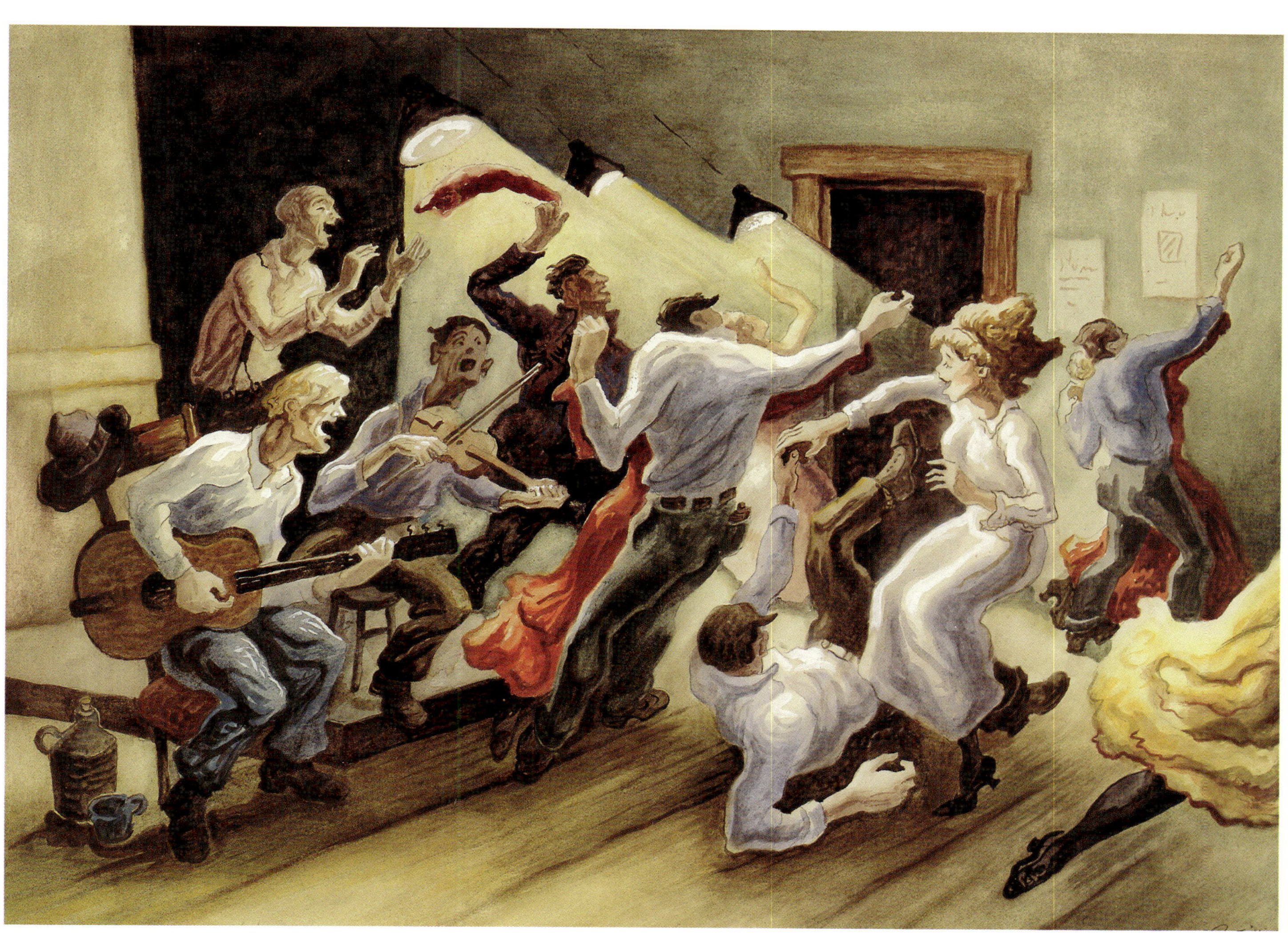

John Steuart Curry
1897–1946

The Return of Private Davis
1928–40
oil on canvas
37 1/2 x 51 1/2 inches
signed and dated lr:
JOHN STEUART
CURRY/1931
The Warner Collection
Tuscaloosa, Alabama

John Steuart Curry joins Thomas Hart Benton and Grant Wood as the primary Regionalist painters. At a time when many artists were turning to abstract modes of expression, this group steadfastly advocated an idealized realism that glorified the people and the land of rural America. Curry was born in Dunavant, Kansas, of Scottish-Irish farmers. His art education included the Kansas City Art Institute, the Art Institute of Chicago School of Art, and Geneva College in Pennsylvania, as well as training with the illustrator Harvey Dunn. Curry was a magazine illustrator from 1919 until 1926, when he traveled to Paris to study. Upon his return a year later, he began to paint the landscape and people of his native Kansas.

The Return of Private Davis was inspired by the funeral of a high school friend who was killed in the Argonne in 1918. The body of Private Davis was one of the first to be brought back to Kansas after the war. Despite the fact that the painting refers to a specific soldier, Curry was more interested in showing the broad effect the tragedy of World War I had on ordinary Americans. Beyond the mourners and flag-draped coffin, the sky opens up over a vast landscape that may suggest the importance and permanence of the land in the life of the community. Although this painting is dated 1931, it was begun in 1928 and exhibited several times during the 1930s before being completed in 1940, reflecting Curry's tendency to continually rework his canvases.

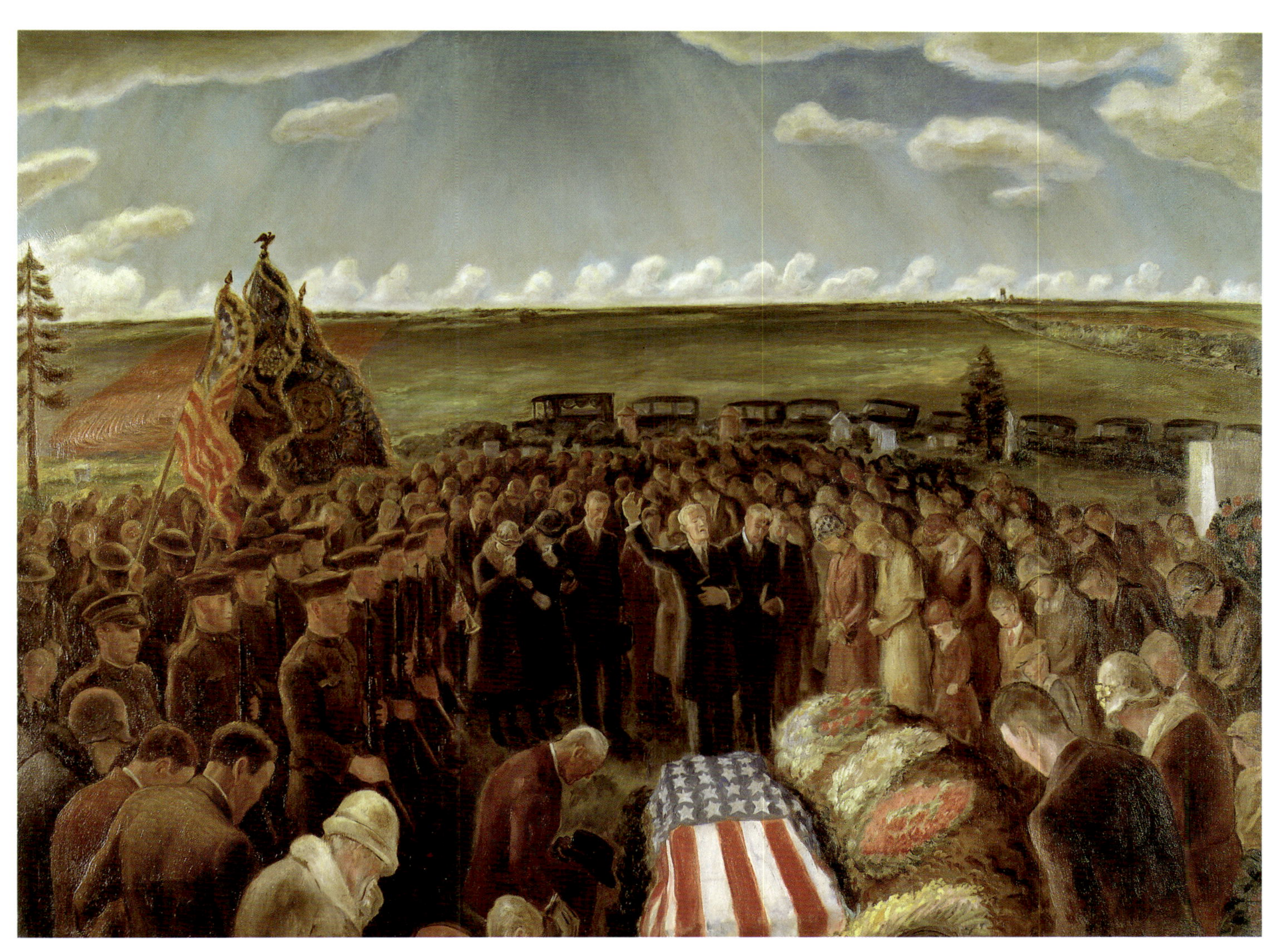

Grant Wood
1891-1942

Arbor Day
1932
oil on panel
25 x 30 inches
signed and dated lr:
Grant Wood 1932
William I. Koch Collection

Grant Wood, along with fellow painters Thomas Hart Benton and John Steuart Curry, led the Regionalist movement, which promoted American idealism and a national aesthetic of realism. Wood's form of regionalism espoused a deliberately naive technique. His stylized scenes of Iowa are captured in a sharp, decisive manner using a meticulous method. This time-consuming technique limited his productivity. Born in Anamosa, Iowa, Wood attended Iowa State University and the Art Institute of Chicago School of Art. He served in the army in World War I, before traveling to Paris, where he studied at the Académie Julian. His first important commission was executed in 1927, but it was his painting *American Gothic* of 1930 that ensured his fame.

Special rituals were favorite topics for the Regionalist painters. *Arbor Day* depicts an annual event in which a teacher and her students plant a tree near the schoolhouse. The immaculate surfaces and dollhouse-like structures are typical of Wood's style. He reduces everything to round or rectilinear shapes with no irregular edges. This results in a profusion of decorative patterns, which are particularly striking in the road and the rolling hills. Sharp light and high-key color emphasize Wood's meticulously rendered forms. *Arbor Day* memorializes the rural America where life centered around the land and the white one-room schoolhouse was a dominant feature of the landscape.

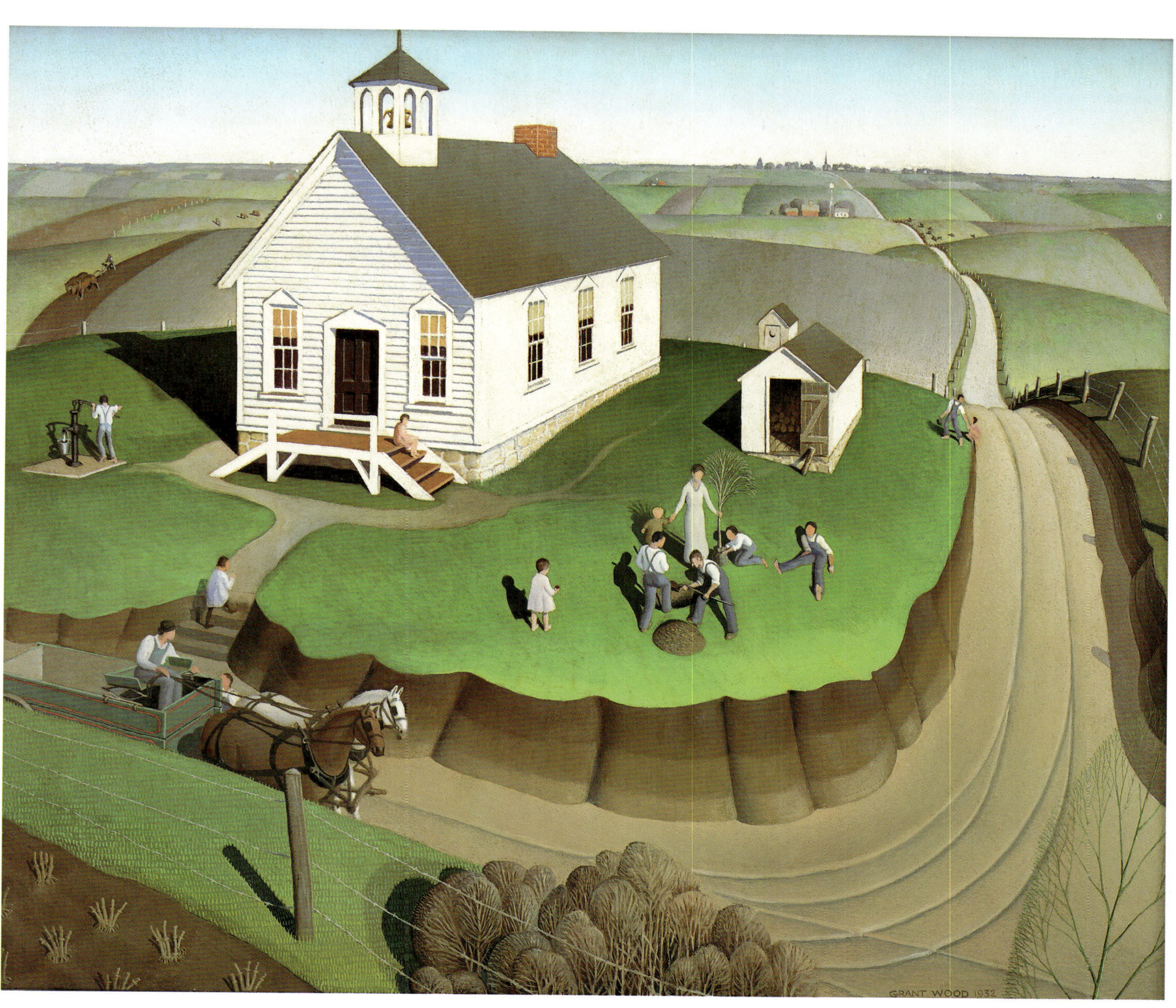

Edward Hopper
1882-1967

Dawn Before Gettysburg
c. 1934
oil on canvas
15 x 20 inches
signed lr: E. Hopper
The Warner Collection
Tuscaloosa, Alabama

128

While Thomas Hart Benton championed the virtue and vitality of American life, Edward Hopper is best known for scenes infused with the loneliness and alienation that can also be part of the American experience. He was born in Nyack, New York, and became a student of Robert Henri in the early 1900s. From 1906 to 1910 he lived in Paris and then settled in New York City. Hopper was a successful etcher before receiving recognition as a realist painter. His images of banal urban scenes or stark landscapes are powerful observations of the period in which he lived. They have become symbols of the human condition in twentieth-century America.

The Civil War scene *Dawn Before Gettysburg* is an unusual subject for Hopper, who rarely painted historical themes. Yet his presentation of soldiers anticipating a battle is not so very far from his views of twentieth-century urban America. Although the painting is filled with people, there is a strong feeling of isolation, as the soldiers do not communicate with each other. Their common bond is apprehension and fear. The brightly lit sky and dark landscape set up a contrast that is echoed in the white house and deep blue uniforms. The starkness of these flat, geometric shapes adds to the scene an icy stillness and a sense of intense anxiety.

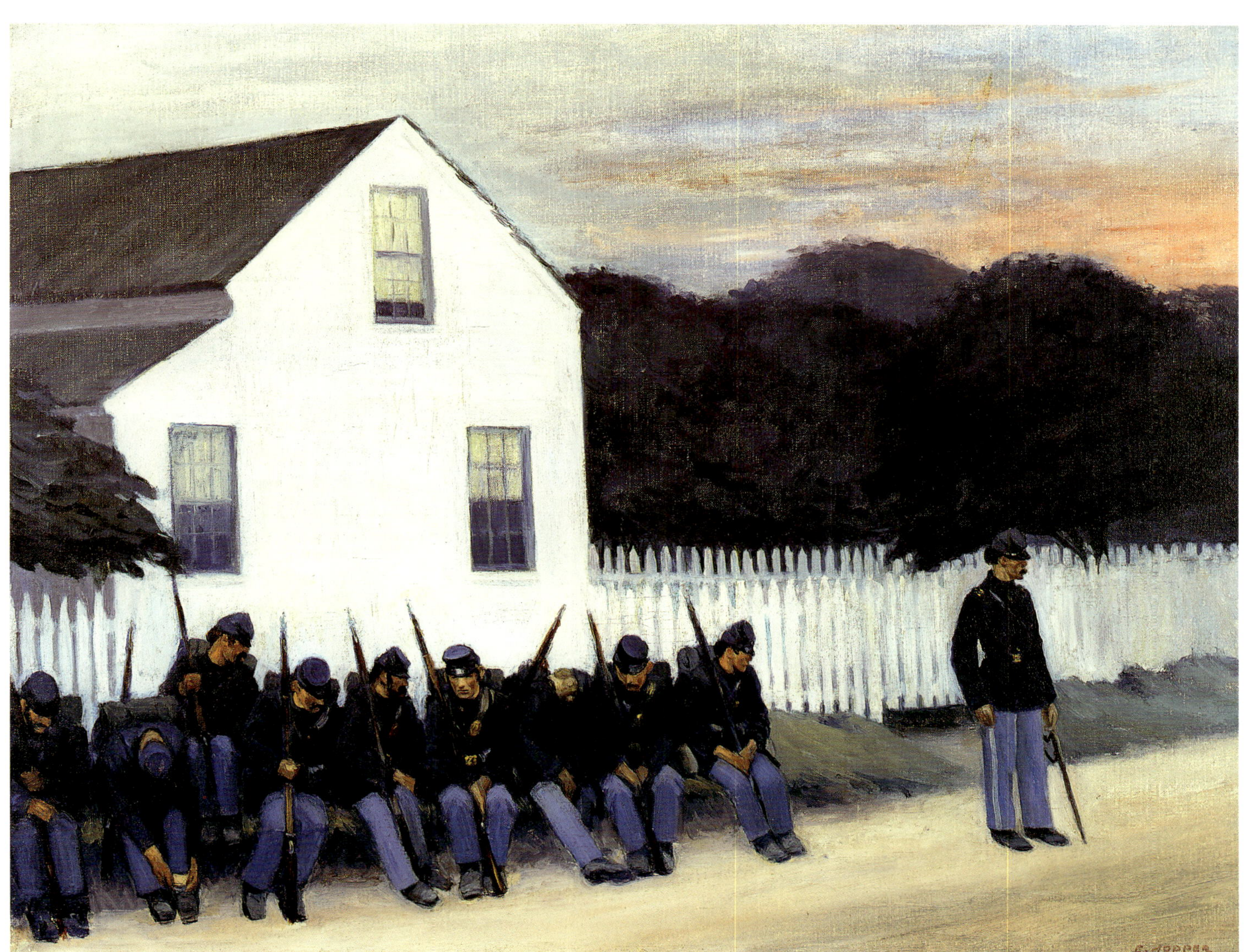

The Seawatchers
1952
oil on canvas
29 1/4 x 39 1/4 inches
signed lr: Edward Hopper
Spring Creek Art
Foundation, Inc.

130

In his later paintings, Hopper maintained his emphasis on light, his interest in geometric forms, and the powerful suggestion of men and women alienated from their environment. This detachment is particularly disturbing in *The Seawatchers*, since waterside resorts are usually associated with vacations and pleasant experiences. Hopper's view of the New England coast is anything but festive. Despite the strong sunlight, the brisk wind that blows the drying towels makes the sea appear cold and uninviting. Two people stare intently and silently at the ocean, unable to communicate with each other. The barrier separating them is suggestive of the isolation that Hopper felt existed between the individual and society. During the last fifteen years of his life, he further eliminated details and concentrated even more directly on the abstract designs produced by strong contrasts of light and shadow. Hopper's sense of pattern is particularly evident in the configuration of the house, patio, sky, and sea. When asked what he was after in his paintings, Hopper replied, "I'm after me."

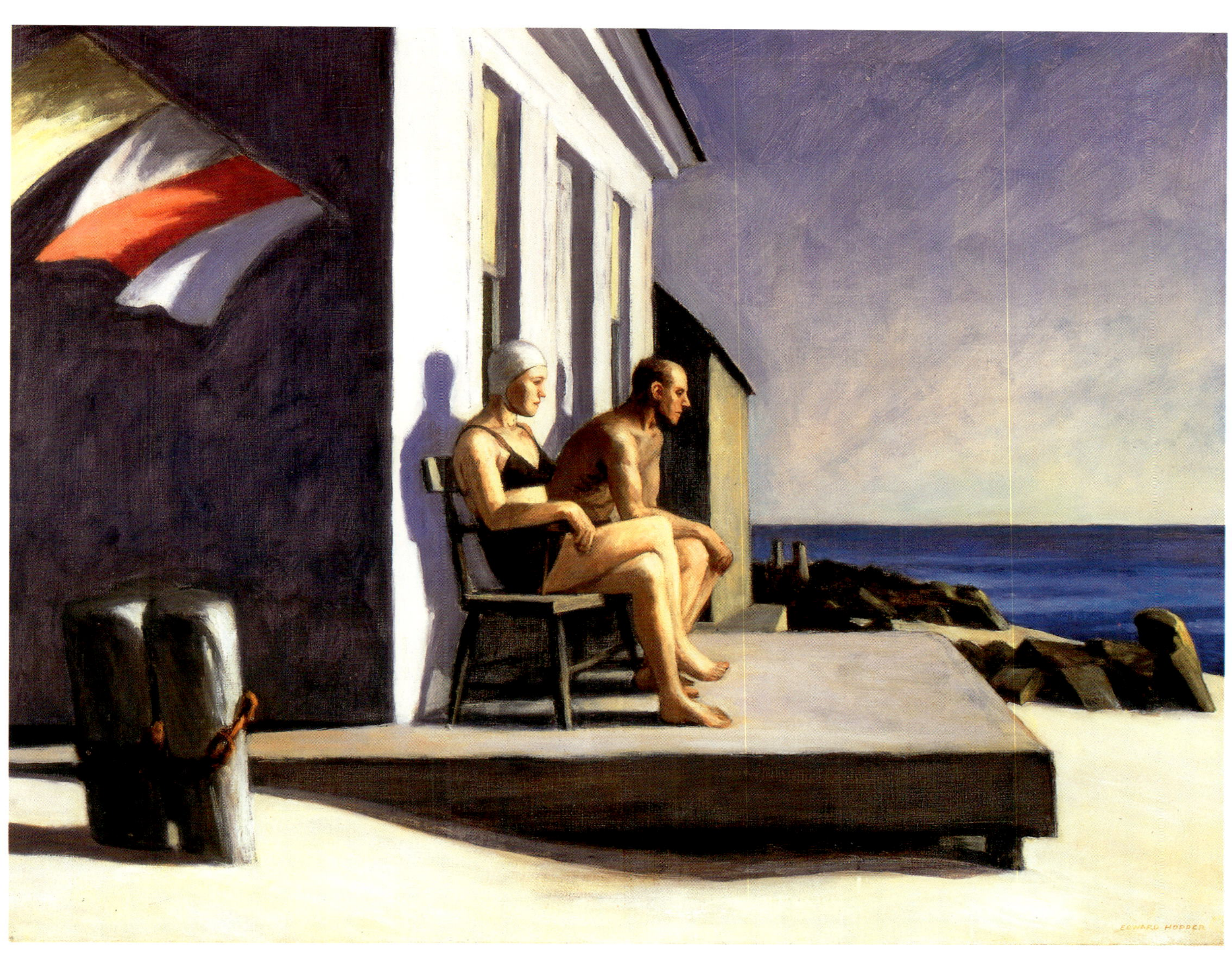

Charles E. Burchfield
1893-1967

Glory to God
1953
watercolor on paper
47 x 47 inches
signed with monogram lr
of central panel: CEB
The Warner Collection
Tuscaloosa, Alabama

Few American artists have responded to the landscape with as much emotion or personal expression as Charles Burchfield. In his watercolors nature is hauntingly strange and powerful, and he takes reality to the edge of abstraction in an attempt to evoke the universal mystery of the landscape. Born in Ashtabula Harbor, Ohio, and raised in the nearby town of Salem, Burchfield studied at the Cleveland School of Art under Henry G. Keller, who encouraged his interest in design and pattern. He was also influenced by Chinese and Japanese art as well as Hindu and Buddhist mythology. In the 1920s Burchfield moved permanently to Buffalo, New York. Although he painted a few oils, watercolors were his preference. He sometimes added ink, pencil, and other media to obtain the results he desired. Burchfield's watercolors provide a melancholy and foreboding view of the rural landscape that is reminiscent of Edward Hopper's approach to his urban subjects. The personal and expressive aspects of their art influenced the work of the American abstract expressionists of the late 1940s and 1950s.

Glory to God was painted for a church and formed in the shape of a triptych altarpiece. Burchfield composed his central landscape panel to resemble a cathedral, suggesting the presence of God with a star-shaped sun. The bare trees in this spiritual landscape allude to the Crucifixion. Their converging shadows lead inside the churchlike structure toward an infinite space beyond. The work captures what Burchfield called "the agonizing mystery of infinity. It is impossible ever for man to comprehend it, but it is always there in the background of my life."

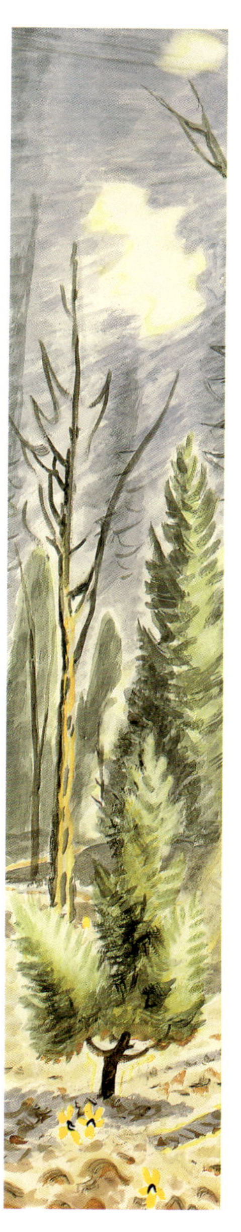
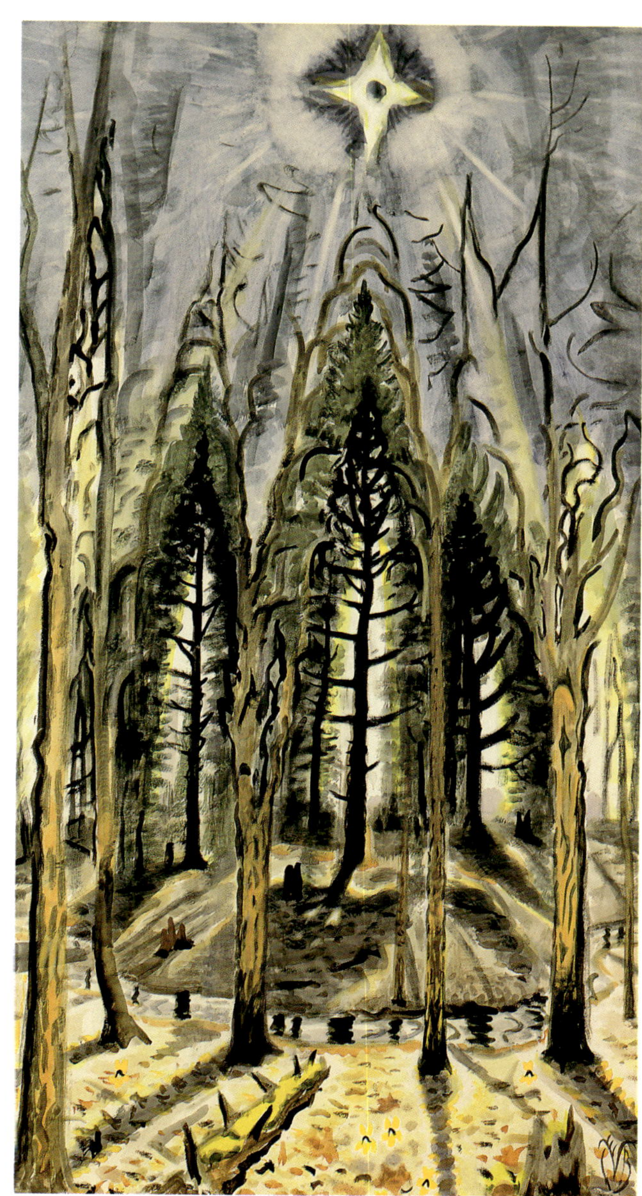
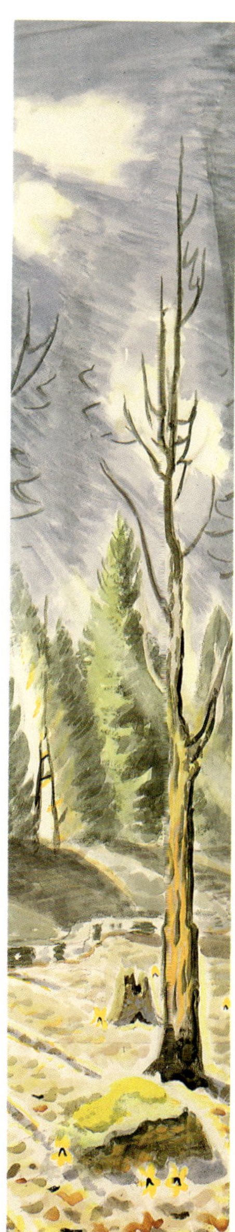

Georgia O'Keeffe
1887-1986

Black and White
1930
oil on canvas
36 x 24 inches
Whitney Museum of
American Art, New York
50th Anniversary Gift
of Mr. and Mrs. R.
Crosby Kemper

Georgia O'Keeffe was a major exponent of modernism in America. Her style, based on clear colors, hard edges, and magnified views, embraces a wide range of subjects that reflect her unique perception of her environment. O'Keeffe was born in Sun Prairie, Wisconsin, and raised in Virginia. She studied at the Art Institute of Chicago School of Art and the Art Students League, but it was Arthur Wesley Dow's class at Columbia University Teachers College that proved most influential. His interest in the principles of oriental art made a lasting impression on the young artist. O'Keeffe moved to Canyon, Texas, in 1916, where she began painting abstract compositions inspired by her exposure to the plains landscape. Another influence on O'Keeffe's work was photographer and gallery owner Alfred Stieglitz, who was a mentor to many of America's early modernist painters and later became the artist's husband. O'Keeffe moved to New York City in 1918, and by the mid-1920s she was painting the urban landscape. She began spending summers in New Mexico in 1929 and settled there after Stieglitz died in 1946.

In the late 1920s and early 1930s O'Keeffe created some of her most severe abstractions. These works were limited in color, occasionally almost monochromatic, with their entire emphasis on crystal-clear forms. *Black and White* has its roots in O'Keeffe's abstractions of the Texas plains and her paintings of New York skyscrapers. In this canvas, she captures the essence of the skyscraper by distilling its soaring shape into a white triangle set against the blackness of the night sky. In its austerity, the sharply contoured image adds an element of anxiety to the composition. The dynamic emphasis on form endows the painting with a cosmic grandeur and characterizes much of O'Keeffe's approach to her subjects drawn from nature.

Georgia O'Keeffe
1887-1986

Yellow Jonquils, No. 3
1936
oil on canvas
30 1/4 x 40 1/4 inches
The R. C. Kemper
Charitable Trust and
Foundation and the
Enid and Crosby Kemper
Foundation

In 1916 O'Keeffe became the head of the art department at West Texas State Normal College in Canyon. This isolated setting was the early inspiration and an enduring source for her paintings of landscapes and other natural subjects. In 1924 O'Keeffe began a series of greatly enlarged images of leaf and floral forms, initiating the style for which she is best known. These studies paralleled the exploration of close-focus camera views by Stieglitz and other photographers.

Yellow Jonquils, No. 3 exemplifies O'Keeffe's exaggerated floral images, which are taken out of their environment and depicted in a highly detailed manner. She often created series based on a single theme, which was frequently a motif in nature that in successive paintings she transformed into an almost abstract image. Although three jonquil paintings are known, there were possibly five works in the series. In *Yellow Jonquils, No. 3* O'Keeffe takes the viewer into the private world of nature. The blossoms fill the canvas with their delicate contours, vivid color, and magnified forms. O'Keeffe's arrangement summons an energy and exuberance that threaten to break the bounds of the composition. She explains her motives for these paintings: "If I could paint the flower exactly as I see it no one would see what I see because I would paint it small like the flower is small. So I said to myself—I'll paint what I see—what the flower is to me but I'll paint it big and they will be surprised into taking time to look at it—I will make even busy New Yorkers take time to see what I see of flowers."

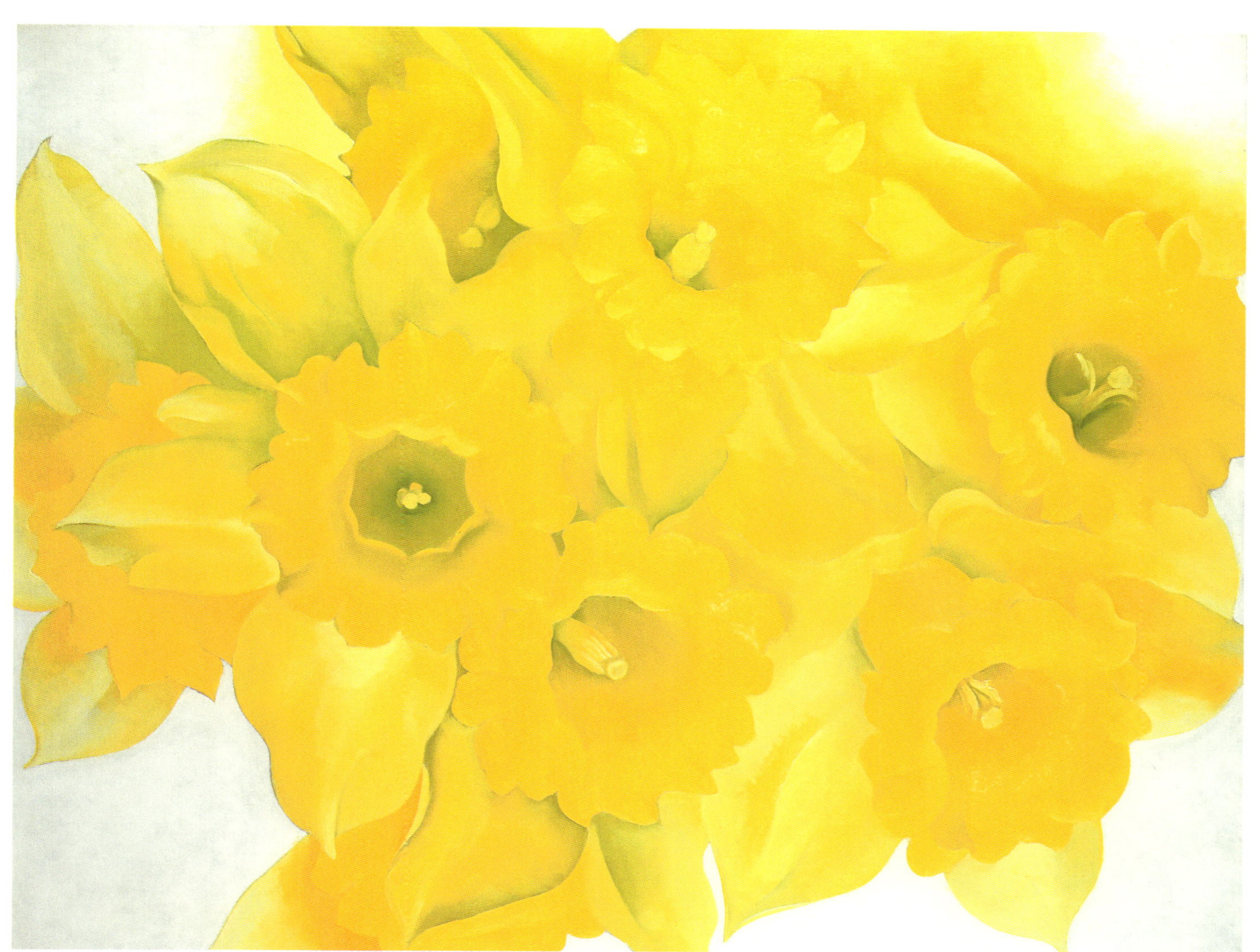

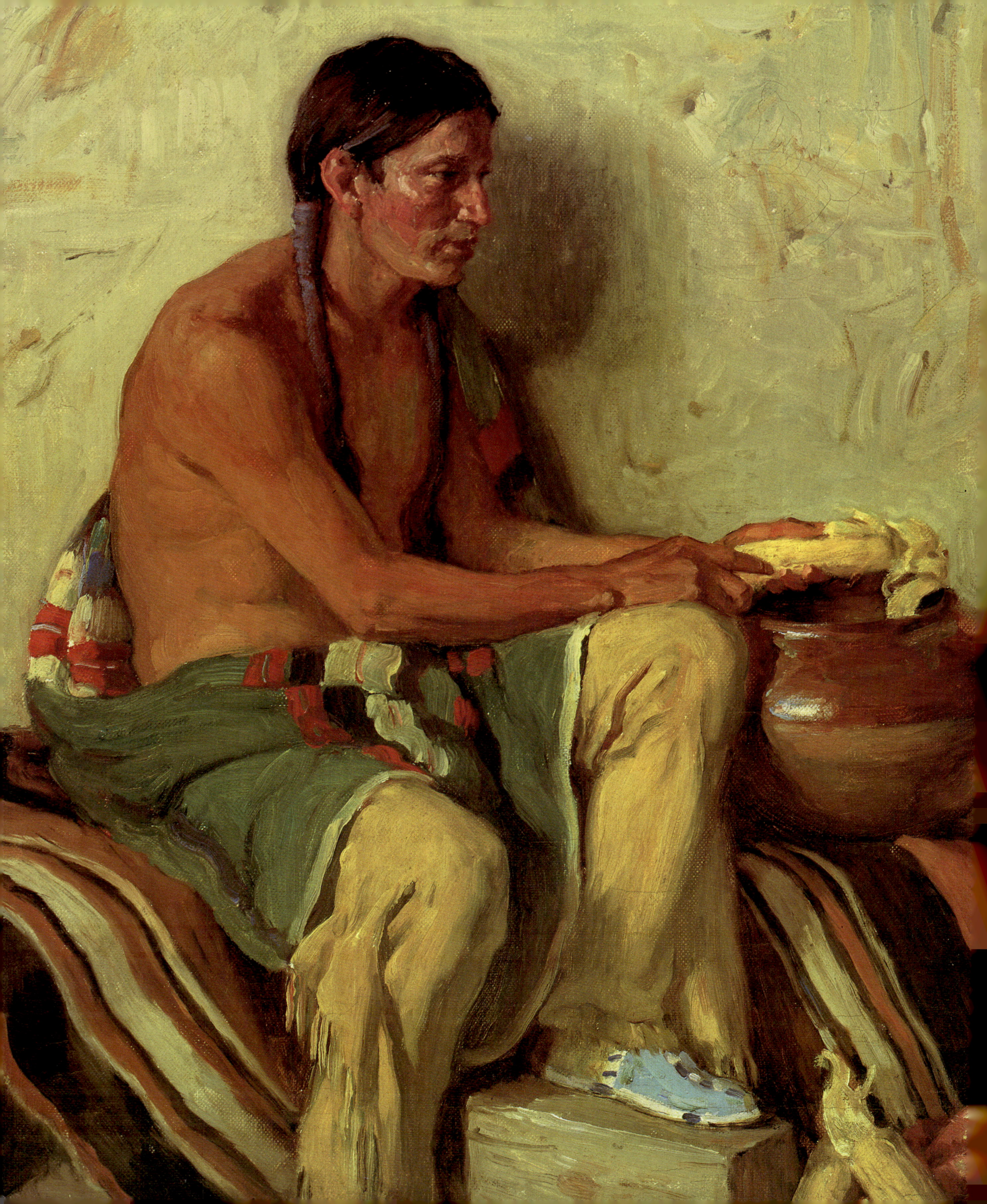

WESTERN AMERICAN ART
1822 - 1991

American Traditions: Art from the Collections of Culver Alumni

Petalesharro
c. 1822
oil on panel
17 1/2 x 13 3/4 inches
The Warner Collection
Tuscaloosa, Alabama

A native of Newport, Rhode Island, Charles Bird King had his first formal art training in the New York studio of Edward Savage. In 1805 he traveled to London to study at the Royal Academy with Benjamin West, a prominent American artist famous for historical painting. King returned to America seven years later, eventually settling in Washington, D.C., where he opened his own gallery. He quickly developed a solid reputation as a portrait painter and had as clients many of the local government officials. In 1821 the War Department commissioned King to paint portraits of visiting Native American chiefs as part of a documentary project initiated by Thomas L. McKenney, superintendent of Indian trade in Georgetown. From 1821 to 1842 he painted over one hundred such portraits; all but four were destroyed in a disastrous Smithsonian fire in 1865. His work has been preserved through copies that he made for himself and through hand-colored lithographs published by McKenney and James Hall in their three-volume *History of the Indian Tribes of North America.*

Petalesharro was a member of a delegation of sixteen Native Americans, mostly Pawnee, who visited Washington in the winter of 1821–22. The Pawnee chief is depicted with an eagle feather headdress decorated with ermine tails, and a Monroe "peace medal," presented to him by a representative of the government. *Petalesharro* was one of the earliest formal portraits of a Plains Indian wearing his native garments. This is one of five extant copies produced by King from the original *Petalesharro.*

M. K. D.

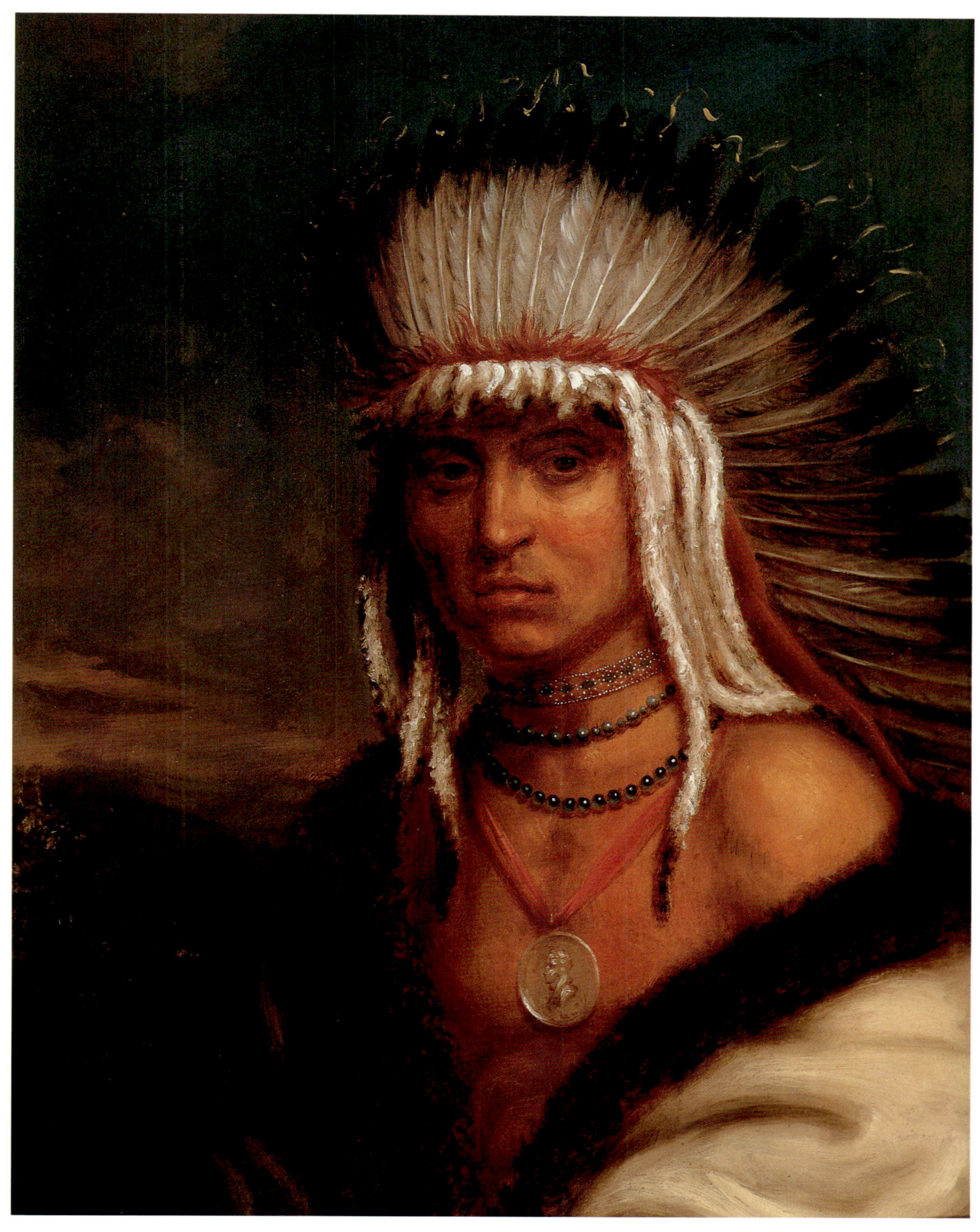

Charles Bird King
1785-1862

Pushmataha
c. 1824
oil on panel
17 1/2 x 13 3/4 inches
The Warner Collection
Tuscaloosa, Alabama

142

King created the majority of the portraits in the McKenney and Hall publication; other artists included Henry Inman and James Otto Lewis. The finished paintings were displayed in Washington as part of the government's "Indian Gallery."

Pushmataha, a Choctaw warrior chief, led his tribal delegation to Washington in 1824 to negotiate the sale of portions of Mississippi farmlands; he was welcomed by the president, secretary of war, and members of the cabinet. Pushmataha was one of the few visiting chiefs who chose to be portrayed wearing a Euro-American suit rather than his traditional native clothes. The chief died in Washington after a brief illness, as he had predicted earlier to members of his tribe. He was buried with full military honors in the Congressional Cemetery. This painting is the only extant copy made by King.

M. K. D.

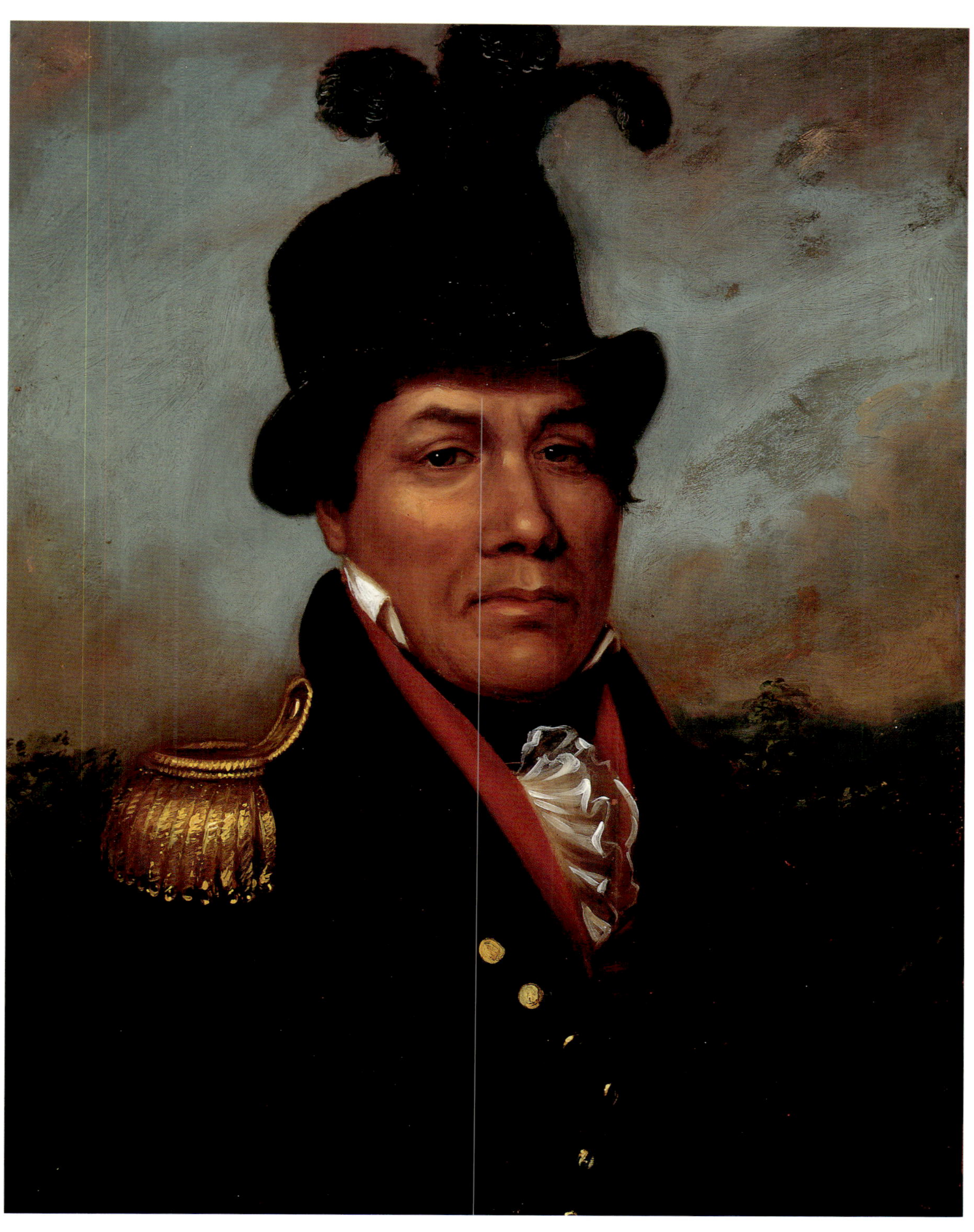

Charles Bird King
1785-1862

Makataimeshekiakiah
(Black Hawk)
c. 1833
oil on panel
24 x 19 3/4 inches
The Warner Collection
Tuscaloosa, Alabama

Black Hawk, a Sauk and Fox chief from Illinois, came to Washington in April 1833 as a prisoner of war, but he was welcomed as a military hero. He had led a band of Sauk and Fox against government troops in the upper Mississippi Valley, in a war that was later named after him. His warriors were defeated in August 1832, and within a few days Black Hawk surrendered. After a brief imprisonment at Fort Monroe, Virginia, Black Hawk and five other members of his tribe toured the northeastern states. They soon became national celebrities, much to the embarassment of President Jackson.

Black Hawk is shown wearing a brilliant roach made of porcupine guard hairs dyed red, and a Jackson "peace medal." This is the only copy King made of the portrait, which was destroyed in the Smithsonian fire.

M. K. D.

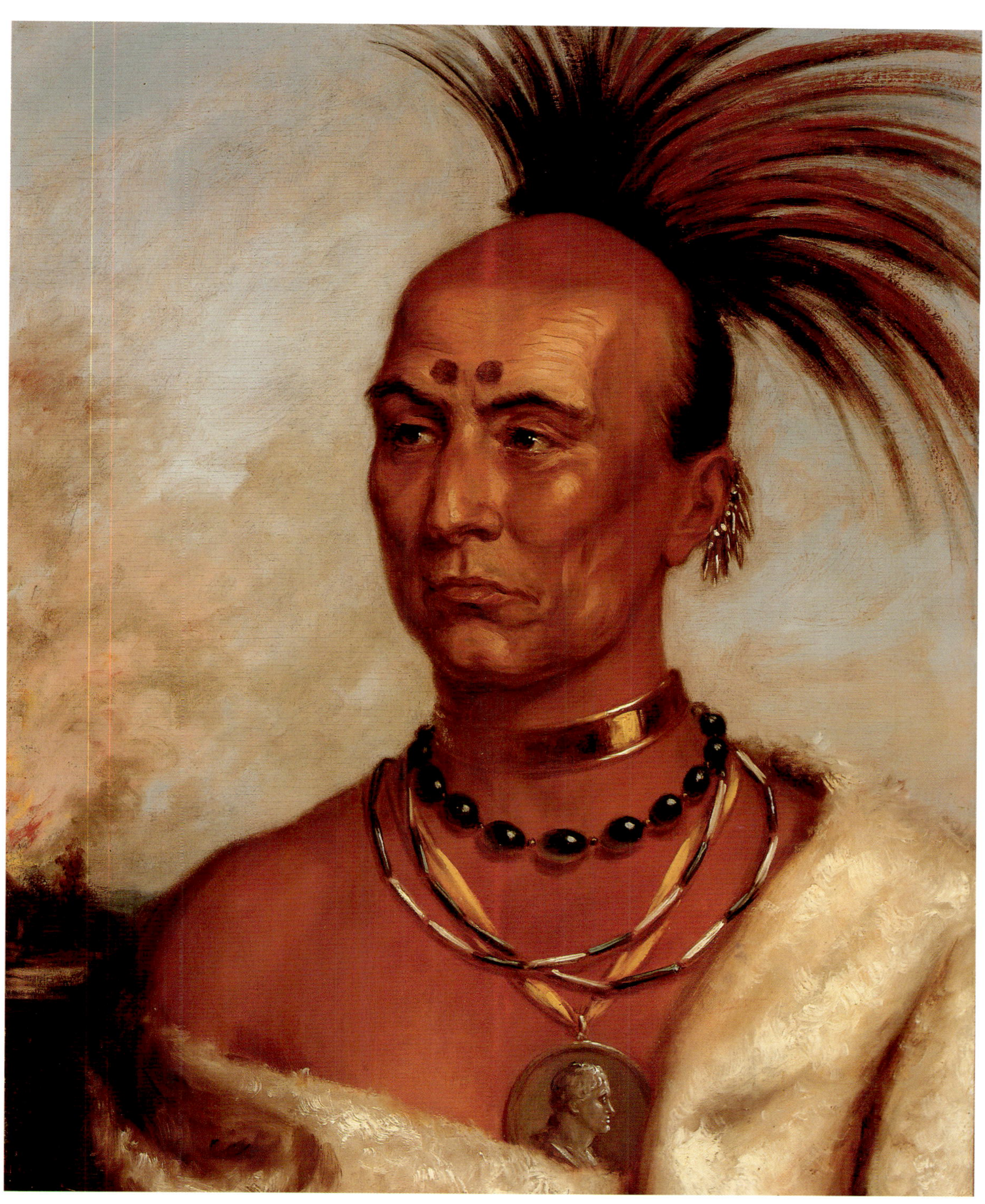

George Catlin
1796-1872

Interior of a Mandan Lodge
c. 1832
oil on canvas
23 1/4 x 28 inches
The Warner Collection
Tuscaloosa, Alabama

George Catlin preferred the outdoors and hunting, but at his father's request he trained for the law. At the same time, he taught himself to paint portraits. After informal study in the 1820s at the Pennsylvania Academy of the Fine Arts and in the studios of John Neagle and Thomas Sully, Catlin gave up his legal practice to devote himself to painting. Influenced by a visit to Charles Willson Peale's new museum, which included a display of Indian artifacts acquired in the West, and by witnessing an official delegation of American Indian tribal leaders enroute to Washington, Catlin decided to specialize in history painting and to document what he thought were the vanishing Native Americans. In 1830 he moved to St. Louis to begin painting the native inhabitants on the lower Missouri River. Numerous trips north and west in the next decade provided subjects for hundreds of Indian portraits and genre studies.

Catlin visited the Mandan Indians for the first time in 1832, during a two-thousand-mile voyage to the headwaters of the Missouri River. Catlin's paintings (and those of his contemporary, Karl Bodmer) of Mandan chiefs and medicine men, buffalo dances, village games, war councils, and ceremonies provide valuable visual documents of this Northern Plains culture, for in 1837 almost all of the Mandan Indians died from smallpox.

M. K. D.

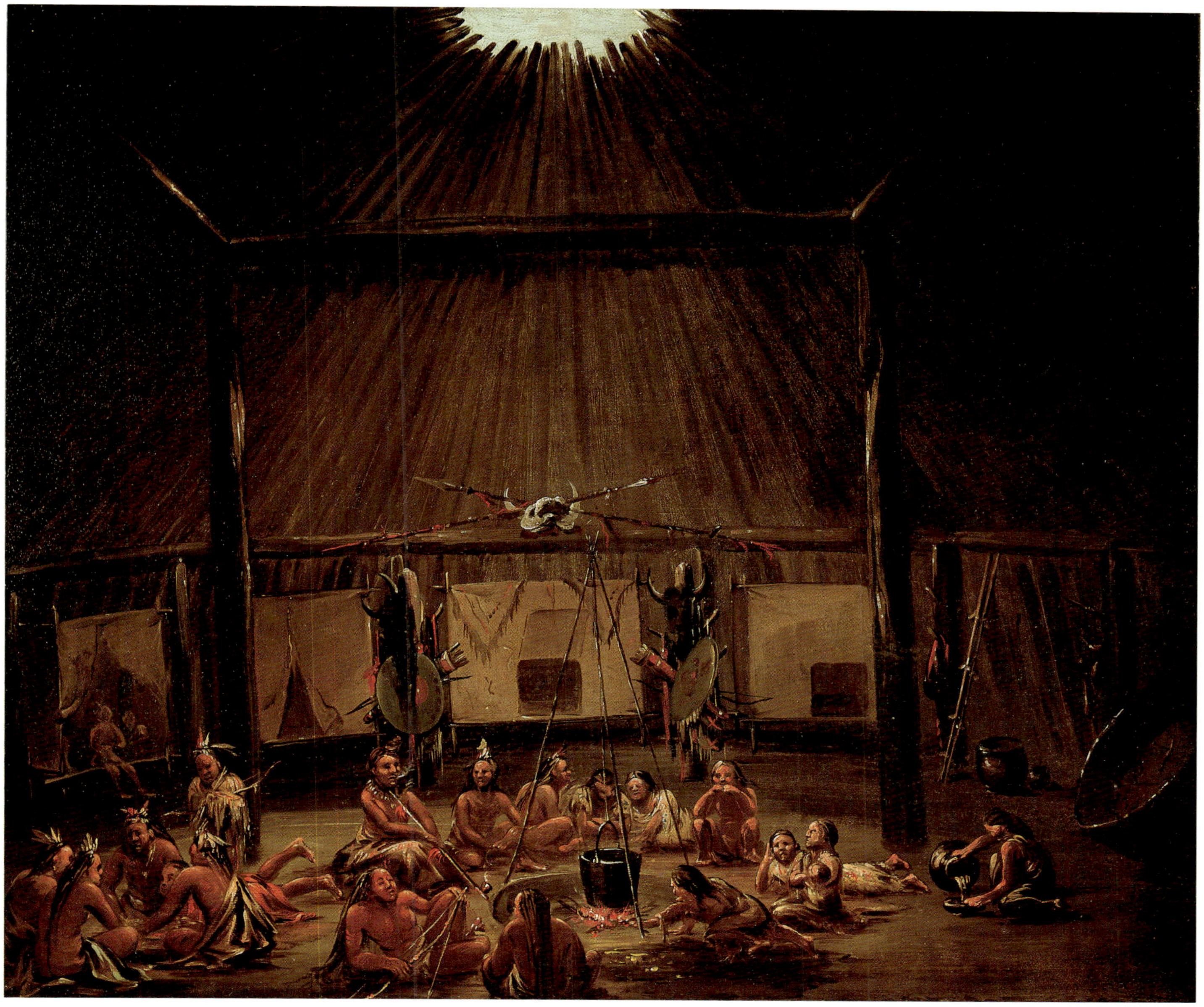

*Battle Between Sioux, Sauk
and Fox*
c. 1846
oil on canvas
25 3/4 x 32 inches
The Warner Collection
Tuscaloosa, Alabama

In 1839 Catlin developed what he called his "Indian Gallery," which included not only his paintings, but also numerous Indian objects and a Crow tipi. In the 1840s the Catlin Gallery, usually accompanied by an entourage that presented native dances, demonstrations of craft and skill, and lectures, traveled through England, Ireland, and Scotland and to Paris. For years Catlin tried, without success, to sell his Indian paintings to the United States government. He finally sold them to an American manufacturer, whose heirs, ironically, later donated them to the Smithsonian Institution. During the 1850s Catlin continued to travel, visiting Central and South America on three different occasions as well as the American Northwest. By 1857 Catlin had painted most of the Indians of South America. Catlin was the most prolific eyewitness recorder of Native Americans, and until his death in 1872 he championed their cultures.

In this dramatic painting of a deadly battle between the Sioux and the Sauk and Fox tribes, set against a panoramic Western landscape, Catlin has captured the sense of action and danger. In his obsession to record every detail of Indian life before it disappeared forever, Catlin often worked very quickly and sketchily. The somewhat awkward proportions of his figures and horses here betray his self-training, but his passion and concern for his subject add a sense of charm and naiveté.

M. K. D.

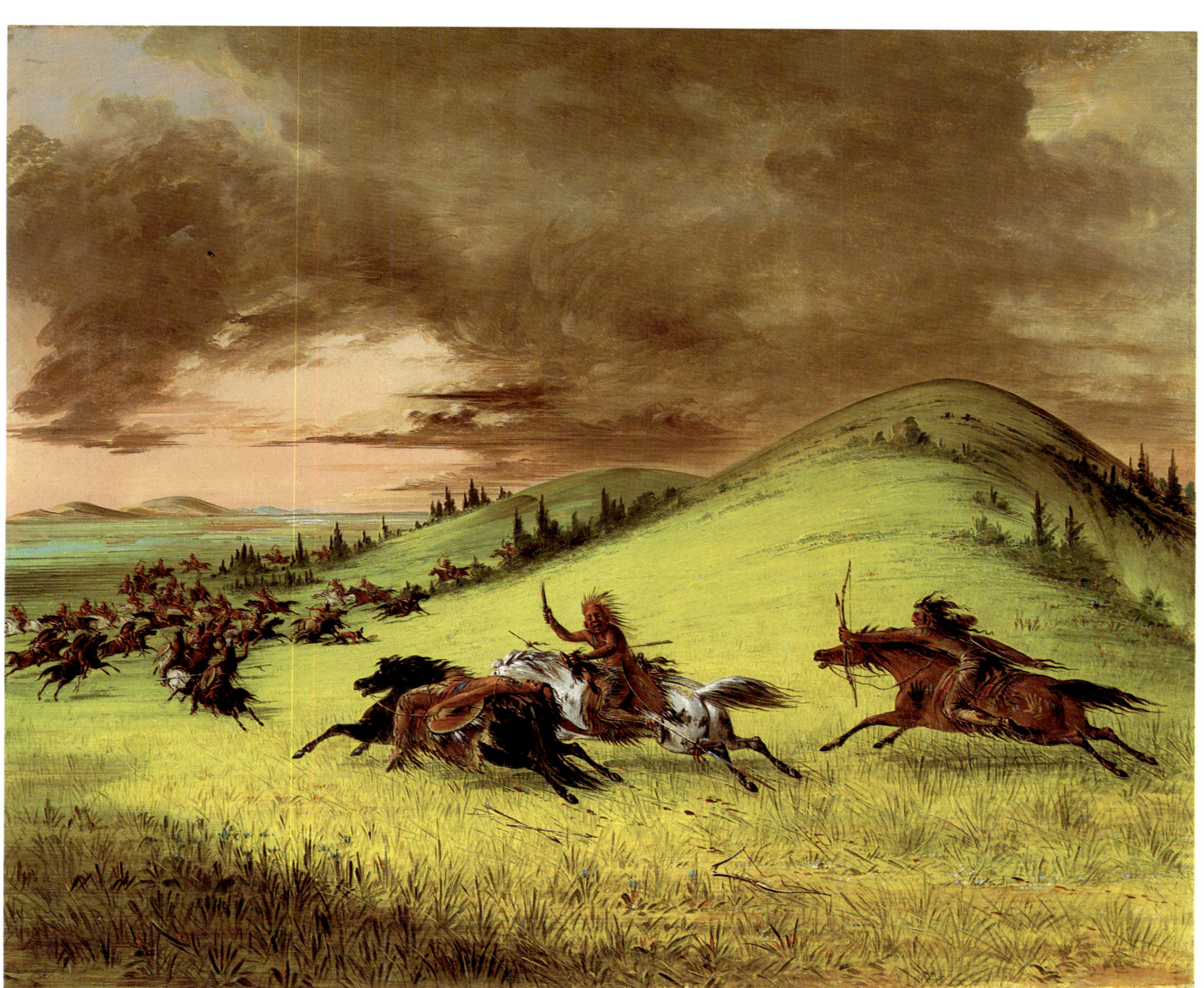

Seth Eastman
1808–1875

Sioux in Council
c. 1848
oil on canvas
35 x 25 inches
The Warner Collection
Tuscaloosa, Alabama

Seth Eastman was one of several early American artists concentrating on genre scenes of the American Indians; others include George Catlin, Charles Wimar, and Alfred Jacob Miller. Unlike the others, however, Eastman was a career soldier, having graduated from West Point in 1829. Art to him was an enjoyable hobby, and he did not have to rely on drawing and painting as a profession.

Eastman's army career provided many years of contact with Native Americans, and he usually managed to get assignments that allowed time for drawing and painting. After brief duty in the Michigan Territory, Eastman returned to West Point, where he was an assistant teacher of drawing from 1833 to 1840. He then was stationed again in the West, serving for over seven years at Fort Snelling (present-day Minneapolis), in the homeland of the Santee Sioux. Subsequent assignments included various frontier outposts, with intermittent duty in Washington, D.C. During the 1850s Eastman was assigned to the Bureau of Indian Affairs in Washington, and he spent five years illustrating Henry R. Schoolcraft's six-volume *Indian Tribes of the United States*, which had been commissioned by the federal government. After officially retiring from the army in 1863, Eastman received further commissions from Congress to paint scenes of Indian and frontier life for the Capitol and for House committee rooms.

Eastman's close assocation with native tribes, his fluency in the Sioux language, and his deep respect for native cultures gave him access to ceremonies and activities not usually available to Anglos. His hundreds of sketches and paintings developed during his military assignments are valuable both artistically and ethnographically.

In this council scene, eight Sioux are having an intense argument, as evidenced by the gesturing arms and angry faces. Bright yellows and whites help emphasize the central figure, who is wearing a "peace medal," indicating he had visited Washington, D.C., and had been received by an official of the United States government. The closely contained group is set within a limited woodland space, through which we have a glimpse of blue sky in the upper right.

M. K. D.

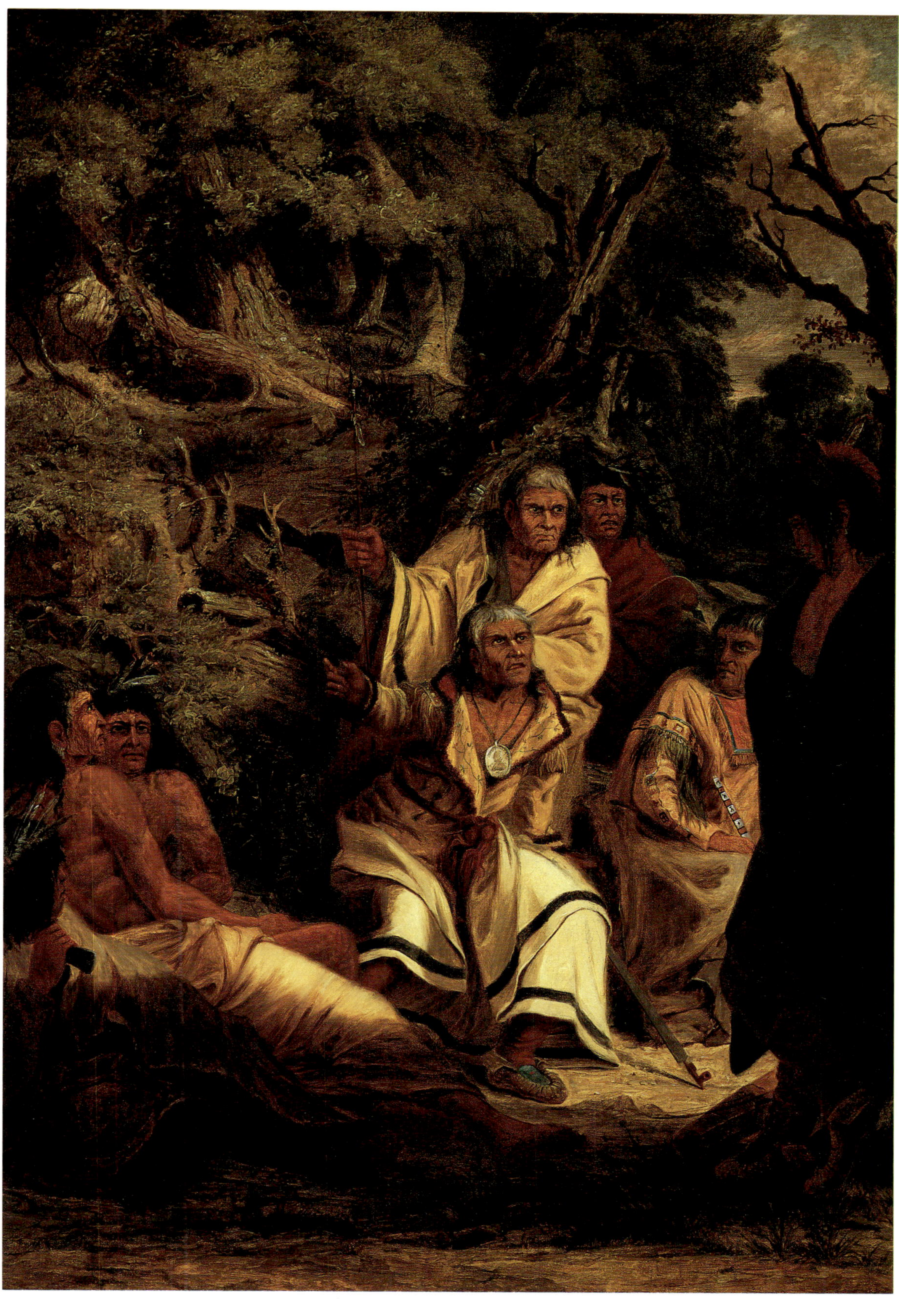

Karl Bodmer
1809-1893

Buffalo Hunt
c. 1840
oil on canvas
13 x 30 inches
The Warner Collection
Tuscaloosa, Alabama

In 1832 Prince Alexander Philipp Maximilian of Wied Neuwied, Germany, embarked on a two-year exploration of the territories of the upper Missouri River. This remarkable scientist-scholar had hired a young artist, Karl Bodmer, to document the people and places they would encounter.

Born in Zurich, Switzerland, in 1809, Karl Bodmer received formal training in drawing, painting, and engraving from his uncle, J. J. Meier, a well-known landscape artist. Bodmer's exacting attention to detail and his careful observation made him a perfect choice to accompany the prince. Through hundreds of oil paintings, watercolors, and sketches of the natives living along the upper Missouri, Bodmer provided both a reliable and beautiful pictorial record of North American Indian cultures—cultures that were rapidly changing as European settlement expanded westward.

Maximilian and Bodmer returned to Europe in July 1834 and devoted the next few years to publishing Maximilian's journals and Bodmer's images. Bodmer's watercolors of the northern landscape, frontier settlements, native customs and ceremonies, daily life, and tribal leaders and chiefs were reproduced as lithographs and aquatints and widely distributed in both Europe and America. Bodmer never returned to America; he spent the rest of his life living and working in the Barbizon forest, outside Paris.

M. K. D.

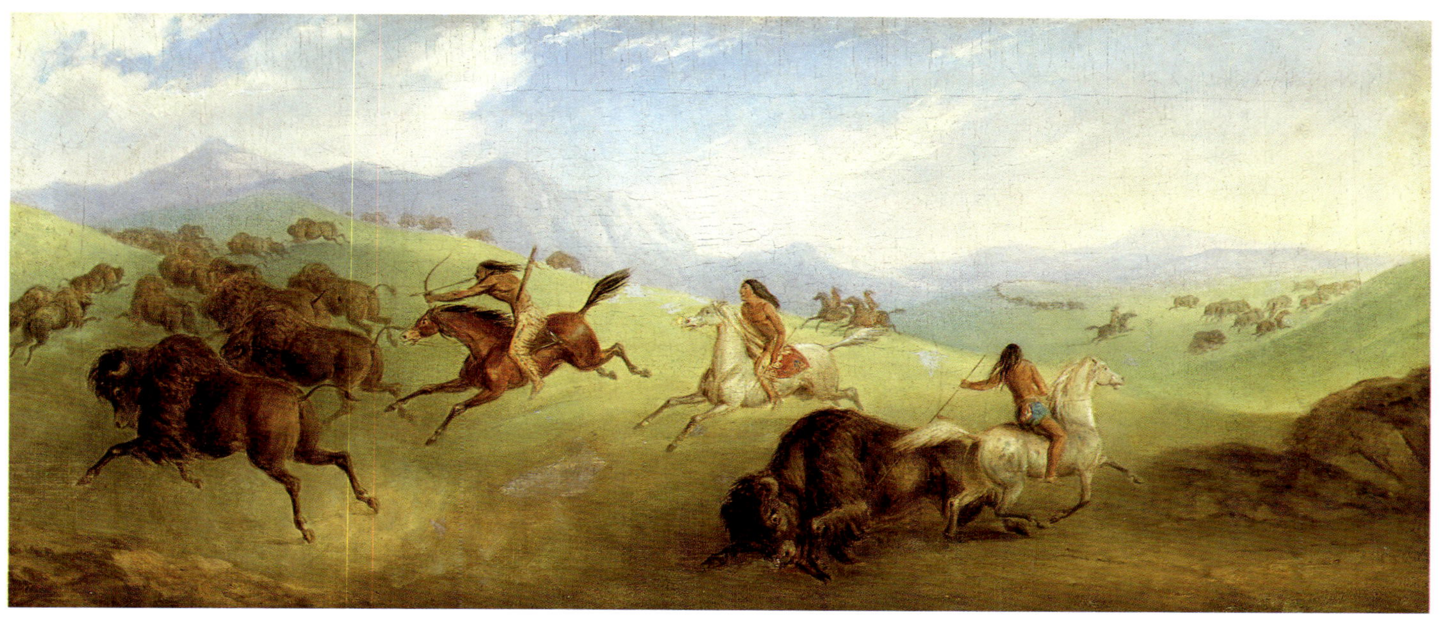

Alfred Jacob Miller
1810-1874

The Snake Indians
1840
oil on canvas
18 x 24 inches
The Gund Collection
of Western Art

154

Alfred Jacob Miller, the only artist to paint the Rocky Mountain fur trade from firsthand experience, was born in Baltimore, Maryland, to a wealthy family. After studying portrait painting with Thomas Sully in 1831–32, he toured Europe for almost two years, studying at the Ecole des Beaux-Arts in Paris and at the English Life School in Rome, where he was the only American student. When he returned to the United States in 1834, Miller opened a portrait studio in Baltimore, which slowly failed. In 1836 he moved to St. Louis and established a new studio—this time with more success. The following year he was hired by the Scottish nobleman and adventurer Captain William Drummond Stewart to accompany him to the last great fur traders' rendezvous, at Green River, Wyoming. While traveling with Stewart, Miller made hundreds of drawings and field sketches. For years to come, he used these studies to develop formal paintings, often creating several versions of the same subject.

Of all the native tribes he encountered during the journey to Green River, Miller most admired the Snake Indians: "Their horses and equipments [sic] were better . . . they were more friendly, sociable, and hospitable." In this dramatic painting, a Snake (Shoshone) chief, mounted on his restless white horse, is starkly silhouetted against a pale, cloud-filled sky. The proud chief, a mounted companion, and the dark promontory fill the foreground in the left half of the painting; they balance the deep space leading to distant mountains on the right. This composition became very popular, and Miller painted several variations.

M. K. D.

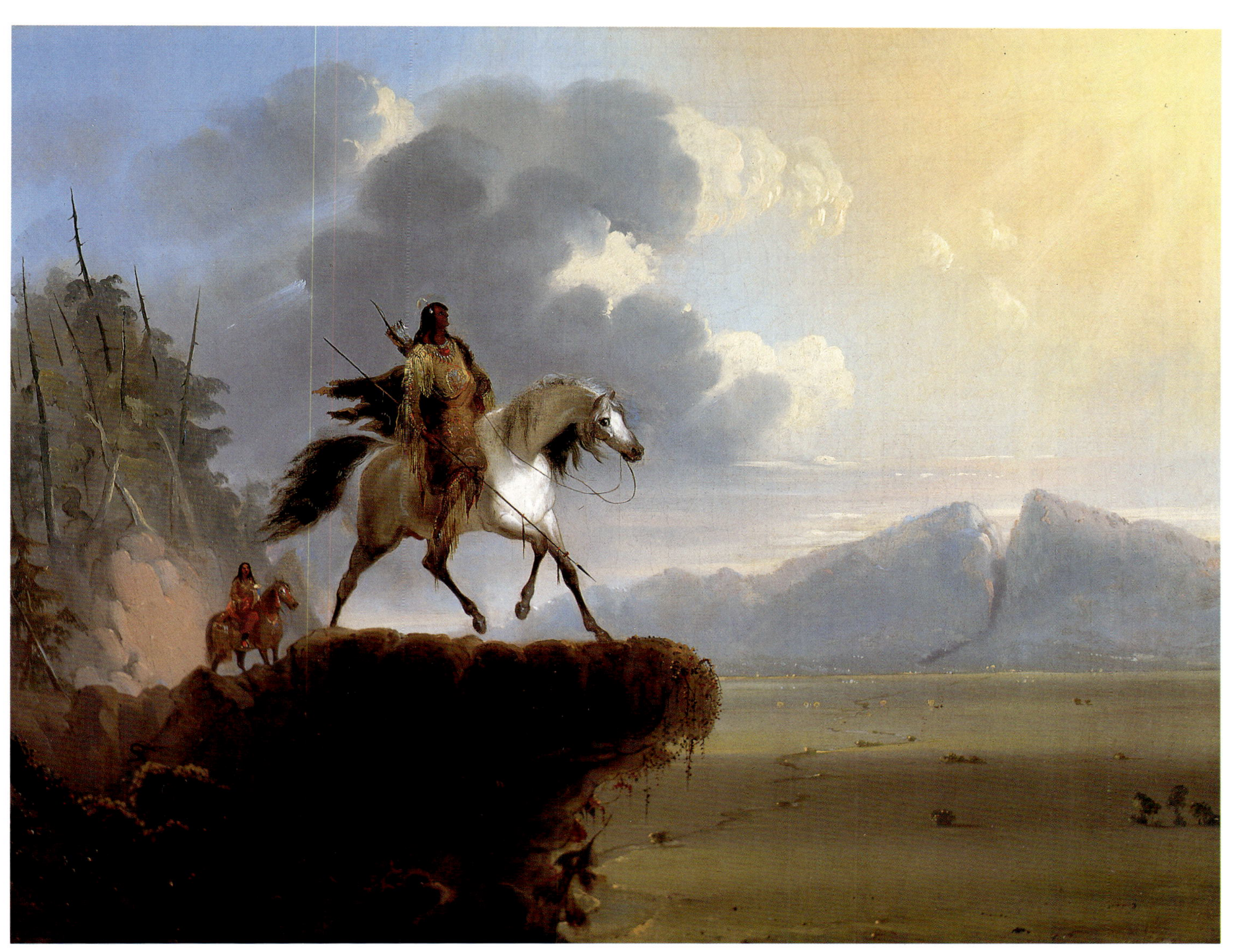

The Thirsty Trapper

1850
oil on canvas
24 x 20 inches
signed and dated lr:
A. MILLER/1850
The Warner Collection
Tuscaloosa, Alabama

Three years after accompanying Captain Stewart to the rendezvous of 1837, Miller moved to Scotland to work exclusively for the Scottish adventurer. During his two-year stay, from 1840 to 1842, at Stewart's Murthly Castle, he produced decorative scenic oils based on favorite incidents from the trip and a portfolio of pen and ink, wash, and watercolor sketches. In 1842 Miller returned to his native Baltimore, where for the rest of his life he painted portraits, some religious subjects, and Western scenes experienced firsthand in 1837.

In this romanticized treatment of a familiar scene on the plains, a mounted trapper and his partner are eagerly awaiting a drink from a horn offered by a native woman, dressed in pale, fringed buckskin. *The Thirsty Trapper* is one of several versions of this subject that Miller created; others are titled *Receiving a Draught of Water from an Indian Girl* and *The Halt*. The low horizon reinforces the vastness of the flat prairies and makes the two trappers seem vulnerable. The woman's graceful, demure pose reflects the classical training Miller received at the Ecole des Beaux-Arts in Paris. The large white horse, which frequently appears in Miller's paintings, is a tribute to his patron, who rode such a horse during the 1837 expedition.

M. K. D.

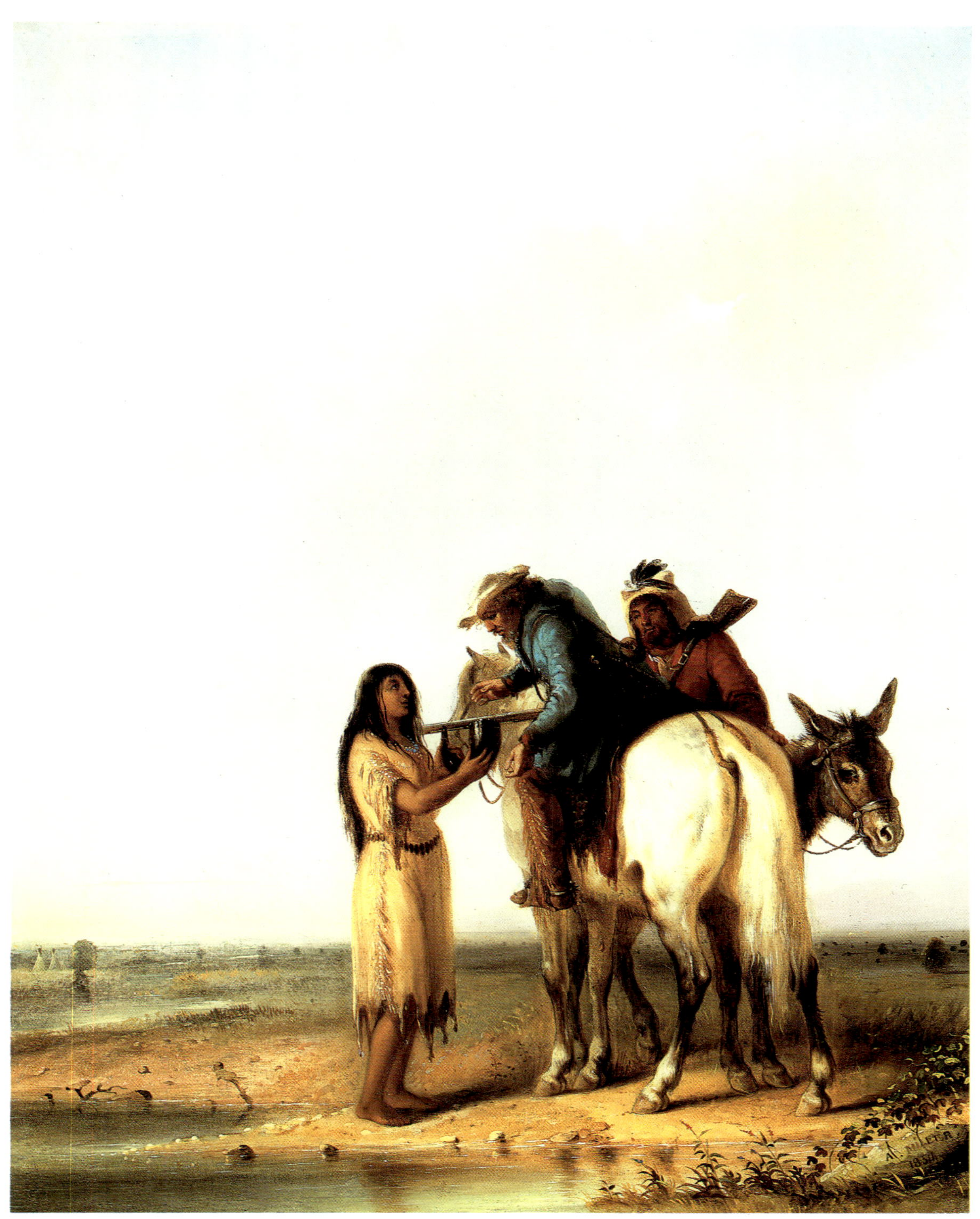

Alfred Jacob Miller
1810-1874

The Lost Greenhorn
1851
oil on canvas
16 x 20 inches
signed and dated lr:
A. Miller/1851
The Warner Collection
Tuscaloosa, Alabama

158

Miller's Western subjects include landscapes, Native American portraits and genre scenes, buffalo hunts, trappers and other visitors to the rendezvous, animal studies, and imaginary scenes.

In this tragicomic image of a lost tenderfoot, Miller presents a sense of hopelessness and despair, as the rider looks in vain across the flat prairies for a recognizable landmark. The painting is based on a specific incident. When John, the English cook who accompanied the 1837 expedition to the rendezvous, bragged about his accomplishments as a buffalo hunter, Captain Stewart, who never ignored boasts, took it as an immediate challenge. John responded by riding out of camp to prove his abilities. When he had not returned after two days, hunters were sent out to rescue the frightened cook. This became one of Miller's most popular images; he painted several different versions that were reproduced as lithographs.

M. K. D.

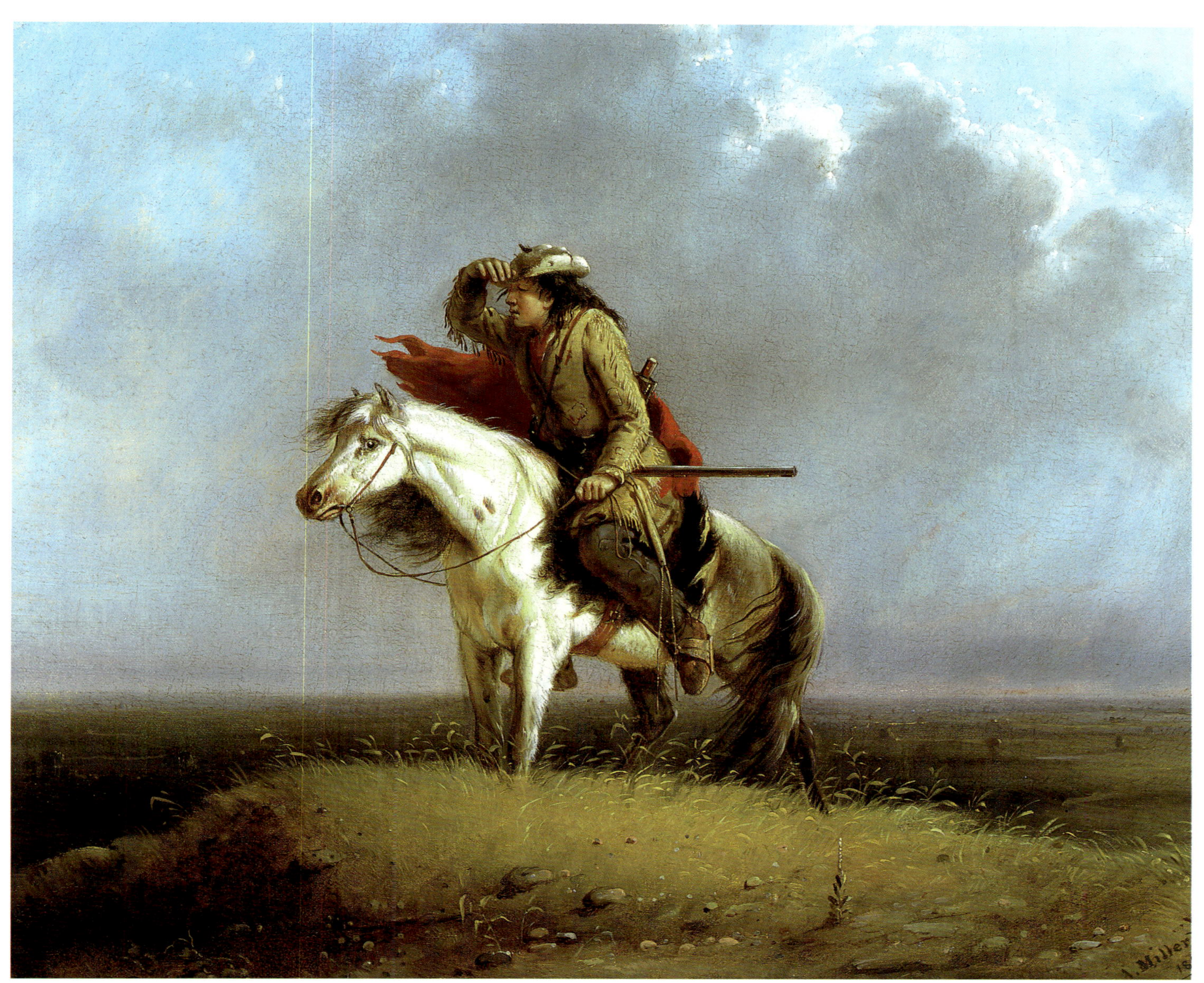

(Studio of)
George Caleb Bingham
1811-1879

Trappers Return
c. 1851
oil on panel
4 x 6 1/2 inches
The Warner Collection
Tuscaloosa, Alabama

George Caleb Bingham, born in the Shenandoah Valley in Virginia, was raised in the Missouri Territory, in what became central Missouri. Largely self-taught, he worked primarily in Missouri, with brief stays in Washington, D.C., and Düsseldorf, Germany. Though he initially earned a living by painting portraits, Bingham became famous for his genre scenes of the riverboat traffic on the Mississippi and Missouri rivers. He documented the everyday social and political activities of the flatboatmen and traders moving up and down the rivers and of the residents of the small towns lining their shores. Known as "the Missouri painter," Bingham captured on canvas the vitality, ambition, and spirit of the nineteenth-century American frontier.

This small painting, by a student or follower of Bingham, directly echoes the composition of Bingham's most famous work, *Fur Traders Descending the Missouri*, painted in 1845. The pose, garments, and colors of the father and son; the profiled dugout canoe with its wrapped cargo; the background of trees, including a dead tree trunk, blurred in the river mist; even the rock and logs in the river interrupting its smooth flow—all are faithful to the original work. Only the pet bear cub, chained to the prow of the boat, has been changed; an indeterminate package has taken its place.

M. K. D.

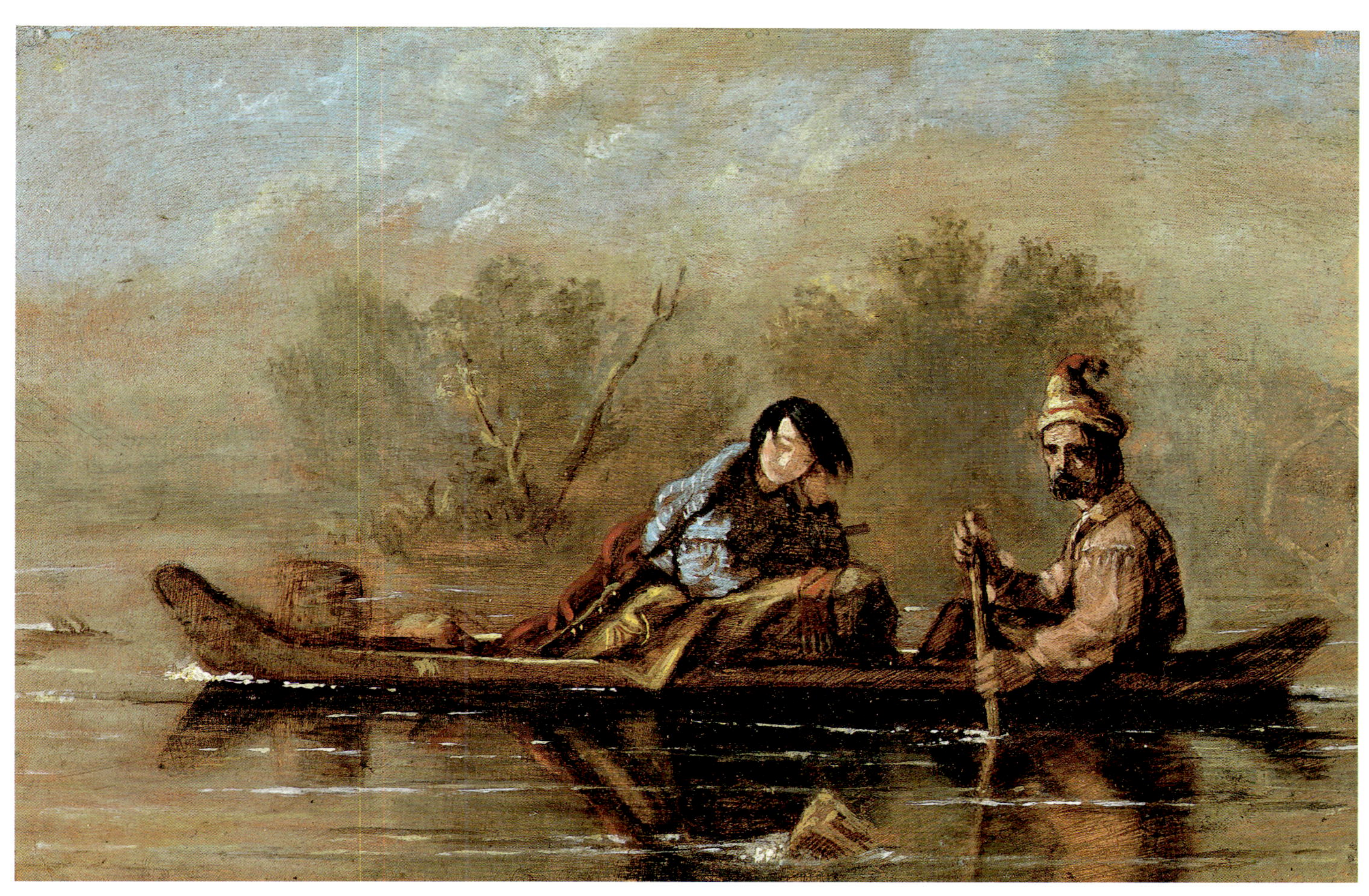

The Trappers
c. 1856
oil on canvas
8 3/4 x 12 inches
The Warner Collection
Tuscaloosa, Alabama

162

William T. Ranney, noted for his American genre and history paintings, was born in Middletown, Connecticut. After his father's death Ranney served a seven-year apprenticeship with a North Carolina tinsmith. In 1833 he gave up tinsmithing and moved to Brooklyn, New York, to study drawing and painting. Three years later, after the fall of the Alamo, Ranney interrupted his art studies to join the army of the Republic of Texas. During his months in Texas Ranney became intrigued by the colorful dress, manners, and lifestyles of the trappers and mountain men who had joined the revolution.

Ranney returned north in 1837 and established a portrait studio, first in New York and later in New Jersey. His Hoboken studio was a replica of a pioneer's cabin and was filled not only with his paintings, but also with his large collection of frontier artifacts. By the late 1840s Ranney was concentrating on Western subjects: trappers and hunters and Anglo pioneers moving to the West. Ranney joined the growing list of American genre artists, which included William Sidney Mount and George Caleb Bingham; in 1850 he was elected to the National Academy of Design. Mount was so impressed with Ranney's work that he finished several incomplete canvases found in the artist's studio after his death from consumption at age forty-four.

In this painting Ranney portrays two trappers, silhouetted against a glowing sky, as the early American heroes extolled in art and in literature at mid-century—independent, self-reliant, adventuresome, and willing to risk daily dangers as they roam the Western landscape. This is a smaller, more colorful version of a painting with a similar title in the Joslyn Art Museum in Omaha, Nebraska. The brilliant pinks and yellows of the sky are repeated in the reflections in the water and in the distant mountains; strong yellow highlights help define the two mountain men and their horses. Ranney characteristically includes splashes of bright red, here seen on saddle blankets, a scarf, a belt, a portion of a horse's headstall, and a pack cover.

M. K. D.

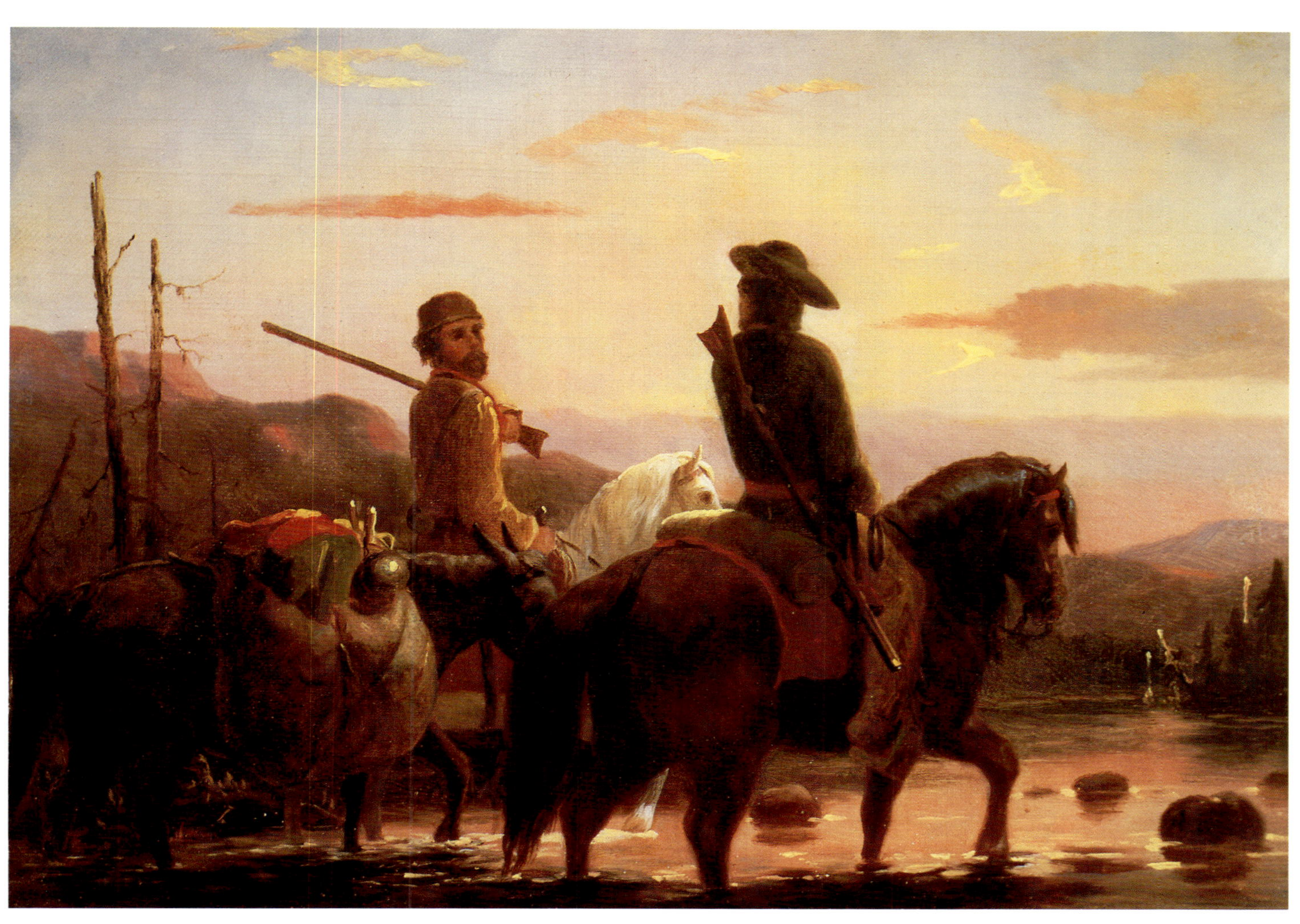

William Tylee Ranney
1813-1857

The Pioneers
oil on canvas
24 x 36 inches
signed lr: W. Ranney
The Warner Collection
Tuscaloosa, Alabama

Ranney's experience in the West was limited to his few months of duty in the Republic's army (and possibly a return visit to Texas in the early 1840s), but it provided the inspiration for the scenes he developed ten years later in his New Jersey studio. Ranney, who was much more interested in painting the daily activities of trappers and pioneers than in documenting frontier history or describing the spectacular landscape of the West, was one of the earliest artists to portray pioneer families. In this painting, the Easterners looking for a new life capture the spirit of optimism so prevalent at mid-century. The West was seen as a new Eden, with endless opportunities; Anglo pioneers were filled with the spirit of Manifest Destiny. Ranney seldom made references to the grave difficulties that might be encountered on the Overland Trail—disease, starvation, thirst, marauding Indian tribes, vagaries of weather, and losing the way.

The static composition suggests a timeless belief in the rewards of good intentions and hard work. The smiling woman (primly seated sidesaddle), the protective husband with his trusty rifle, the faithful dogs, and the sheltered children are all very carefully delineated, reflecting Ranney's drawing skills. The solid forms of the figures, the horse, and the oxen are brightly lit, as they pause on their journey west. Only the small black-and-white dog in the foreground is active on the flat, open prairie.

M. K. D.

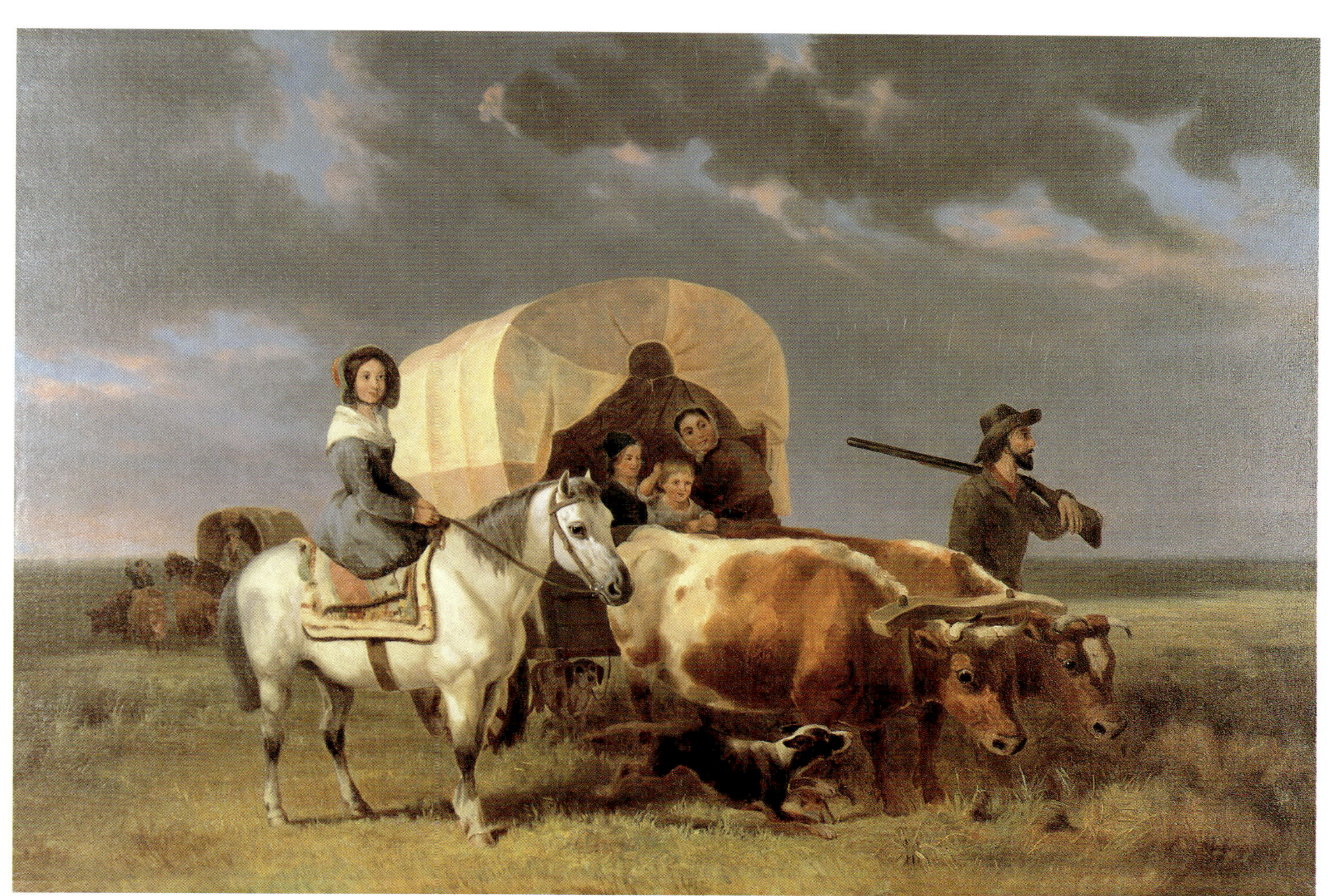

John Mix Stanley
1814–1872

Indian Telegraph
1847
oil on canvas
21 x 31 inches
signed and dated ll:
John Mix Stanley/1847
The Warner Collection
Tuscaloosa, Alabama

John Mix Stanley was born in Canandaigua, New York, where for the early part of his life he painted decoration as a coachmaker's apprentice. In 1834 Stanley moved to Detroit, Michigan, where he became a sign painter and later studied under portrait painter James Bowman.

Like George Catlin, Charles Wimar, and Charles Deas, Stanley was drawn to the West by a fascination with Native Americans. By 1842 he was portraying Indian life around the vicinity of Fort Snelling in Minnesota. Later that year he traveled to Fort Gibson, Oklahoma, then on to Texas, New Mexico, California, and eventually Hawaii. His sojourns also included accompanying the Pacific Railroad Survey in 1853–54, which started in Saint Paul, Minnesota, and passed through North Dakota, Montana, Idaho, and Washington.

Stanley's excursions enabled him to amass a considerable collection of Indian portraits and scenes. He hoped to sell the works to the government, and in 1852 he placed 152 paintings from his North American Indian Gallery collection on exhibit at the Smithsonian Institution. Unfortunately for Stanley, Congress was not interested in acquiring the paintings. A fire at the Smithsonian in 1865 destroyed all but five of the works from the collection. Stanley suffered another setback when subsequent fires at the P. T. Barnum American Museum and at his studio in Buffalo, New York, consumed an unknown number of works.

Stanley's painting *Indian Telegraph* was perhaps one of his most popular images. He recreated it in at least four other versions and in a chromolithograph. The date of this painting indicates that it was possibly done during his trip up the Columbia River. His rendering of two scouting parties, who stand on opposite sides of an enormous valley and communicate by means of smoke signals, not only has narrative drama but also emphasizes the grandeur and immensity of the landscape of the American West.

M. D. L.

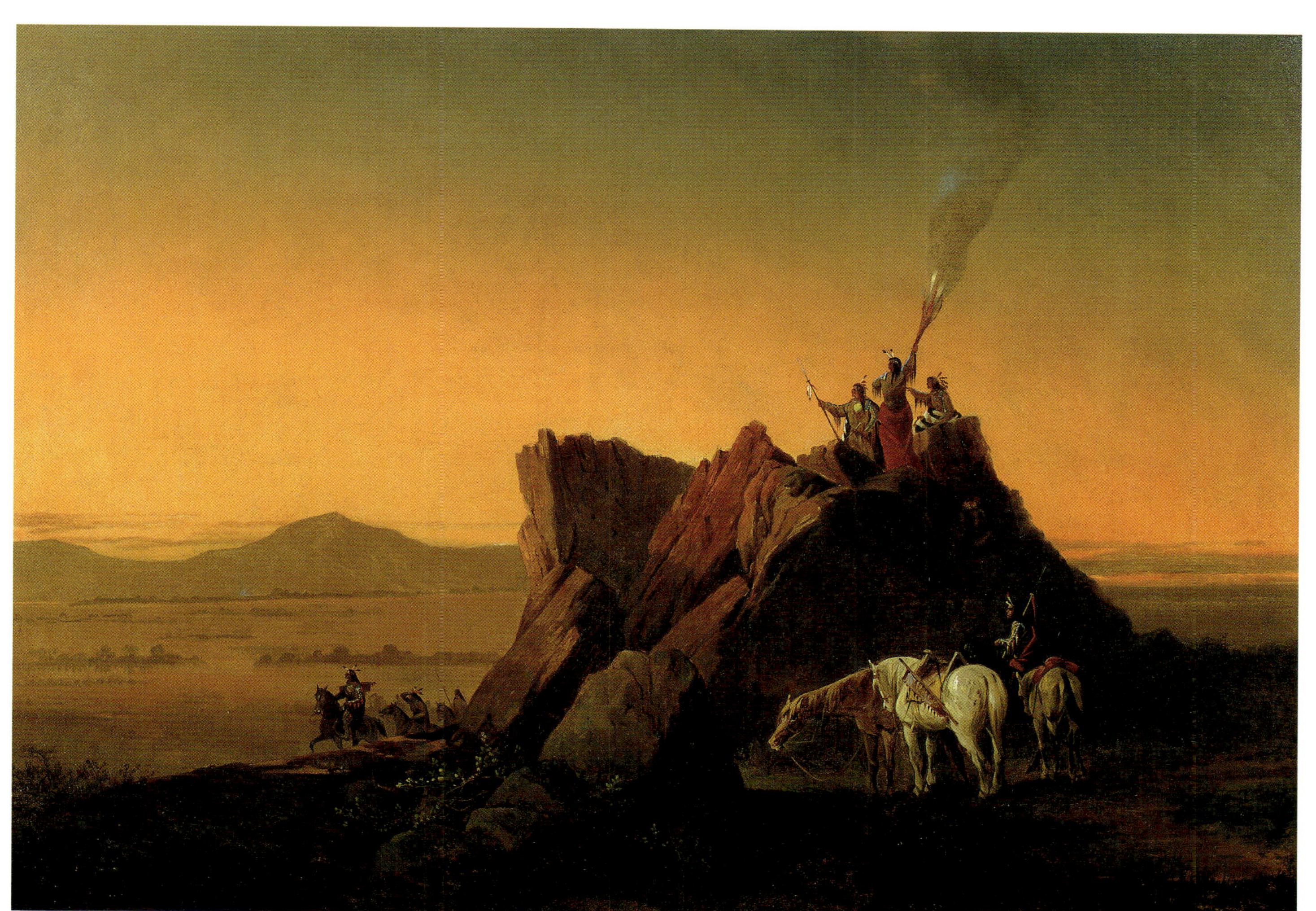

Charles Deas
1818-1867

Figure Group of Sioux
c. 1845
oil on paper
mounted on panel
7 1/4 x 6 inches
The Warner Collection
Tuscaloosa, Alabama

Charles Deas was born and raised in Philadelphia and began his career as an artist in New York City during the late 1830s. After studying briefly at the National Academy of Design, Deas was elected an associate in 1839. Like many artists of the day, he found himself drawn to the West.

Inspired by the images in George Catlin's Indian Gallery, Deas traveled to Prairie du Chien, Wisconsin, in 1840 to visit his brother, a military officer at Fort Crawford. From there he went on a number of hunting, trapping, and military expeditions along the upper Mississippi, the Missouri, and the Platte rivers. In the early 1840s he settled in St. Louis.

During the six years he remained in Missouri, Deas turned his earlier sketches and field notes into some of the most prominent works of his career. His paintings generated considerable interest and were exhibited regularly at the National Academy of Design, the Pennsylvania Academy of the Fine Arts, and the Boston Athenaeum. Deas became known and respected as a chronicler of Indian life, although he occasionally painted landscapes, scenes of trappers and fur traders, and portraits. His paintings often conveyed a sense of melodrama, and by the late 1840s danger and fright were common elements. At this time Deas was becoming increasingly unstable, and at the age of thirty he was judged insane and committed to a New York asylum, where he remained until his death.

One feature that differentiated Deas's paintings from those of previous chroniclers of Indian life was his careful illustration of Native American culture and tradition. This is evident in the painting *Figure Group of Sioux,* which depicts a proud father giving his son a riding lesson. Among the Lakota (Sioux), boys were taught by their parents to be great warriors. The horse and horsemanship played an important role in Lakota warrior societies, and at an early age boys also learned how to make and use bows, knives, and ropes. The son depicted here, for instance, would join other boys in playing war games and displaying their skills as horsemen.

M. D. L.

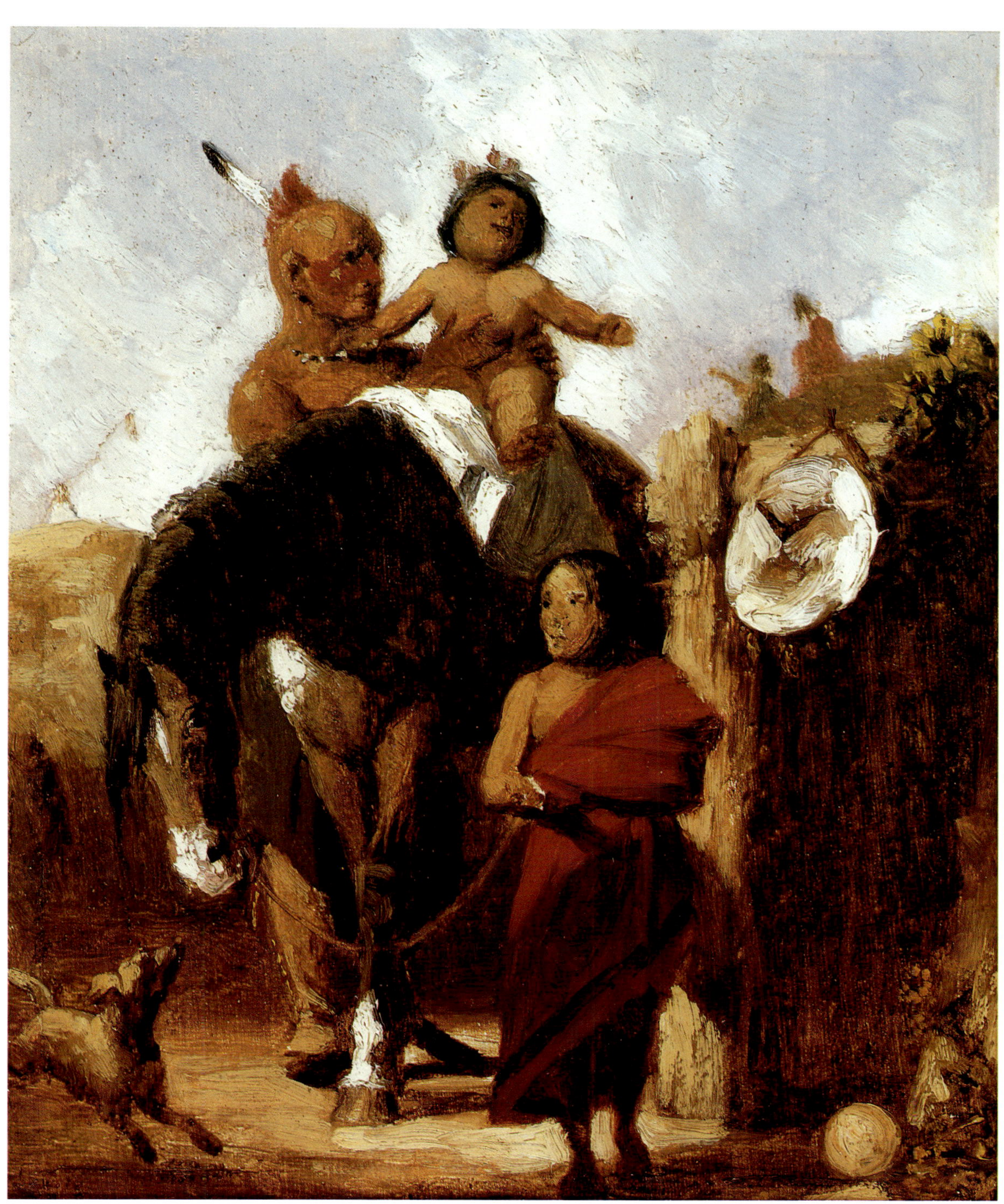

Charles Wimar
1828-1862

Indians Pursued by
American Dragoons
1855
oil on canvas
33 x 46 inches
signed, inscribed, and
dated lr: Charles Wimar/
Dusseldorf 1855.
The Warner Collection
Tuscaloosa, Alabama

Born in Siegburg, Germany, Charles Wimar emigrated to America with his mother when he was fifteen. The family settled in St. Louis, on the edge of the Western frontier, where his stepfather had opened an inn. Native Americans were frequent visitors to the area, trading furs and buying supplies, and Wimar soon developed what became a lifelong fascination with them and their ways of life. He served a six-year apprenticeship with a local painter, Leon Pomarede; together they traveled up the Mississippi River, sketching the landscape and the native inhabitants. In 1852 Wimar returned to Germany and studied at the Düsseldorf Academy under Josef Fay, and, later, under another German-American artist, Emanuel Leutze. The Düsseldorf Academy was the leading art school at that time; most instructors encouraged large-scale dramatic paintings, preferably with historical themes. Wimar became known as "the Indian painter," partly due to his dark coloring and his penchant for buckskin clothing, and partly due to his choice of subjects—American Indian activities. He drew on published prints and books by George Catlin, literary references by frontier authors such as James Fenimore Cooper, and on native garments and objects he had requested from his family.

In this emotional scene, painted in Düsseldorf, Plains Indians are fleeing in terror from heavily armed and mounted soldiers. Wimar has compressed the action into the foreground, with the dragoons advancing relentlessly across the picture plane from right to left. One dying warrior, his back arched in agony, is framed against the brilliant sunset. Garments, uniforms, and accessories are meticulously and accurately described, reflecting Wimar's German training.

M. K. D.

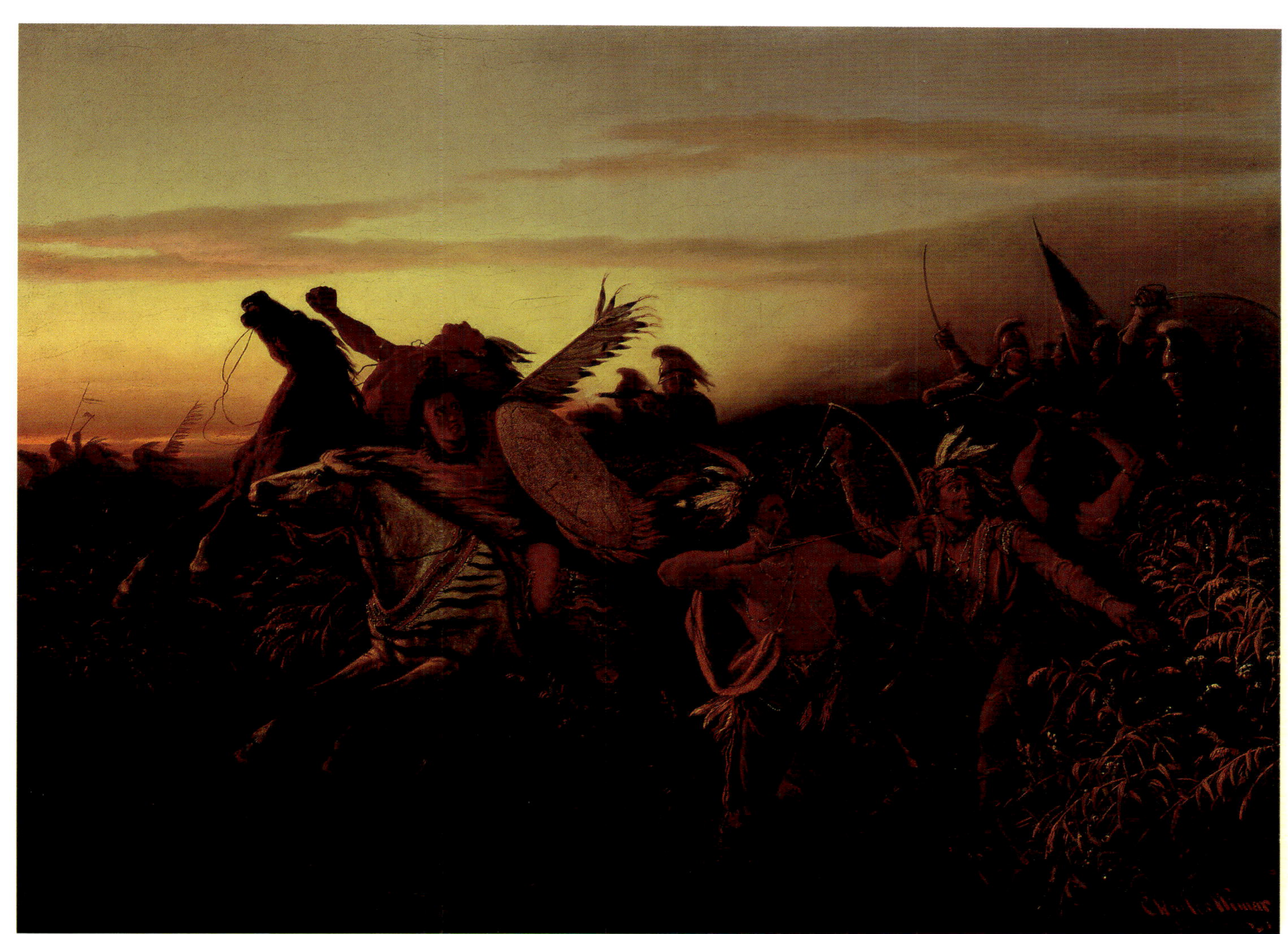

Charles Wimar
1828-1862

Funeral Raft of a
Dead Chieftain
1856
oil on canvas
11 1/4 x 16 inches
signed and dated lr:
Carl Wimar 1856
The Warner Collection
Tuscaloosa, Alabama

When Wimar returned to St. Louis in 1856, after four years of study in Düsseldorf, his painting style quickly loosened. He continued to focus on the activities and ceremonies of the Native Americans, but he found that the city had changed while he was in Germany; most of the Native Americans he had admired and studied so much had moved west and north, and seldom ventured into the city. During the next few years Wimar traveled extensively along the Missouri and Yellowstone rivers, sketching and photographing the tribes, the landscape, and the wildlife of the Northern Plains. He also avidly collected native clothing, weapons, and utensils as resource material for his paintings. His largest and most important commission also proved to be his last: he was hired to paint four large historical murals for the dome of the St. Louis courthouse. While working on these, he contracted tuberculosis and died, at age thirty-four, soon after their completion. Wimar and other early frontier artists, such as George Catlin, Karl Bodmer, and Alfred Jacob Miller, were firsthand witnesses to the rapidly changing lifestyles of the American Indians. As such, they provided an invaluable documentation of the continent's history, as well as a unique artistic legacy.

In this romantic depiction of the funeral journey of a dead native chief, Wimar has staged the scene dramatically under a glowing sky, with a crescent moon high above a few scattered clouds. Framed against the pale yellows and oranges, two Indians pole the raft through the river, while a third kneels as a guard over the chief's body. Wimar has formally centered the raft and has pushed it to the immediate foreground, heightening the emotional intensity. The brushwork is broad and free, and the artist has barely suggested glittering highlights on feathers and jewelry in the faint light.

M. K. D.

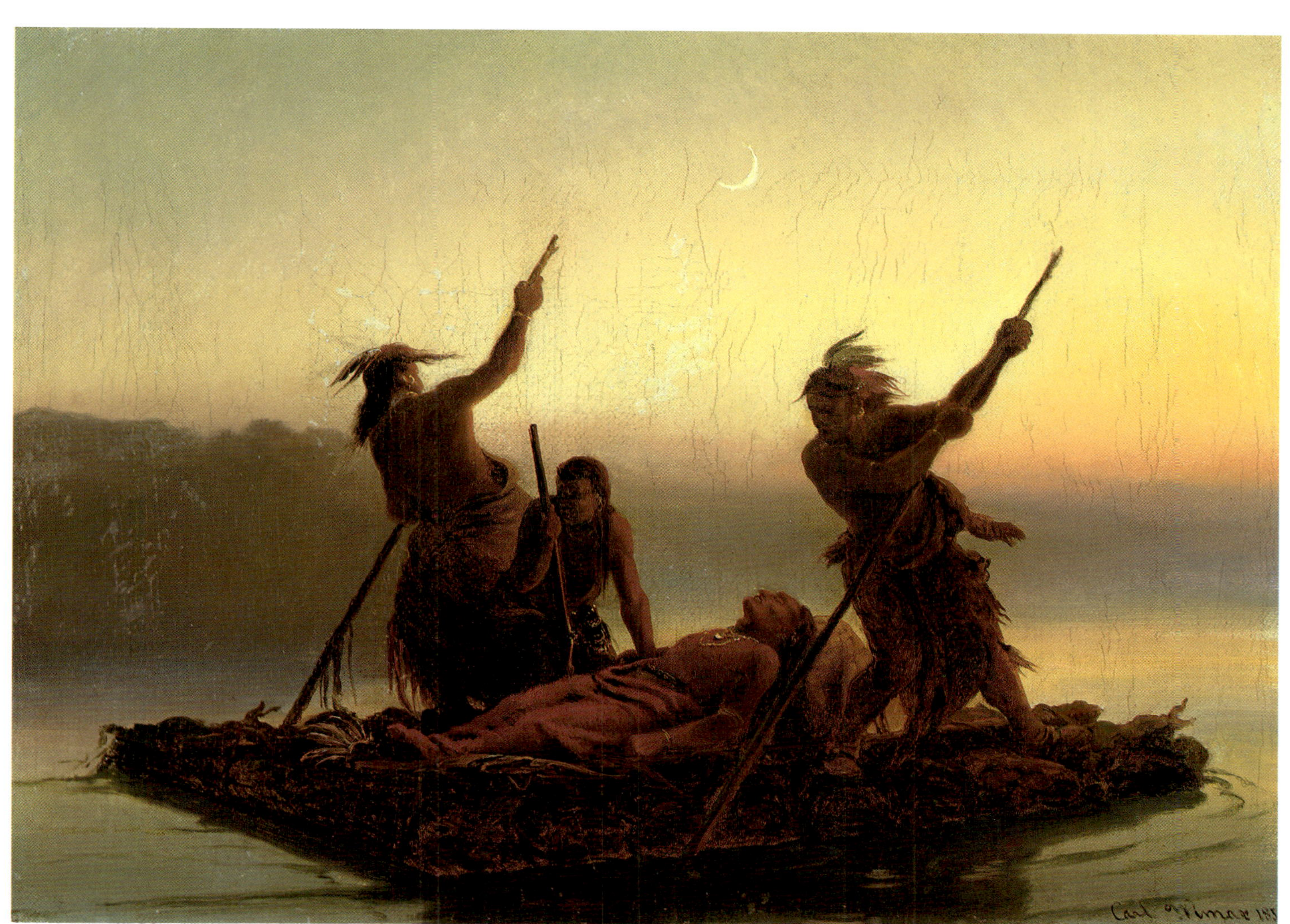

High Sierras
oil on canvas
22 x 30 inches
signed ll: ABierstadt
K. S. "Bud" Adams, Jr.

Despite his German birth and European training, Albert Bierstadt is best known for his panoramic landscapes of the American West—the Rocky Mountains, the Sierra Nevada range, and, especially, Yosemite Valley. Sketches and studies produced in oil and watercolor during three extensive trips west provided Bierstadt with dramatic subjects for most of his life. He traveled into the Sierras on several occasions with a variety of people, including Clarence King, geologist and director of the government's Fortieth Parallel Survey, and Collis P. Huntington, vice-president of the Central Pacific Railroad.

In this dramatic landscape, the majestic snow-covered Sierra peaks tower over a central valley, partially obscured by low-hanging clouds. The foreground is more sharply focused, with the diagonal hillside on the left balancing detailed trees on the right. While Bierstadt presents the Sierras as almost overpowering, he does not suggest anything fearful or foreboding in the landscape. The viewer may be dwarfed by the size of the mountains, but, at the same time, he or she is invited into the wilderness.

M. K. D.

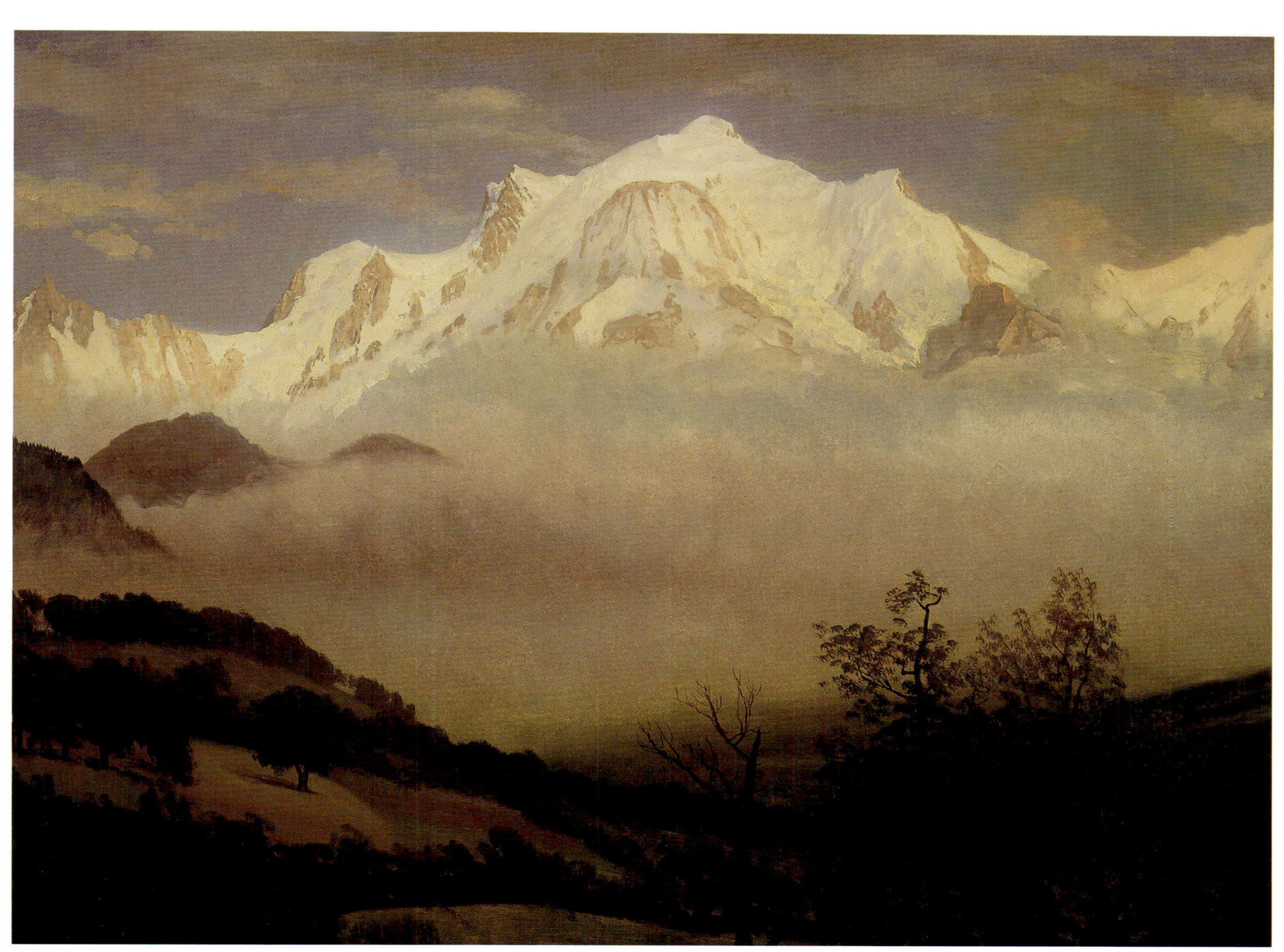

Albert Bierstadt
1830-1902

A Halt in the Yosemite
1870
oil on board
16 7/8 x 24 inches
signed and dated ll:
ABierstadt/70
The Gund Collection
of Western Art

Bierstadt's first visit to Yosemite Valley was inspired by the striking photographs of Carleton E. Watkins, which he saw on display in a New York gallery in 1863. Later that year Bierstadt spent seven weeks exploring the valley, as well as Oregon and the Columbia River area. Scenes from Yosemite Valley provided Bierstadt with subject matter for the rest of his life, and for the next two decades his name was synonymous in the mind of the public with panoramic images of the spectacular Yosemite landscape, portrayed under a wide variety of light and atmospheric conditions.

Perhaps because Watkins and other photographers had already photographed Yosemite's natural wonders, Bierstadt felt free to depart from absolute reality and to adjust cliffs, trees, waterfalls, and other landmarks to suit his compositional requirements. This was a freedom unknown to earlier artists documenting the landscape of the West.

In this view of the towering granite pillars of Yosemite, Bierstadt has added tiny detailed figures and horses in the right foreground to emphasize the enormous height of the distant cliffs. Alternating bands of light and shadow add to the drama of the scene: bright sunlight helps define the horses, trees, and dead branches in the foreground; diffused shadows obscure the middle view; and bright sunlight strikes the base of the cliffs, contrasting with the dark somber sky.

M. K. D.

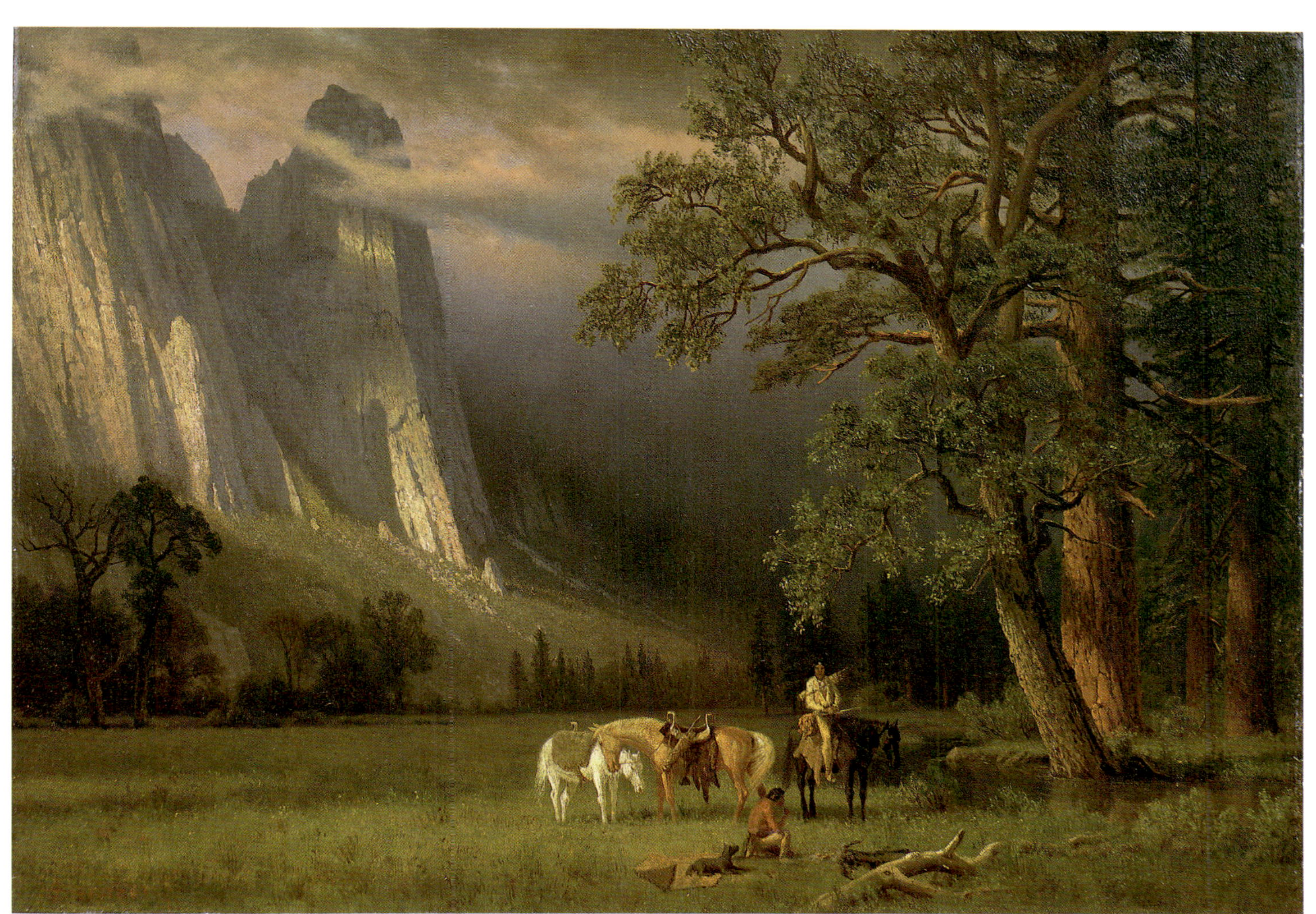

Albert Bierstadt
1830-1902

Donner Lake
c. 1871
oil on canvas
26 x 36 inches
signed lr: ABierstadt
The Warner Collection
Tuscaloosa, Alabama

While living in California in 1871 and 1872, Bierstadt worked on a variety of Western subjects, including the Sierra Nevada mountains, Yosemite Valley, the Farallon Islands, and Donner Lake. He painted several different versions of the lake, located at the foot of the fateful pass in the high Sierras. In the winter of 1846–47 the Donner party, a group of emigrants traveling to California, were trapped on these shores by an early snow. The few who survived reported horrific stories of starvation and cannibalism. Twenty years later, this same pass presented the greatest challenge to the eastward movement of the Central Pacific Railroad, as Chinese and Irish laborers blasted track beds out of canyon walls. To celebrate this technological feat, Collis P. Huntington, who directed the railroad construction, commissioned Bierstadt in 1871 to paint an immense canvas of Donner Lake.

In this smaller version, the tranquil image of the lake belies the earlier tragedy. The quiet lake reflects the golden haze of the setting sun; the dark, diagonal shoreline and slender trees contrast with the glowing colors. The angles of the distant mountain on the left and the descending hillside on the right converge on a small boat with passengers; these figures, plus a dog on the shore, provide a sense of scale against the grandeur of the mountain setting. Bierstadt has created a warm, habitable locale, with no hints of mystery or tragedy.

M. K. D.

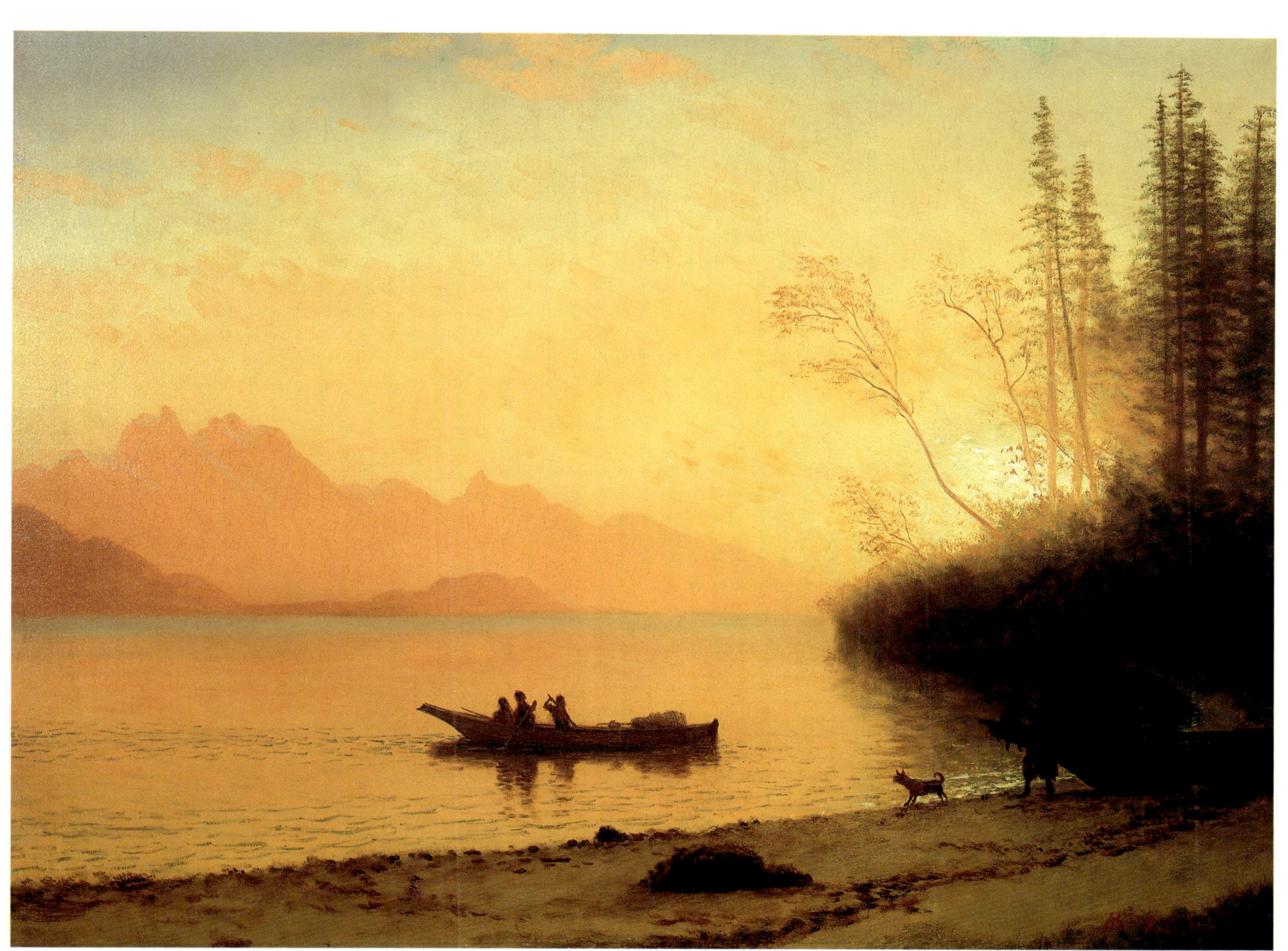

Thomas Moran
1837-1926

Green River Cliffs, Wyoming
1881
oil on canvas
25 x 62 1/4 inches
signed and dated lr:
TMORAN./1881
Spring Creek Art
Foundation, Inc.

Thomas Moran moved with his family from Bolton, England, to Philadelphia when he was seven years old. He first worked as a wood engraver and then watercolorist, before he turned to painting in oils in 1860. On return trips to Europe during the 1860s, he studied old master paintings, particularly those by the English romanticist J. M. W. Turner.

In the spring of 1871 Moran was hired to illustrate an article about Yellowstone territory for *Scribner's Monthly*. He was so intrigued that he petitioned to join F. V. Hayden's U.S. Geological Survey of the Territories, leaving that summer. This became the first of his many trips west.

Moran painted this version of the Green River cliffs of western Wyoming ten years after that first visit. To emphasize the grandeur and majesty of the scene, Moran silhouetted the dark middle ground against the brilliant yellow and orange cliffs in the distance. Tiny figures of Native Americans on horseback reinforce the enormity of the space. A diagonal path, with a cropped horse in the immediate foreground, makes this idyllic scene accessible. The dramatic contrast of light and dark, the intense colors, and the sun setting in the distant haze all contribute to this romantic Edenic image.

M. K. D.

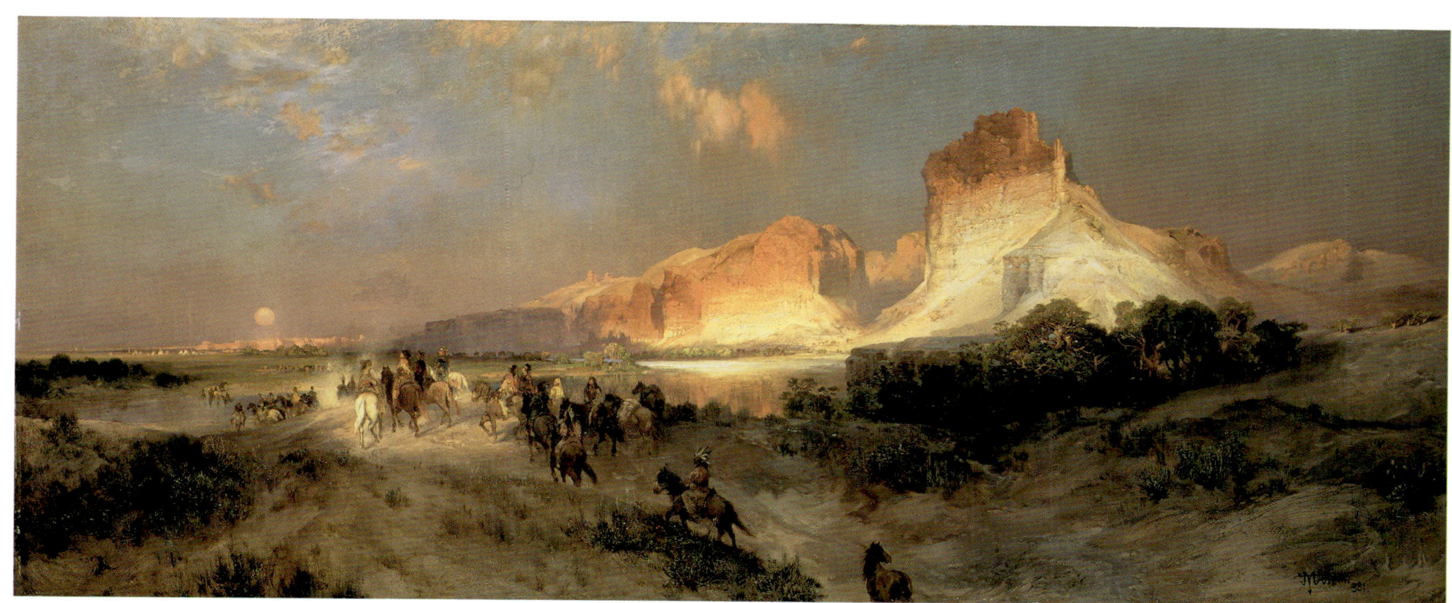

Thomas Moran
1837-1926

Green River in Wyoming
1899
oil on canvas
10 x 14 inches
signed and dated lr:
TMoran.1899
The Warner Collection
Tuscaloosa, Alabama

Moran's field sketches and watercolor studies from the Hayden expedition helped convince Congress to establish a system of public parks, and on March 1, 1872, Yellowstone National Park was created.

The spectacular cliffs lining Green River had been the subject of Moran's first field study on the 1871 trip. They continued to fascinate him for the rest of his life, inspiring as many as forty paintings over the next three decades. This version of the towering rock formations was painted twenty-eight years after his initial visit.

M. K. D.

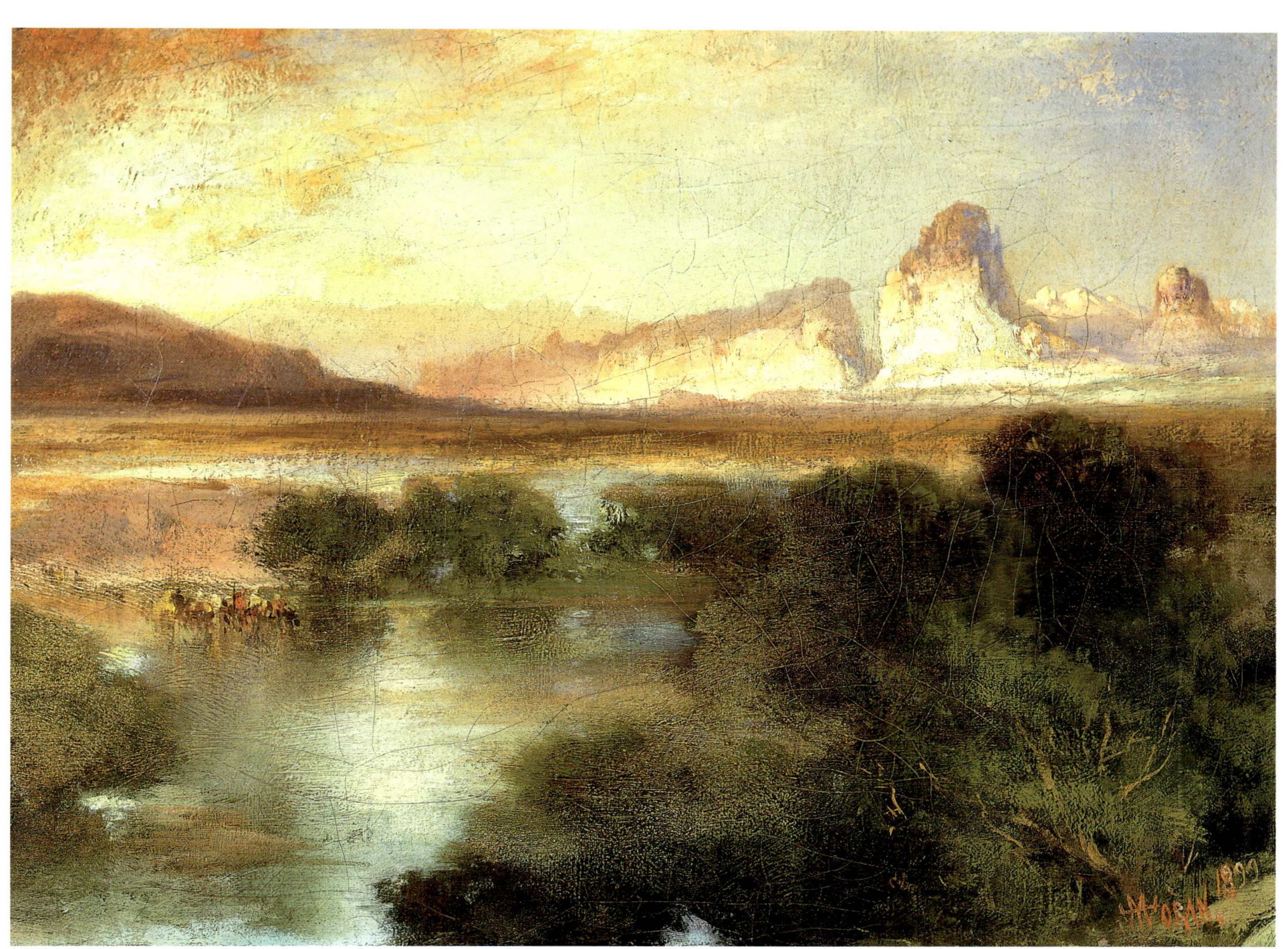

Thomas Moran
1837-1926

Canyon Mists: Zoroaster Peak,
Grand Canyon
1914
oil on canvas
40 x 30 inches
signed and dated ll:
TMORAN/MAY 1914
Anonymous Collector

Moran first visited the Grand Canyon in 1873 as a member of the John Wesley Powell expedition. Powell, who had been exploring the Colorado River and its territories since 1867, hired Moran for this trip after seeing some of his Yellowstone images in *Scribner's.* Reproductions of Moran's field studies of the Grand Canyon were also published and distributed widely.

Although Moran painted scenes from his travels in Europe, Mexico, and the eastern United States, his Western images were most popular with the American public and constitute his greatest artistic achievement. His two monumental paintings *The Grand Canyon of the Yellowstone* and *The Chasm of the Colorado* were the first American landscapes by an American artist to be purchased by Congress; they hung prominently in the Capitol until 1936. Two Western sites were subsequently named after the artist: Mount Moran in the Teton Range and Moran Point, Arizona.

In this dramatic view of the Grand Canyon, the sunlit cliffs, fog-filled gorges, and turbulent sky hint at the climatic changes that can occur so suddenly. The detailed rocks and scattered trees in the immediate foreground reinforce the vastness of the canyons leading back to the spotlit summit of Zoroaster Peak. As with many of his paintings, Moran chose a specific viewpoint and then somewhat freely manipulated chasms, buttes, and other elements. The result is a creative composite that is accurate in its details but emphasizes the grandeur and awe-inspiring character of the Grand Canyon.

M. K. D.

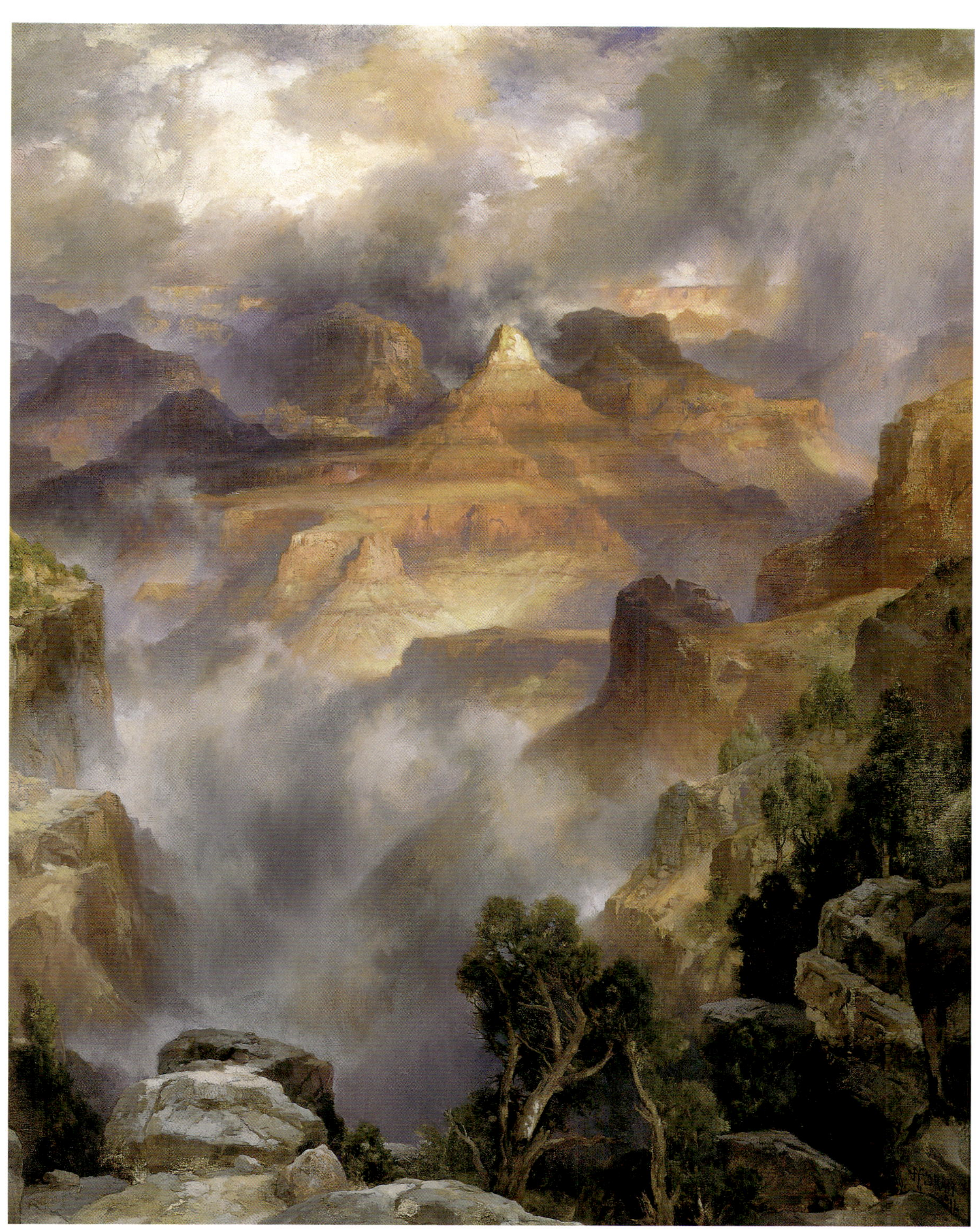

Henry F. Farny
1847-1916

Indians Moving Camp
1898
oil on canvas
22 x 40 inches
signed and dated lr:
H·F·FARNY·1898
The Gund Collection
of Western Art

Political refugees from France, the Farny family emigrated to Warren, Pennsylvania, and then to Cincinnati, Ohio. In Cincinnati Henry apprenticed with a lithographer, and by 1865 his own illustrations were published in *Harper's Weekly*. After studying art for three years in Europe, Farny returned home to pursue a career in illustration. Subsequent journeys to the West resulted in his first renderings of Native American life and the Western landscape.

Like many of his contemporaries, Farny reacted to the intense light of the Western landscape by brightening his palette. Eventually, his colors became almost impressionistic in hue.

Farny brought his finely honed observational skills and his training as an illustrator to bear on his compositions. He uses unusual croppings to vary the viewpoint in his paintings. In *Indians Moving Camp*, for example, many of the background objects have been cropped to create a vast landscape. This involves the viewer in the painting by creating an illusion that important objects lie outside the borders of the painting.

Farny also creates a sense of balance and stability in his paintings. The horse and trees in the right background of *Indians Moving Camp* are balanced by the group of Indians and horses in the left background. The main figure, standing off-center in the foreground holding a rifle, is stabilized and framed by the large rocks that Farny placed slightly behind and around him.

J. L. C.

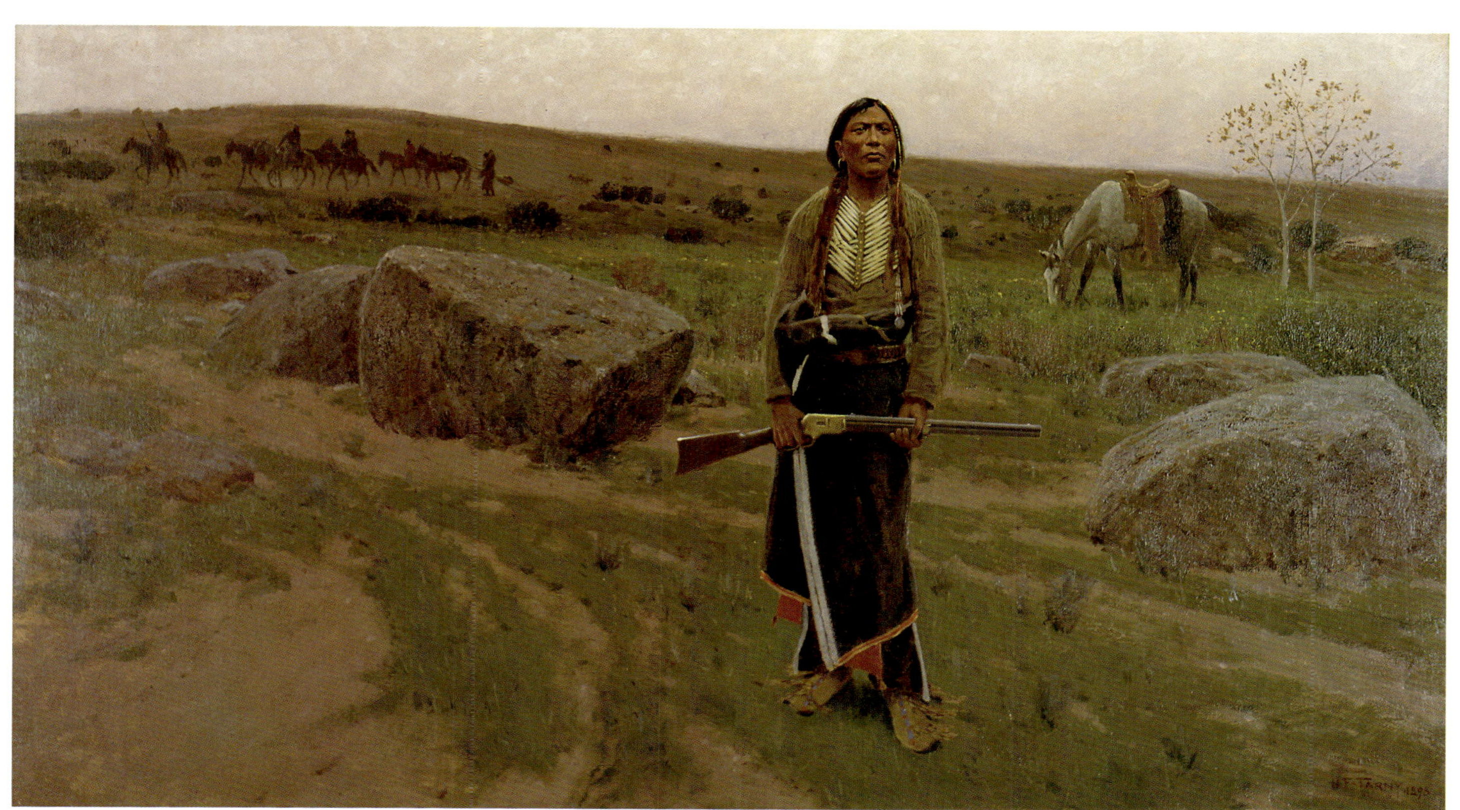

Henry F. Farny
1847–1916

The Return to Camp
1903
gouache on paper
12 1/2 x 8 inches
signed and dated lr:
-FARNY-/-1903-
The Warner Collection
Tuscaloosa, Alabama

188

When he returned to his studio in Cincinnati from his trips to the West, Farny brought with him a collection of American Indian objects and over one hundred photographs. These objects and photographs helped Farny to recreate with historical accuracy the images still fresh in his mind. By 1890 he focused his paintings on the diverse civilizations living in the West, and he became known for his realistic portrayals of American Indian cultures.

The Return to Camp depicts a cold, winter hunting scene of an Indian leading his horse down the snowy mountainside to camp. The deer carcass on the back of his horse provides evidence of the day's success. Farny creates the feeling of a vast landscape by cutting off background objects, such as trees and large rocks. Placed within this environment, the man's impassive expression instantly evokes a sense of solitude. Farny's honest renderings of life in the West, with their lack of sensationalism, place him in a class distinctive from many other nineteenth-century American painters.

J. L. C.

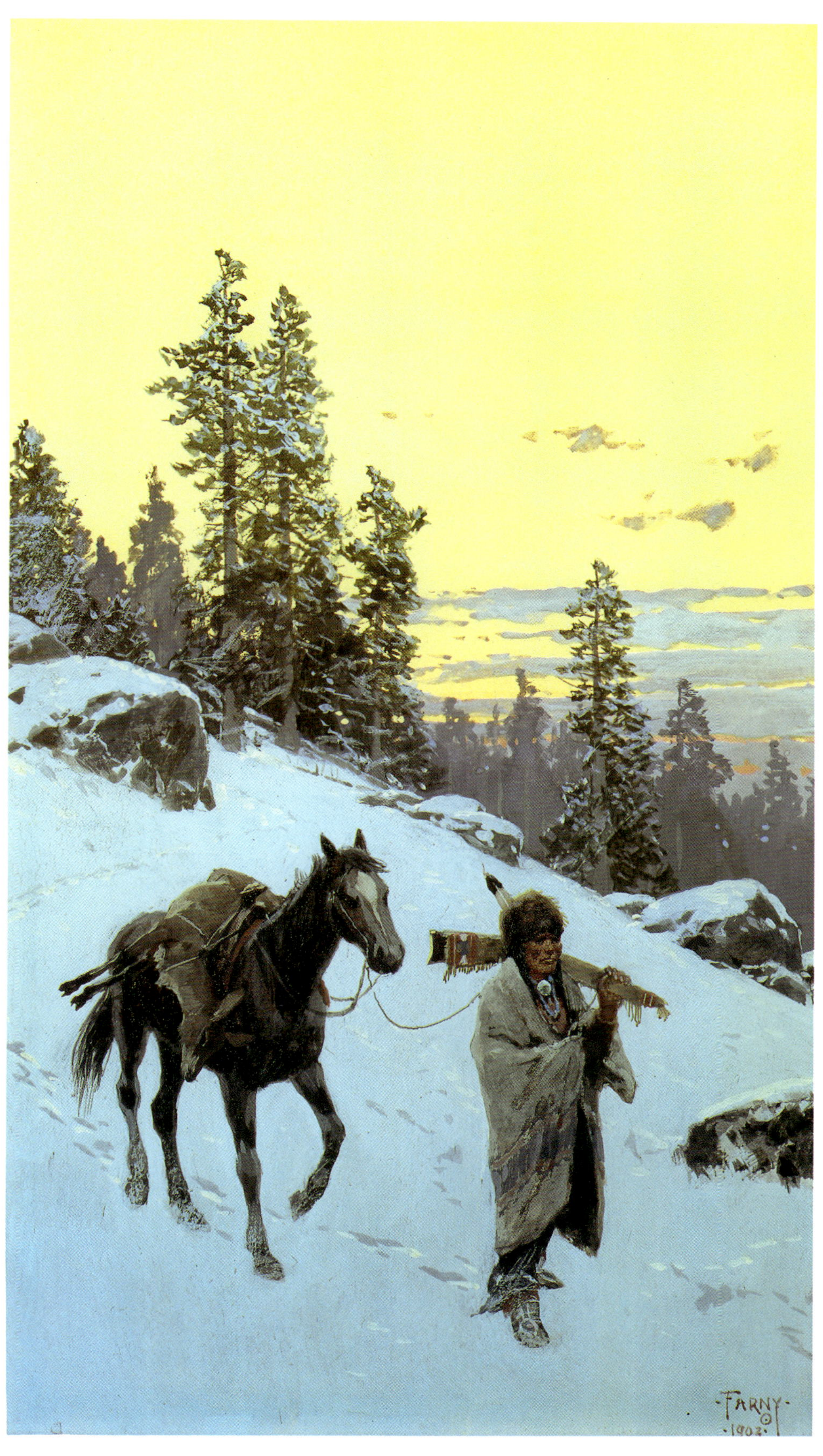

George de F. Brush
1855-1941

Seated Indian
oil on canvas
4 3/4 x 7 3/4 inches
signed ll:
Geo De Forest Brush
The Warner Collection
Tuscaloosa, Alabama

George de Forest Brush is known primarily for his Renaissance-inspired images of mothers and children, but during the 1880s he created a small body of remarkable Western paintings.

Raised in Connecticut, Brush received his earliest artistic training from his mother, an amateur painter. As a young child visiting New York City, he met the frontier artist George Catlin and saw his Indian Gallery. From 1871 to 1874 Brush studied at the National Academy of Design in New York City. He then went on to Paris and worked for six years in the studio of Jean Léon Gérôme; Gérôme's academic style of careful modeling and precise draftsmanship was a strong influence in the development of Brush's artistic style.

Brush returned to America in 1880 convinced that he should focus on painting American subjects. In 1881 he traveled to California, Wyoming, and Montana with his brother, camping among the Arapaho, Shoshone, and Crow. Brush greatly admired the American Indians and their ways of life, and he believed they had a direct relationship with the timeless classical past.

In this small oil study, a lone hunter leans on his hands, as if unable to rise; he looks pensively across the snowy landscape to a cluster of tipis in the distance. A thick grove of barren trees blocks the view on the left, while the right side of the painting opens up to deep space.

M. K. D.

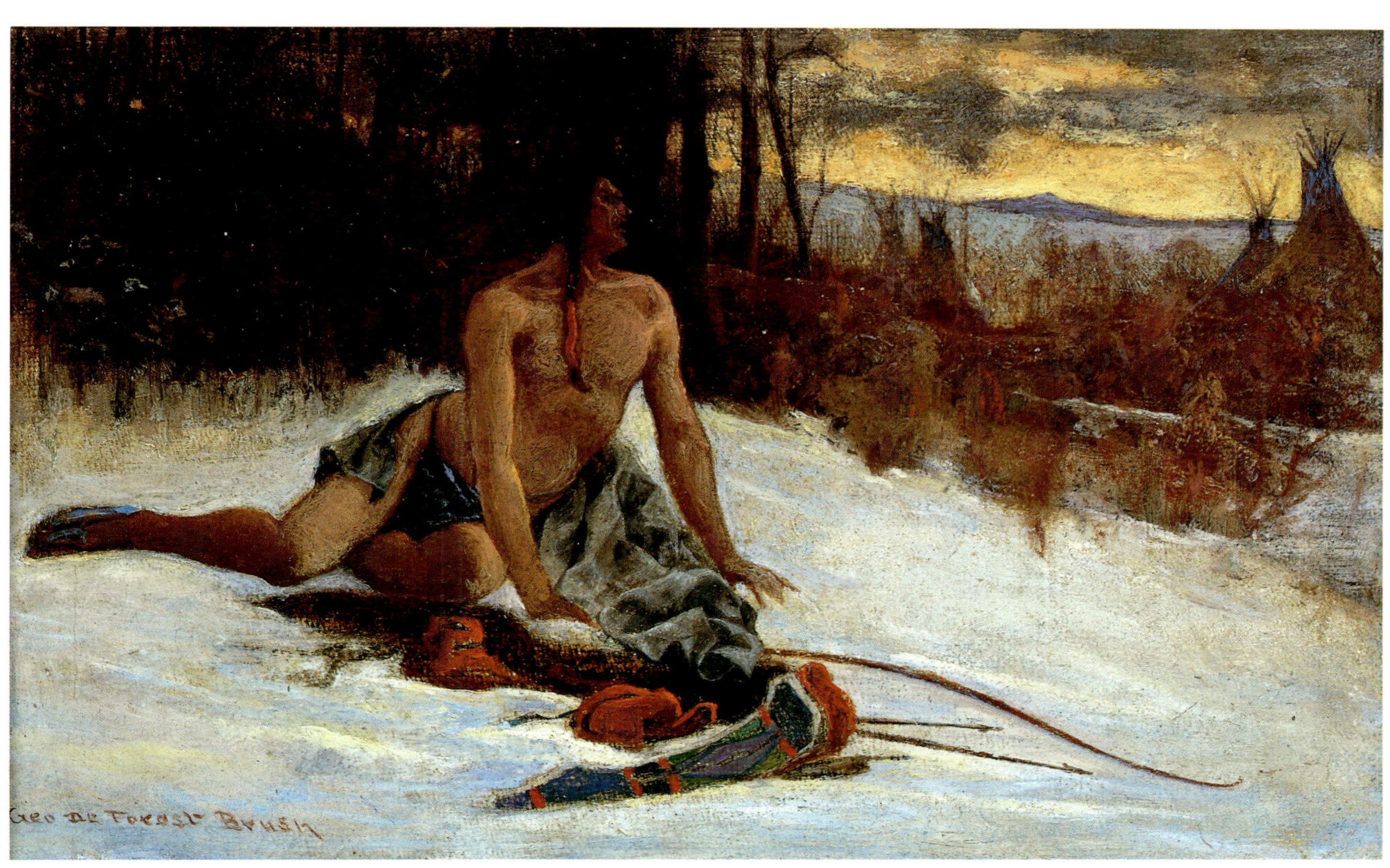

Geo de Forest Brush

George de F. Brush
1855-1941

The Shield Maker
1890
oil on canvas
11 x 16 inches
signed and dated ll:
Geo. De.F. Brush/1890
The Warner Collection
Tuscaloosa, Alabama

Brush usually painted his Native American subjects in solemn, contemplative scenes, in which they are wholly involved in some craft, such as building a pot, weaving a rug, or painting a hide. His figures are idealized and romanticized, and thus quite unlike more popular images of them as hunters or warriors riding across the plains. Unconcerned with the authenticity of garments, settings, or accessories, he consciously tried to relate his subjects to what he called the eternal truths of old master paintings.

By 1890 Brush was no longer painting Native Americans. According to his daughter, he was so distressed at their treatment by the federal government that he turned instead to sentimental portraits of women and children.

In this colorful painting a native craftsman, wearing nothing but a copper armband, is quietly plucking feathers from a dead flamingo to add to the shield he is making. The setting for this figure, who is totally absorbed in his work, is painted in subdued earth tones. Brush then enhances the image with the brilliantly colored bird and a leopard-skin rug. The anatomical detailing and the careful draftsmanship reflect Brush's adherence to Gérôme's academic teachings.

M. K. D.

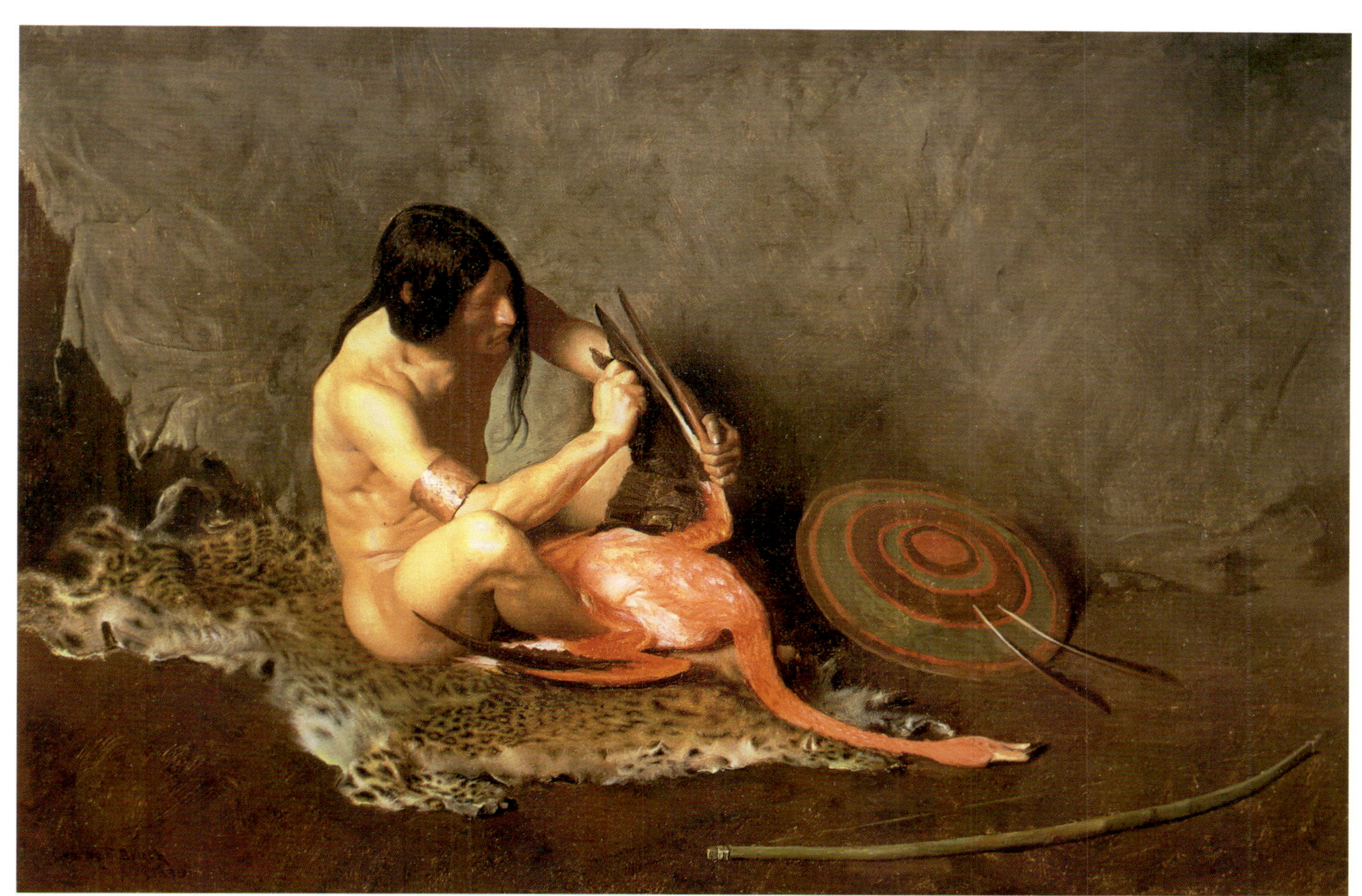

William Gilbert Gaul
1855–1919

Exchange of Prisoners
oil on canvas
34 x 44 inches
signed ll: Gilbert Gaul
The Warner Collection
Tuscaloosa, Alabama

William Gilbert Gaul, born in Jersey City, New Jersey, began his education at Claverack Military Academy. From 1872 to 1876 he studied at the National Academy of Design in New York City under L. W. Wilmarth. Traveling west in the 1880s, he began his study of military activities and American Indians. He was commissioned by *Century* magazine to illustrate an article detailing the battles and commanders of the Civil War. He was also one of five agents who took the 1890 census among the American Indians. His observational techniques and close attention to detail earned Gaul his reputation as the "foremost American painter of battle scenes."

Exchange of Prisoners reflects just one aspect of the life he witnessed during his excursions in the American West. Gaul's concern for detail and accuracy is evident in the soldiers' uniforms, which are alike, yet worn in a manner unique to each man. He cleverly captures feelings of curiosity and hesitancy by having men peer out windows and lurk behind fence posts. In this painting, as in others, Gaul uses details and precision to bring everyday occurrences in the West to the attention of the rest of America.

J. L. C

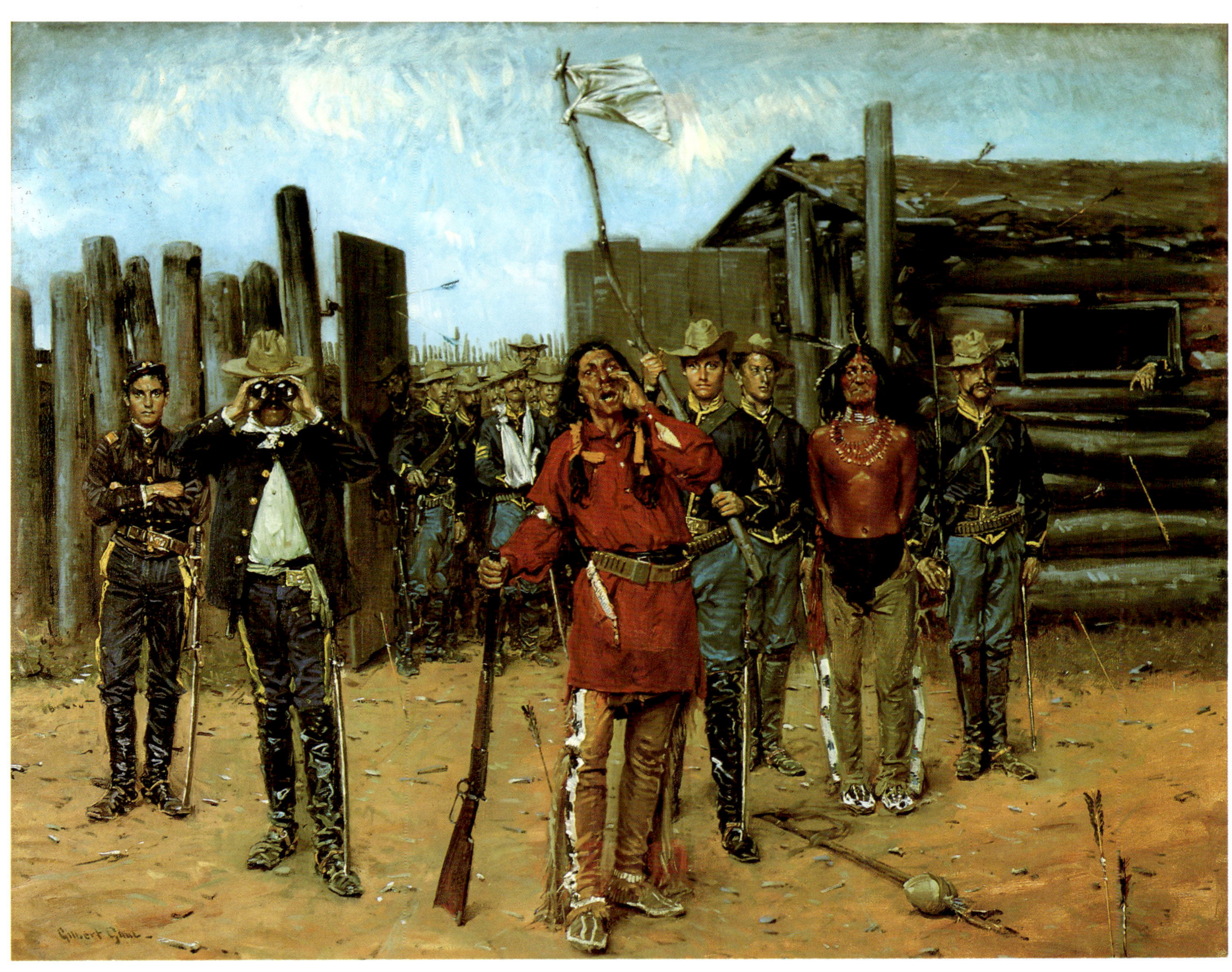

Joseph Henry Sharp
1859-1953

Young Chief's Mission
oil on canvas
4 1/2 x 6 inches
signed lr: JHS
Mr. and Mrs. Jon R. Stuart

Joseph Henry Sharp had his first contact with American Indians as a young child growing up in small river towns in southern Ohio. After studying and working in Cincinnati for eight years, he spent an additional year at the Antwerp Academy in Belgium. In 1883 he traveled to the American West, where he sketched and painted the Native Americans in the Santa Fe and Columbia River areas.

During the next several years Sharp spent his time studying, painting, and teaching in Cincinnati, Europe, and western America. On his second trip west, in 1893, he visited Taos, New Mexico, for the first time. His enthusiastic description of that remote village inspired several other young American artists to visit the Southwest.

This oil study of four standing figures, cropped above the knees, depicts a quiet but intense dialogue between two of the men. Sharp loosely defines the figures with bold, confident strokes. The decorative detailing on the hide shirt on the far left provides a bright contrast to the more somber hues of the blanketed Pueblo Indians. The dark hats are silhouetted against an unidentifiable background of pale yellows, ochres, and yellow-greens.

M. K. D.

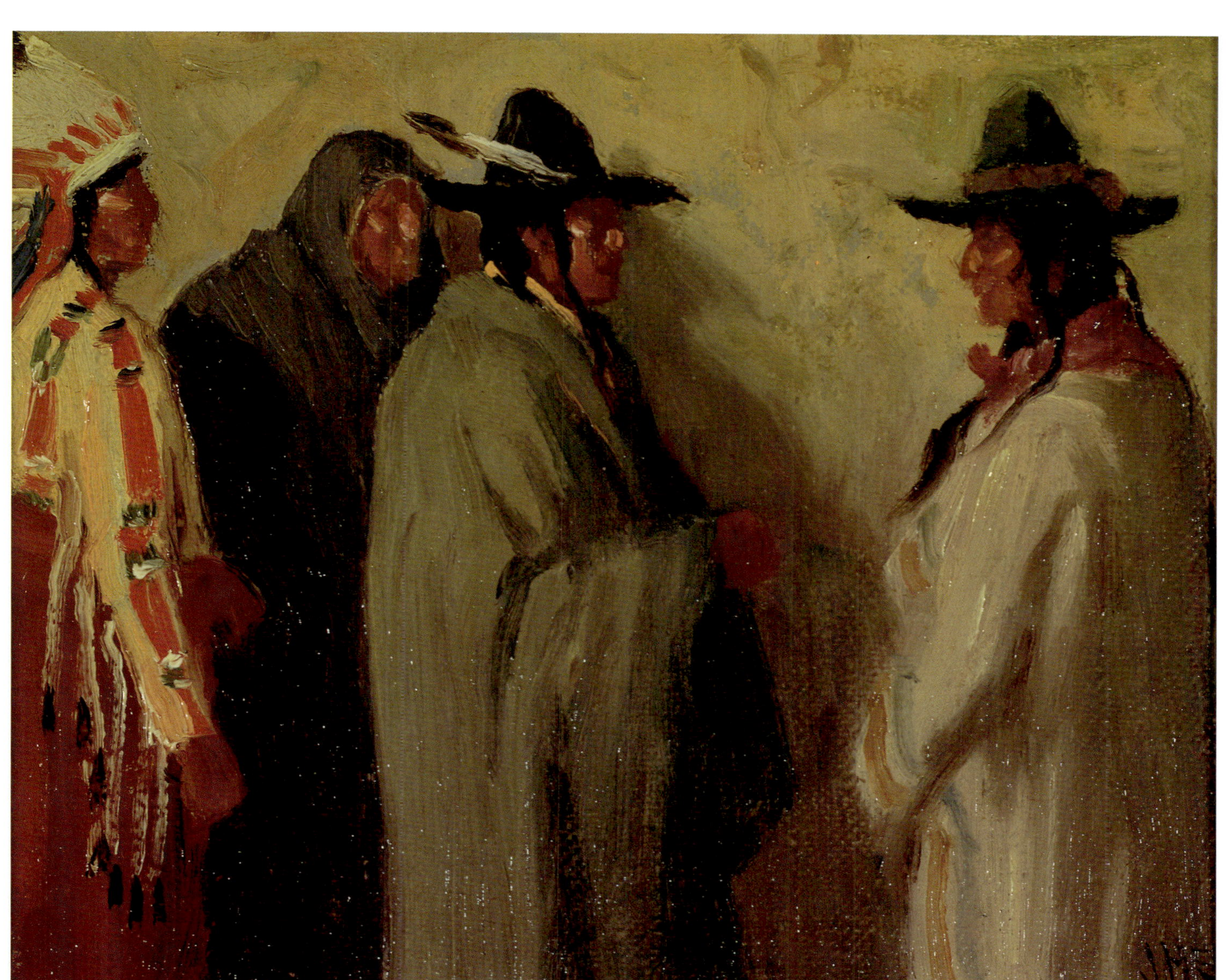

Joseph Henry Sharp
1859-1953

Hunting Son
oil on canvas
20 x 24 inches
signed lr: JHSHARP
Mr. and Mrs. Jon R. Stuart

In 1899 Sharp began working in Montana, where he photographed and sketched the local Indians and the many visitors to the old Custer battlefield near the Little Big Horn River. For over fifteen years Sharp wintered in Montana, painting portraits and studying the traditions and ceremonies of the Crow, Blackfeet, and Sioux Indians. His artistic reputation was established when the Smithsonian Museum purchased eleven of his portraits of Plains Indians.

Sharp's lifelong goal was to record the changing cultures of the Native Americans. His hundreds of portraits of western Indians often evoke a longing for an earlier way of life and express the difficulty in reconciling their traditional heritage with the modern Anglo world.

In this quiet study of a seated Plains Indian, Sharp has balanced the figure against a cropped blanket, feathered bonnet, and drum. Sharp commented on using the local natives as models: "Though the Plains Indians are not disinclined to pose, you must never count upon getting a second sitting from any of them. Almost all my portraits are painted from one sitting."

M. K. D.

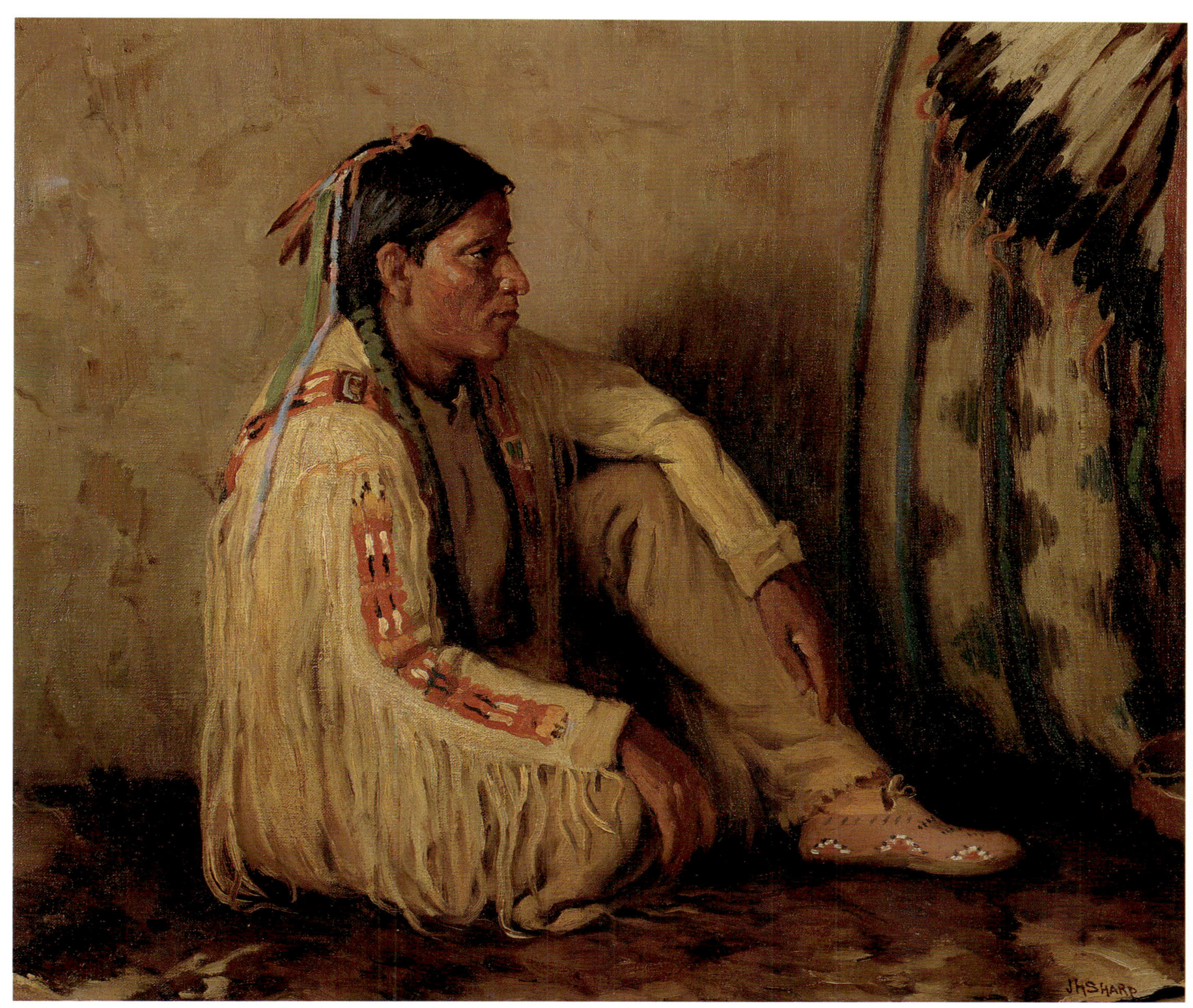

Joseph Henry Sharp
1859-1953

Shelling Corn
oil on canvas
20 x 24 inches
signed ul: JHSHARP
K. S. "Bud" Adams, Jr.

Sharp resigned his teaching position in Cincinnati in 1902 to spend more time traveling in the West and painting Native Americans. In 1909 he set up a studio in an old Penitente chapel in Taos, across the road from Kit Carson's house; in 1912 he moved to Taos permanently. Three years later Sharp helped found the Taos Society of Artists. Although known primarily for his Native American subjects, Sharp also painted landscapes, seascapes, and flower still lifes.

Using a vivid palette, Sharp in this painting portrays a local Taos Indian shelling corn into a large San Juan pot. He seats the model against the back wall, painted very freely in subdued grays and ochres. The intense green blanket, yellow leggings, and purple braid wraps and drape play against smaller patches of bright colors—red, light blue, and lavender. The striped blanket covering the wooden bench adds a strong decorative pattern to this richly painted genre scene. Sharp cropped the Indian's right leg, leading the viewer into the setting and adding a quiet sense of intimacy.

M. K. D.

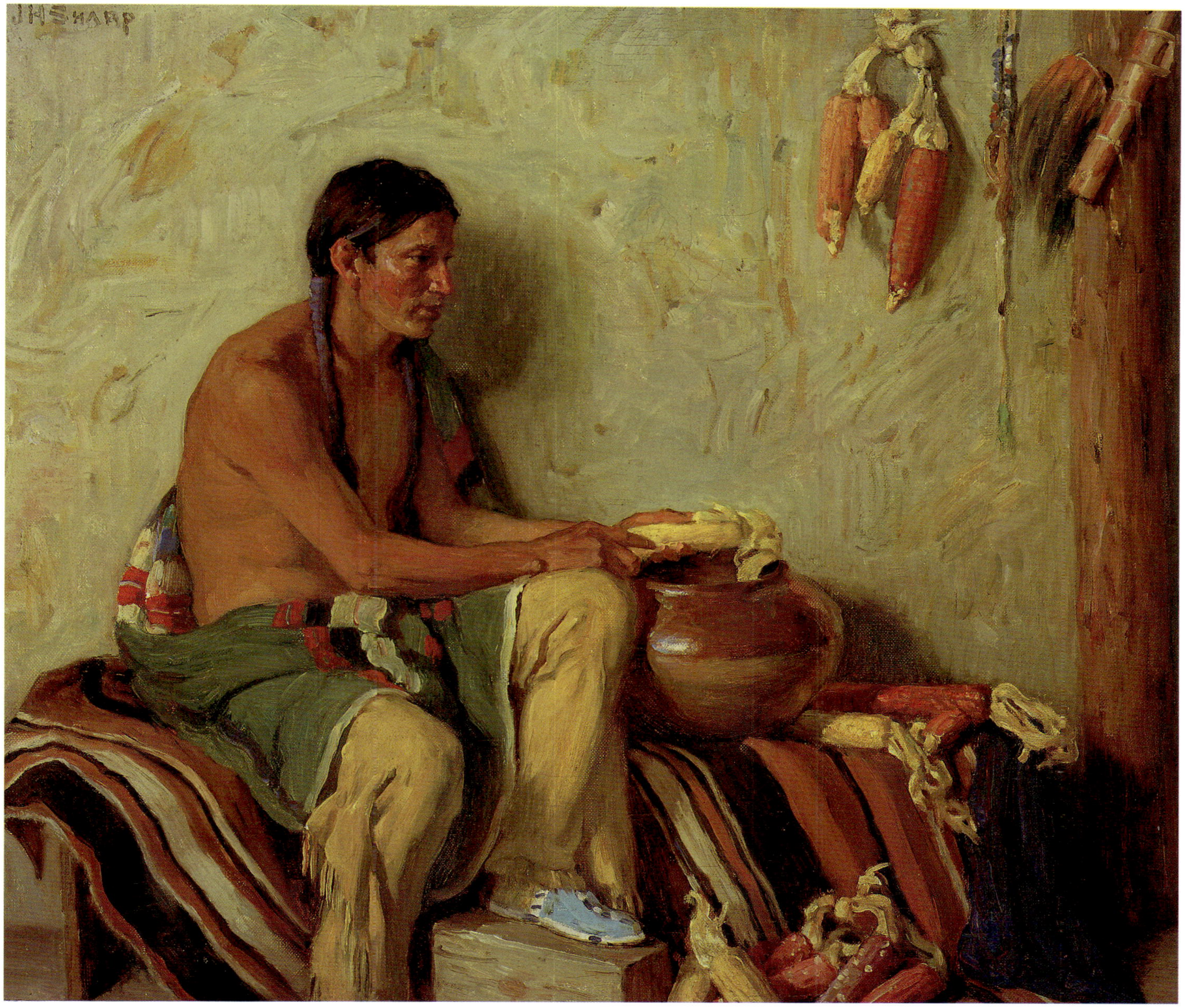

Edwin Deming
1860-1942

An Indian Competition
oil on canvas
32 x 60 inches
signed lr: E.W.DEMing
The Dicke Collection
New Bremen, Ohio

When he was a teenager Edwin Deming, who was born in Ashland, Ohio, and raised in western Illinois, traveled to Oklahoma to observe and sketch the local American Indians. Though his parents wanted him to become a lawyer, Deming was determined to be an artist. He sold his belongings to raise the money to study at the Art Students League in New York City. When he finished in 1884, he spent a year studying in Paris.

In 1887 he began his thirty-year study of Native American life, in which he extensively observed the Apache, Pueblo, Blackfoot, Crow, and Sioux cultures. Deming, his wife, whom he married in 1882, and their six children were adopted by the Blackfoot Indians, who named them the "Eight Bears."

Deming made a name for himself as an artist-historian because he combined artistic ability with his vast knowledge and deep understanding of Native American life, cultures, and religions. He conveyed his observations not only as a painter, but also as an illustrator, sculptor, and writer.

An Indian Competition is typical of Deming's subject matter and composition. The poses of the figures display his grasp of human nature: the competitor is stiff and rigid, while the observers are relaxed yet interested. The V-shaped composition highlights the action. Color is muted, except for the sparks of red leading the viewer through the composition.

J. L. C.

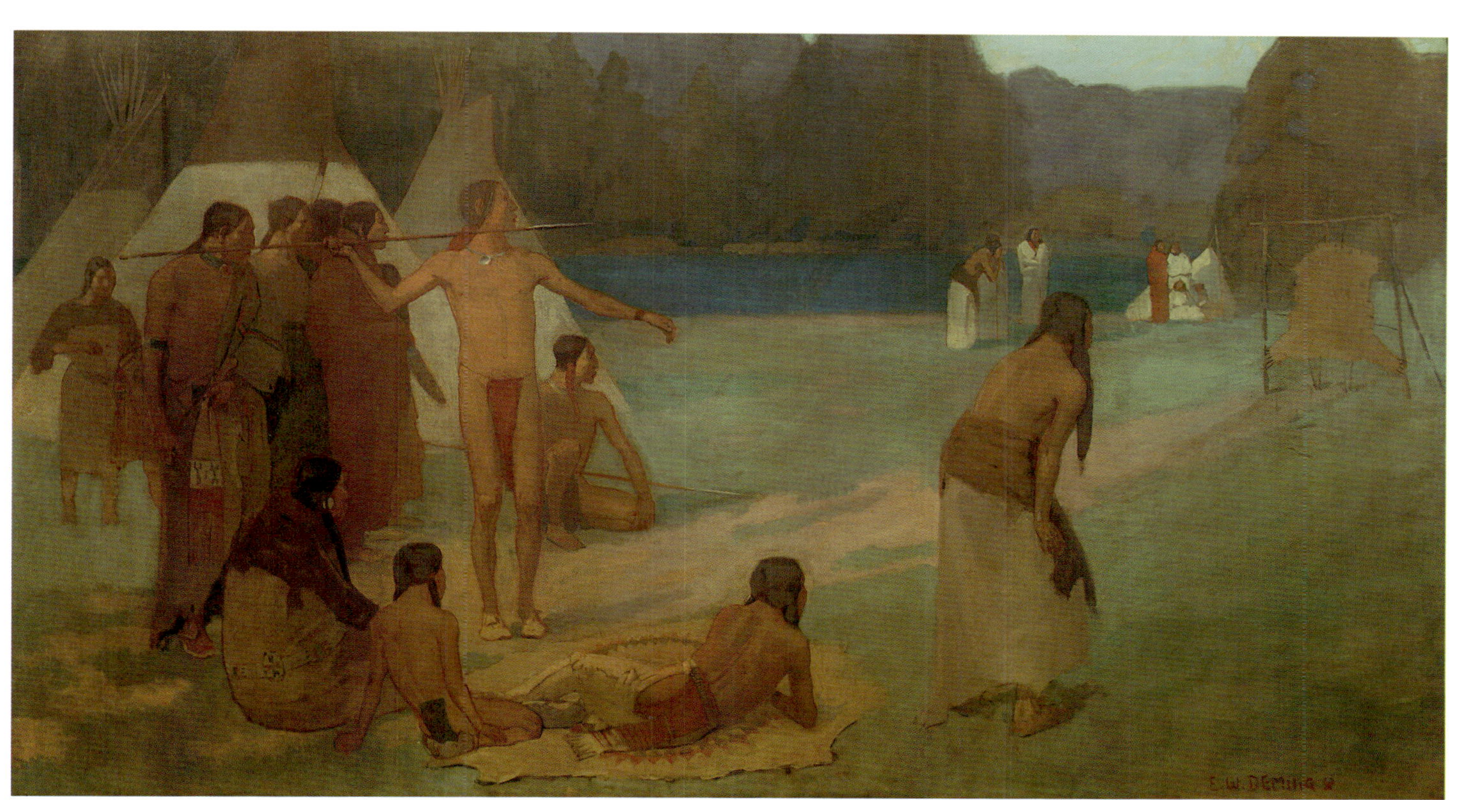

Frederic S. Remington
1861-1909

204

Buffalo Soldier
1888
line and wash drawing
24 x 18 1/2 inches
signed and inscribed lr:
Frederic Remington./
Arizona- inscribed lr:
M.S."Buffalo Soldiers"-
-A Study from Life.-
The Gund Collection
of Western Art

In 1886 Frederic Sackrider Remington traveled to the Arizona Territory; while there he became a close friend of Lieutenant Powhatan Clarke, who was serving frontier duty in the U.S. Army. Remington discovered that Clarke had risked his life to rescue a wounded black corporal, one of the famed "Buffalo Soldiers." He illustrated the heroic episode and sent the drawing to *Harper's Weekly*, where it was published as the frontispiece to the August 21, 1886, issue. This was just one of many studies Remington made of the black servicemen.

Buffalo Soldiers were members of the all-black Ninth and Tenth Cavalry regiments, which served in the West from 1866 to the early 1890s. They kept the peace between Native Americans and Anglo settlers, pursued outlaws and cattle rustlers, escorted stagecoaches and trains, and built and repaired frontier posts. The nickname Buffalo Soldiers was first used by Native Americans in 1867; the term is generally thought to suggest a similarity between the soldiers' dark curly hair and the coat of the buffalo. Because the buffalo was so important to the Plains Indians, the name was considered a sign of respect, and soldiers of both regiments accepted it proudly.

In this sensitive drawing of a Buffalo Soldier, Remington presents a dignified cavalryman, who carefully directs his mount down a very steep slope. Characteristically, Remington has captured the action at a precarious moment, as the horse proceeds cautiously. The sharp diagonal of the hillside, which is barely suggested with a pale wash, the rigidly braced forelegs, the angled posture and outstretched arm of the rider—all reinforce the image of a hazardous descent.

M. K. D.

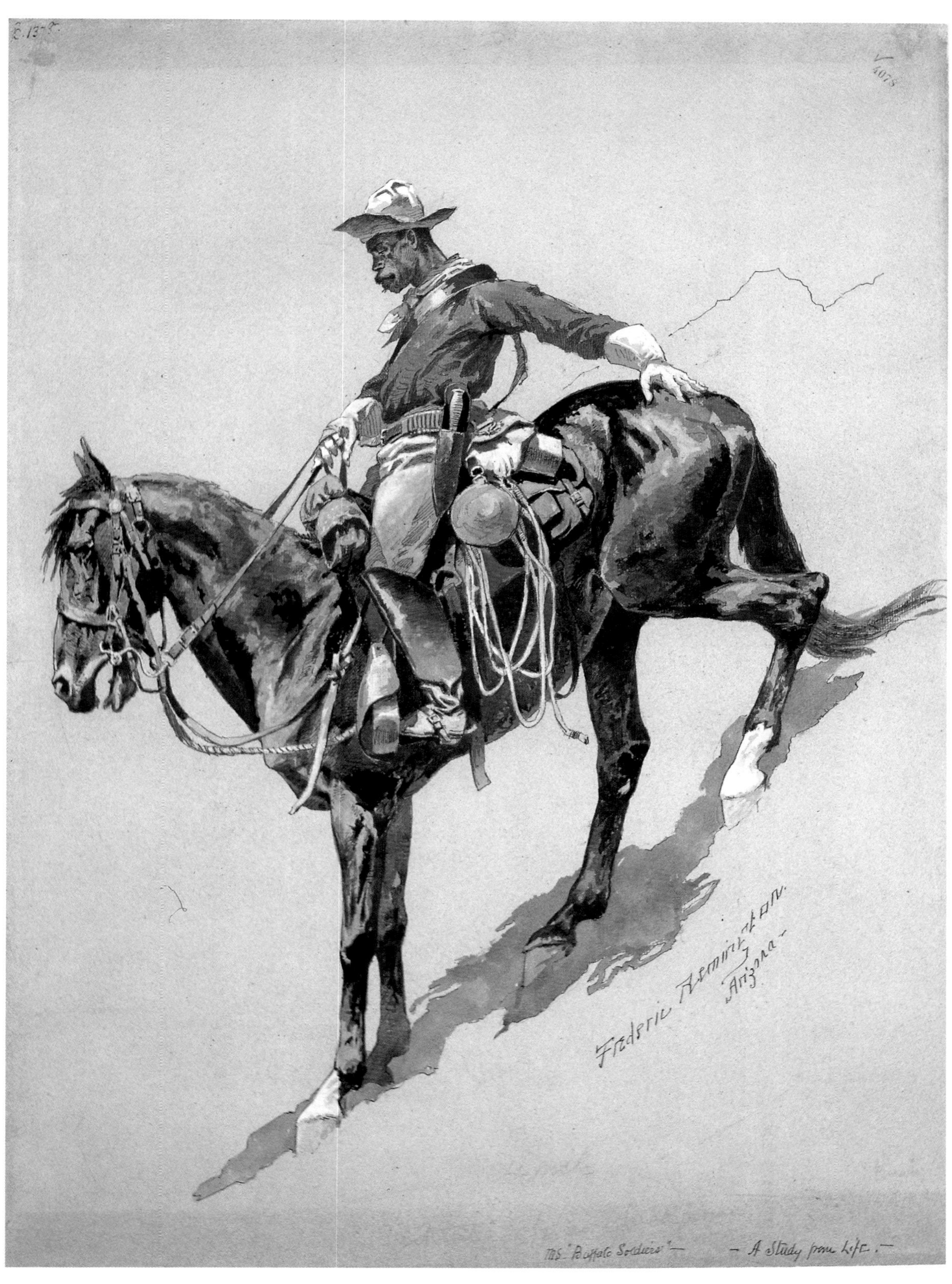

Frederic Remington. Arizona.
MS. "Buffalo Soldiers" — — A Study from Life. —

Frederic S. Remington
1861-1909

The Bronco Buster
c. 1895
oil on canvas
35 x 23 inches
signed lr: FREDERIC
REMINGTON
K. S. "Bud" Adams, Jr.

206

Throughout the 1890s Remington's paintings and drawings of Western life and adventures, particularly those of cowboys, found a large and enthusiastic audience. His ability to produce iconographic figures, such as this cowboy breaking a fresh bronco, came to represent the idea as much as the reality of the American West. Breaking horses was one of Remington's favorite subjects during this period of his career. The contest between man and animal, complete with its physical danger, allowed Remington to express his attitudes about the life and nature of the West in a single, concise event. As typical as the subject of the painting is Remington's contrasting of the bright, blue, and cloud-sculpted sky with the yellowish, brown Southwestern landscape.

M. W. D.

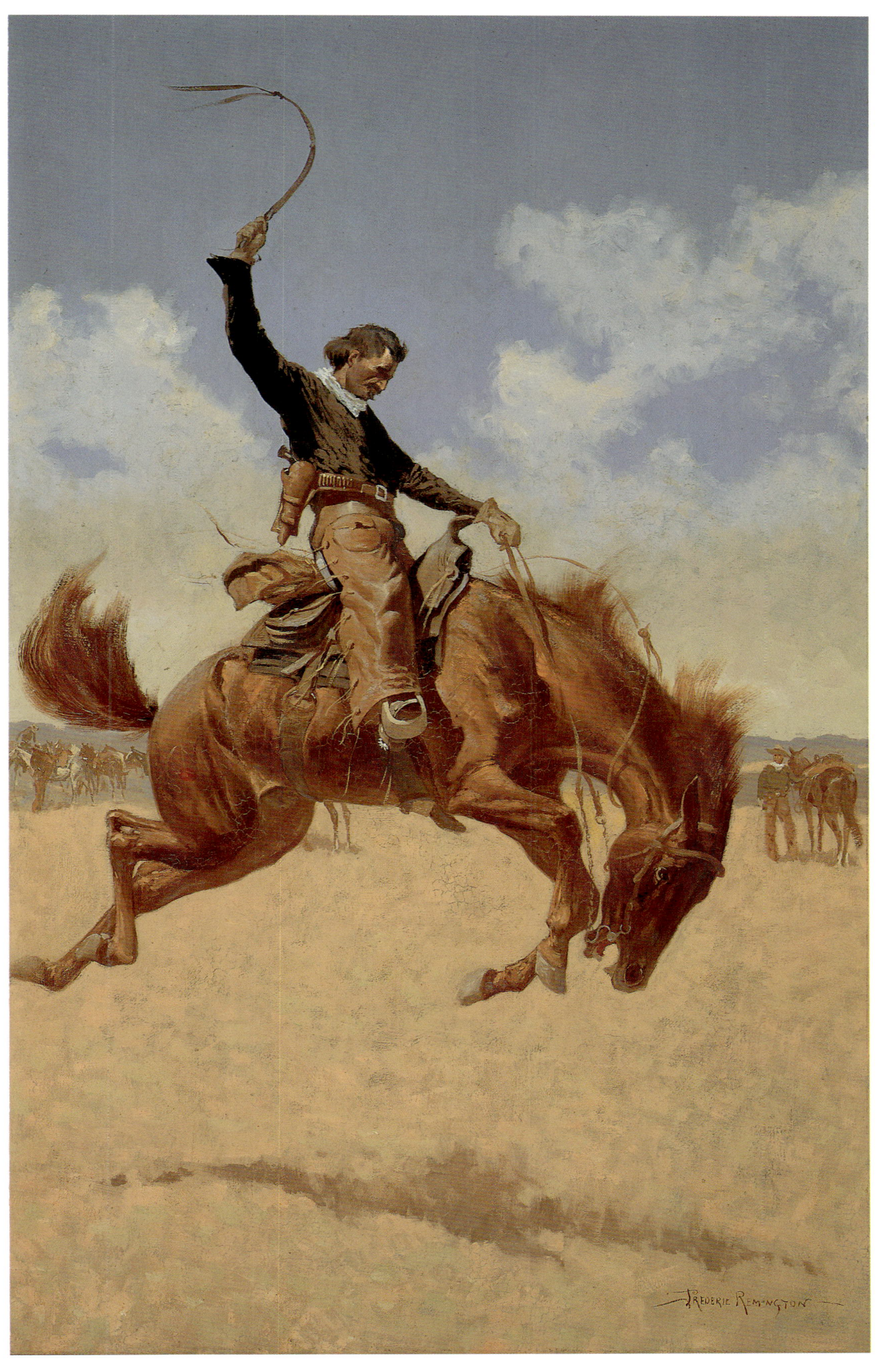

Frederic S. Remington
1861-1909

Coming to the Call
1905
oil on canvas
27 x 40 1/8 inches
signed ll:
Frederic Remington
William I. Koch Collection

Wishing to break away from his reputation as an illustrator, Remington in 1903 negotiated a lucrative agreement with *Collier's* magazine. He would be paid a thousand dollars for the reproduction rights to twelve paintings per year for four years. In addition, the magazine gave him absolute freedom in choosing his subjects. The paintings would be reproduced in color as two-page spreads without any accompanying text. The contract allowed Remington to venture in new directions in both subject and technique. Increasingly influenced by impressionism, by 1905 Remington was experimenting with light and tone, as well as with non-Western subjects.

  Coming to the Call represents a major advance in both areas. Painted in upstate New York, its working of light, reflection, water, and shadow is indicative of Remington's continuing maturation as an artist.

M. W. D.

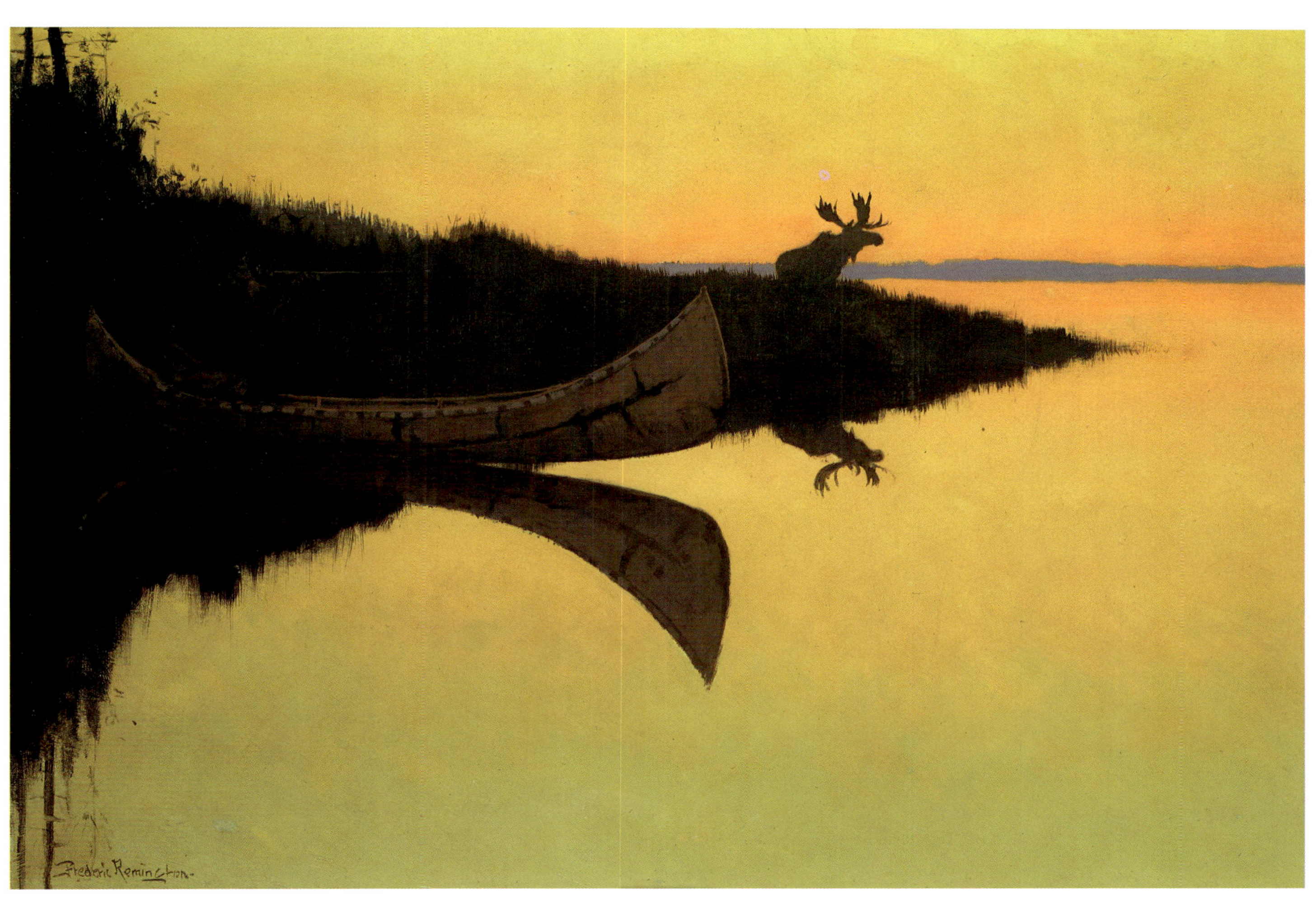

Charles Schreyvogel
1861-1912

Doomed
c. 1901
oil on canvas
25 x 34 inches
inscribed, dated, and
signed ll: Copyright/1901/
by/Chas. Schreyvogel
signed lr: Chas. Schreyvogel
K. S. "Bud" Adams, Jr.

Born in New York City to German immigrant parents, Charles Schreyvogel, like many other prominent Western artists, was a lifelong Easterner. In 1886 he left New York for Munich, Germany, to study with Carl Marr and Frank Kirchbach. Upon his return to the United States he became enthralled with the Wild West of Buffalo Bill Cody and his traveling entourage, and he began sketching and painting the characters and events depicted in these performances.

Schreyvogel eventually made his first trip west in 1893. The paintings he completed after this trip did not sell, and he returned to portraiture and lithographic work to support himself and his wife Louise. He continued to paint Western action scenes and to make yearly trips west, during which he collected both artifacts and stories that would later become the basis for paintings he executed in his New Jersey studio.

Schreyvogel's Western paintings are characterized by one or two dominant figures, carefully composed and pushed to the foreground. The influence of Cody's Wild West is evident in his work, especially in his depiction of dramatic, action-packed, life-and-death confrontations between cavalry soldiers and Indian warriors or, as in *Doomed*, of a buffalo hunt, a favorite subject for many Western artists.

R. B. T.

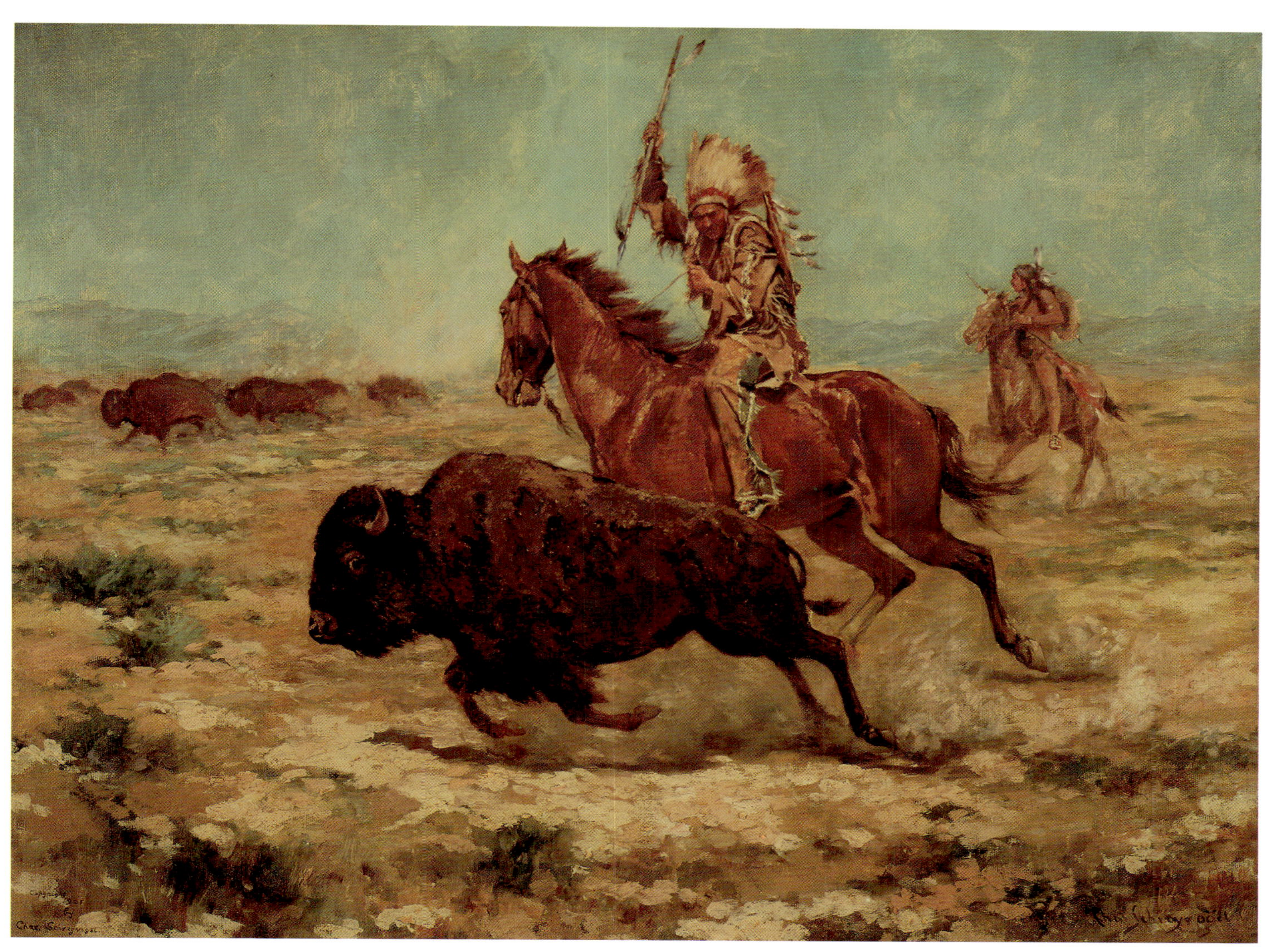

Charles Schreyvogel
1861-1912

Fight to the Finish
c. 1912
oil on canvas
34 x 25 inches
signed, inscribed, and
dated lr: Chas Schreyvogel/
Copyright/1912
K. S. "Bud" Adams, Jr.

In 1900 Schreyvogel entered a painting titled *My Bunkie* in the annual exhibition of the National Academy of Design. Unexpectedly, this painting was awarded the prestigious Clark prize and ensured Schreyvogel almost instantaneous success.

With his new-found success came bitter criticism of his work by the preeminent Western chronicler of the day, Frederic Remington. Never having had a rival such as Schreyvogel, Remington launched public attacks on the authenticity of Schreyvogel's work. Military veterans, among them Teddy Roosevelt, who had become an admirer of his work, rallied in defense of Schreyvogel's accuracy, and Remington's diatribes were eventually dismissed as petty jealousy.

Remington and Schreyvogel remained rivals until Remington's death in 1909. Three years later, after contracting blood poisoning from a chicken bone that lodged in his gum, Charles Schreyvogel died in Hoboken, New Jersey. His slow and deliberate style, along with his penchant for in-depth research, resulted in a relatively small body of work, fewer than eighty paintings.

R. B. T.

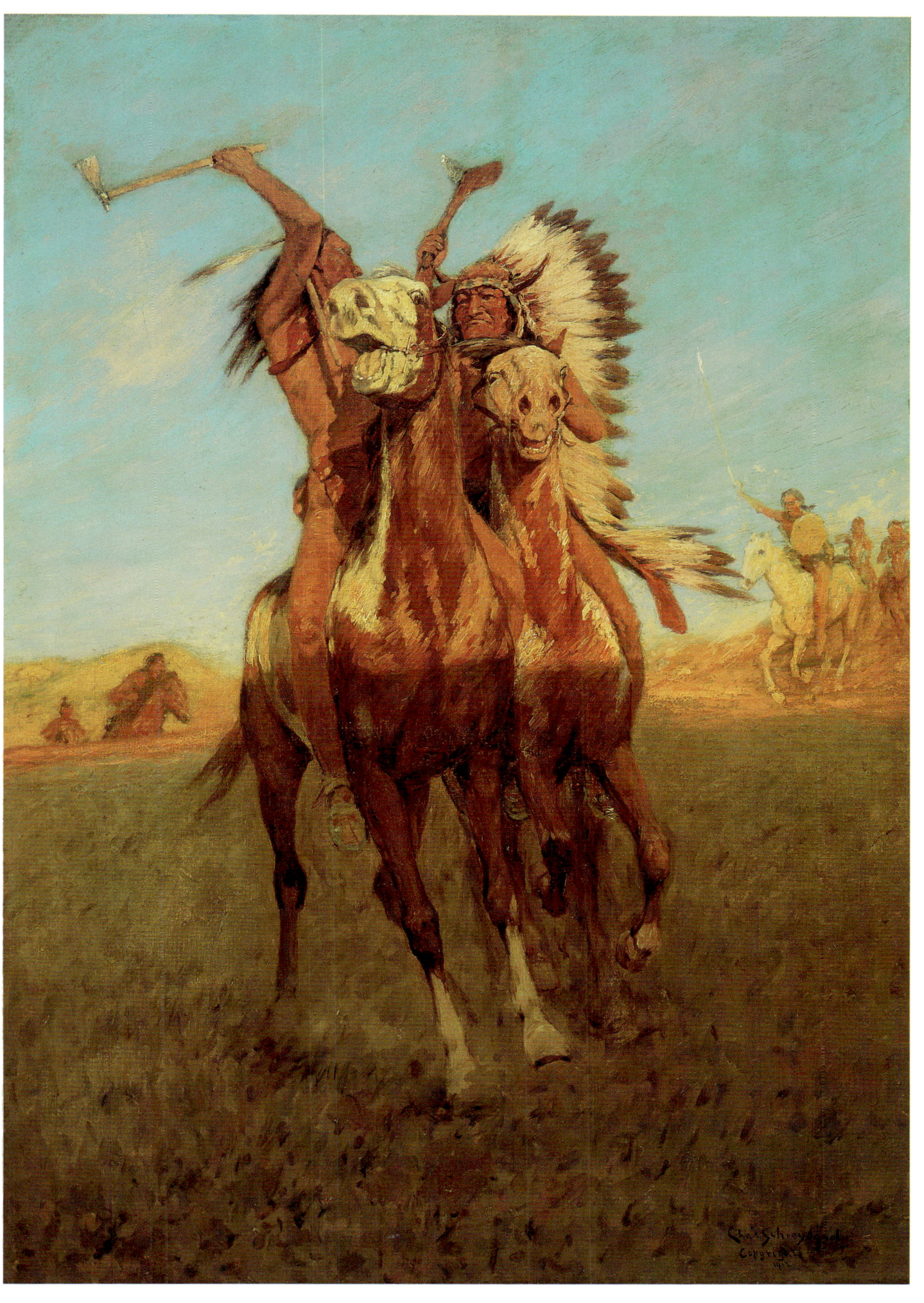

Cyrus Edwin Dallin
1861-1944

Appeal to the Great Spirit
1912
bronze
height 40 inches
signed and dated
on top of base:
© C. F. Dallin 1912
William I. Koch Collection

Cyrus E. Dallin was born in a log cabin in Utah, in a pioneer settlement surrounded by friendly Ute Indians. As a young boy he played many games with his Ute friends; some of these games used objects made out of clay from a local riverbank. After their games were finished, the boys often sat around modeling bison, horses, antelope, and other prairie animals from this clay. Dallin's lifetime commitment to sculpture and his involvement with Native American cultures developed from these childhood activities.

With money earned from working in a silver mine plus the financial support of friends, Dallin went to Boston in 1884 to study sculpture. His skills improved rapidly, and he soon opened his own studio, where he specialized in portrait busts and small Native American figures. In 1888 he traveled to Paris for the first time to further his training at the Académie Julian. One year later, when Buffalo Bill's Wild West Show came to Paris, Dallin took the opportunity to make clay studies of many of the Indian performers. He returned to the United States in 1891 and began a long and successful career as a sculptor, specializing in American Indian subjects.

Over a period of twenty years, 1889–1909, Dallin developed four equestrian statues for what he called his "Indian cycle," which depicts the changing relations of the Indian and the white man. *Appeal to the Great Spirit*, the final sculpture in this series, presents a romanticized image symbolizing the defeat of the Indians and their tragic loss of homelands and lifestyles. A Plains Indian sits astride a motionless horse with his back arched, his face turned to the skies, and his arms outstretched in a universal gesture of supplication. *Appeal to the Great Spirit* was cast in several different sizes; another cast of this sculpture is installed on the grounds of Culver Academies, a gift from the class of 1930.

M. K. D.

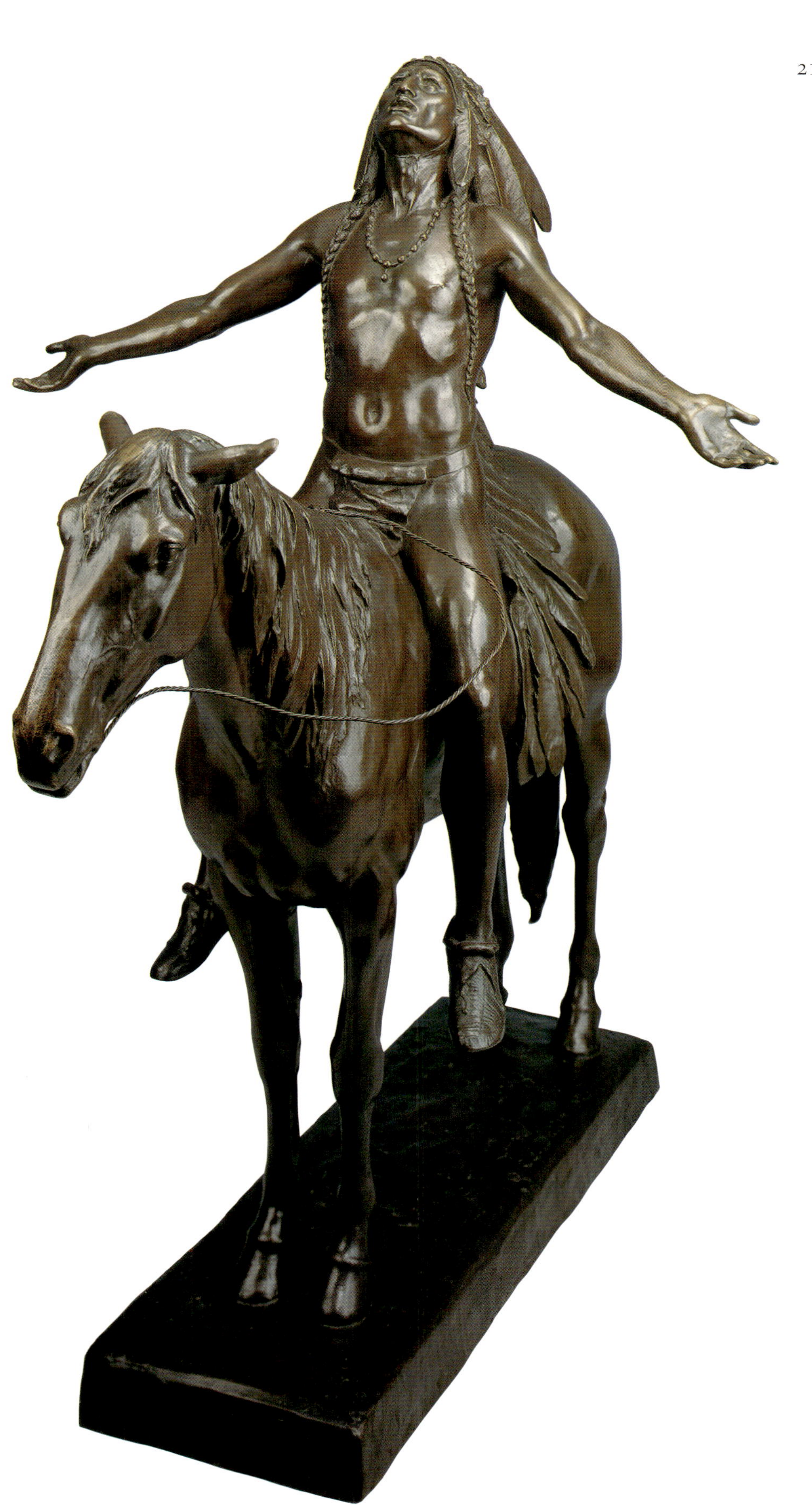

Charles Marion Russell
1864-1926

Start of a Roundup
1898
watercolor on paper
14 1/2 x 20 1/2 inches
signed and dated ll:
C M Russell/1898
K. S. "Bud" Adams, Jr.

Born to wealthy parents in St. Louis, Charles Marion Russell exhibited early on two traits that would dominate his life and work: an innate ability to draw and model and an intense interest in the American West. In an attempt to satisfy his Western yearnings and to encourage him to put those longings behind him, Russell's parents sent him to work on a friend's sheep ranch in Montana when he was sixteen.

Although his career as a sheep rancher was brief, his love affair with Montana and the West never ended. By the mid-1880s Russell was working as a night wrangler, which allowed him plenty of time during the daylight hours to sketch and draw. His subjects were the people and events that he saw around him. By 1890 his reputation locally as an artist had grown enough to convince him to pursue an artistic career full time.

Start of a Roundup shows Russell's early fondness for portraying a fairly large group of characters caught up in the excitement and drama of cowboy life.

M. W. D.

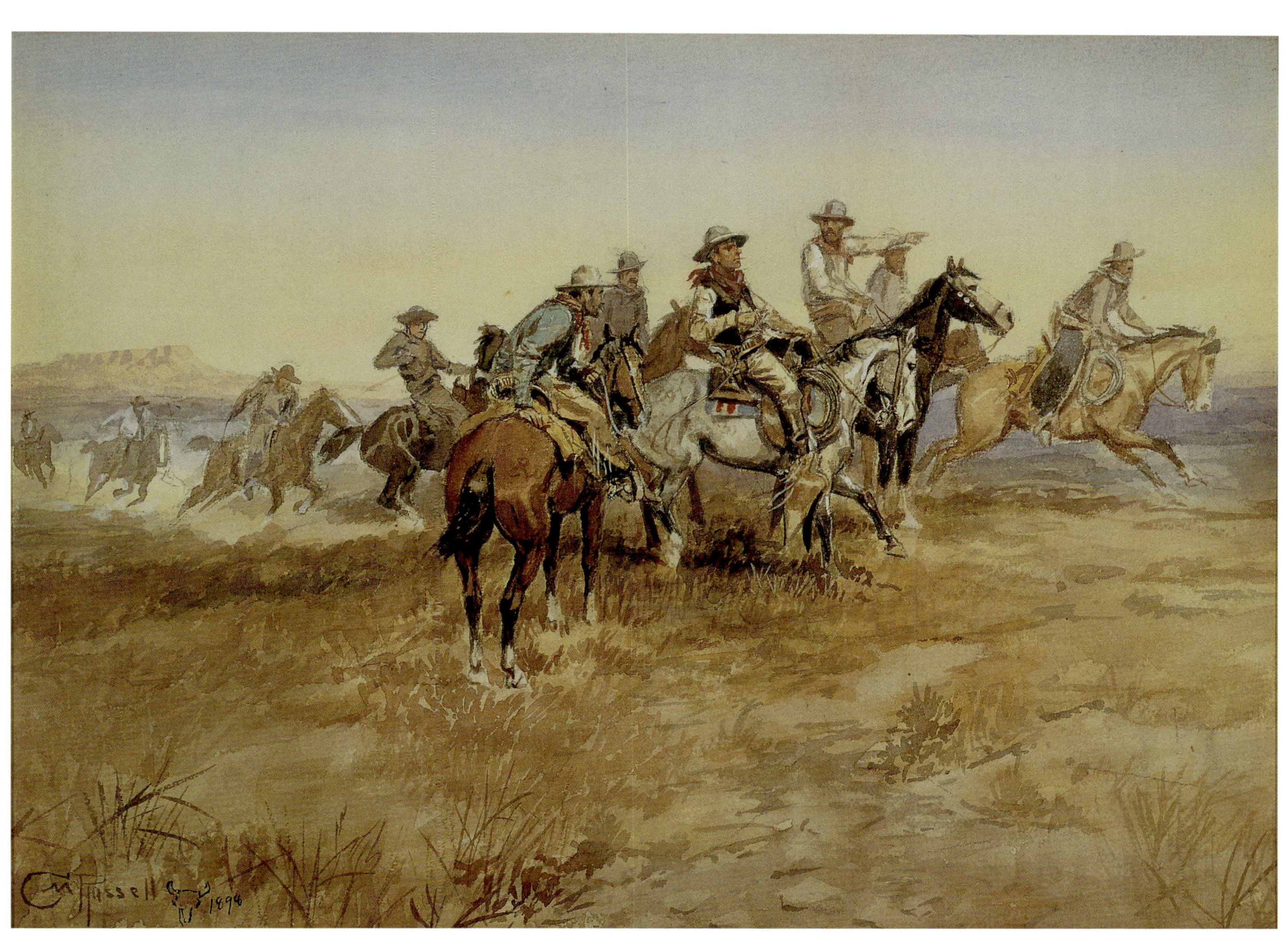

Charles Marion Russell *On the Prowl*
1864-1926 1898
watercolor on paper
14 1/2 x 20 1/2 inches
signed and dated ll:
C M Russell/1898
K. S. "Bud" Adams, Jr.

218

While Russell's early reputation was made on his depiction of cowboys, round-ups, and the life in Western towns, he was drawn throughout his career to portraying American Indians. Russell felt such an affinity for the Indians of the Northern Plains that he once said that the highest compliment that could be paid him was to mistake him for an Indian. Painting Indians in their natural surroundings and engaged in typical activities also gave Russell the opportunity to portray Montana during a historical period that he felt was superior to his own age. While Russell spent a great deal of time with Northern Plains tribes from his arrival in Montana in 1881 until his death in 1926, the majority of his paintings of Indians are set in an earlier time, before settlement reached the northern Rockies.

M. W. D.

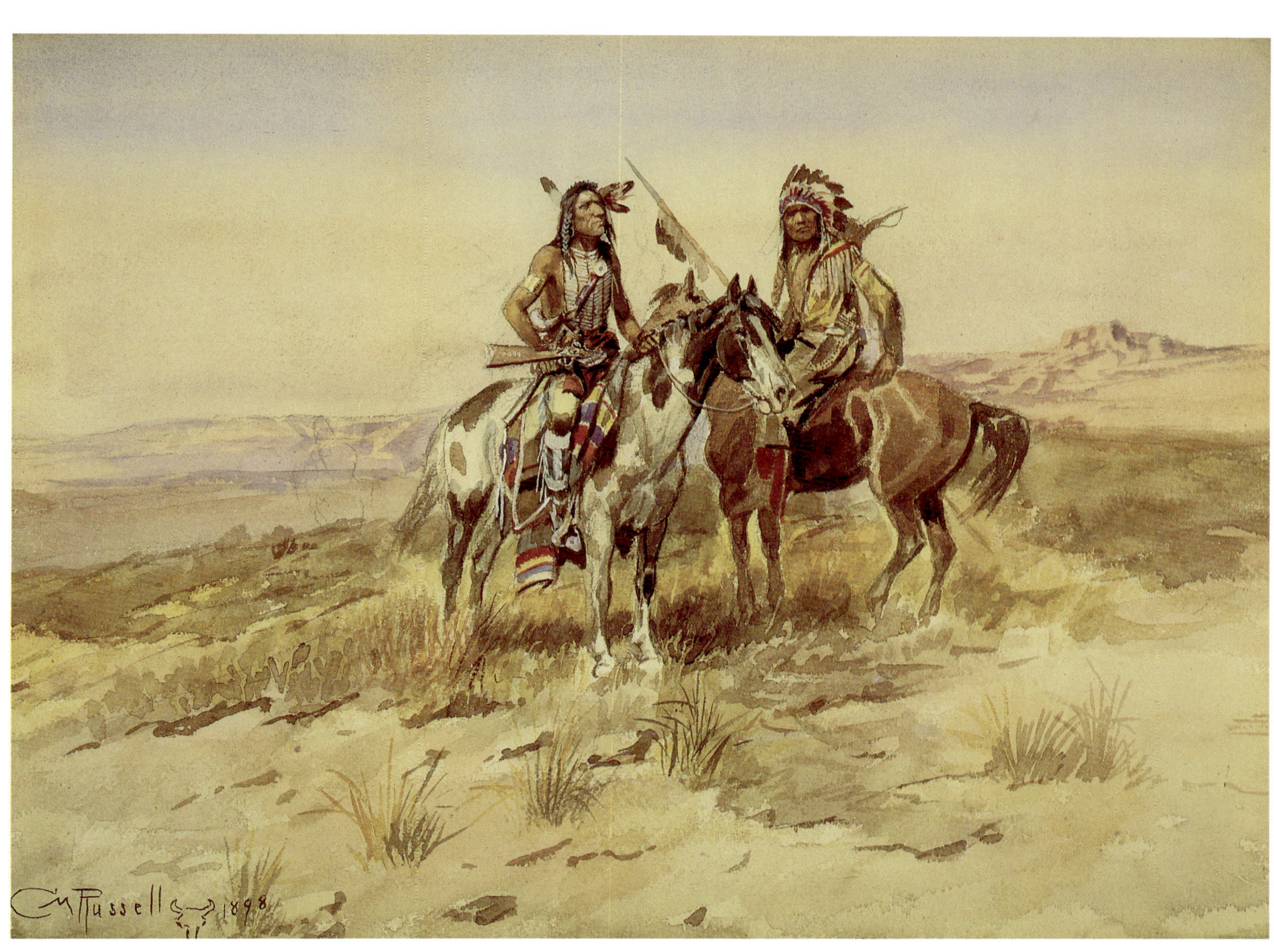

Charles Marion Russell
1864-1926

The Scouting Party
1898
oil on board
9 x 15 1/2 inches
signed and dated ll:
C M Russell/1898
K. S. "Bud" Adams, Jr.

220

As Russell gained experience as a painter, he began to focus on individual figures rather than groups. Here he uses a simple triangular composition: the mounted Indian and his shadow merge into the foreground of the painting and are balanced by another triangle of rocks. The painting illustrates not only Russell's reliance on fairly simple compositional devices, but also his interest in the cycles of American Indian life.

M. W. D.

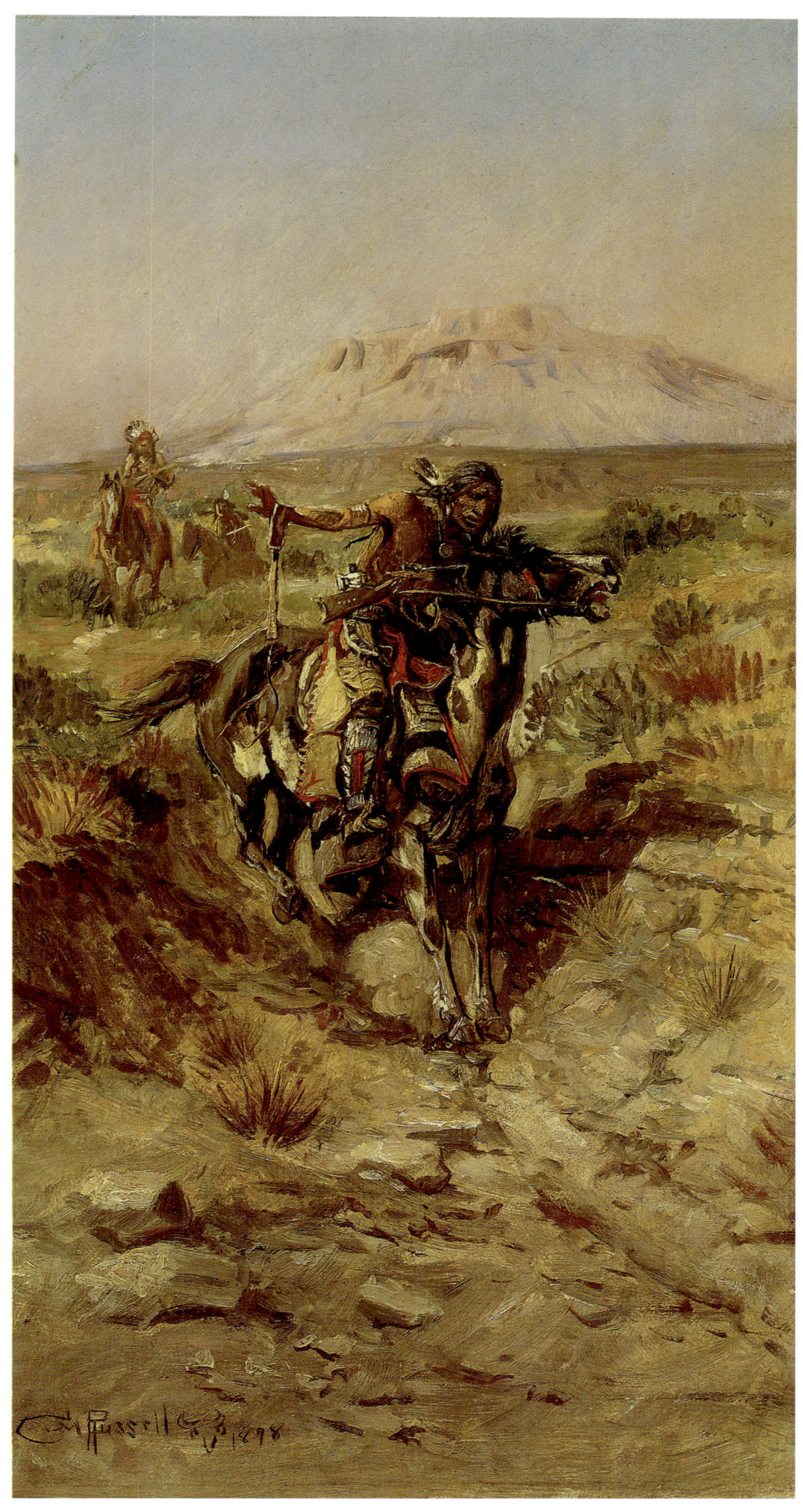

Whoop Up Trail
or *Tribe in a Snowstorm*
1899
oil on canvas
24 x 36 1/2 inches
signed and dated ll:
C M Russell/1899
William I. Koch Collection

222

By the end of the nineteenth century, Russell was well established nationally as a painter and illustrator. He owed his success in part to Nancy Cooper, an ambitious young woman from Kentucky, whom he married in 1896 and who became his business manager. Through disciplined management skills and astute marketing, she soon developed an audience for Russell paintings in the East as well as throughout the West.

In the bleak *Whoop Up Trail*, painted primarily in grays and browns, Russell depicts a Plains tribe moving across the prairies through a winter storm. The snow has blotted out all indications of background or horizon, and small touches of blue in the hoarfrost, horses' breath, and shadows reinforce the sense of penetrating cold. Two central riders—one on a spotted brown and white horse, the other on a black horse—form the focal point; they are portrayed with the greatest amount of detail, the strongest colors, and the brightest accents. Flanking riders have less intense hues and fewer details. The remaining tribal members, straggling into the left distance, are briefly suggested with grayed colors and abbreviated brush strokes.

M. K. D.

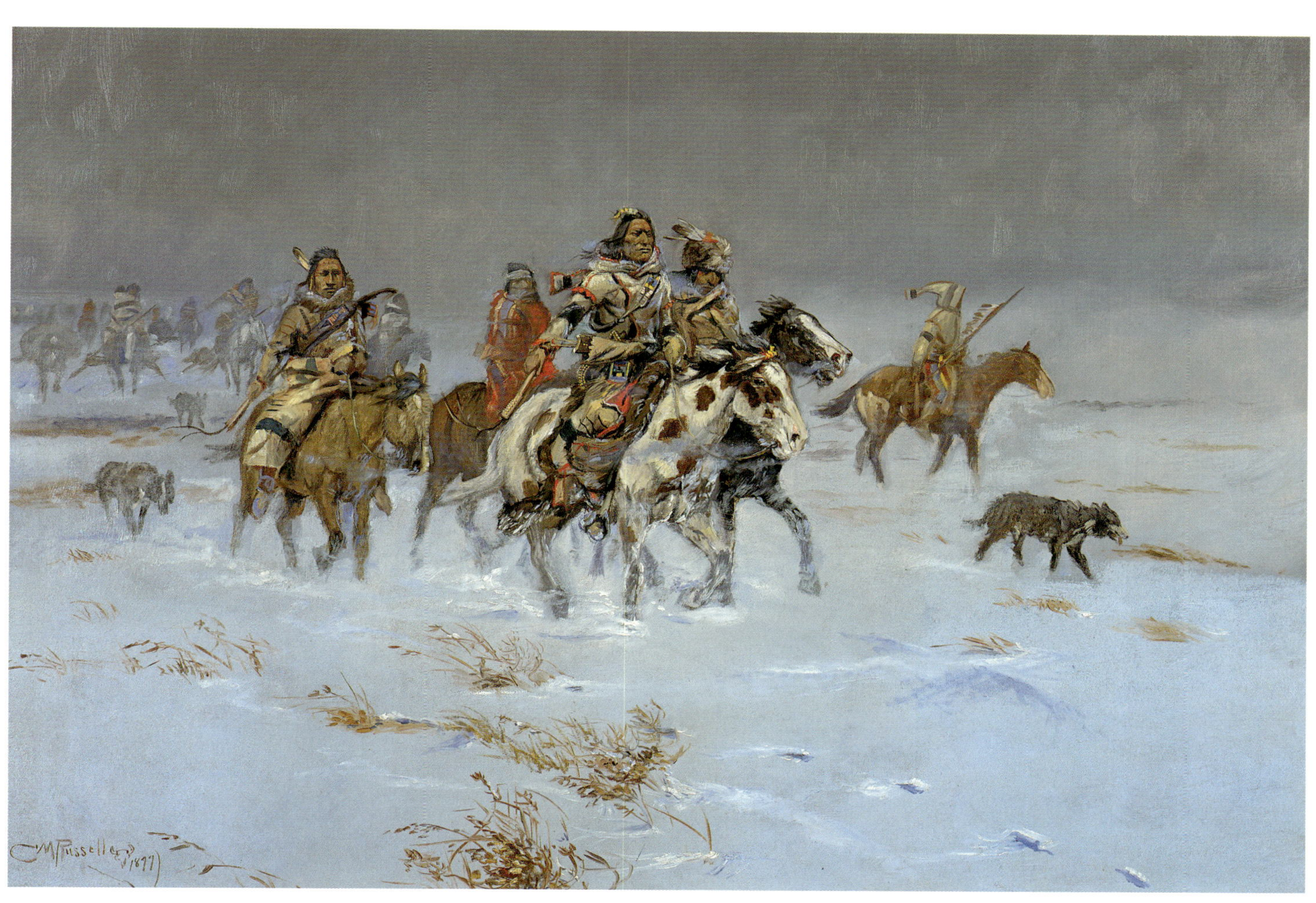

Charles Marion Russell
1864-1926

Crippled but Still Coming
(A Dangerous Cripple)
1913
oil on canvas
30 x 48 inches
signed and dated ll:
C M Russell/1913/©
The Gund Collection
of Western Art

224

Russell was famous for his ability to tell a story, whether in person or on canvas. This painting, which presents a frightening story with an unforeseeable outcome, was purchased by Judge James Bollinger of Davenport, Iowa, directly from the artist. Later, according to legend, while Russell was visiting Bollinger, he discovered that the judge's young son Steve wanted to become a cowboy and would use a Circle S brand. Russell immediately borrowed brushes and paint from the child and added that brand to the shoulder of the white horse.

Russell set this scene against the rocky terrain of Gunsight Pass in Glacier Park, Montana. A lone hunter turns back for one more shot at an angry, wounded bear, as the terrified horses frantically scramble down the mountainside. The strong diagonal of the mountain, the off-center triangle of horses and rider, and the implied line of fire add to the tension of this dramatic image.

M. K. D.

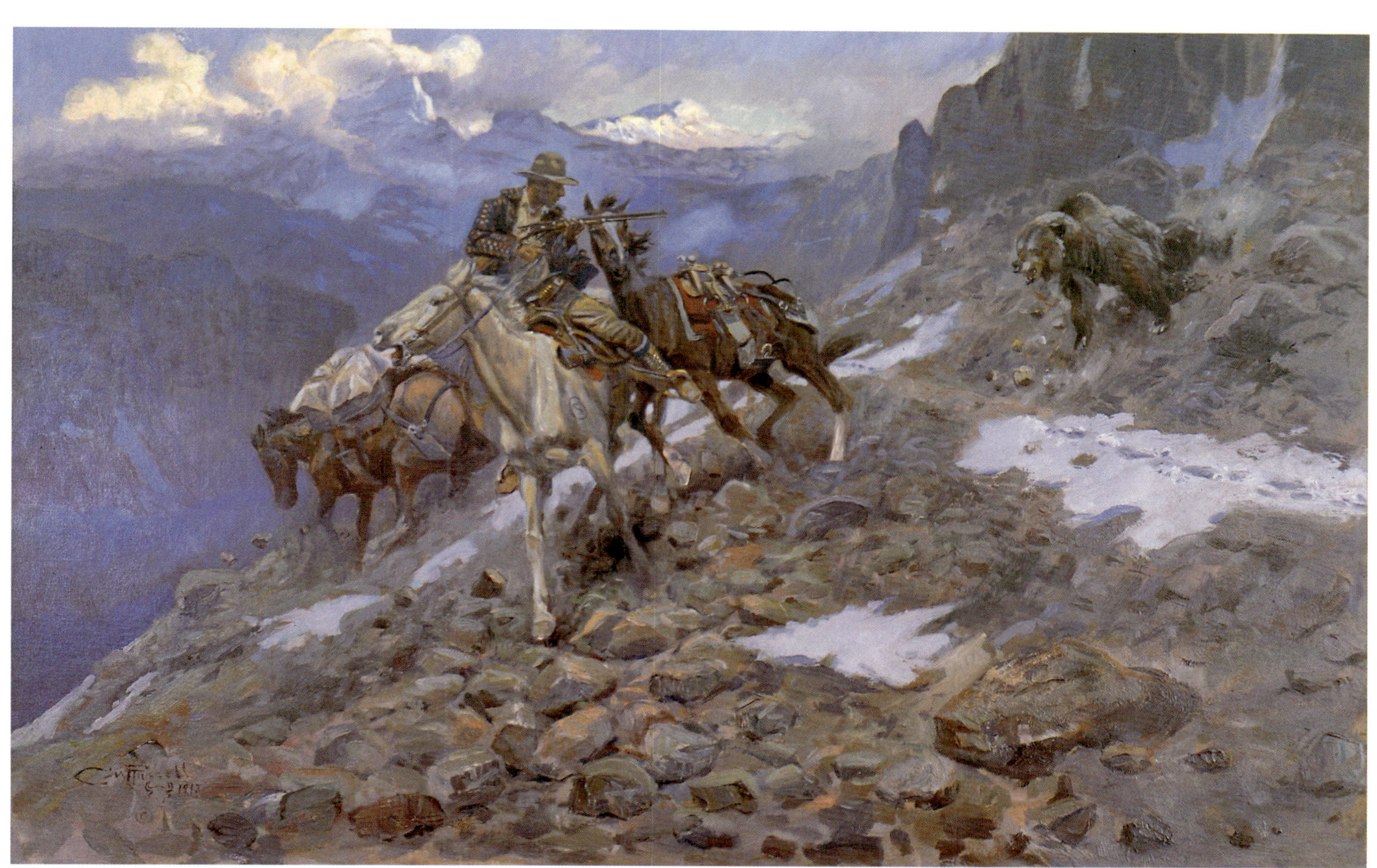

226

The moving of an Indian camp was a recurring and important subject in Russell's art. For him
the Indian way of life was marked by an appreciation for the natural environment and a keen
ability to adapt to the climate and resources. While Indian men pursued bison herds, it was the
responsibility of the women to maintain and transport the camps. In such scenes Russell often
showed several generations of family members, all working in harmony with both each other
and nature.

M. W. D.

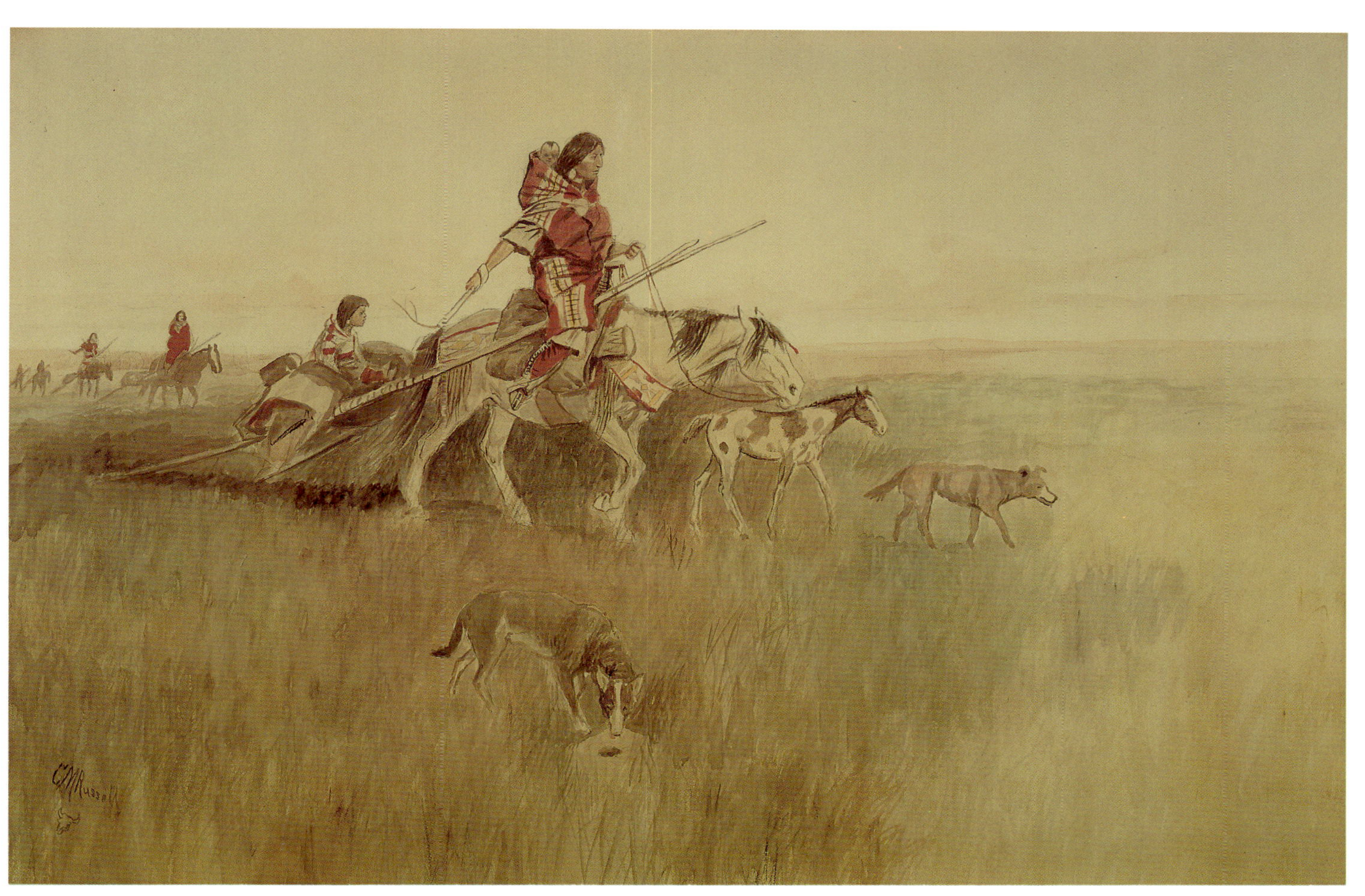

Charles Marion Russell
1864–1926

Indian on Horseback
c. 1915
watercolor on paper
15 3/4 x 20 inches
signed ll: C M Russell
K. S. "Bud" Adams, Jr.

228

Some of Russell's best paintings are small watercolor studies of individual Indians, such as this one. While the background is always the familiar countryside around Great Falls, Montana, Russell's careful details and authenticity focus our attention on the figure. Russell was a collector of American Indian material as well as a painter, and he often used items from his personal collection in his paintings, taking care never to mix objects from different tribes.

M. W. D.

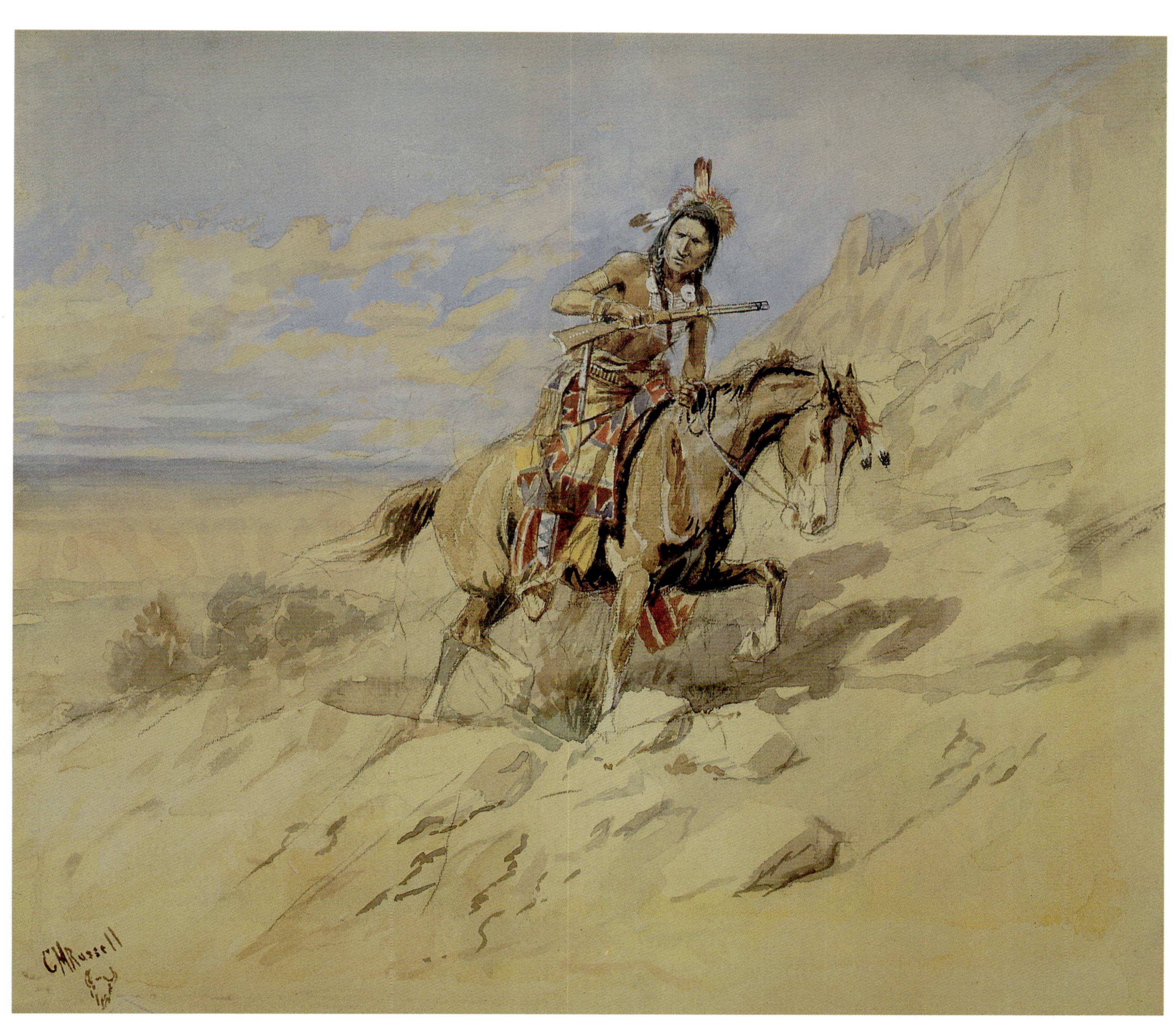

Charles Marion Russell
1864-1926

Trail of the White Man
or *Wagon's Dust Cloud*
1925
oil on canvas
24 x 36 inches
signed and dated ll:
C M Russell/1925
William I. Koch Collection

230

In *Trail of the White Man*, painted the year before his death, Russell presents both a favorite subject and a familiar composition. Six mounted Plains warriors, framed against a pale sky, have paused in their journey across the prairie to study the tracks of the men they are following. The small band of horsemen forms a shallow triangle slightly off-center to the right. A diagonal rut meanders across the prairie from the center foreground around the horses on the right. The vibrant blues, pinks, and purples of the distant mountains and the intense yellows and oranges reflected from the sun are characteristic of Russell's late paintings.

M. K. D.

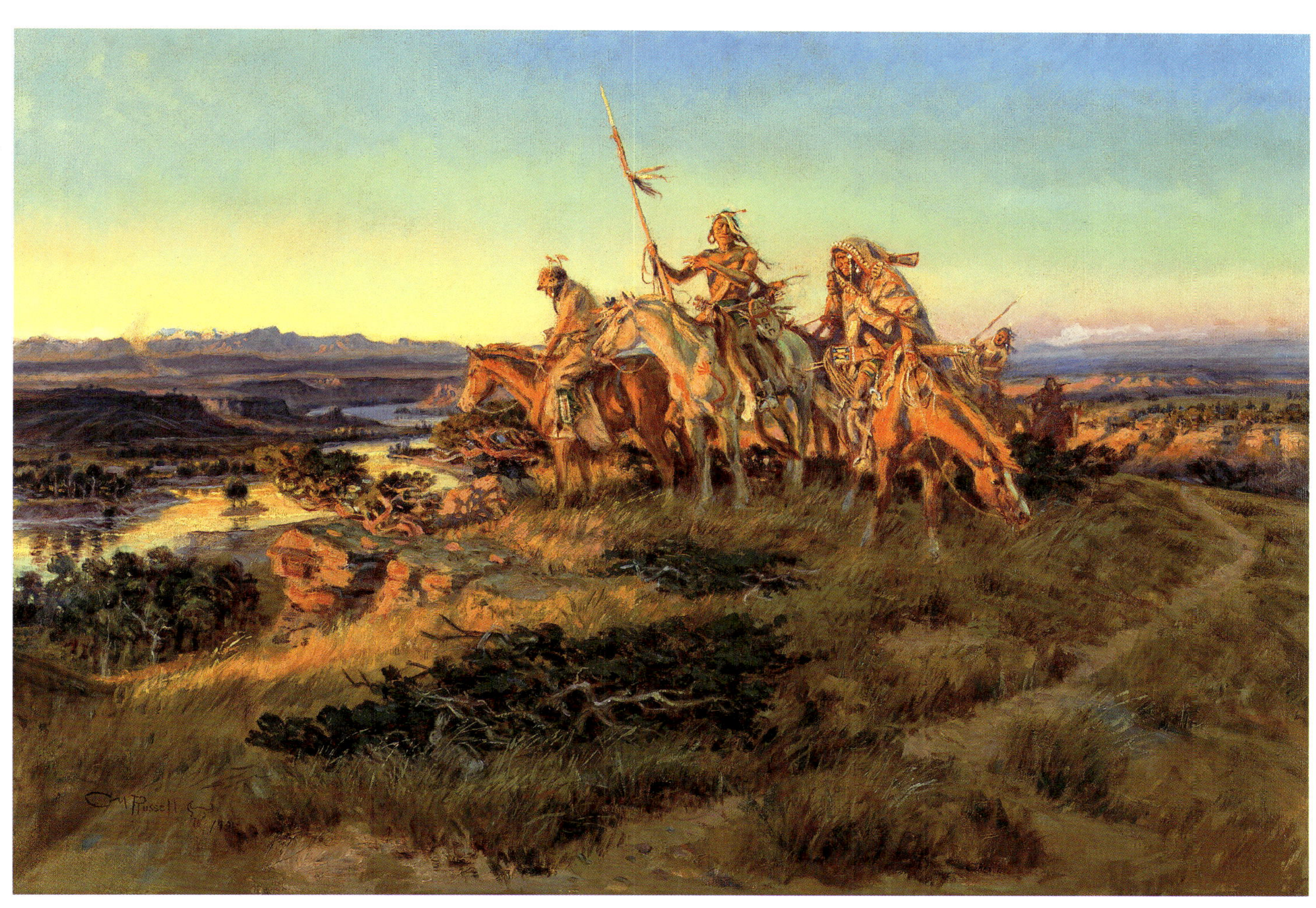

Eanger Irving Couse
1866-1936

The Hunter
oil on canvas
30 x 36 1/4 inches
signed ll: E·I·COUSE·
K. S. "Bud" Adams, Jr.

E. I. Couse was born in 1866 in the remote logging and lumbering town of Saginaw, Michigan. As a teenager he earned money for art school by painting barns and houses and by completing portraits of local Chippewa Indians. After formal study in Chicago, New York, and Paris, Couse established a solid reputation in both the United States and France. Throughout his life, Couse was intrigued by Native Americans and by the American West.

In 1902 he first visited Taos, New Mexico, and was fascinated by the intense blue New Mexican sky, the old town, and the local pueblo villages. This visit changed the direction of Couse's artistic career: the Pueblo Indians provided suitable subjects for his romantic and idealistic tendencies, and the influence of the Southwest light gradually led to a brighter palette.

Couse's favorite subjects were the Taos Indians, and he frequently painted a single Indian involved in an ordinary, everyday activity. In *The Hunter*, a lone man stands behind a tree, in shadow, and quietly tracks small game moving through the sunlit aspen forest. Couse was especially intrigued by the opportunities for rich color combinations; here he plays the dark colors of the hunter and the tree trunk against the dappled white bark of the aspen trees.

M. K. D.

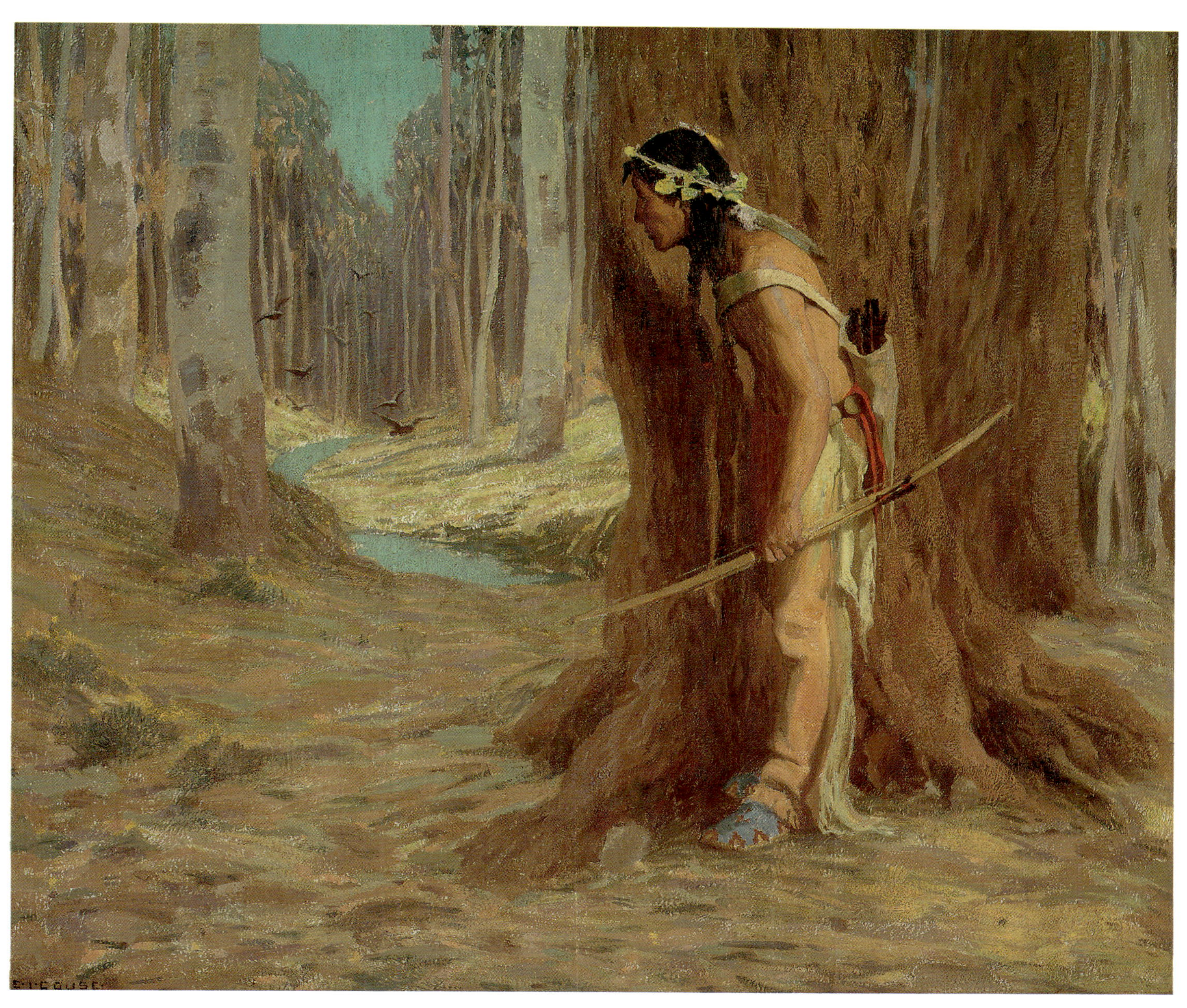

Eanger Irving Couse
1866-1936

The Potter
oil on canvas
24 x 30 inches
signed ll: E·I·COUSE·N.A.
The Culver Educational
Foundation
Gift of Homer I. Lewis '38
and Peter Pauls Stewart '37

To promote the Southwest as a tourist mecca, the Santa Fe Railway commissioned paintings featuring the landscape and peoples of New Mexico; these were reproduced on widely distributed calendars. In 1903 the railway, as part of the project, offered Couse and his family free passage to the Southwest. He soon became one of the railway's preferred artists, and over the years he produced twenty-three calendar images.

In this quiet genre study, a native craftsman is set against an undefined background and painted with broad, thick brush strokes. He holds a large San Juan pot, while a smaller Santa Clara blackware pot is on his right. A sense of stillness pervades the scene. The squatting pose used here is characteristic of many of Couse's paintings: the pose was designed to fit into the horizontal format required for calendar images.

M. K. D.

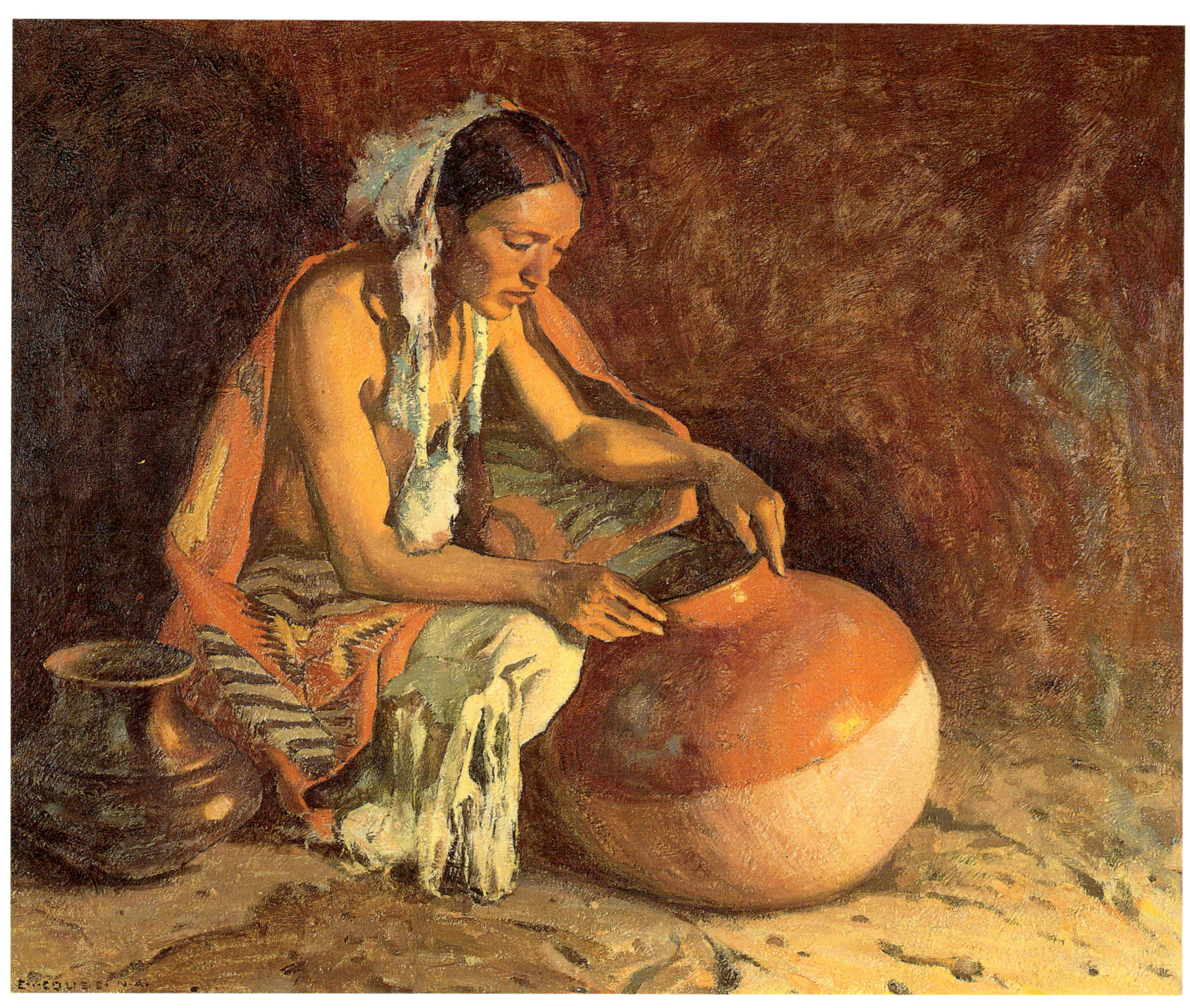

Eanger Irving Couse
1866-1936

Lovers
c. 1906
oil on canvas
30 1/4 x 36 1/4 inches
signed ll: E·I·COUSE·
K. S. "Bud" Adams, Jr.

From 1905 to 1928 Couse summered in Taos, where he sketched Indians within their natural landscape setting. During the winter he worked with models in his New York studio and finished large canvases based on his outdoor sketches. When the Taos Society of Artists was organized in 1915, Couse was elected the first president. He became a permanent resident of Taos in 1928.

The romantic image of two lovers in a canoe was inspired by the courtship of one of his models. With his characteristic lack of concern for cultural accuracy, Couse chose to depict the couple in a non-Pueblo birchbark canoe. He asked two of his favorite Taos Pueblo models, Tonita and Ben Lujan, to sit and kneel in his studio as if in a canoe; he then added wooden boards to suggest the sides of the canoe and the paddle. The background was also completed in the studio, with careful references to his black-and-white site photographs and field studies.

M. K. D.

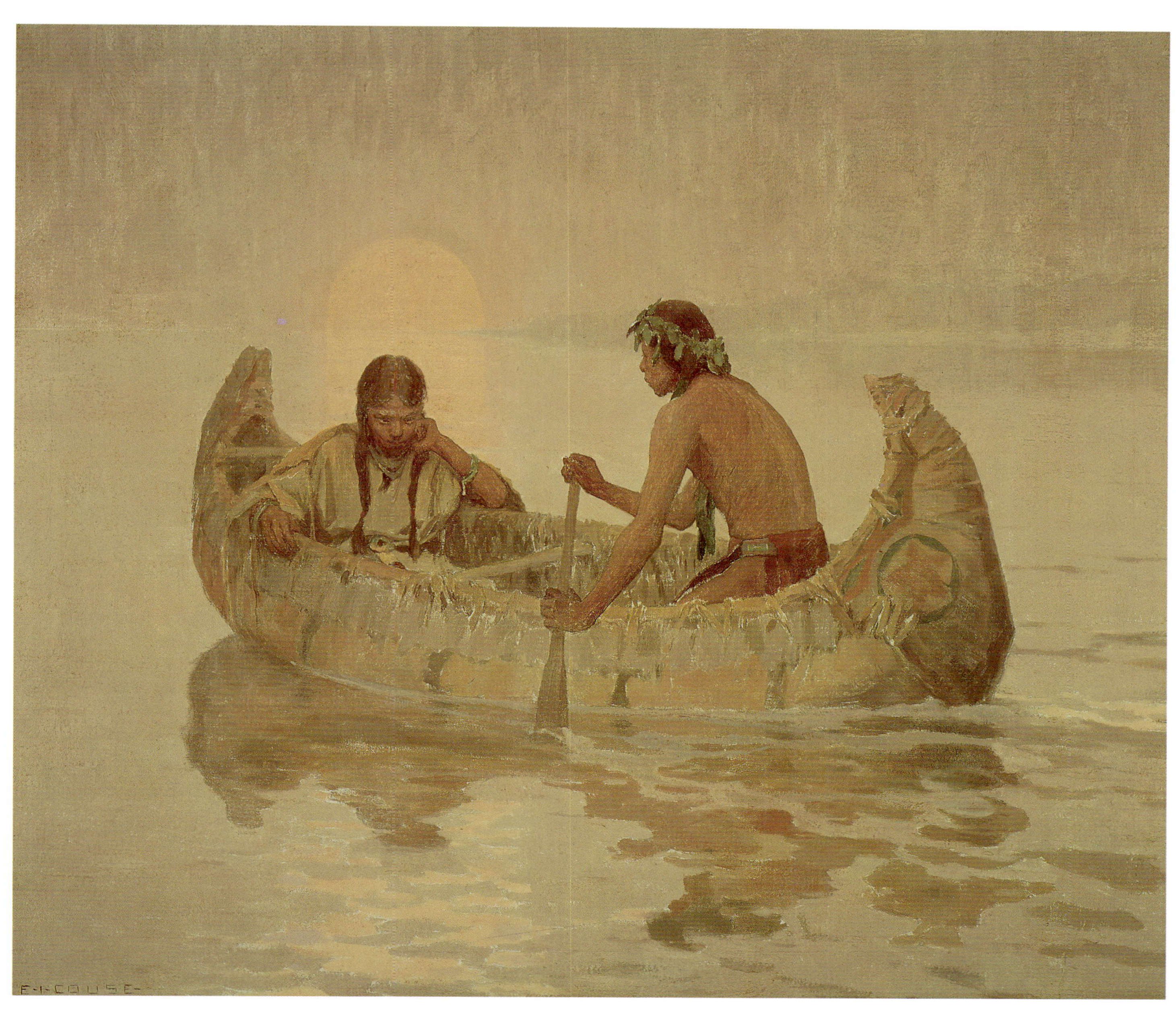

William R. Leigh
1866-1955

The Shield
1940
oil on canvas
40 x 60 inches
signed and dated lr:
W. R. LEIGH·1940
K. S. "Bud" Adams, Jr.

William Robinson Leigh was born and raised on a plantation in West Virginia that had been largely destroyed during the Civil War. Early struggles with poverty left him with lifelong feelings of inadequacy and bitterness. His formal art training was funded primarily by his uncles and included three years of classes at the Maryland Institute of Art in Baltimore, followed by twelve years of work and study at the Royal Academy of Fine Arts in Munich.

Leigh returned to America in 1896. He found, to his great disappointment, that the meticulous realist style he had perfected in Munich was more suited to a career as a commercial illustrator than to that of a fine artist. He was soon accepting regular assignments from *Scribner's Magazine*, *Collier's*, and *McClure's*.

When he visited New Mexico for the first time in 1906, Leigh felt that the peoples and landscapes of the Southwest were exactly what he had been seeking. Although still accepting illustration assignments, Leigh began to focus on Western genre paintings, determined to become a frontier artist.

In this large painting of a Southwest showdown, Leigh has drawn on his experience as an illustrator to create a dramatic narrative. The accurate details, superb draftsmanship, strong colors, and carefully organized composition reflect the influence of his Munich training.

M. K. D.

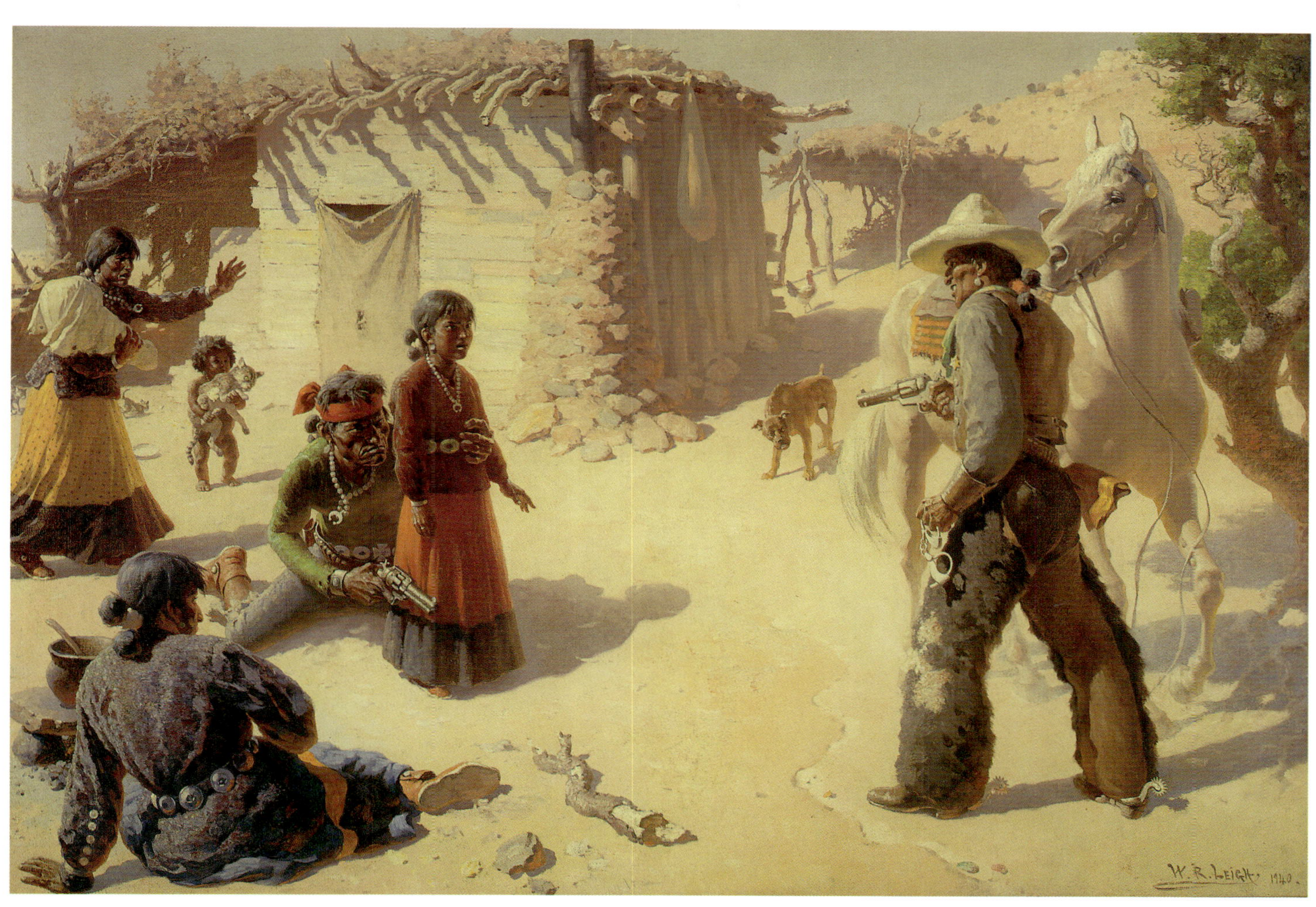

Grizzly's End
1948
oil on canvas
25 x 40 1/4 inches
signed and dated ll:
©/W. R. LEIGH·1948·
K. S. "Bud" Adams, Jr.

240

Although Leigh was dedicated to painting the subjects of western America, he maintained his permanent residence in New York City. Extensive travels, including twenty-five trips to the West and Southwest and two prolonged trips to Africa, provided him with a steady supply of field studies and sketches to be used in developing full-scale paintings.

As Leigh neared the age of seventy, he began to get the recognition as a fine artist that had eluded him for so long. The last two decades of his life were his most productive. In a 1944 New York exhibition of his paintings, Leigh was linked with Frederic Remington and Charles Russell as the third of the three great painters of the Old West. Leigh was elected an associate of the National Academy of Design in 1953 and an academician in 1955.

Grizzly's End provided Leigh with the opportunity to combine two of his favorite subjects—western cowboy life and big game. Using a dramatic triangular format, Leigh shows the ignominious defeat of a wild grizzly. Strong diagonals reinforce the struggles of the hunter and horse and the alert postures of the dogs.

M. K. D.

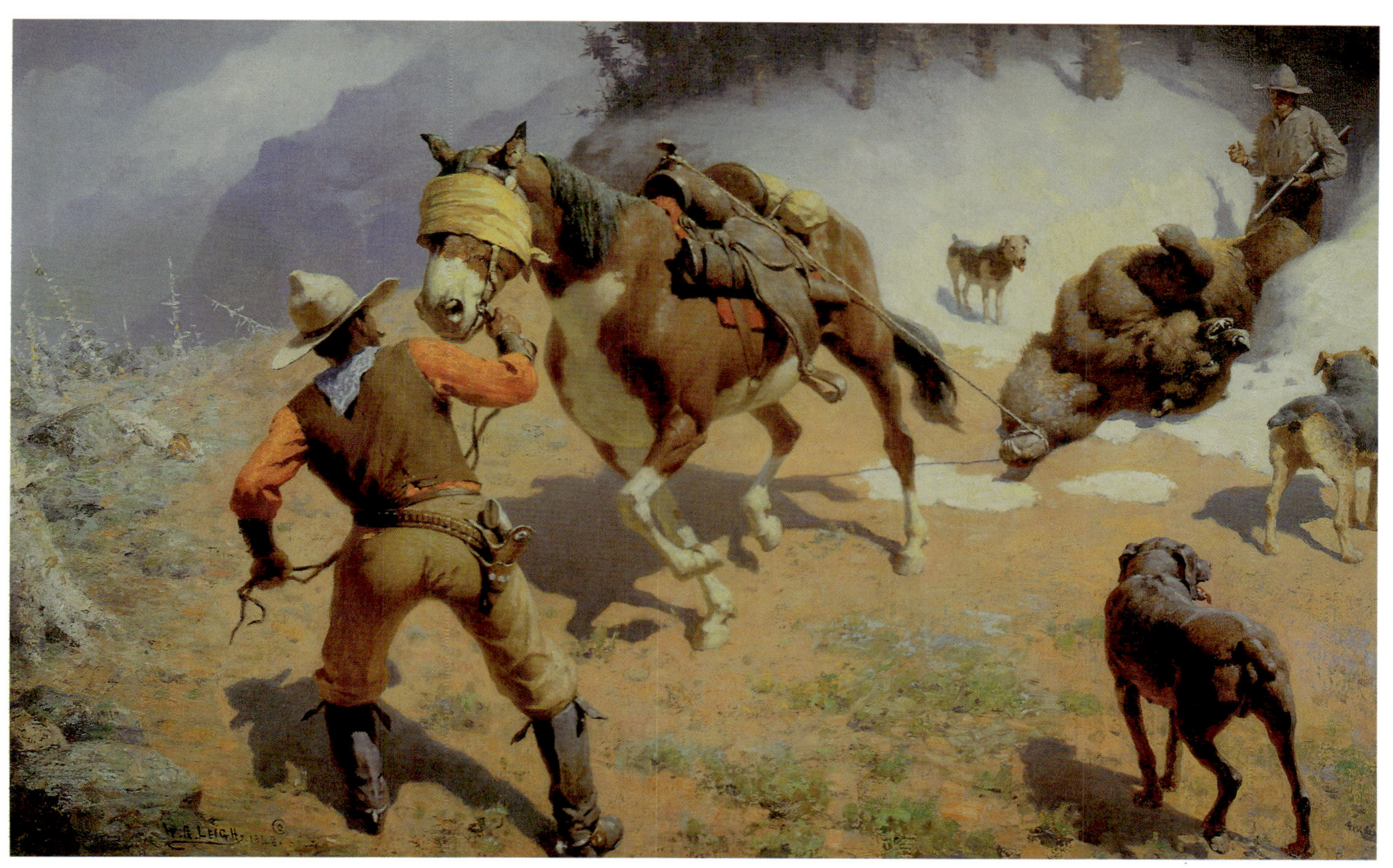

Carl Rungius
1869-1959

Early Thaw
oil on canvas
30 x 46 inches
signed lr: C-Rungius
Mr. and Mrs. Jon R. Stuart

A native of Berlin, Germany, Carl Rungius was already an accomplished artist, avid naturalist, and outdoorsman when he first visited the United States in the early 1890s. By 1894 he had established himself as an illustrator of hunting, fishing, camping, and other outdoor scenes. His work appeared in such periodicals as *Forest and Stream*, *Outing Magazine*, and *Everybody's Recreation*.

Rungius traveled extensively in the American West and the Canadian Rockies, where he hunted and studied big game animals. In 1904, having grown dissatisfied with magazine illustration, he decided to devote his full energies to painting wildlife subjects. His stature as the "preeminent painter of North American big game" is evidenced by his friendship with President Theodore Roosevelt, accolades from Frederic Remington, his election to associate and full membership in the National Academy of Design, and by the large number of collectors who still pursue his work today.

In this work, typical of Rungius's early paintings, the viewer is brought face to face with the majesty of a bull moose—in its habitat and on its terms.

R. B. T.

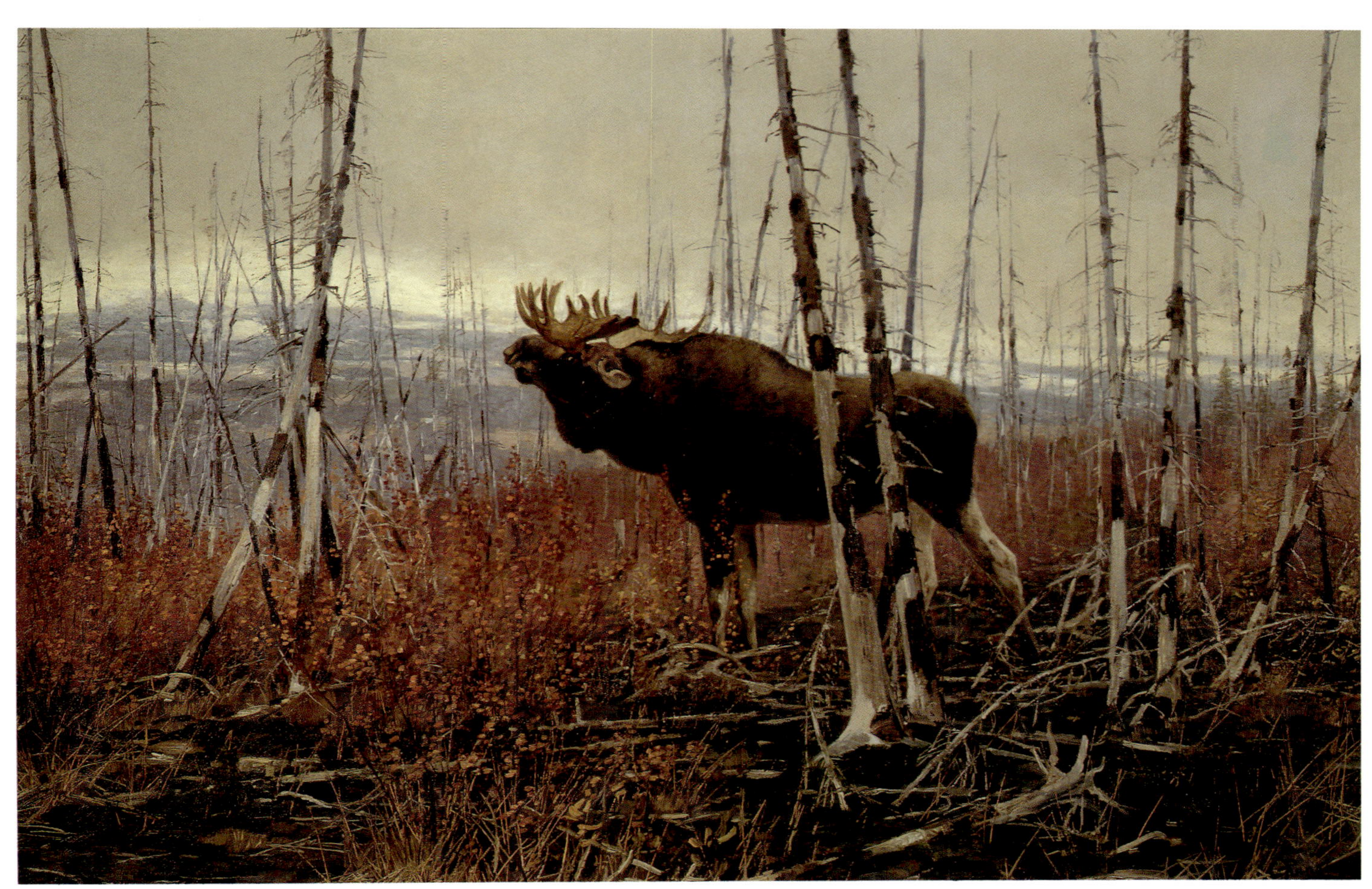

Chief Blackbird
c. 1903
bronze
height 18 inches
inscribed lr:
CHIEF/BLACK/BIRD/
OGALALLA/SIOUX
William I. Koch Collection

Adolph Alexander Weinman was born in Karlsruhe, Germany, and at the age of ten emigrated to America with his mother. He began his formal art training with an apprenticeship under Frederick Kaldenberg and later enrolled in classes at Cooper Union and the Art Students League in New York City. By the age of nineteen Weinman was studying under or working with many of the prominent sculptors of the day, including Philip Martiny, Charles Neihaus, Olin Levi Warner, and Daniel Chester French. During this period of artistic development, Weinman acquired a strong interest in Native Americans as subjects for art. He saw the indigenous people as noble and heroic and was one of the first to create bronze portraits of Indians.

The portrait *Chief Blackbird* is one of Weinman's best-known works. Blackbird was a Lakota chief and a member of Colonel Cummings's Wild West Show. While the show performed at Coney Island and Madison Square Garden in New York City, Weinman used a number of the Indians in the troupe, including Blackbird, for studies. His mastery of intricate linear patterns is well illustrated throughout the sculpture.

M. D. L.

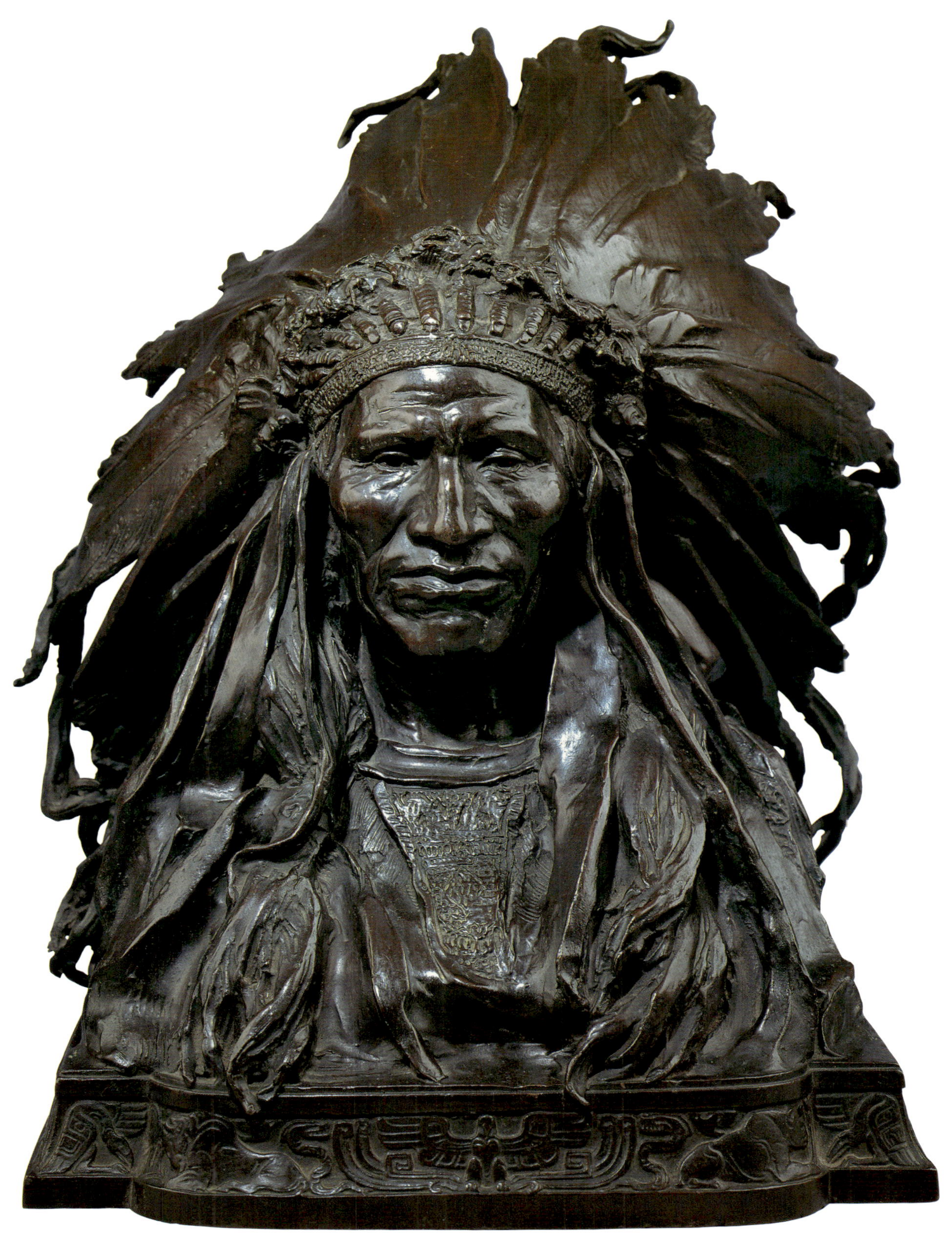

Edward Borein is best known for his small watercolors and etchings that poignantly illustrate the life of the American cowboy. This was a subject he knew very well, as he was born and raised in the typical western cowtown of San Leandro, California. As a child, Borein watched large cattle herds driven by Mexican *vaqueros* parade through town almost daily. Increasingly fascinated by the cowboy, he learned the tricks of the trade—how to set a horse, throw a rope, and drive cattle. While working as a cowhand on ranches throughout the West, Borein also began honing his skills as an artist, continually recording his personal experiences in sketches and drawings.

By 1900 Borein's interest in art drew him to Oakland, where he established a studio in his parents' home. He began work as an artist for a local paper and a story illustrator for magazines such as *Sunset*. A few years later he moved to New York City. Soon his works began appearing as illustrations for stories on the West in *Harper's*, *Collier's*, and *The Saturday Evening Post*. Looking for a way to make his work more accessible to collectors, Borein developed an interest in etching that led him to enroll in classes at the Art Students League, where his teachers included Childe Hassam and Vojtech Preissig. By the time he left New York City in 1919, he had established himself among Eastern art critics as an accomplished etcher.

Borein returned to California and in 1921 settled in Santa Barbara, where he remained for the rest of his career. Although he would continue to work and display his etchings, he began to concentrate on watercolors.

Cowboys Riding is typical of the work produced by Borein during this period. It is simple in style yet authentically characterizes the spirit and routine of cowboy life. The pale yellow, green, and brown colors clearly depict the arid environment of southern California; and Borein has accurately described cowboy dress and equipment. In *Cowboys Riding*, as in his other works, Borein painted from personal experience and always with the thought of leaving "only an accurate history of the West, nothing else but that," as he noted in a letter to a friend in 1930.

M. D. L.

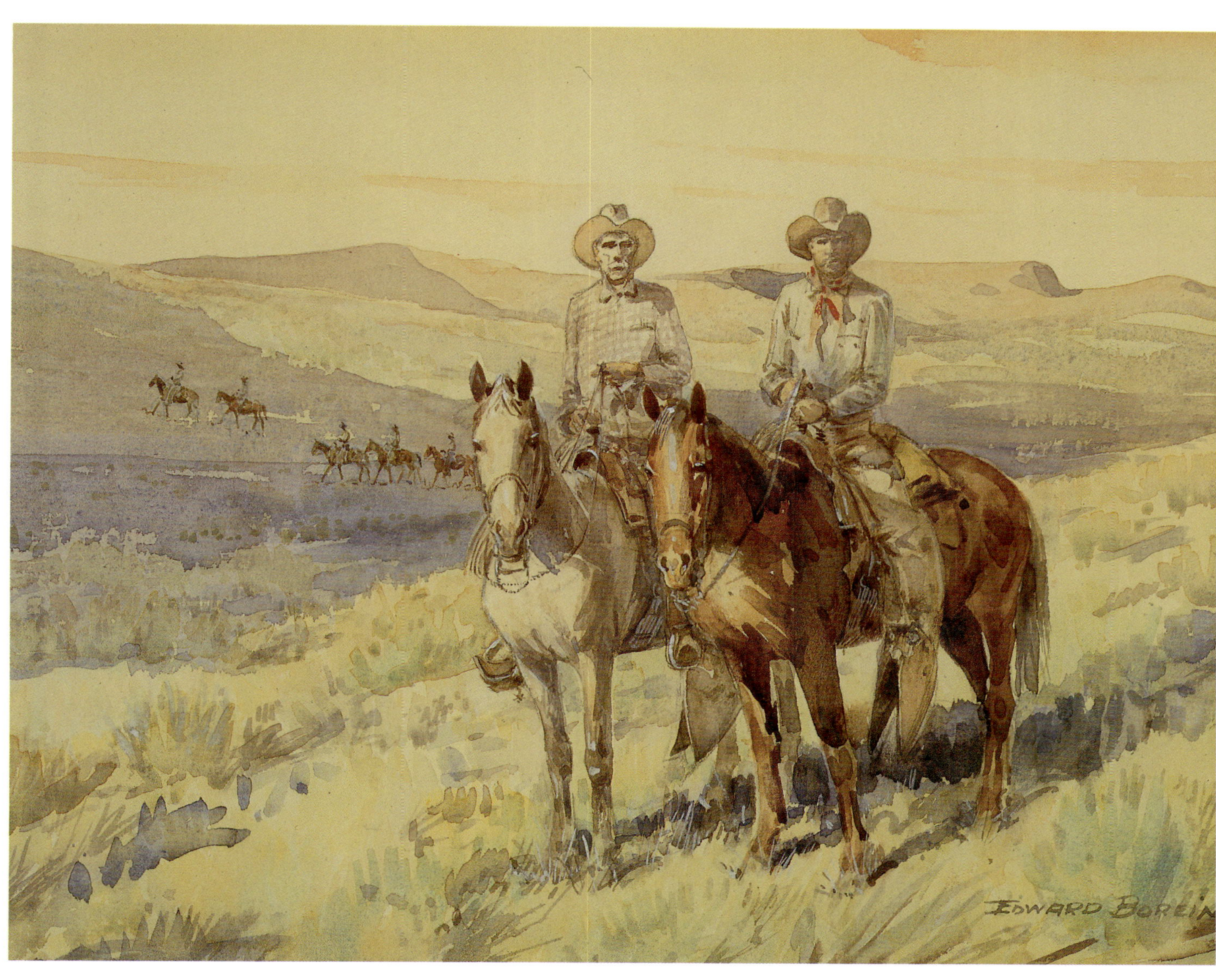

Passing Herd and Storm
1921
oil on canvas board
16 x 20 inches
signed, inscribed, and
dated ll:
MAYNARD·DIXON/
Sandhill Camp. May 1921
inscribed lr: Love to
Winona/from D.L. & M.D.
Mr. and Mrs. Jon R. Stuart

Born in the San Joaquin Valley of California, Maynard Dixon taught himself to sketch and draw. Eagerly desiring a life as an artist, he sent samples of his work to his childhood idol Frederic Remington. When Remington responded with encouragement, Dixon enrolled at the Mark Hopkins Institute of Art in San Francisco. By the middle of 1893 he had grown dissatisfied with formal art training and quit school. Over the next two years he roamed the Southwest, living the life of a cowboy. In 1895 he returned to San Francisco to work as a newspaper and magazine illustrator. After the earthquake of 1906 Dixon moved to New York City, where he successfully sold illustrations to such periodicals as *Scribner's*, *Collier's*, and *McClure's*. By 1912 he had become disillusioned with city life and the demands of magazine art editors and returned to California, where he increasingly devoted his time to easel and mural painting.

Thoroughly involved in the cultural life of San Francisco, Dixon befriended such noted Western artists as Charles Russell, Edward Borein, and Harold Von Schmidt. His apartment/studio became the gathering place for an eclectic group of artists and writers. In the 1920s and 1930s Dixon's style changed markedly. His exposure to the tenets of modernism and his heightened awareness of social concerns resulted in paintings that emphasized man's relationship to the land, particularly the desert Southwest. His paintings were now characterized by simplified architectural forms, strong compositions, and a vibrant palette— a combination of cubism and realism.

In 1939 Dixon and his third wife, artist Edith Hamlin, gave up their California home and moved to Tucson, Arizona, where Dixon continued to work on both easel paintings and murals until his death in 1946.

Passing Herd and Storm is typical of Dixon's work up to the early 1920s. In this impressionistic rendering of a trail drive, Dixon has placed the trail riders and herd far back on the horizon, thus giving greater compositional importance to the vast Southwestern landscape and passing storm.

R. B. T.

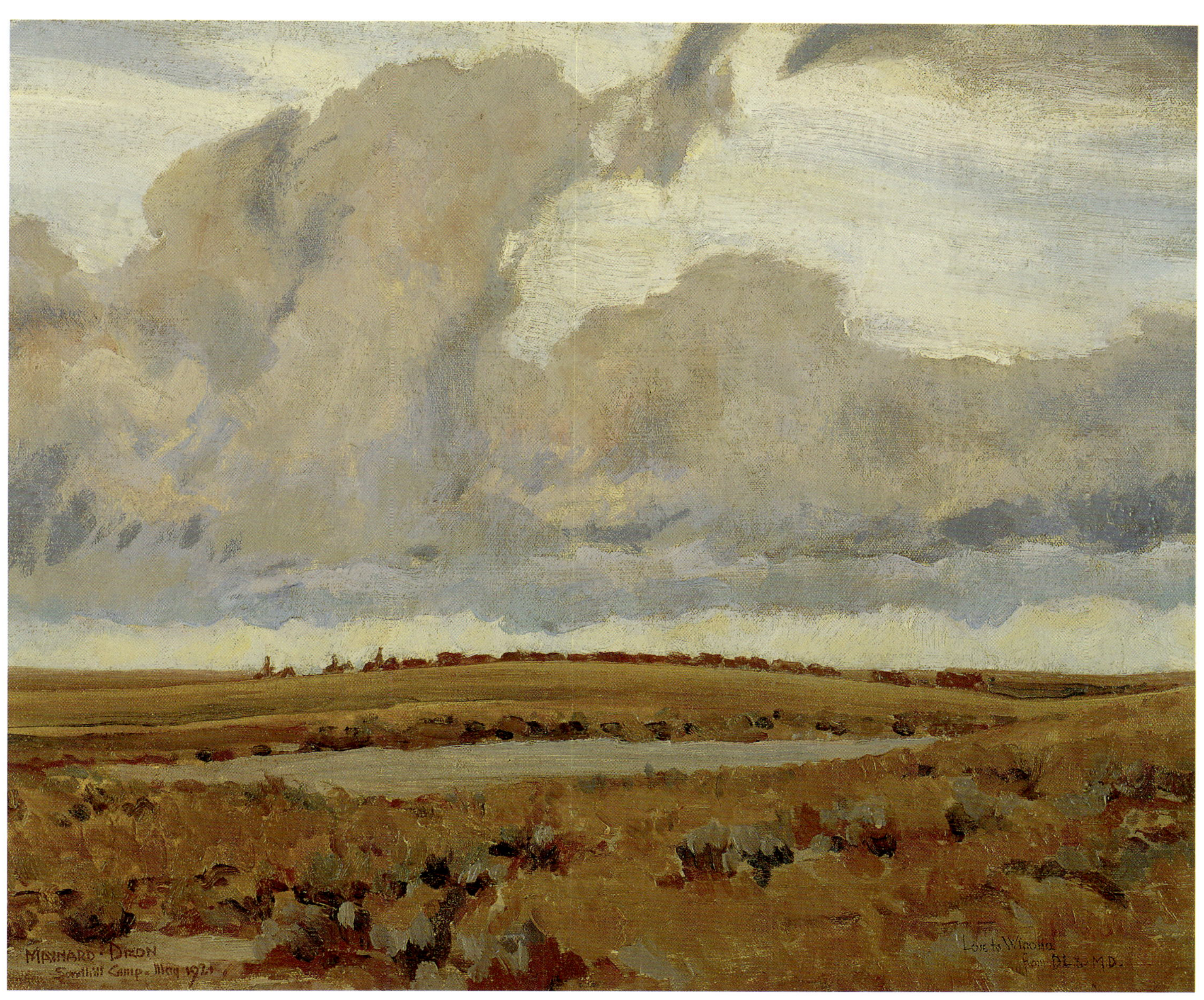

Walter Ufer
1876-1936

Angling, Early Autumn
oil on canvas
25 x 30 inches
signed ll: wufer
Mr. and Mrs. Jon R. Stuart

Walter Ufer was born in Louisville, Kentucky, of German immigrant parents. He first studied art with his father, a skilled steel engraver, and then at seventeen began an apprenticeship with a lithographer in Hamburg, Germany. After three years of study in Hamburg and Dresden, Ufer returned to Louisville and began a career as a graphic artist. In 1900, determined to concentrate exclusively on fine art, he went to Chicago to study; he later studied in Munich. When his work was displayed in Chicago upon his return from Germany in 1914, it attracted the attention of former mayor Carter H. Harrison. In exchange for finished works, Harrison and a group of his friends subsidized several yearly trips to Taos for Ufer and his wife. In 1917 Ufer was invited to join the Taos Society of Artists. For the remainder of his life, Ufer divided his time among Chicago, New York, and Taos.

Once Ufer had been introduced to the New Mexico landscape and cultures, he focused primarily on portraits and genre studies of the local Native Americans. He quickly abandoned his dark Munich palette for the lighter and brighter colors of the Southwest, and he built his compositions with short, bold brush strokes and thick, rich pigments. In this quiet landscape composition, the lone figure of a Southwest Indian is an integral part of the forest.

M. K. D.

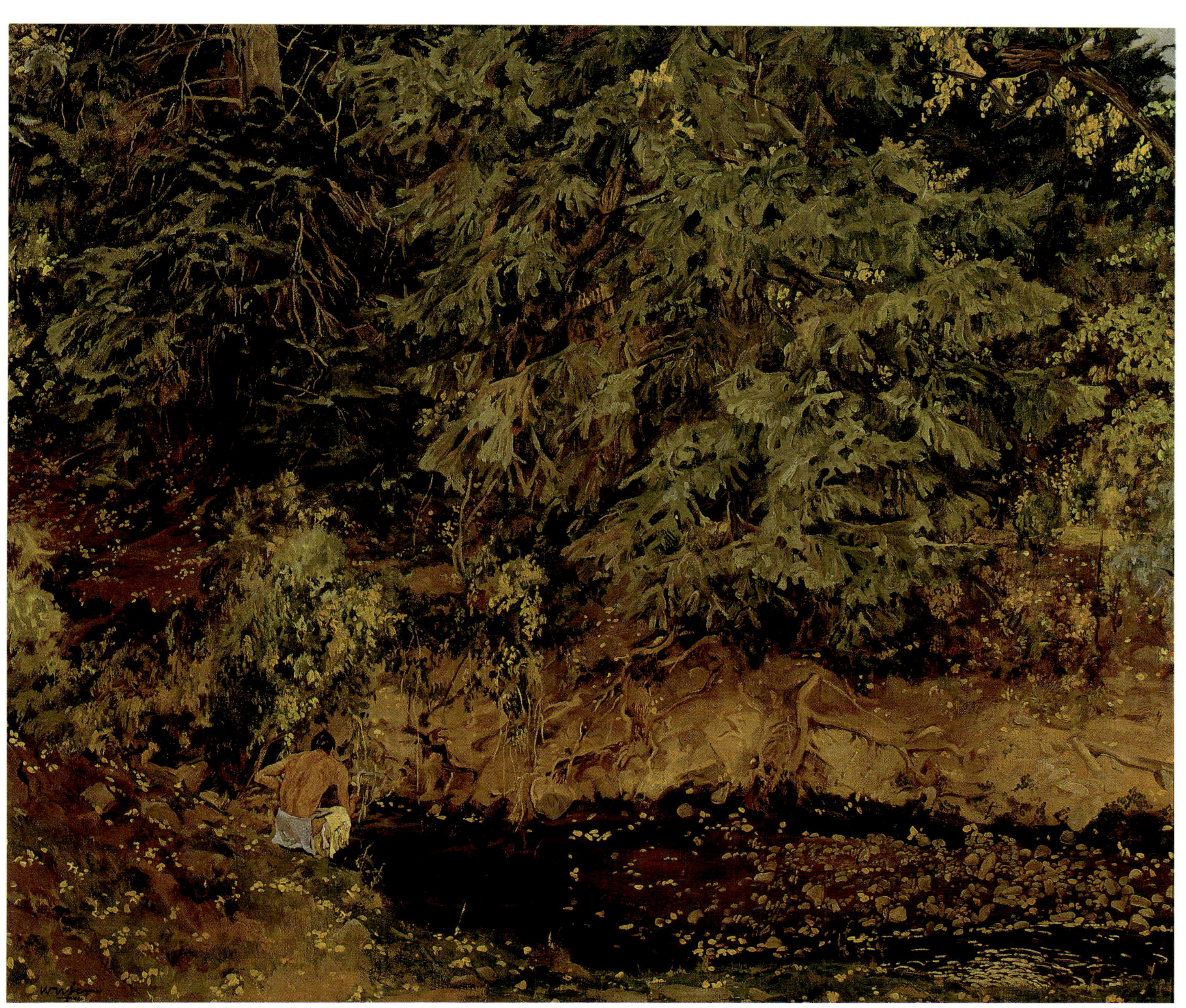

The Scouts
1911
watercolor and gouache
on board
14 x 22 1/2 inches
signed and dated lr:
O.C.SELTZER./1911
K. S. "Bud" Adams, Jr.

252

Born in Denmark in 1877, Olaf Carl Seltzer migrated while a teenager to Great Falls, Montana, with his mother. Although he had trained early as an artist at the Danish Art School in Copenhagen, he worked in Montana as a cowboy and railroad machinist. He continued to paint as a hobby and was encouraged by his neighbor, Charles M. Russell, whose style he greatly admired and emulated. When he was forty-four, he turned his attention full time to painting. Like Russell, he had a great interest in Northern Plains Indians and strove to portray them in their ordinary pursuits before the coming of Europeans to the mountains.

M. W. D.

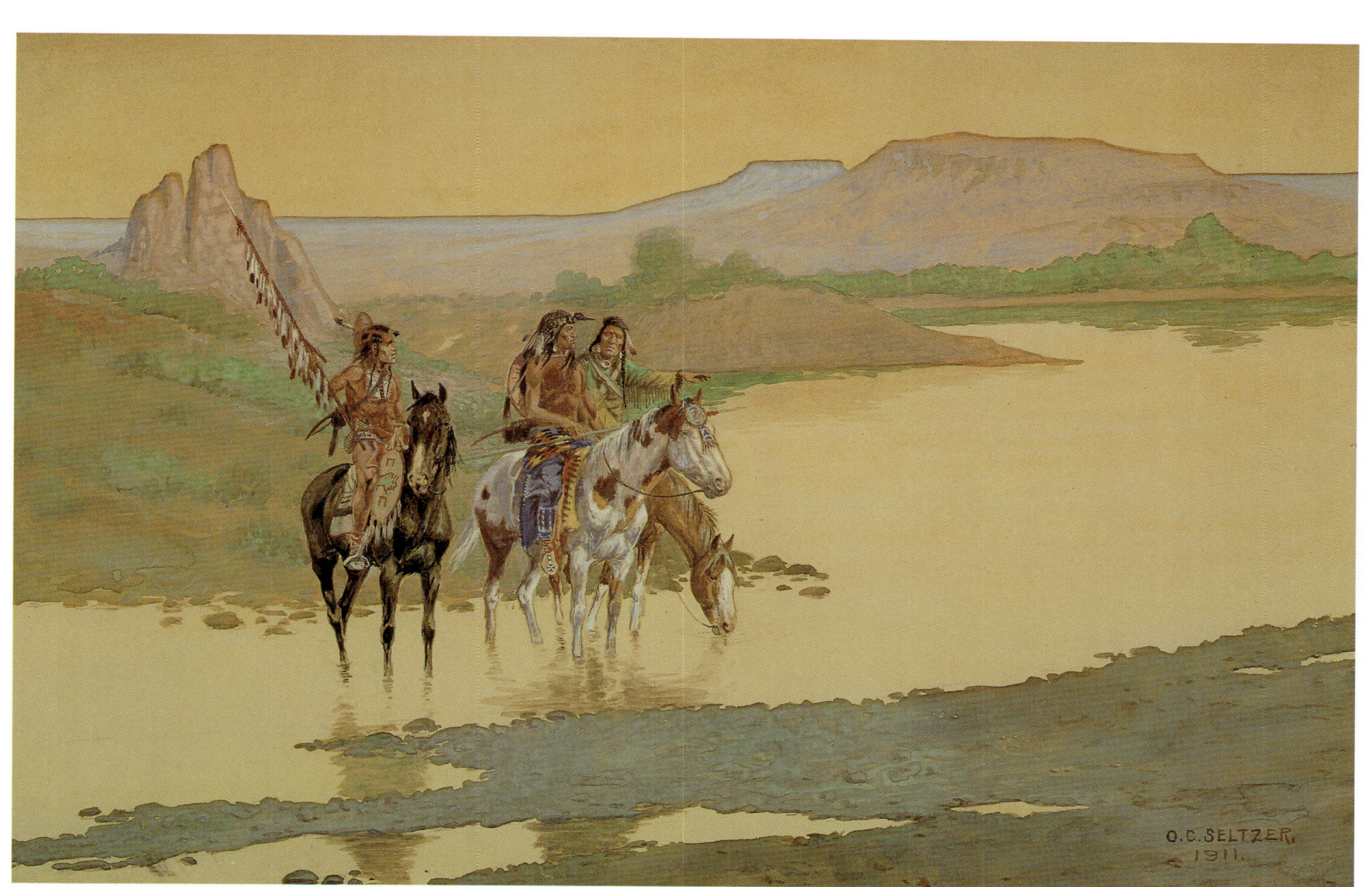
O.C.SELTZER
1911

Olaf Carl Seltzer
1877-1957

Scouting Party
watercolor on board
10 x 15 inches
signed ll: O.C.SELTZER.
K. S. "Bud" Adams, Jr.

Seltzer was greatly influenced by Russell in both style and subject. Russell, in fact, was one of his staunchest supporters and often said that he had learned as much from Seltzer about the proper use of color as Seltzer had learned from him about other aspects of Western painting. In general, Seltzer's palette was brighter than Russell's, and his later work shows more mastery of draftsmanship than his mentor's.

M. W. D.

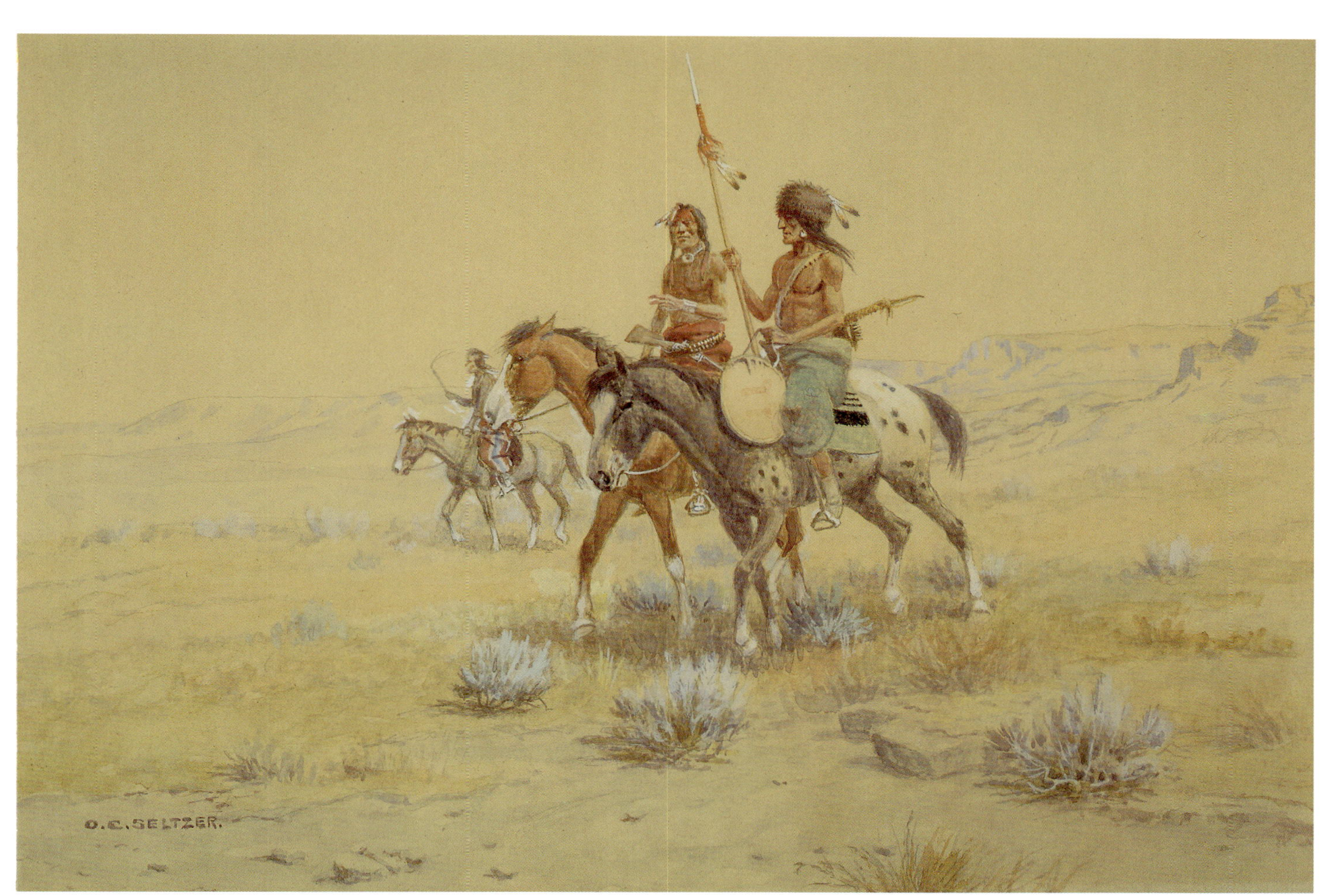

Olaf Carl Seltzer
1877-1957

Prairie Sentinel
watercolor on board
12 x 16 3/4 inches
signed lr: O.C.SELTZER.
K. S. "Bud" Adams, Jr.

Seltzer often chose to portray individual Indians with careful attention to the authenticity of dress and possessions. Likely as not the objects in his paintings were drawn from his studio collection. They often were reminders of an earlier time, but aspects of the cultures they reflect were still much in evidence during Seltzer's years in Montana.

M. W. D.

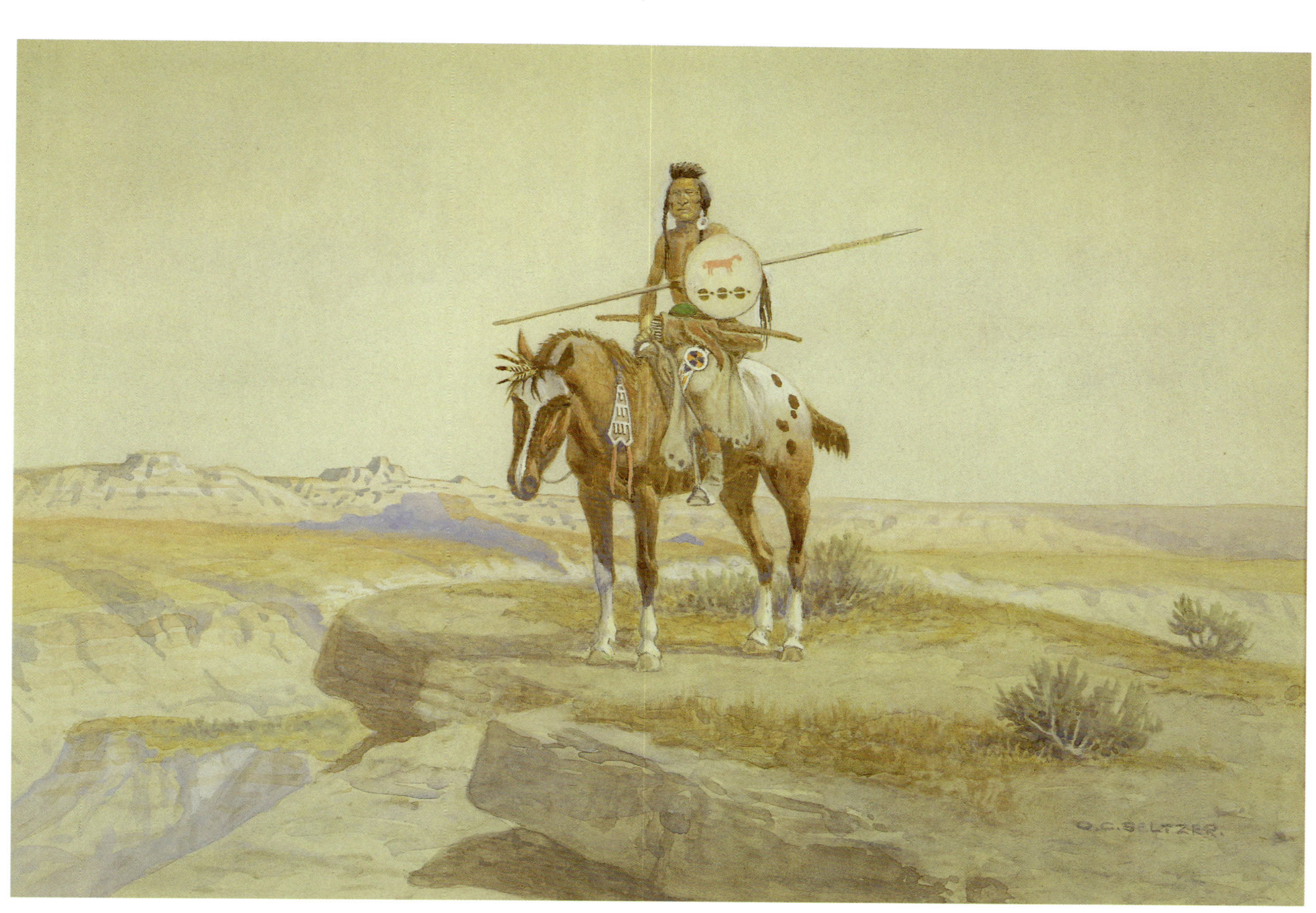

Olaf Carl Seltzer
1877–1957

Untitled
c. 1925
watercolor on paper
10 x 14 inches
signed ll: O.C.SELTZER.
Mr. and Mrs. Jon R. Stuart

While he did not turn to painting as an occupation until rather late in life, Seltzer found success almost immediately. Perhaps due in part to the great popularity of his mentor, Charles Russell, who died five years after Seltzer entered art as a career, Seltzer's works were consistently in demand. Focusing almost entirely on the people of Montana, both American Indians and European settlers, Seltzer's work can be seen as a visual history of the rapidly vanishing "Old West."

M. W. D.

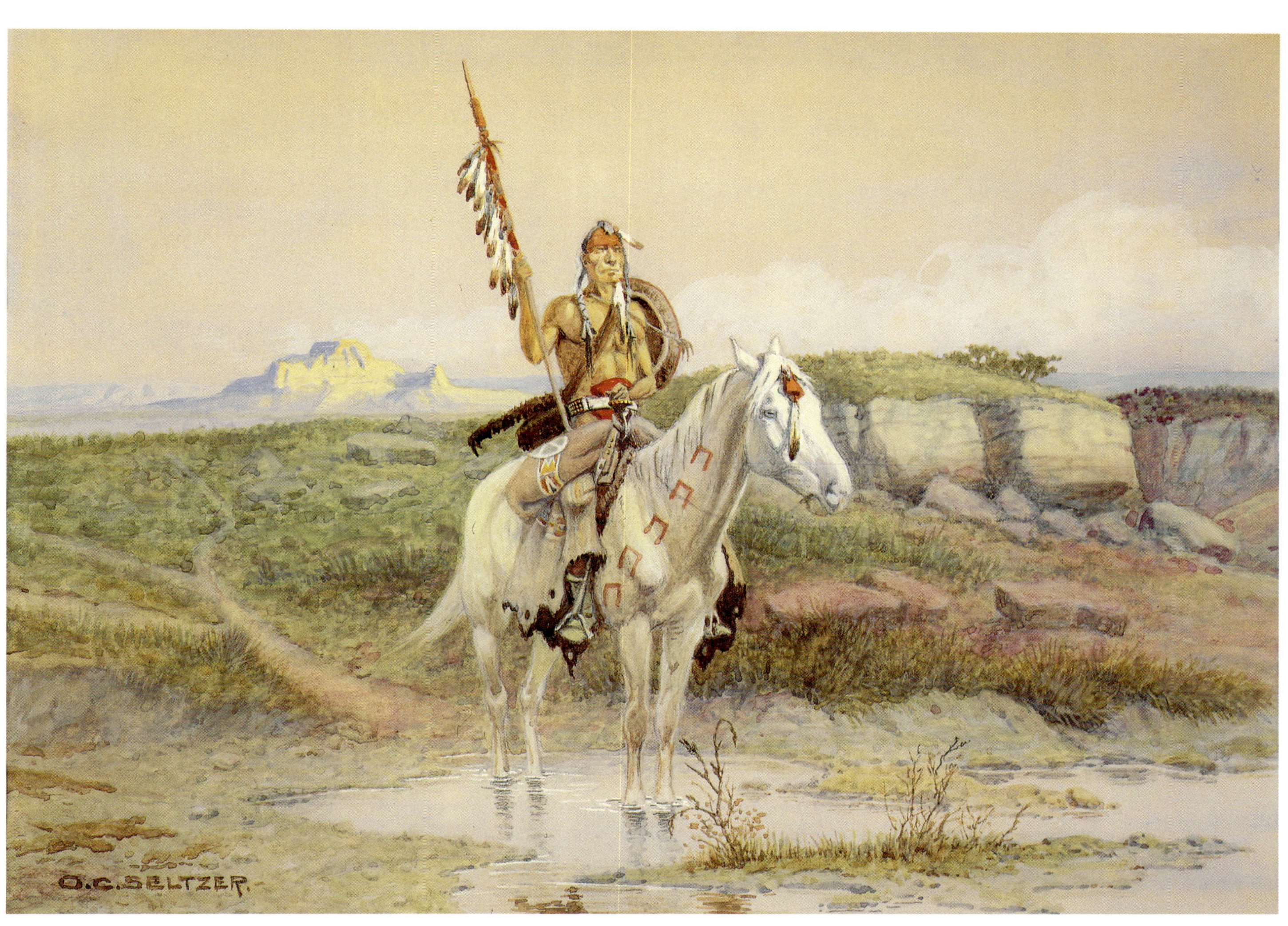
O.C.SELTZER.

E. William Gollings
1878-1932

Roping a Steer
oil on canvas
30 x 23 inches
signed lr: Gollings
K. S. "Bud" Adams, Jr.

Born in Idaho, near his father's mining camp, William Gollings was raised in rural Michigan and New York by his grandmother. When his father remarried, eight-year-old Gollings rejoined him in Idaho; in 1890 they moved to Chicago. As a child Gollings industriously studied Frederic Remington's magazine illustrations in *Harper's Weekly*, and he continually drew cowboys and horses on his slate. In 1896 Gollings left his family to slowly work his way back west; he held a variety of jobs, though much of the time he worked as a sheepherder or cowboy. In 1903, at age twenty-five, he taught himself to paint with oils after ordering a set by mail from Montgomery Ward. He then studied briefly at the Chicago Academy of Fine Arts, where he won a scholarship for composition. For several years he divided his time between painting and working as a cowhand, but by 1909 he could support himself full time as an artist. He spent the rest of his life painting genre scenes of cowboys and cattle ranch life in Wyoming.

In his painting of a subject familiar to all cowhands, Gollings has captured a very dynamic moment. Strong diagonals intersect on the surface of the painting as well as in space—the straining body of the steer, the taut ropes, the steer's shadow, and the angles of the two horses. The high horizon puts the viewer in the immediate foreground, watching a second lasso about to encircle the steer's head.

M. K. D.

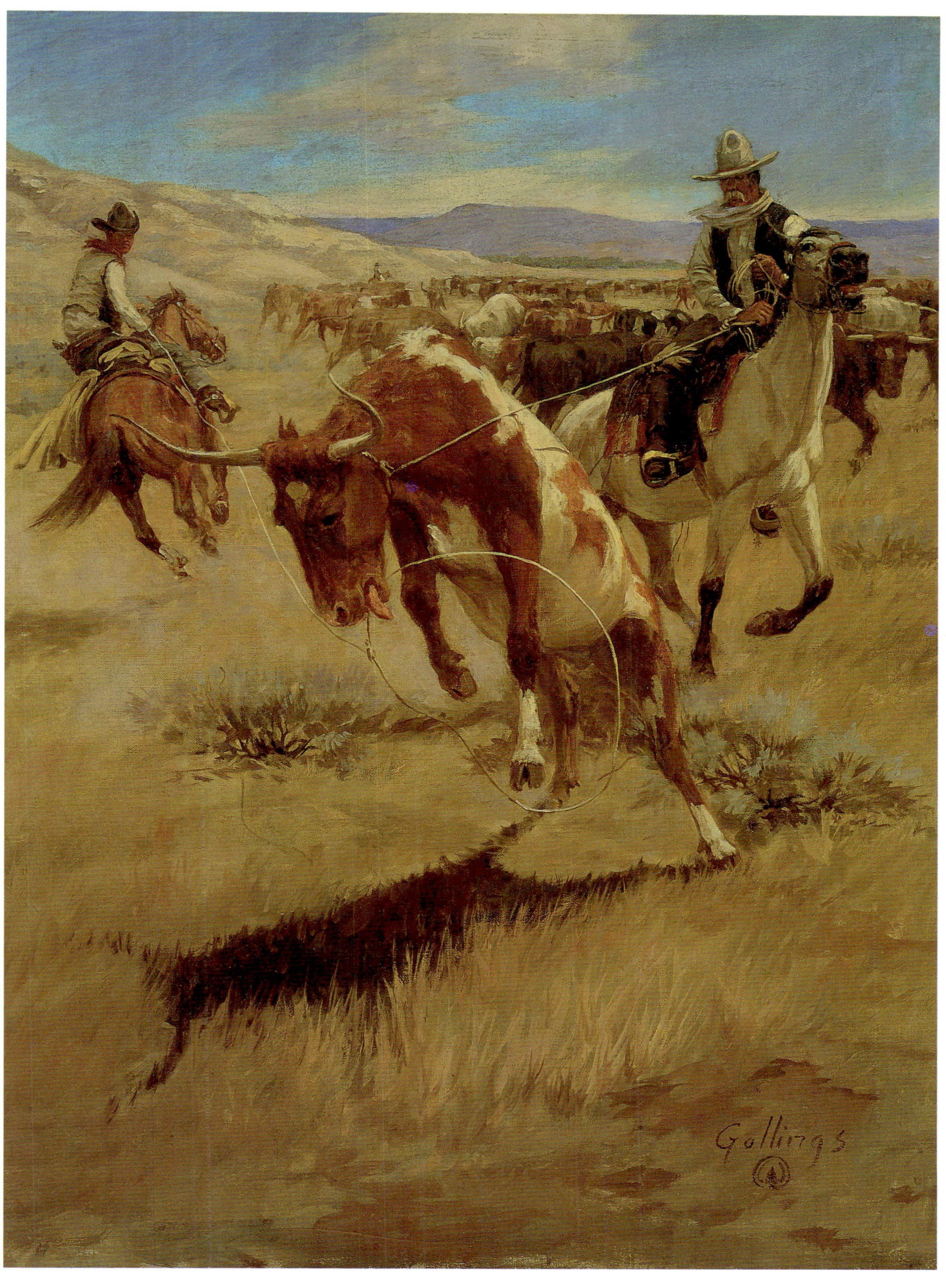
Gollings

Cowpuncher
oil on board
14 x 14 inches
signed ll:
W. Herbert DunTon
Mr. and Mrs. Jon R. Stuart

262

While William Herbert Dunton was growing up in Maine, his life was dominated by a keen interest in the American West and a great love of the outdoors. When he was sixteen he quit school and took a job in order to save enough money to finance a trip west. In 1897, after spending a year in the West, where he worked as a cowboy and hunter, he returned to the East and settled in Boston. He enrolled in the Cowles School of Art, where he studied with Andreas M. Andersen, William Ladd Taylor, and Joseph Rodefer DeCamp. By the turn of the century Dunton's career as an illustrator was well underway, and he had made several more trips west. In 1911 he attended the Art Students League under the tutelage of Frederick Coffay Yohn, Frank Vincent DuMond, and Ernest Blumenschein.

By 1912 Dunton had grown increasingly dissatisfied with illustration as a career and had discussed his feelings and options with Blumenschein. Upon the recommendation of Blumenschein, Dunton visited Taos, New Mexico. Two years later he moved there permanently. After his move to Taos Dunton only occasionally painted commissioned illustrations, and in the early 1920s he gave it up completely.

The striking natural light and breathtaking scenery of New Mexico proved an irresistible attraction for Dunton. With other artists who were also drawn to New Mexico—among them Oscar Berninghaus, Blumenschein, Eanger Irving Couse, Bert Geer Phillips, and Joseph Henry Sharp—he founded the Taos Society of Artists in 1915.

While his colleagues in the Taos Society often portrayed local Hispanics and Native Americans in their work, Dunton remained true to his interest in the Old West, albeit in a less narrative style. Dunton scholars have noted that his early Taos paintings are characterized by a heightened awareness and use of light, a brightened palette, and a more deliberate brush stroke, perhaps reflecting the influence of French impressionism and the growing interest in plein-air painting. *Cowpuncher*, probably a composition for a larger painting, is typical of Dunton's work during this period, which features figurative images, centered on the canvas against a sunlit landscape. *Cowpuncher* is a tribute to the hardy, self-confident men Dunton identified as the settlers of the Old West.

R. B. T.

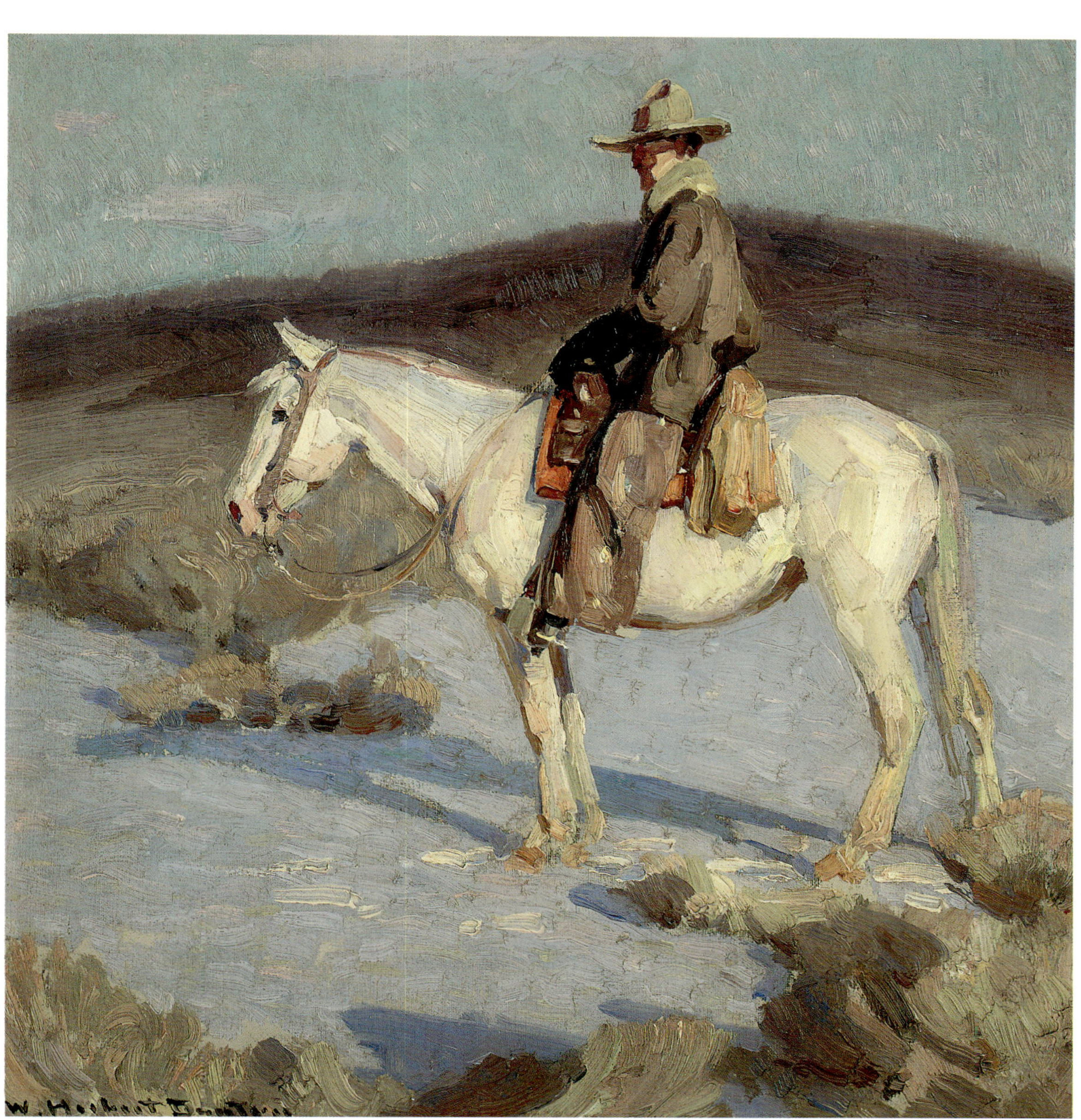

W. Herbert Dunton
1878–1936

Composition for
"Black Bear and Aspens"
c. 1928
oil on canvas
14 x 14 inches
signed ll: DunTon
Mr. and Mrs. Jon R. Stuart

The work of the last decade of Dunton's life is characterized by a shift in style away from the bright plein-air work of his early Taos years. He completed these carefully composed renderings in his studio, using simplified forms, repetitive patterns, and bold color.

During this period Dunton returned to a subject that had fascinated him throughout his life—the bear. His large bear paintings include *Mother Bear and Three Cubs*, *Timberline*, *The Mountain Mother*, and *Fall in the Foothills*, all completed in the early 1930s. *Fall in the Foothills* would eventually be chosen by Franklin Delano Roosevelt to hang in the White House. *Composition for "Black Bear and Aspens"* is a preparatory work for a larger canvas completed in 1933. The deep, rich colors and soft forms create gentle curvilinear rhythms throughout this small painting. The effect is a harmonious image that combines both grace and boldness in Dunton's distinctive style.

R. B. T.

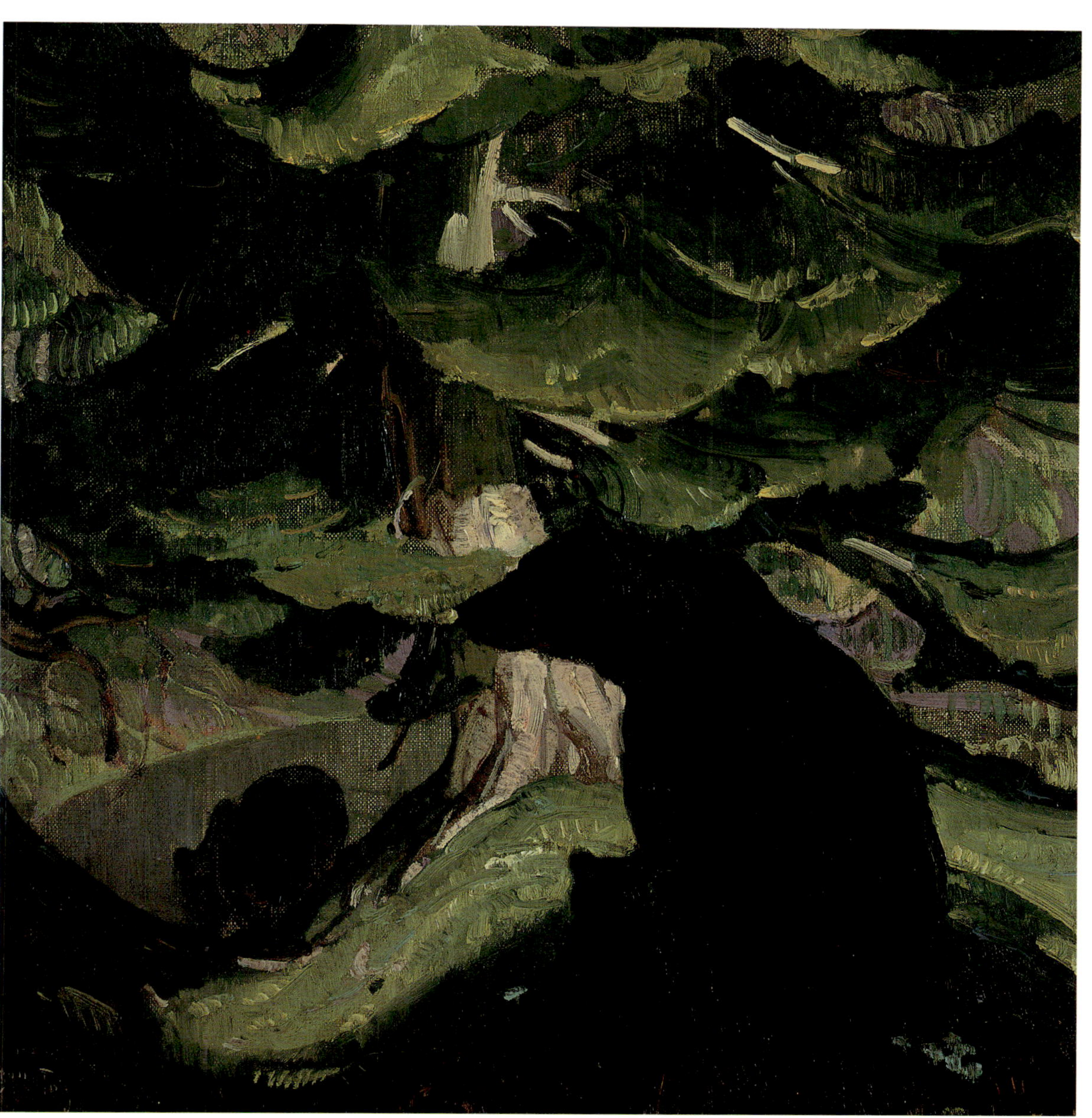

W. H. D. Koerner
1878-1938

Lumbertown Sheriff
1934
oil on canvas
30 x 42 inches (vignette)
signed mr: WHDK
Phillip M. Knox,
Class of 1966

William Henry Dethlef Koerner was born in Lunden, Germany, and grew up in Clinton, Iowa, where his family emigrated in 1880. His career began in 1896 when he was hired by the *Chicago Tribune* as a staff artist at the weekly salary of five dollars. He attended the Art Institute of Chicago School of Art and the Francis Smith Art Academy. In 1905 he moved to New York City to attend the Art Students League and two years later moved to Wilmington, Delaware, to study with Howard Pyle. His fellow students in Wilmington included Harvey Dunn, Frank Schoonover, and N. C. Wyeth.

From 1910 to 1935 Koerner's illustrations appeared in all the leading magazines, but the majority, over 1,500, were painted for *The Saturday Evening Post*. Koerner often utilized the vignette technique. Vignettes—uncluttered, borderless paintings in which the colors fade toward the edges—serve as design elements used to break up the flow of text on the page. *Lumbertown Sheriff* is a vignette Koerner painted to illustrate John P. Marquand's "Winner Takes All," a story serialized in five issues of *The Saturday Evening Post* in 1934.

R. B. T.

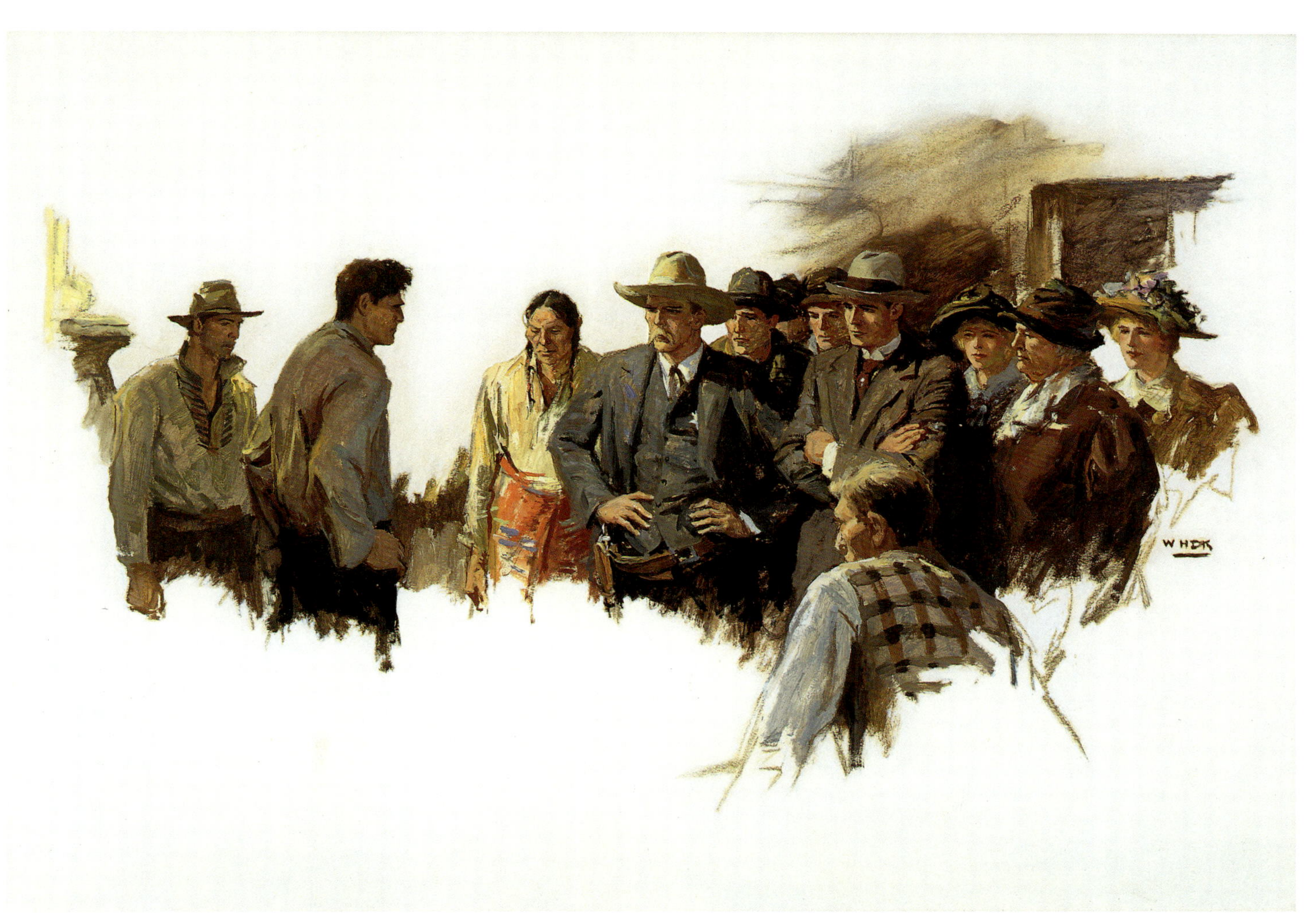

Leon Gaspard
1882-1964

Aspen Trees and Taos Indians
oil on canvas board
20 x 15 inches
signed ll: Leon Gaspard
Mr. and Mrs. Jon R. Stuart

Leon Gaspard was born in Vitebsk, a large town west of Moscow. As a young boy he accompanied his father, a retired Russian army officer, on fur-trading trips to Siberia and drew little sketches of the people and scenes about him. In Vitebsk Gaspard and fellow student Marc Chagall trained under Julius Penn. He also studied in Odessa and Moscow before going to Paris, where he studied at the Académie Julian. His first one-man show resulted in the purchase of thirty-five sketches by a New York collector.

During World War I Gaspard was seriously injured while acting as an aerial observer for the French aviation corps. In 1916, after a long recuperative process, Gaspard joined his wife in New York City. Because of his poor health, Gaspard's doctor recommended a warmer climate. Gaspard and his wife moved to Santa Fe, New Mexico, where his love for the country returned. In the summer of 1918 the Gaspards moved once again, this time to Taos. Gaspard found the combination of mountains and deserts, Indians and Hispanic villagers to be a beautiful and colorful subject for his canvas.

Gaspard's palette is bright with free, loose brushwork that creates a freshness throughout his oeuvre. In *Aspen Trees and Taos Indians* he depicts a dense forest in a variety of green hues. The vegetation is created with sweeping brushwork that gives it a vibrant, alive look. The small Indian figures provide a sense of scale that creates a feeling of monumentality in this small piece. Here as in many other works, Gaspard captures a fleeting moment and gives it a sense of time and place.

J. L. C.

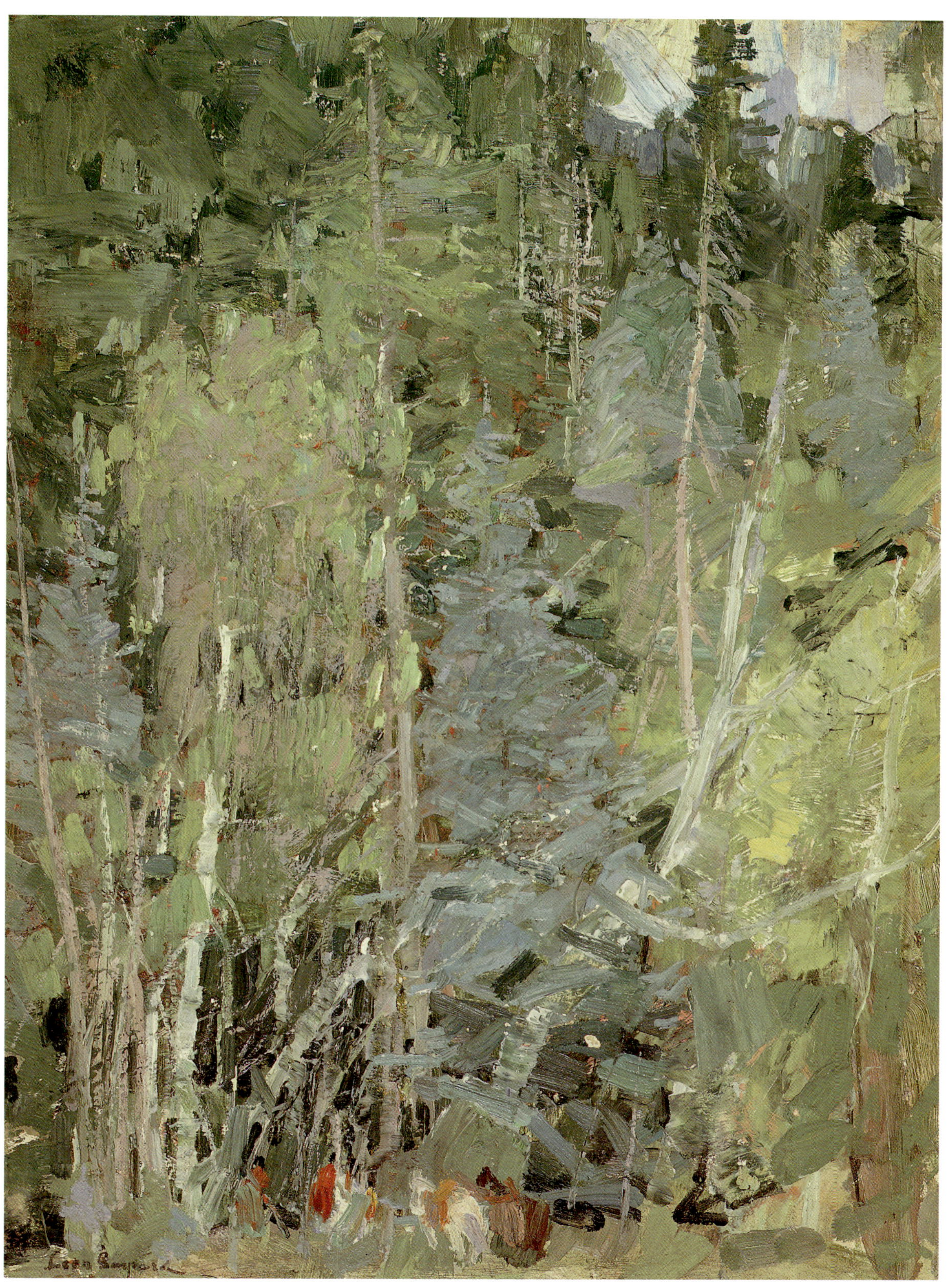

*"Nothing Would Escape Their
Black, Jewel-Like, Inscrutable
Eyes" (The Guardians)*
1911
oil on canvas
46 1/4 x 37 1/8 inches
signed ll: N.C.WYETH
The Warner Collection
Tuscaloosa, Alabama

270

Newell Convers Wyeth, patriarch of the artistic Wyeth family, was one of America's foremost, and most prolific, illustrators. Wyeth studied with Howard Pyle in Wilmington, Delaware, and later in Chadds Ford, Pennsylvania, in the Brandywine River valley. Among his fellow students were such noted artists as Harvey Dunn, W. H. D. Koerner, and Frank Schoonover.

Fascinated by the myth of the American West, and undoubtedly influenced by the illustrations of Frederic Remington, Wyeth in his early works depicted the people and places of the rough-and-tumble frontier. In both 1904 and 1906 Wyeth traveled west to research picture assignments for *The Saturday Evening Post* and *Scribner's Magazine*. The memories and experiences of these trips, plus a collection of props, provided him with a wealth of inspirational material that lasted for the remainder of his career. He produced in excess of three thousand illustrations for magazine articles, books, calendars, advertisements, and murals. This painting is one of two that were commissioned by *Harper's Monthly Magazine* in 1911 to illustrate Gouverneur Morris's tale "Growing Up."

R. B. T.

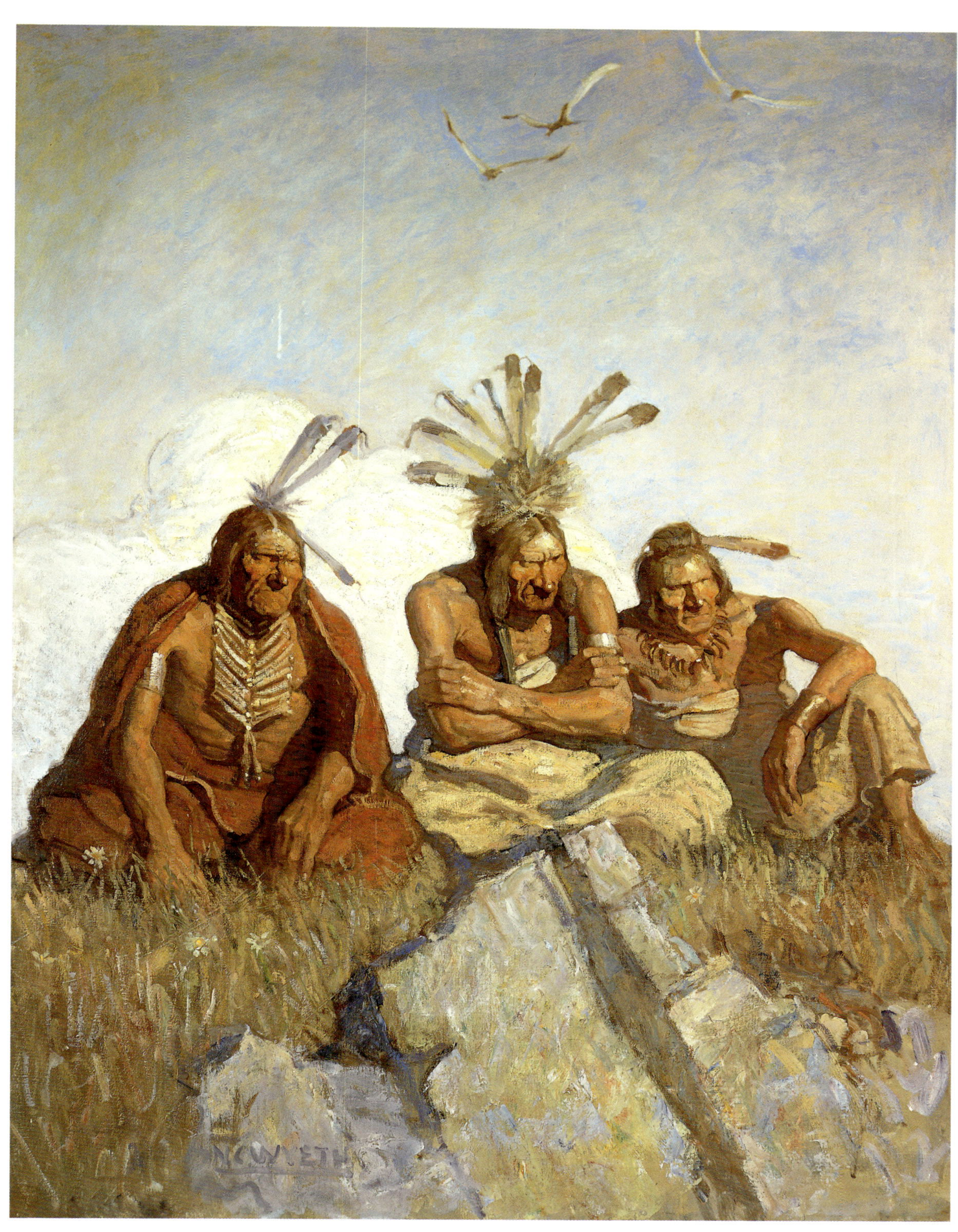

Edgar Alwin Payne
1883–1947

Lake Louise, Canada
c. 1929
oil on canvas
20 x 24 inches
signed ll:
EDGAR PAYNE
Mr. and Mrs. Jon R. Stuart

Edgar Payne left his native Washburn, Missouri, at an early age and drifted from place to place, working as a house and sign painter. By 1907 he had landed in Chicago, where he studied for a short time at the Art Institute School of Art and began making a living painting stage scenery and department store backdrops.

Best known for his majestic Western landscape paintings, Payne made his first trip to the West between 1909 and 1911. He settled in California, where he married Elsie Palmer, an aspiring young artist. His biggest achievement during this period was a large series of decorative canvases for the Congress Hotel in Chicago, which he painted in Glendale, California, with the help of several artist friends.

The couple moved for a short time to Chicago, where together they painted murals for theaters, courthouses, and civic buildings throughout the Midwest. One of their earliest surviving works was commissioned for the Hendricks County Courthouse in Danville, Indiana. The mural, a depiction of the liberation of Vincennes, Indiana, was completed in 1913 and still hangs on the south wall of the Circuit Courtroom. (Another mural done by the Paynes was commissioned for the Clay County Courthouse in Brazil, Indiana.)

The Paynes moved back to California around 1915 and eventually established a studio in Laguna Beach. Although the couple traveled extensively throughout the United States and Europe, California remained home. For the next thirty-five years, Edgar played a prominent role in the evolution of Western landscape painting. He won several distinguished awards, including the 1920 Martin Cahn Prize from the Art Institute of Chicago, an honorable mention in the 1923 Paris salon, and the 1928 Ranger Fund Purchase Award. He was also instrumental in the establishment of the Laguna Art Gallery (now the Laguna Beach Art Museum) and served as the Laguna Art Association's first president.

Payne's affinity for the majestic mountain scenery and his mature mastery as a landscape artist are readily apparent in the painting *Lake Louise, Canada*. While it vividly projects the rugged, formidable solitude of such places, the painting also reveals Payne's technical skills, which range from intricate designs and linear patterns to the broad, bold impressionistic brush strokes seen in this painting.

M. D. L.

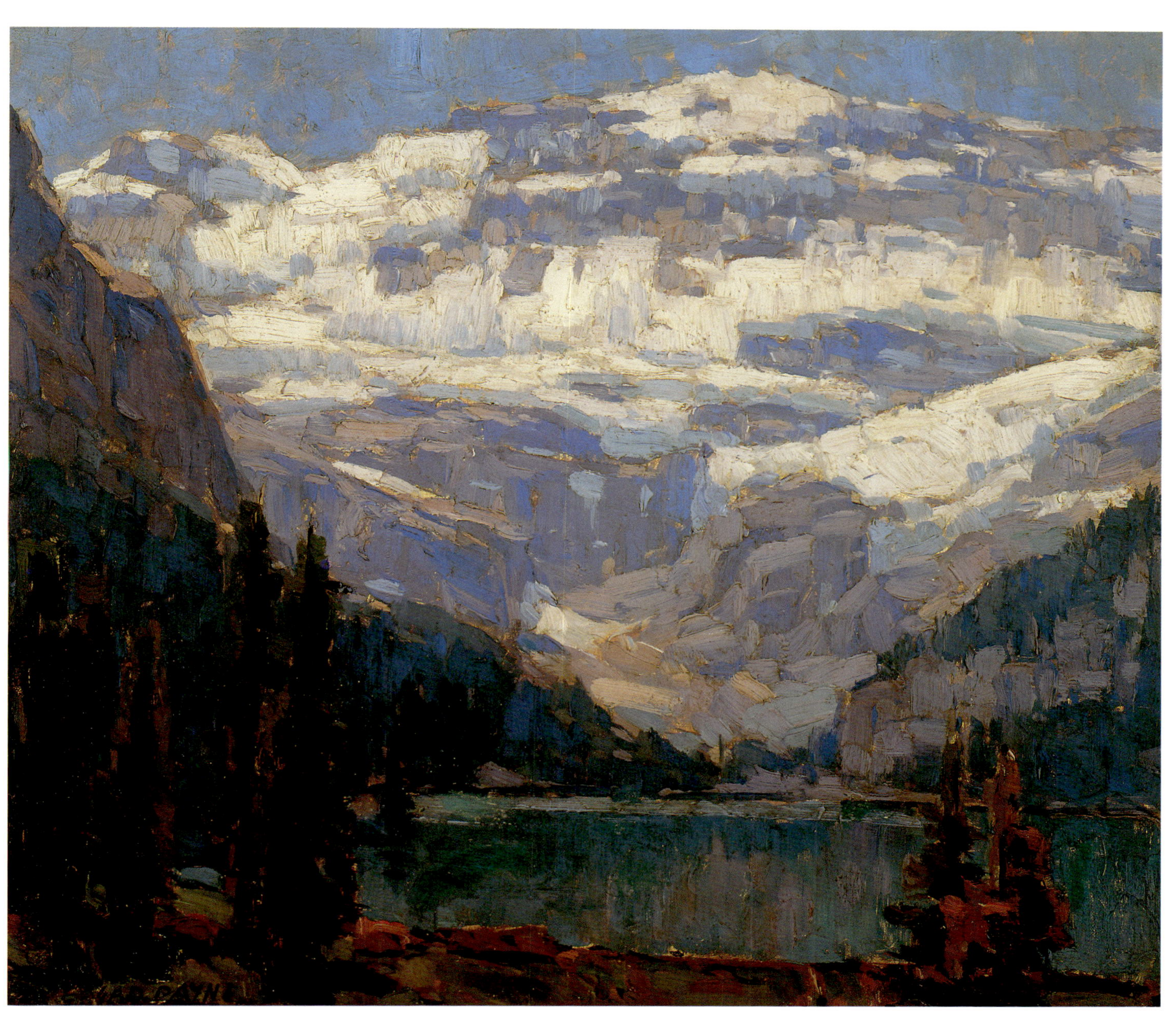

Edgar Alwin Payne
1883–1947

Arizona Sky
c. 1935
oil on canvas
25 x 30 inches
signed ll:
EDGAR PAYNE
Mr. and Mrs. Jon R. Stuart

In 1916 Payne received a commission from the Atchison, Topeka and Santa Fe Railroad to depict the scenic landscape along the company's southwestern route. It was during this time, with his numerous treks into New Mexico and Arizona, that Payne began to experiment with color and technique.

As illustrated in *Arizona Sky*, Payne often successfully combined in his works a number of painterly approaches. Here the sky is brushed in bold strokes and is projected as part of the foreground. The contrast of shadows and intense light plus the intricate patterns of the landscape provide a strong linear presence. The four riders serve to highlight the scale and the spatial connection between land and sky.

Among Payne's many accomplishments are an important book on landscape painting, *The Composition of Outdoor Painting*, published in 1941, and a documentary film, *Sierra Journey*, about his beloved mountains. The film draws on his experience and knowledge of the mountains and his appreciation as an artist of their grandeur and beauty.

M. D. L.

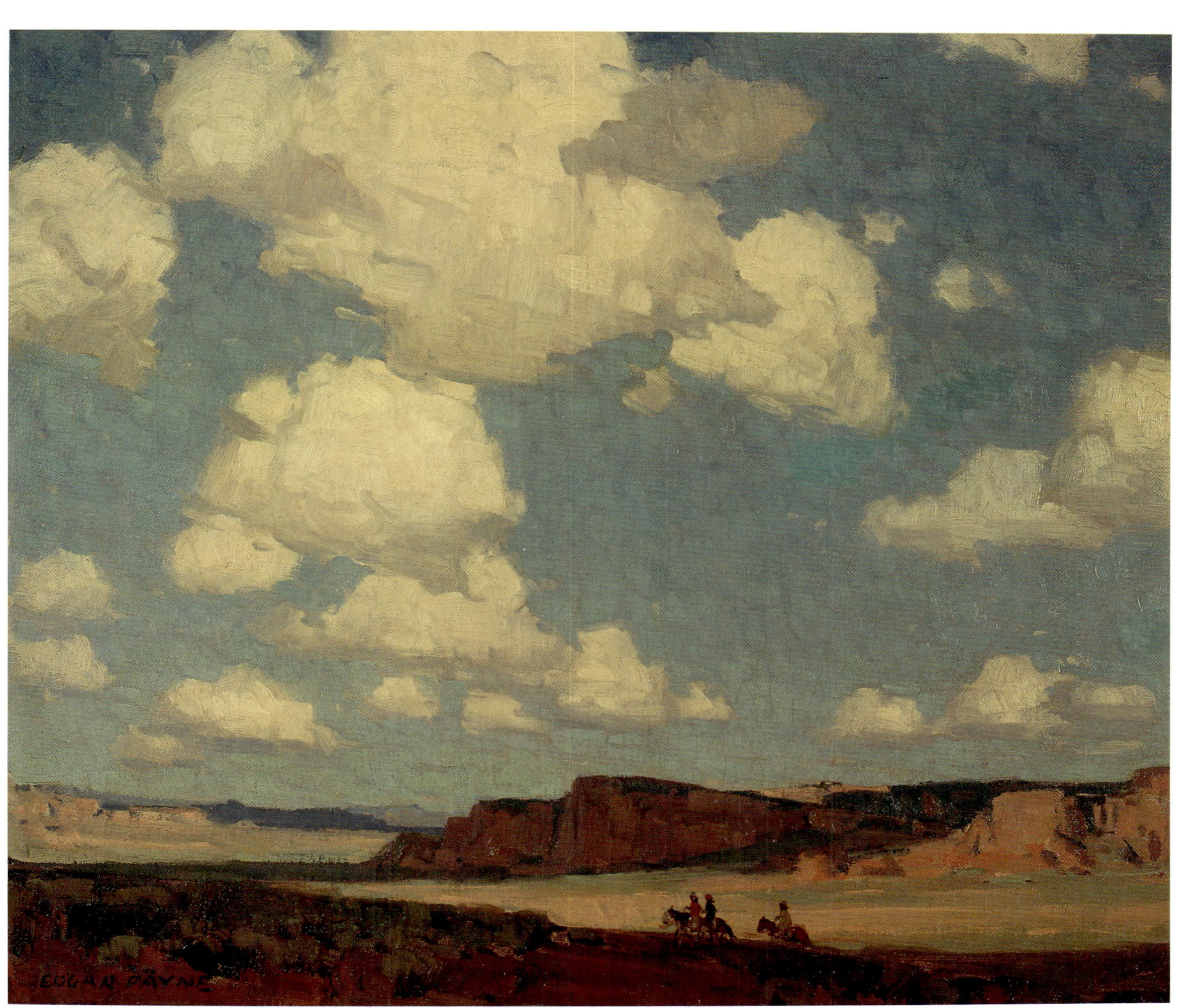

E. Martin Hennings
1886-1956

Land of Enchantment
oil on canvas
16 x 20 1/4 inches
signed ll:
E Martin Hennings
K. S. "Bud" Adams, Jr.

Ernest Martin Hennings was one of the last artists to become a member of the Taos Society of Artists. He was born in Penns Grove, New Jersey, to a family that had emigrated from Germany; two years later the family moved to Chicago. Hennings showed an early aptitude for drawing, and a visit to the Art Institute of Chicago when he was thirteen so captivated him that he was determined to become a professional artist. After graduating with honors from the Institute's School of Art, he briefly tried a career in commercial art, but this proved unsatisfactory. He toured Europe, spending several months studying at the Munich Academy with fellow Chicagoans Victor Higgins and Walter Ufer, but was forced to return home in 1915 because of World War I. Hennings's subsequent success in Chicago attracted the attention of the former mayor, Carter H. Harrison, who offered to sponsor his travel to Taos, New Mexico, in exchange for some paintings. (Harrison had previously made the same arrangements with Higgins and Ufer.) In 1921 Hennings moved permanently to Taos, and, three years later, joined the Taos Society of Artists. Until his death at age seventy, most of his paintings focused on the landscape and people of northern New Mexico.

In this panoramic sweep of sage-covered desert, mountains, and sky, Hennings conveys his love of the unique Southwestern landscape. The brilliant sunlight and ever-changing clouds provided endless poetry and drama for his work. Hennings preferred to work outdoors and added only the final details back in his studio.

M. K. D.

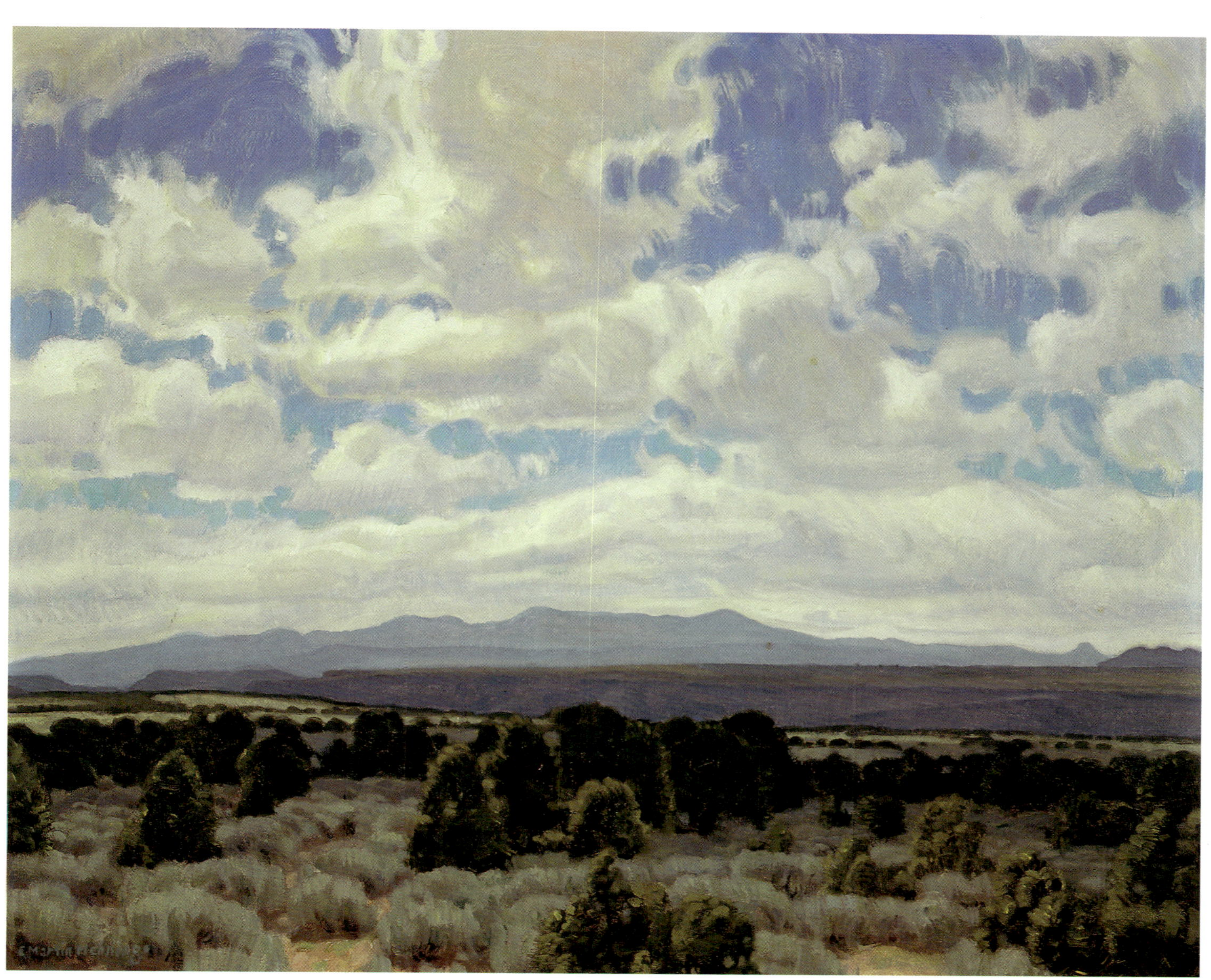

Kenneth Pauling Riley
b. 1919

Welcome Shade
1980
oil on board
40 x 24 inches
signed and dated ll:
Kenneth Riley/1980/©
K. S. "Bud" Adams, Jr.

Kenneth Pauling Riley, raised in small towns in Missouri and Kansas, spent many weekends and summers at the farm of his maternal grandparents. At the age of fourteen, he took his first arts and crafts class from Olive Rees, who in 1938 was instrumental in his enrolling in a three-year program at the Kansas City Art Institute. There he met MarCyne Johnson, a fellow art student, whom he married in 1941 after receiving a scholarship to attend the Art Students League in New York City. After one year of study he enlisted in the U.S. Coast Guard and served as a combat artist in the South Pacific. When the war ended, Riley pursued a career as an illustrator and was soon working for such magazines as *The Saturday Evening Post*, *McCall's*, *Life*, and *National Geographic*.

In 1966 he traveled to the American West on commission from the National Parks Program. Five years later he took up permanent residence in Arizona and became a full-time fine arts painter. He was greatly influenced by Thomas Hart Benton as well as Harvey Dunn and the Brandywine tradition of illustration. His twenty-five-year experience as an illustrator is evident in his narrative, yet historically accurate, portrayals of the past.

Welcome Shade shows a beautiful layering of space: Riley stacks horse upon horse, then adds a layer of stone, broken by horses and riders, and then a mountain. The psychological result is a very claustrophobic yet cool foreground, which contrasts with the huge, hot, harshly lit upper two-thirds of the painting. The use of color to reflect temperature is a very difficult and sophisticated move. This type of challenge is a hallmark of Riley's work.

J. L. C.

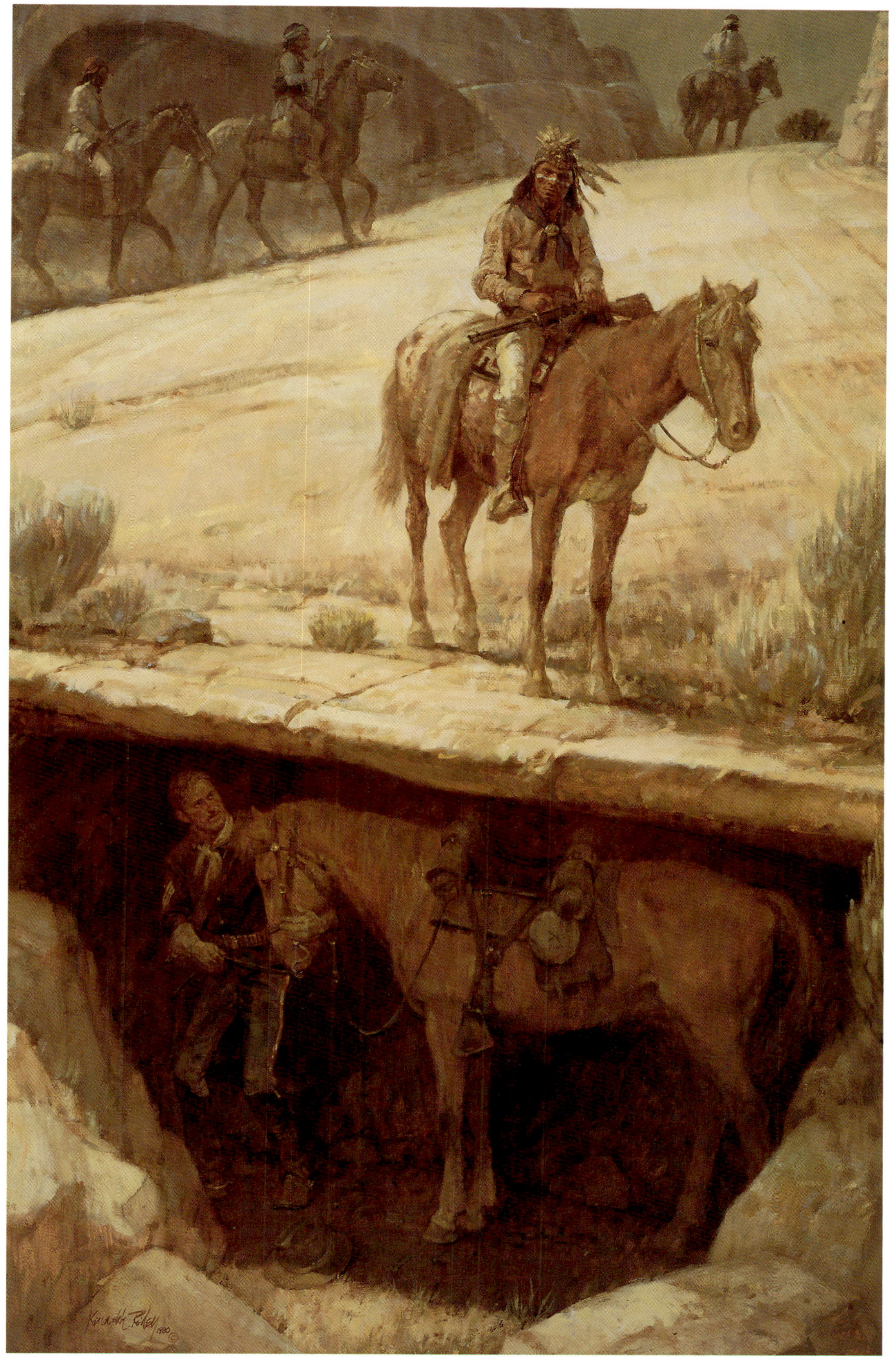

Howard A. Terpning
b. 1927

Speaking Hand of Eagle Kill
1977
oil on canvas
35 x 24 inches
signed and dated ll:
Terpning/77
Anonymous Collector

By the age of seven Howard Terpning decided that he would become an artist. He was encouraged by his mother, an interior decorator, and developed cartooning and portraiture as childhood hobbies. Terpning later studied at the Chicago Academy of Fine Arts and the American Academy of Art. He then served a two-year apprenticeship with the illustrator Haddon Sundblom in Chicago and worked with firms in Milwaukee and New York City before establishing his own studio. For twenty-four years Terpning was a successful free-lance illustrator for such popular magazines as *McCall's*, *Ladies' Home Journal*, *Field & Stream*, *Reader's Digest*, *Good Housekeeping*, and *Time*.

During the summer of 1974 Terpning set aside his career in illustration and painted several images of Native Americans; these proved very successful, and three years later he moved from the East Coast to Arizona to concentrate exclusively on Western painting. Terpning is a member of the Cowboy Artists of America (CAA) and the National Academy of Western Art (NAWA); since 1979 he has received over twenty-one awards in CAA exhibitions (including eight Gold Medals), and the NAWA Prix de West Award.

Terpning continues to focus on the cultures and ceremonies of the Plains Indians—the nomads, the hunters, the warriors, the great horsemen. For this double portrait of two Blackfeet, he created a fictitious character, Eagle Kill, who is dramatically emphasizing his speech with his left hand. The two mounted warriors, defined primarily in dark browns and umbers, almost fill the canvas; they are framed against a lighter prairie landscape, painted with very loose brush strokes.

M. K. D.

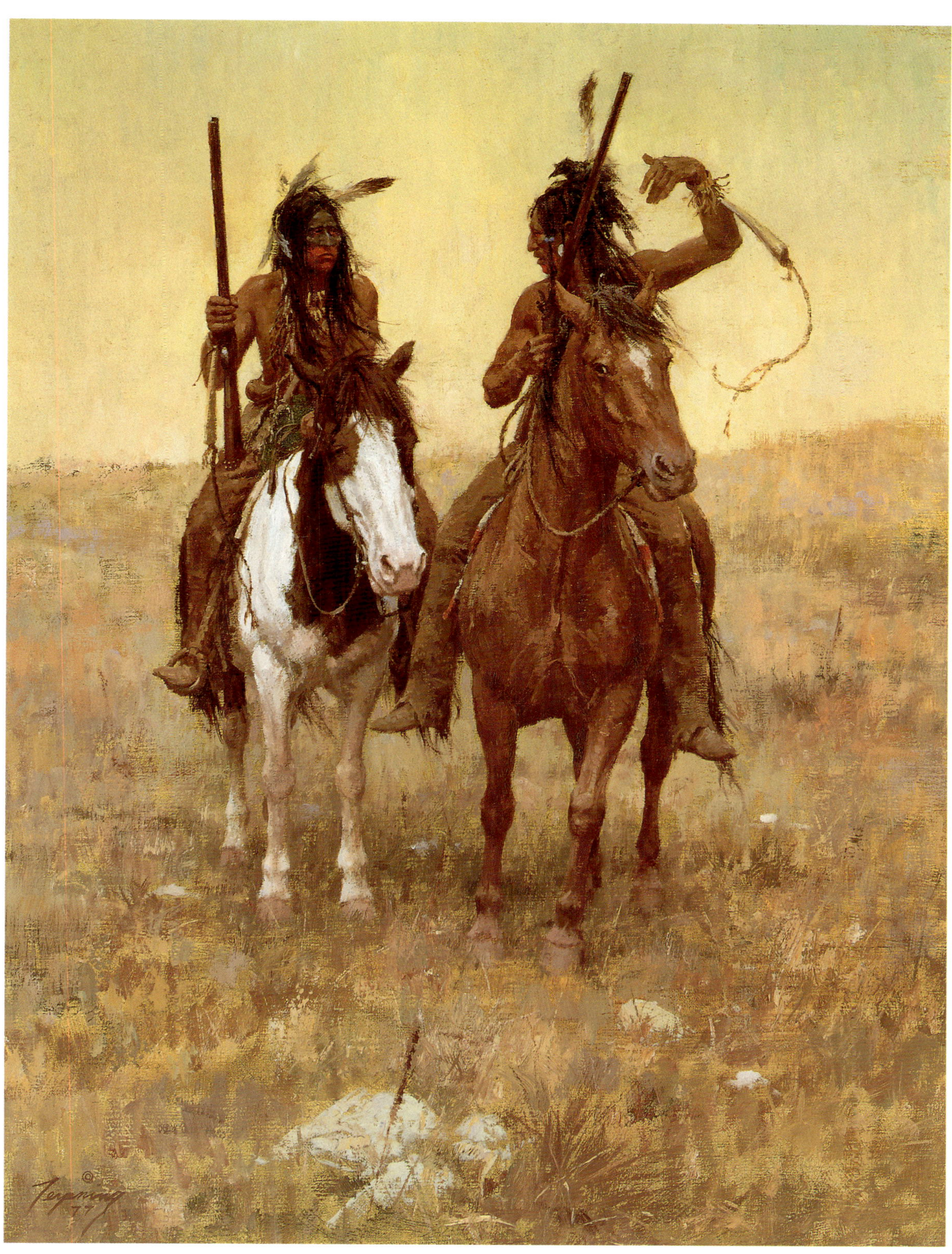

Michael Coleman
b. 1946

When the Land Was Theirs
1978
oil on canvas
32 x 25 inches
signed and dated lr:
MICHAEL COLEMAN -- /
1·9·7·8 VII
Dwight Sutherland

Michael Coleman, a native of Utah, had always wanted to be an artist. He studied art formally at Brigham Young University and at the San Francisco Art Institute but left both schools early out of growing frustration—they were teaching abstraction and he wanted to study realism. His early paintings focused on big game of the American West, and he drew on his experiences as a young boy hunting, fishing, and trapping in the Rocky Mountains. He also created dark, somewhat somber landscapes reflecting the influence of Thomas Moran and the Hudson River School. In the mid-1970s Coleman started working in gouache, an opaque watercolor. His palette lightened considerably, and he began to incorporate figures, particularly Native Americans, into his landscapes. His paintings continue the tradition of the earlier American artists Karl Bodmer and Henry Farny in depicting Plains Indians in their native environment. Coleman spends his summers traveling, attending mountain men rendezvous, camping on Montana reservations, and collecting Indian garments and accessories as source material for his work.

When the Land Was Theirs presents an isolated Plains campsite set in a vast, flat prairie. The low horizon plus the small size of the figures and tipis emphasize the emptiness of the plains and the grandeur of the distant mountain range. Alternating bands of sunlight and shadow reinforce the sense of deep space. The romanticized title evokes nostalgia for the lifestyle of the Plains Indians before the arrival of the European settlers.

M. K. D.

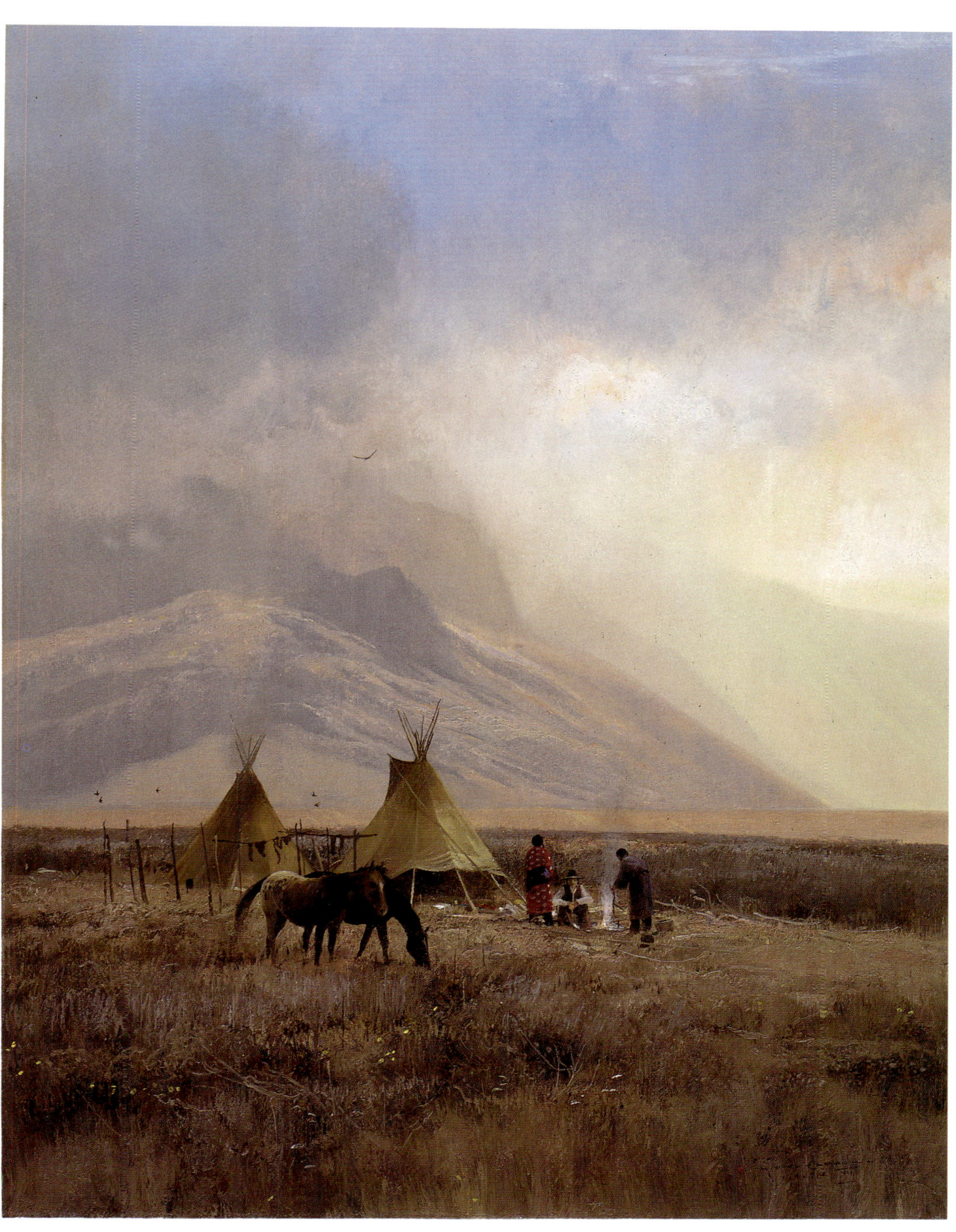

Larry Riley
b. 1947

Great-Grandmother's Doll
1988
oil on panel
16 x 12 inches
signed ll: Larry Riley/©
James W. F. (Class of '66)
and Donna K. Brooks
Collection

284

Larry Riley has been interested in art and in the American West since he was a young child. He and his mother moved to Washington state from his native Canada after the untimely death of his father, a bush pilot. Riley holds degrees in zoology from Washington State University and dentistry from the University of Oregon. He was a practicing dentist for nine years but discovered that painting was his true love. As a full-time artist he concentrates on contemporary images of the traditional American West: mountain men, Native Americans, rodeo participants, and ranchers. He has lived in Arizona for two decades, where he regularly attends rendezvous, rodeos, and Indian encampments, which provide a rich source of material for his paintings.

Great-Grandmother's Doll depicts a young Navajo girl solemnly studying an old family treasure. Her dark, profiled figure contrasts with the pale background, which is indicated only by green and yellow leaves from an unseen bush or tree. The figure is cropped shortly below the waist, a compositional device that helps create an intimate relationship with the viewer. Riley painted the girl, the doll, and all accessories with his characteristic concern for great accuracy and detail.

M. K. D.

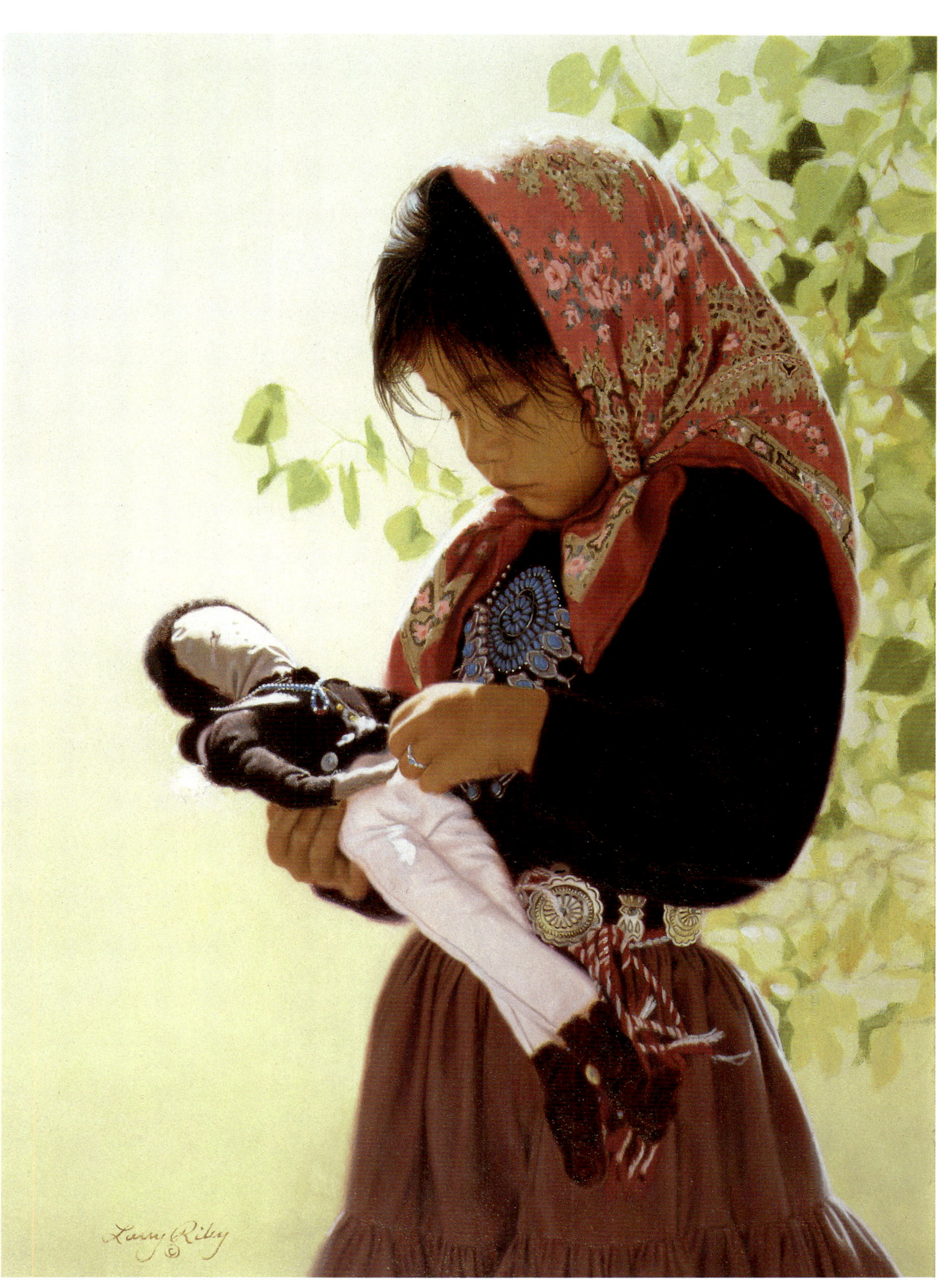

Mike Curtis
b. 1949

Shoreline Descent
1988
bronze with gold and silver
overlay
41 1/2 x 36 inches
signed, dated, and inscribed
on base: Mike Curtis/1988/
Georgia 4/50
H. Ward Lay

Northern Idaho, with its rugged topography, scenic lakes and rivers, and abundant wildlife, provides a perfect location for representational wildlife artists like Mike Curtis. From his studio overlooking Lake Pend Oreille, Curtis watches as nature's cycles are played out in the serenity of his own backyard.

A self-taught artist, Curtis began his career not in the arts but as a natural resource specialist. He is a charter member of the Wildlife Artists of the World and has exhibited throughout the United States. In 1989 he was honored with a commission from President George Bush to produce three sculptures which were then presented by the President to the Chinese government. The works are displayed at the American Embassy and the Cultural Center in Beijing.

During the winter months, Curtis carefully observes the bald eagles diving for fish outside his studio window. In *Shoreline Descent* he has used his careful attention to detail to convey the balance and grace of an eagle in the wild. In addition, Curtis's use of different patinas, as well as careful placement of gold and silver, enhances the color and texture of the bronze.

M. D. L.

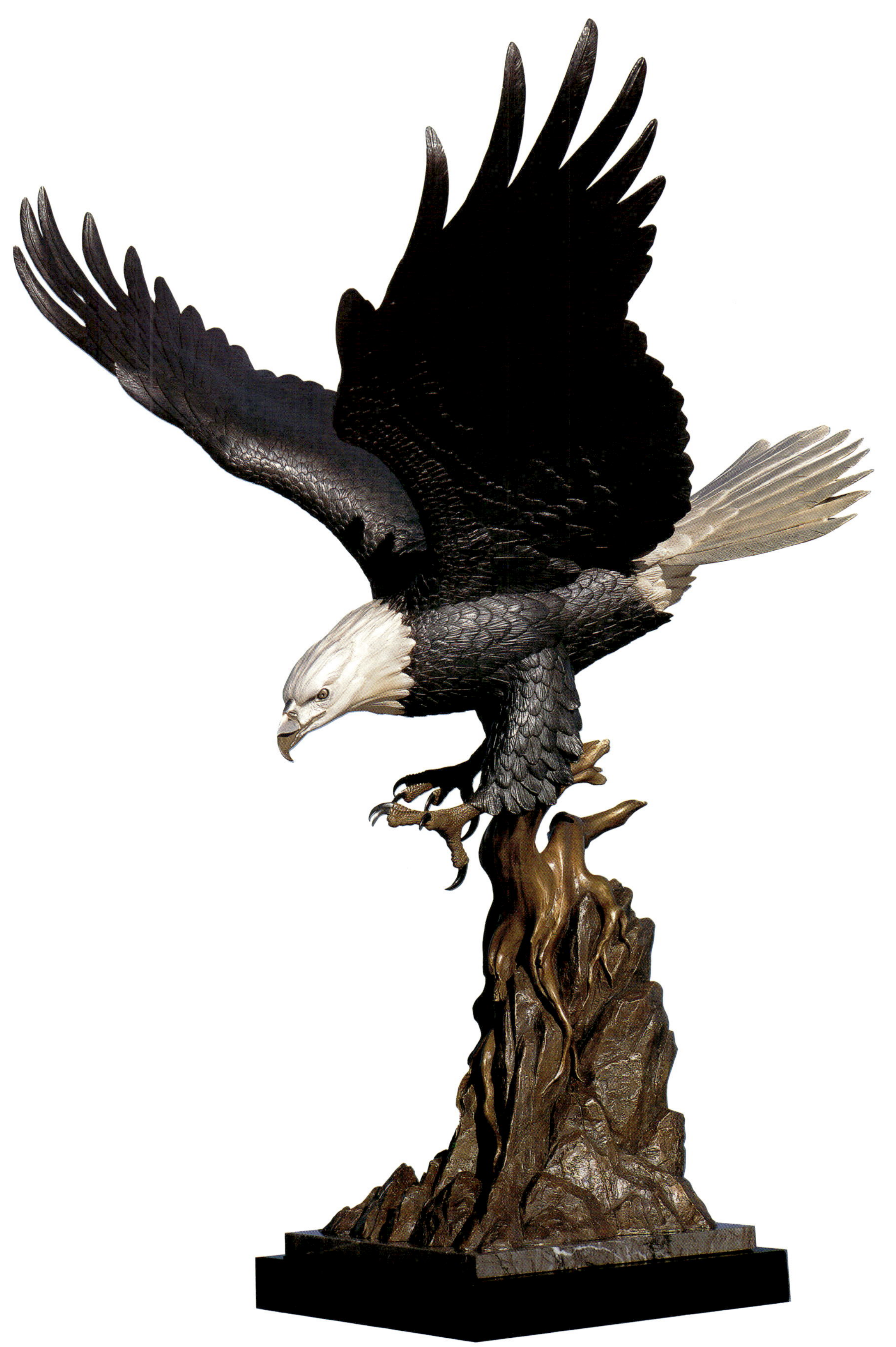

Gary Morton
b. 1951

Unspoiled Water
1990
acrylic on board
16 x 20 inches
signed ll: G. Morton/©
Mrs. Edward Ingersoll

A native of New Mexico, Gary Morton continues a tradition of American Western art begun by such notables as Charles M. Russell and Edward Borein, men who came to paint the life on the western range from direct experience as working cowboys. Before turning his attention full time to painting, Morton worked as a ranch foreman on the Bell Ranch in northern New Mexico. Largely self-taught as an artist, Morton relies on direct observation to capture everyday moments of modern ranch life.

Although Morton works in the representational tradition of nineteenth-century artists of the West, he often takes a more contemporary perspective. *Unspoiled Water* exemplifies this approach. By choosing to portray the two cowboys from above, Morton shifts the viewer's attention to the entire scene: cowboys, horses, and the landscape are linked in one quiet moment of reflection.

M. W. D.

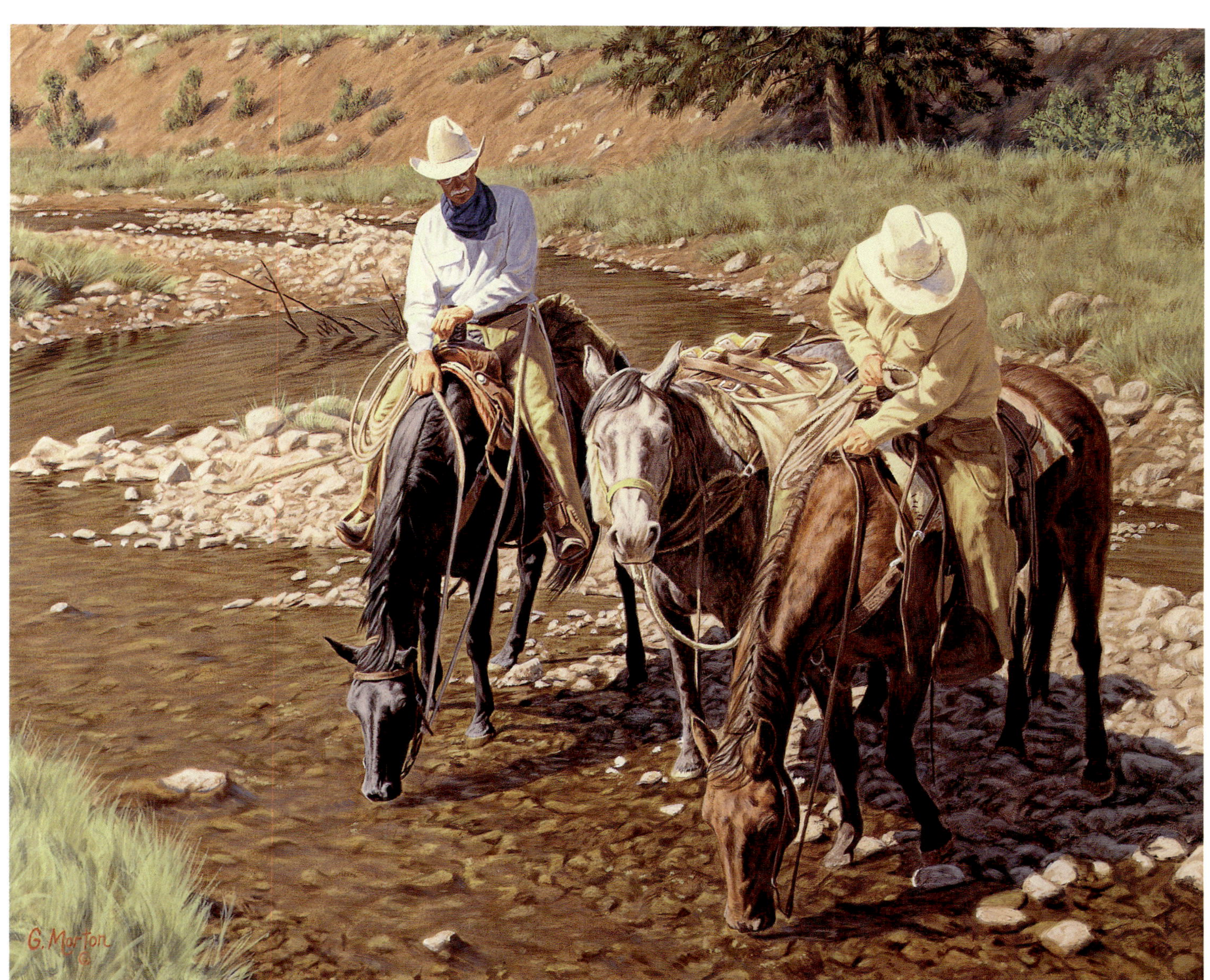

Beginning around 1735, the Crow acquired horses, which enhanced their mobile, hunting lifestyle, acted as commodities for trade, and served as expressions of prestige and wealth. Today, the Crow or Absaroke, as they call themselves, control tribal land in southwestern Montana.

Crow beadwork, highly sought out by collectors of American Indian art, is very distinct. In general, it displays a two-needle overlay stitch that is used to create overall patterns. Several beads are first attached to the surface at its ends only. Then a second needle stitches over the strand of beads at an average interval of every three or four beads to fasten them securely to the foundation.

Crow patterns tend to employ large geometric figures such as triangle, diamond, and hourglass shapes that are often outlined in white beads. The colors in classic Crow beadwork include lavendar, pale blue, yellow, green, and dark blue, and the beads are commonly worked on a red fabric background.

Decorative Crow beadwork is commonly found on horse trappings, like this saddle, saddle pad, bridle, and breast collar. The woman's saddle is identified by its high pommel and cantle. Such a saddle is constructed by stretching wet rawhide over a wooden saddle tree or frame. Tanned hide is used to cover the pommel and cantle, and classic Crow beadwork adorns decorative flaps of red flannel.

Each year Crow Fair, the largest powwow and encampment on the Great Plains, is held at Crow Agency, Montana. One of the highlights is a parade, which culminates in a competition to determine the best outfit of horse trappings. As in earlier times, the Crow consider the horse to be a highly valuable possession.

V. J. C.

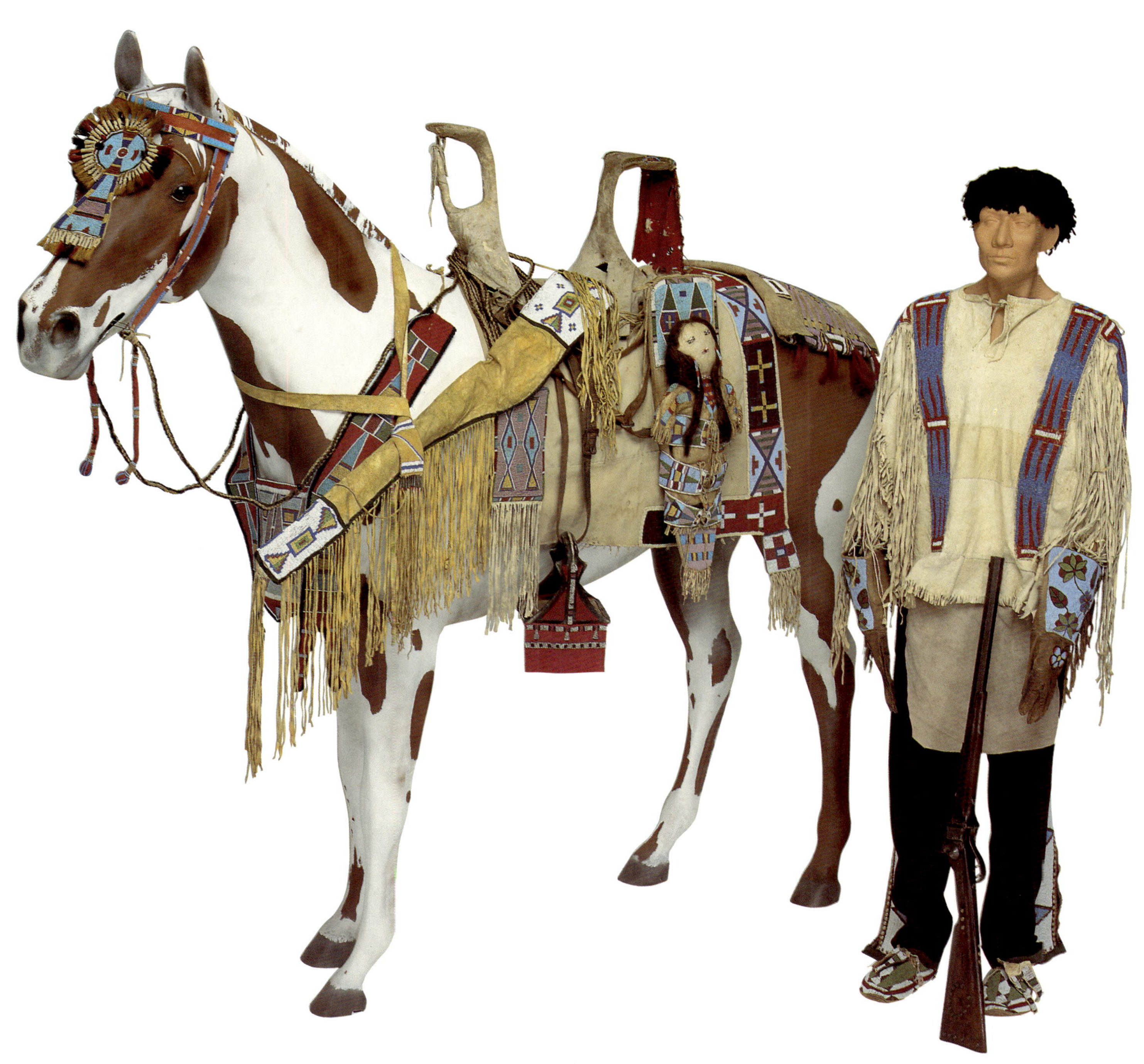

Chris Ravenshead
b. 1957
Tisa Ravenshead
b. 1963
Minneconjou/
Cheyenne River Sioux

Lakota Dress and Cradle
1991
elk hide, dyed porcupine
quills, brass bells and tacks,
red ochre, glass beads, buffalo
fur, feathers, rawhide, wood
60 x 53 and
42 1/2 x 13 x 11 1/2 inches
Ray J. Hillenbrand

The Lakota are one of seven linguistically related bands of western Sioux people with present-day tribal homes on six reservations in South Dakota. Their traditional lifestyle was dependent on the buffalo economy. They lived as nomads, gathering in large groups for summer hunts and ceremonial activities and dispersing into smaller bands during the winter months.

In the past Native American women often had a high degree of economic self-sufficiency, as they made items to be traded or sold. Women who were particularly fine artisans were held in high esteem. Though women traditionally constructed and decorated clothing, today many noteworthy quill- and beadworkers are men.

In a culture where a nomadic lifestyle was the norm, personal items were generally nonbreakable, highly functional, and profusely decorated to satisfy a personal or cultural aesthetic. Elaborately decorated and often prepared and given as gifts honoring the arrival of the newborn, cradles like the one shown here are still very much in use today.

On the Great Plains cradles such as this one are often constructed with a wooden frame and leather strap. The frame can serve to prop the cradle upright, while the strap allows it to be carried on a person's back or hung from a saddle or other secure feature.

This brightly decorated dress was created by husband and wife Chris and Tisa Ravenshead, using traditional materials and construction techniques, yet employing contemporary color. The bright pink porcupine quills adorning the yoke and sleeves of the dress were colored with a commercial dye.

V. J. C.

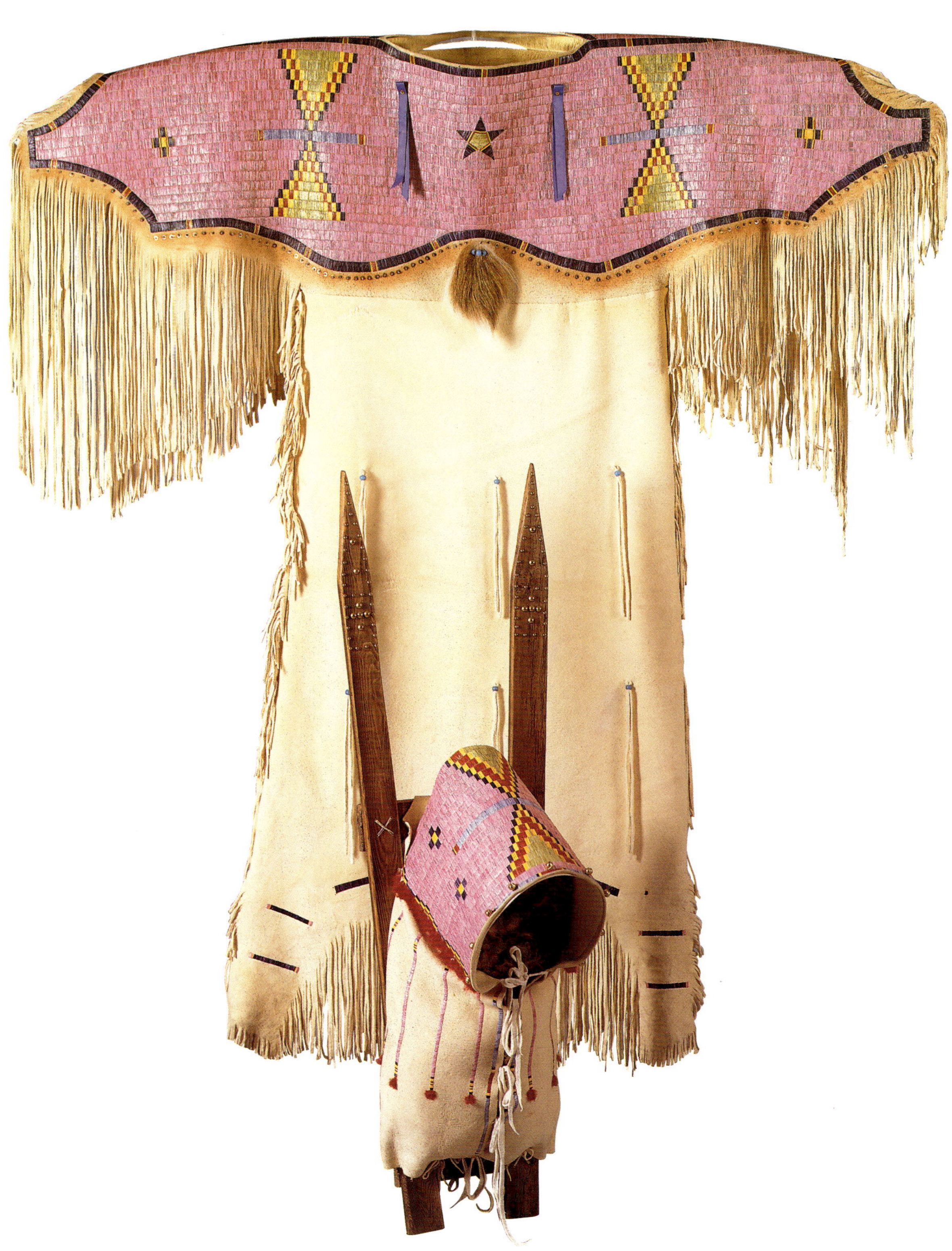

294

With the introduction of glass beads, many tribes reduced their production of porcupine quillwork, in part because of the difficulty in applying quills to the fabric garments that became increasingly common. The Lakota, however, continued a strong tradition of porcupine quillwork and have made many innovations in recent years. The names of certain Lakota individuals or families are nearly synonymous with quality quillwork.

Hide robes have been made for centuries, and while the function is consistent—they are used as an overgarment for protection from the elements or for formal dress—the designs can convey significant messages about the person who wears it. Not only size but also patterns can indicate if a garment was intended for a man or a woman, as Lakota decorative arts were once highly gender specific.

In general, the design elements found on a woman's robe are highly geometric, while those on a man's robe may be representational or abstract. Robes incorporating a geometric box and border design were commonly owned and worn by females. A common male design motif incorporates stylized feathers in the shape of elongated diamonds. Some men's robes are decorated with realistic figures that recount historic events or personal exploits. Paintings of individual American Indians by such artists as Karl Bodmer and George Catlin document many such examples.

This robe utilizes feather designs, but is also reminiscent of box and border in its overall layout. This piece also demonstrates the appliqué decoration typical of such robes. It incorporates porcupine quills, brass bells, feathers, cloth, and paint to create an overall image for a male wearer. The quills are applied to the garment in a band technique. Two separate threads are used at top and bottom under the fold of the porcupine quill to hold it in place. These stitches do not perforate the hide completely, leaving the undecorated surface unbroken.

V. J. C.

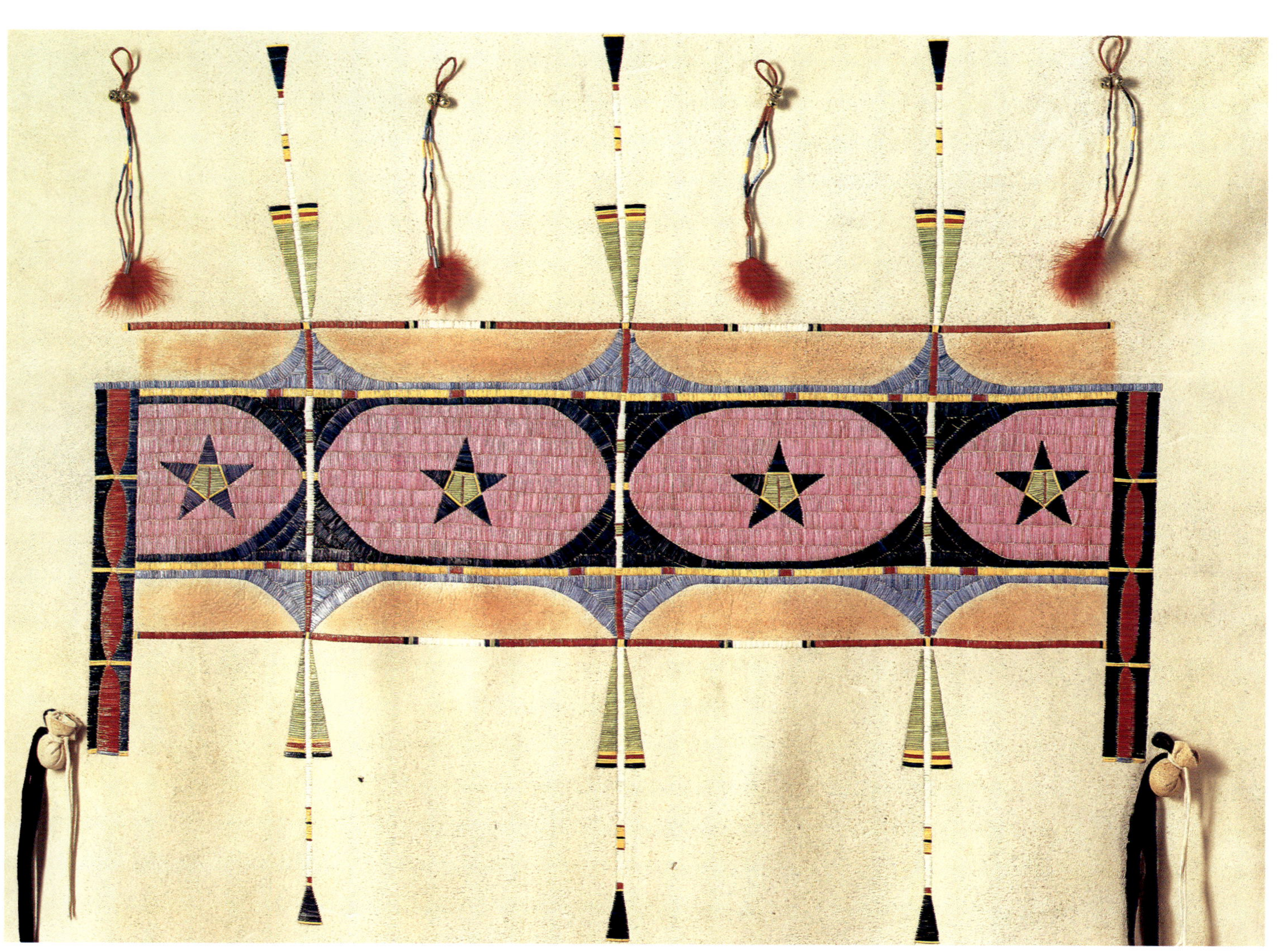

Edward Sheriff Curtis
1868-1952

*Snake Dancers Entering
the Plaza*
1921
photogravure
17 5/8 x 21 3/4 inches
Mr. and Mrs.
Bucky Wharton

296

For thirty years, 1900–30, Edward S. Curtis pursued his personal mission to photograph and document American Indian cultures, which he thought were disappearing forever. During the summers he traveled throughout the West, Southwest, and Northwest, concentrating primarily on portrait studies and genre scenes. He was accompanied by an Indian interpreter, and occasionally by his wife and children. He used a variety of cameras in the field, ranging from a huge 14 x 17 glass plate camera for his earlier photographs to a smaller, more manageable, hand-held model. Winter seasons were spent in Seattle, where Curtis organized his photographs, transcribed his notes, and planned exhibitions and lecture tours of his work. Between 1907 and 1930 he published twenty volumes of *The North American Indian* in a limited edition of five hundred sets, containing both his photographs and his text.

  In his desire for authenticity, Curtis would sometimes stage a scene to recreate a ceremony or special event, and he was always insistent on eliminating any signs of modern culture. This "romanticizing" of the American Indian resulted in criticism from some of his contemporaries and from ethnologists today. Despite these concerns, Curtis's monumental study of over eighty different tribes, resulting in over forty thousand photographs, has provided an invaluable visual document of Native American cultures at the beginning of the twentieth century.

M. K. D.

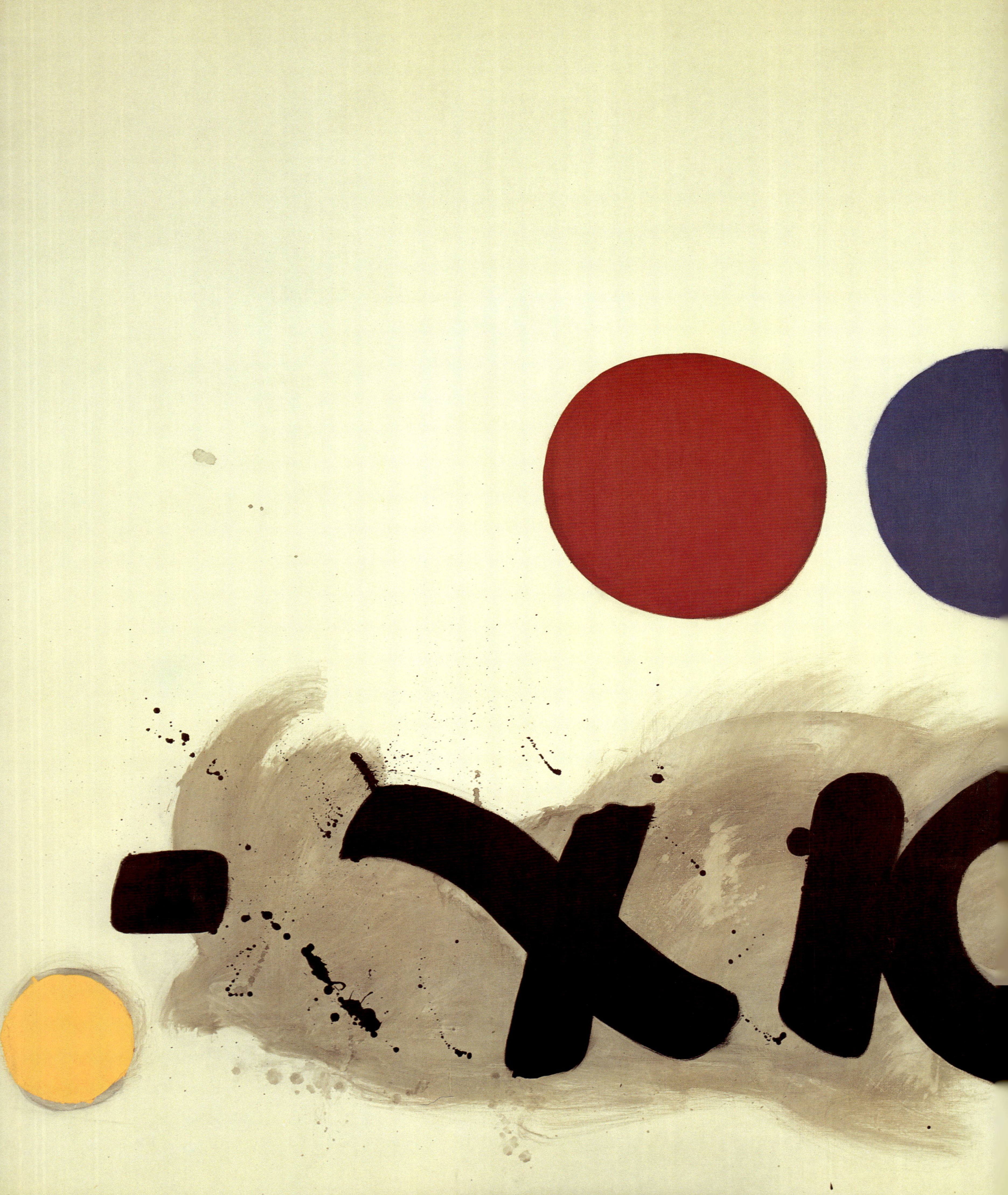

detail of *Red, Blue and Yellow*
by Adolph Gottlieb

INDIANAPO
AMERICAN ART
1953 – 1992
MUSEUM OF
ART •
COLUMBUS
GALLERY

American Traditions: Art from the Collections of Culver Alumni

Urbana
1953
oil on canvas
61 1/2 x 47 1/4 inches
signed and dated lr: RD53
Janet and Craig Duchossois

Richard Diebenkorn was dedicated for four decades to an art that synthesized modernist imperatives with his impressions of his surroundings. His remarkable career began with his study of art at the University of California, Berkeley, in 1943 while on active duty in the marine corps. While he was stationed at Quantico, Virginia, he frequented the Phillips Collection in Washington, D.C., where he saw the works of Pablo Picasso, Georges Braque, Pierre Bonnard, and the most influential artist in his artistic development, Henri Matisse. After his discharge from the marines in 1945, he studied at the California School of Fine Arts (now the San Francisco Art Institute) with Elmer Bischoff, David Park, and Hassel Smith and with visiting faculty Ad Reinhardt, Mark Rothko, and Clyfford Still. He then earned his MFA in 1952 from the University of New Mexico, Albuquerque. Diebenkorn's prodigious work can be loosely divided into three phases: an abstract expressionist period, which includes the approximately seventy paintings of the Berkeley series (1948-55); a gestural figurative period (1955-67), which included still lifes, interiors, and cityscapes (he was the recognized leader of the Bay Area figurative school); and the Ocean Park period, which included over one hundred light-filled abstractions of the Santa Monica neighborhood where he kept a studio from 1966 to 1973.

Urbana was painted while Diebenkorn was teaching at the University of Illinois at Champaign-Urbana, where he found the skies overcast and gray. One inspiration for the painting was the light and landscape of New Mexico. In creating a sense of volume through vibrant colors and fluid, interlacing lines, Diebenkorn also shows the influence of Matisse, whose retrospective he had seen in Los Angeles shortly before painting *Urbana*. The erased, corrected lines—*pentimento*—seen through the patchwork of colors not only reveal the artist's intense creative process, but also produce an illusion of varying depth and tension below the surface. The vertical, architectonic composition and the lighter horizontal band at the top foreshadow his Ocean Park series.

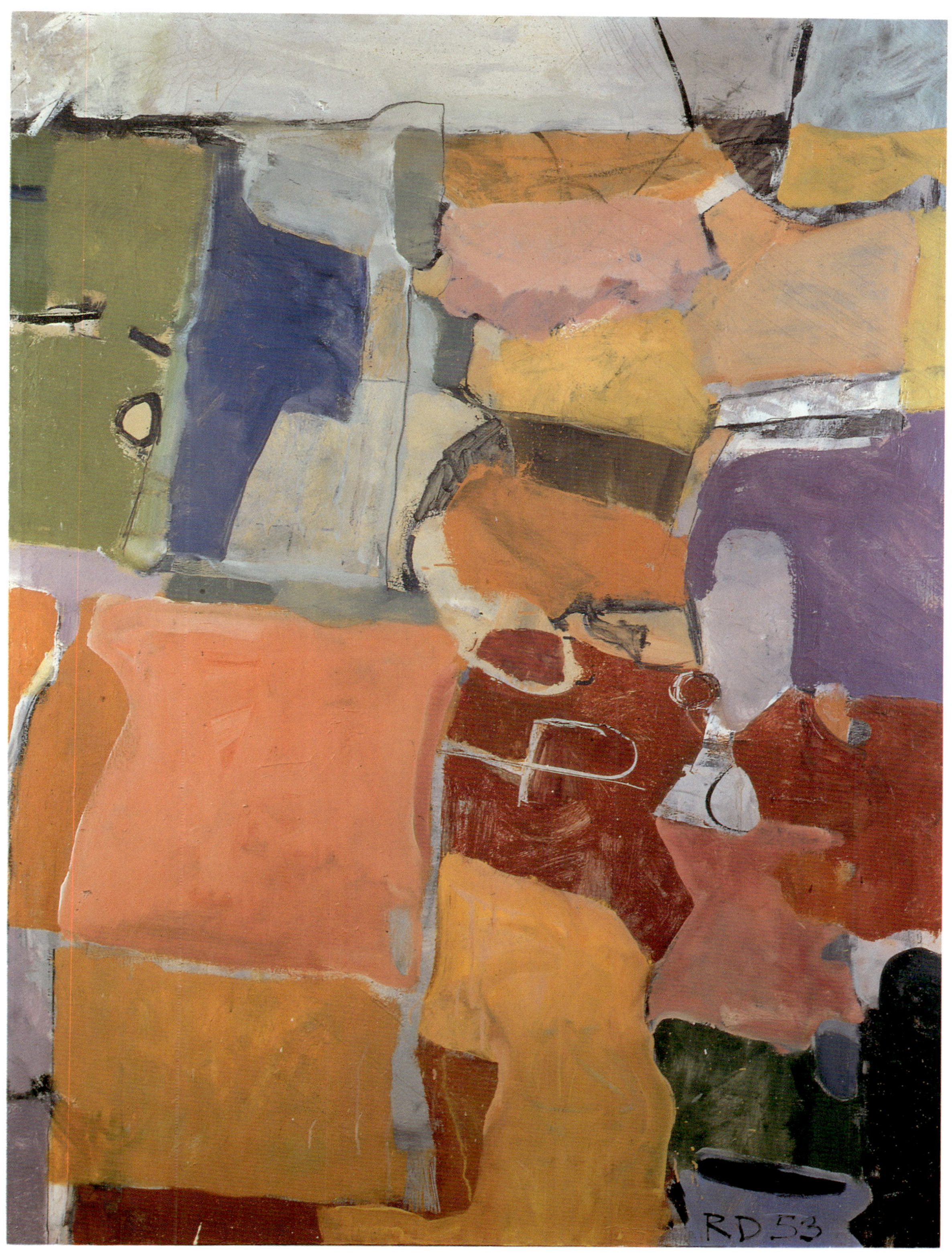

Mark Rothko
1903-1970

Untitled
1955
oil on canvas
91 3/4 x 69 inches
Collection of
Mr. and Mrs. Graham Gund

When he was ten, Mark Rothko, born Mark Rothkowitz, emigrated with his family from his native Divinsk, Russia, to Portland, Oregon. He studied liberal arts at Yale University on a scholarship between 1921 and 1923, and received his only formal art training in 1925-26 under Max Weber at the Art Students League. In 1928 he met Milton Avery when they were both included in a group exhibition at the Opportunity Galleries in New York City, and in the ensuing years Rothko's domestic, seaside, and subway scenes show the influence of his close friend's simplification and reduction of form and color. In 1935 Rothko and Adolph Gottlieb founded The Ten, a loose association of artists who painted in an expressionist mode. From 1936 to 1937 he worked as an easel painter for the Federal Art Project of the Works Progress Administration. In 1945 he exhibited his own surrealist-inspired works at Peggy Guggenheim's Art of This Century Gallery. Three years later Rothko, who believed that there is specific content in abstract art, cofounded the Subjects of the Artists School in New York with Robert Motherwell and William Baziotes. His last major commission was fourteen panels for a chapel donated by John and Dominique de Menil for the University of St. Thomas, Houston (now an interdenominational chapel affiliated with the Institute of Religion and Human Development). The theme of these panels, with their dark colors of black and blood-red, is the Passion of Christ. The chapel was formally opened in 1971, a year after Rothko committed suicide.

In *Untitled* two soft and subtly opposing rectangles—one receding above one expanding—float from their warm, luminous field of orange. There is a radiating inner light, creating for the viewer a spiritual, transcendental experience, in which, according to Rothko, he can "face his mortality and for a moment escape his fate." The scale is large, yet "human and intimate," he says. Rothko's interest in opposition as the basis for the tragic in art was influenced by the German philosopher Friedrich Nietzsche's view of Greek tragedy, which he saw as resulting from the struggle between the Apollonian and Dionysian forces in life. Like that of Gottlieb, Rothko's progression from the use of symbolic imagery to abstract imagery came from his desire to depict subject matter that is, in his words, "timeless and tragic." By 1947 he had eliminated any referential imagery or "obstacles between the painter, the idea, and the observer." In 1950 Rothko developed his restrictive format, characterized by two or three translucent, feathery rectangles placed one above the other. For the remainder of his life, he varied only colors and scale in order to create "a simple expression of human emotions—tragedy, ecstasy, doom."

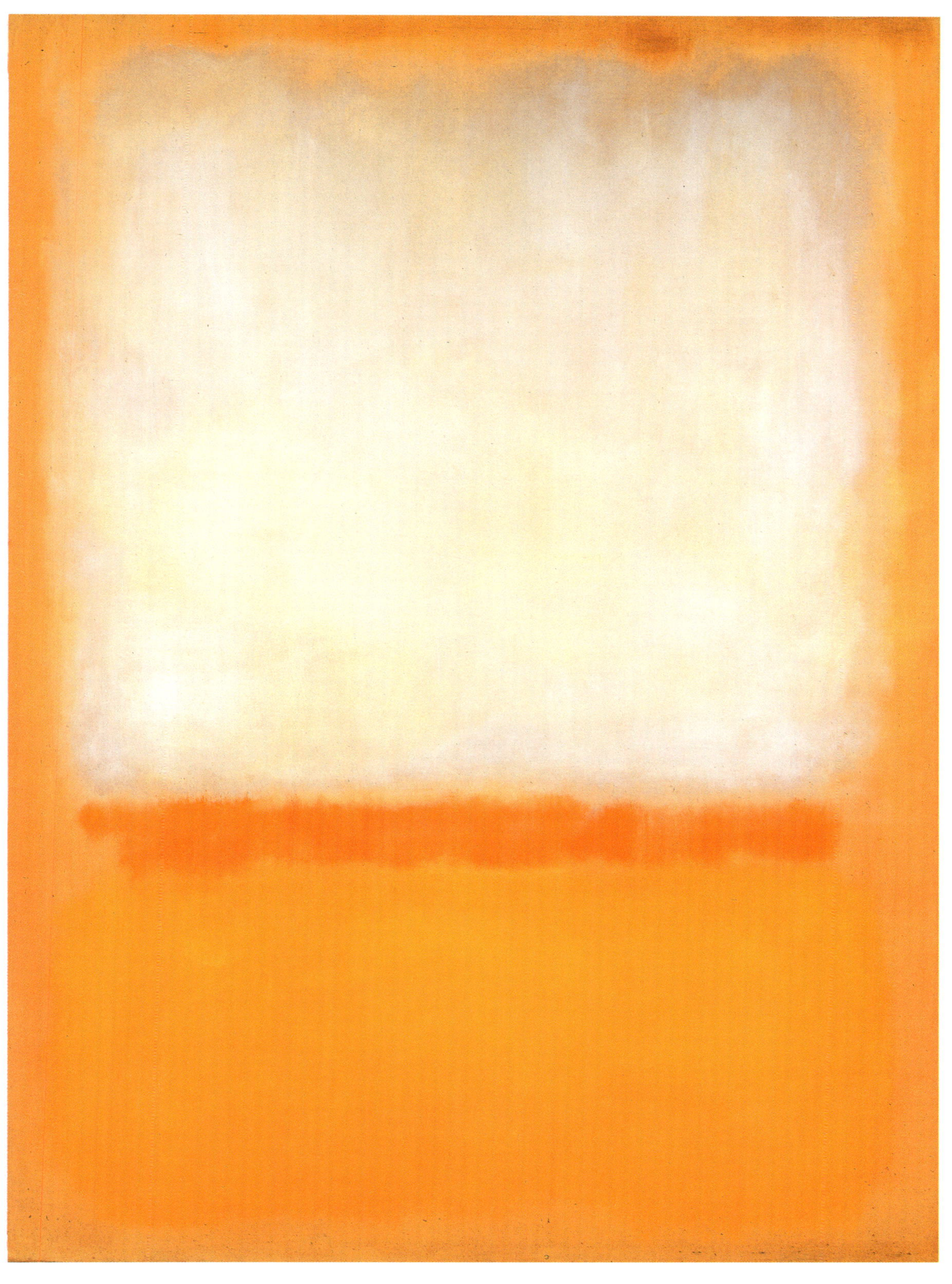

Morris Louis
1912-1962

Beth Heh
1958
acrylic on canvas
90 x 140 inches
Collection of
Mr. and Mrs. Graham Gund

Although he died of lung cancer less than five years after his first solo exhibition in New York City, Morris Louis was a seminal figure in the development of color-field painting. He studied at the Maryland Institute of Fine and Applied Arts in his native Baltimore and then worked in New York City from 1936 to 1940, first in the experimental workshop of the Mexican artist David Alfaro Siqueiros and then as an easel painter for the Federal Art Project of the Works Progress Administration. Back in Baltimore he set up a studio and taught privately, and in 1952, now living near the District of Columbia, he began teaching at the Washington Workshop Center of the Arts. There he met another teacher, Kenneth Noland, who would become an important friend and ally. In 1953 critic Clement Greenberg took the two men to Helen Frankenthaler's studio, where they saw her poured, stained painting *Mountain and Sea* (1952). Louis related Frankenthaler's technique to Jackson Pollock's allover drip paintings of the 1940s—with thinned enamel soaked into raw canvas—and saw it as providing the "bridge between Pollock and what was possible." He abandoned his cubist-inspired paintings for this new method, which, according to Greenberg, freed him "to think, feel and conceive almost exclusively in terms of open color."

Beth Heh is part of Louis's *Bronze Veils* series. He executed the first series of Veils in 1954; in those, he created a fanlike shape by superimposing sheer layers of delicate colors. The second group of Veil paintings, begun in 1958, includes *Beth Heh*, in which rhythmic waves of soft, subdued colors—resting at the base and floating free from the sides and top—produce a monumental and mysterious veil. The absorbing and blending of these colors create an allover wash that has a rich, dark tonality. To achieve this effect, Louis poured thin, quick-drying acrylic paint down an unsized canvas, which was loosely draped over the top of a stretcher, tacked, and then leaned against the wall. Because of the small size of his studio, he had to work in sections. Between the two groups of Veils, Louis gave up the poured and stained method and returned to a mode of abstract expressionism that resembled, according to Greenberg, the gestural marks of Willem de Kooning. Always extremely self-critical, Louis, after his first solo exhibition in New York in 1957, destroyed all but ten of the three hundred paintings he had produced.

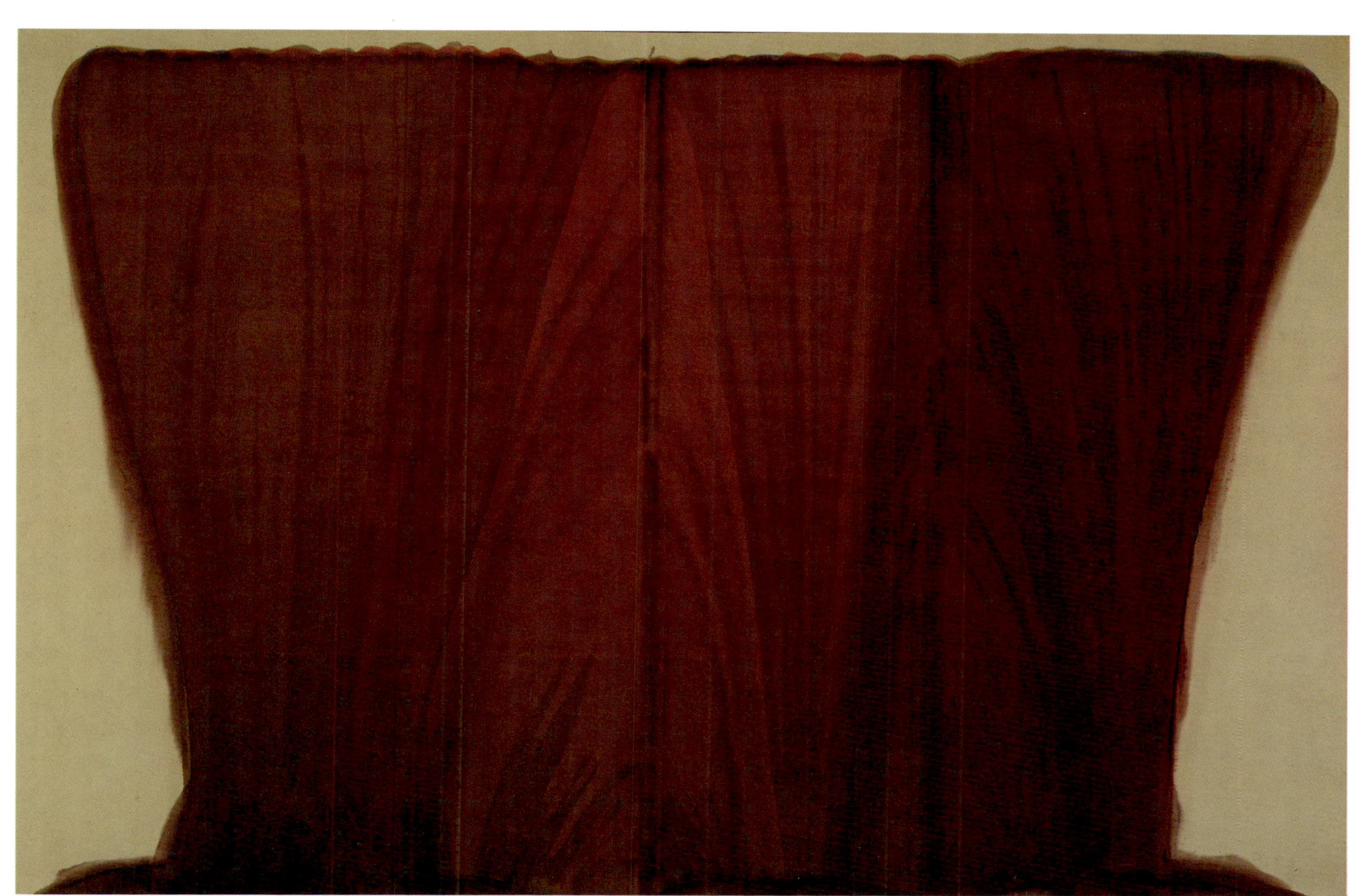

John McLaughlin
1898-1976

#4
1959
oil on canvas
44 x 60 inches
Collection of Mr. and Mrs.
Joseph T. Mendelson

In both his life and art John McLaughlin harmoniously blended Eastern and Western attitudes and beliefs. His carefully composed paintings, with their hard-edged, symmetrical forms, appear to be based on the tenets of Kazimir Malevich's suprematism or Piet Mondrian's neoplasticism. Although McLaughlin did find Malevich's painting *White on White* important because it completely eliminated the object, the philosophical objective of McLaughlin's simple, reductive paintings is the attainment of anonymity, neutrality, and the "marvelous void" he admired in the work of Chinese painters such as Sesshu (1420-1506).

McLaughlin attended the Roxbury Latin School in Boston and the Phillips Academy in Andover, Massachusetts, but was self-taught in art. After graduation he joined the navy and served in World War I. An early interest in collecting Japanese prints led him to travel extensively in Japan and the Far East between 1935 and 1940; during this time he studied Asian languages and art, especially fifteenth- and sixteenth-century Japanese artists. During World War II he served in the intelligence branch of the army; as a major in the Japanese language section, he traveled to China, Burma, and India from 1943 to 1945. After the war, he worked as a dealer of Asian prints in Boston. He did not devote himself fully to painting until he moved to Dana Point, California, in 1946, where he lived until his death in 1976.

Through an extreme economy of means, simplicity, and restraint, McLaughlin has created in *#4* a work of transcendent power. The two halves of *#4* (he did not use titles, which he felt added distorting meaning) are thinly painted in contrasting opaque colors—a gray border with a white center and an orange border with a black center. His composition does not relate to any mathematical proportion, but came from an intense process in which he arranged and rearranged bands and rectangles cut from construction paper. When he was satisfied with the arrangement, he then decided on color and texture. Although each half of *#4* suggests subtle spatial contrasts—one seems to be open and the other to recede—there is unity and equilibrium, as in the Chinese cosmological principle of yin-yang, in which opposites combine to produce one. With this image of quiet opposition, McLaughlin hoped to create a void that would, in his words, "induce or intensify the viewer's natural desire for contemplation."

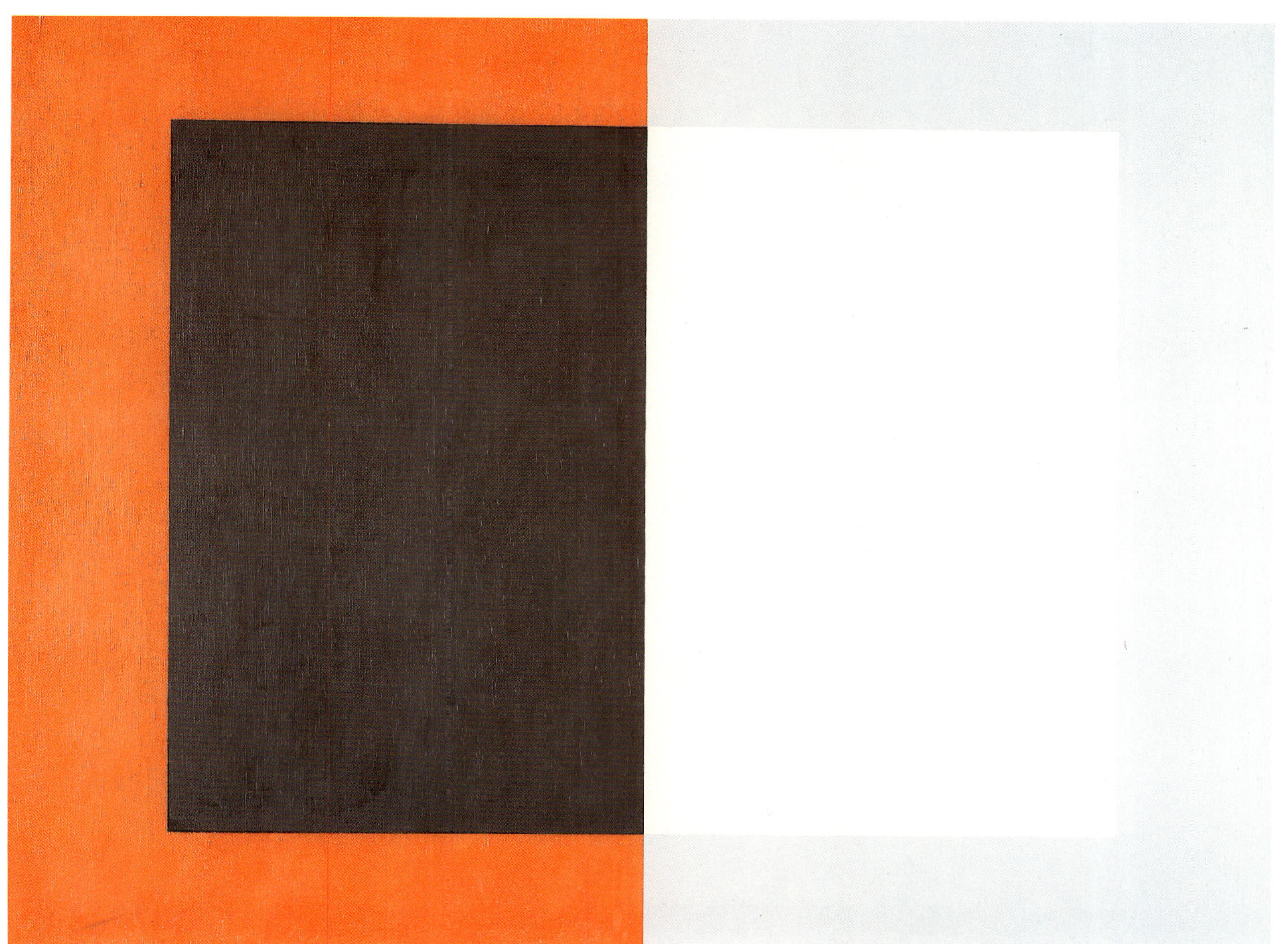

Wayne Thiebaud
b. 1920

Gumball Machine
1961
oil on canvas
25 1/4 x 19 3/4 inches
signed and dated lr:
Thiebaud '61
Mr. and Mrs.
W. A. Moncrief, Jr.

308

Before becoming a painter, Wayne Thiebaud was an animator for Walt Disney, a free-lance cartoonist, and an illustrator and layout designer for the Rexall Drug Company in Los Angeles. After receiving fine art degrees from California State College (now California State University) in the early 1950s, Thiebaud began exhibiting and teaching. He spent his sabbatical year (1956-57) in New York City, where he frequented the Eighth Street Club and joined artists such as Willem de Kooning, Franz Kline, and Barnett Newman in philosophical and theoretical discussions about art. Although impressed by their energized, gestural brushwork and committed to exploring formal values of line, color, and space, Thiebaud could not abandon his interest in the depiction of real objects. Influenced by nineteenth-century realists such as Gustave Courbet and Edgar Degas and masters of light such as Jan Vermeer and Thomas Eakins, Thiebaud sees himself as a "traditional painter," discovering "what the tradition of realism is all about." His presentation of popular imagery—club sandwiches, desserts, candy machines—relates to the technical methods of advertising and display and links Thiebaud to the pop art movement. His greatest interest, however, is the "relationship between paint and subject matter." Thiebaud likes to make the "white, gooey, shiny, sticky oil paint on top of a cake 'become' the frosting."

This painting of an isolated gumball machine radiates a light reminiscent of the boardwalk in Long Beach, California, where Thiebaud spent most of his youth, selling newspapers and working in restaurants in the summer. He especially enjoyed the displays of highly embellished food in the window of the Woolworth's store. With its sharp contrasts of colors, stark blue background, and thick strokes of paint, Thiebaud's *Gumball Machine* literally vibrates, enlivening and heightening our experience of the everyday.

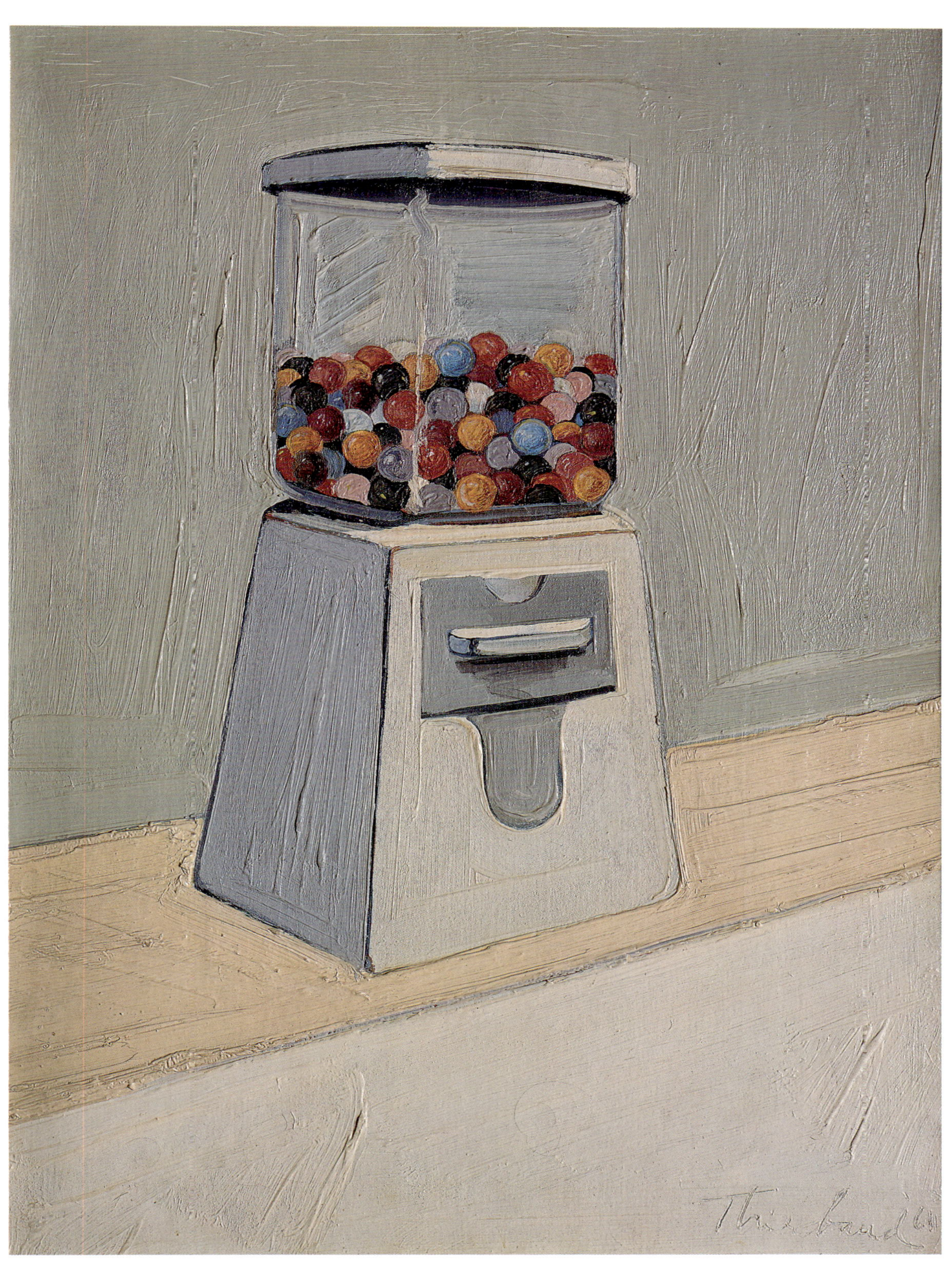

As an artist, teacher, and writer, Josef Albers influenced several generations of American artists. He was born in Bottrop, Westphalia, in 1888, and his pride in craftsmanship was reinforced early on by a father who was a carpenter and a mother who came from a family of blacksmiths. He studied at the Royal Art School in Berlin from 1913 to 1915, the School of Applied Arts in Essen from 1916 to 1919, and with Franz Stück and Max Doerner at the Munich Academy. For thirteen years he was associated with the Bauhaus, an institute founded by architect Walter Gropius in Weimar, Germany, in 1919 and dedicated to abolishing the distinction between the fine and applied arts. As a student, Albers made glass paintings, stained glass, and assemblages in geometric forms, such as a grid from bottle shards and rectangular or square compositions of sandblasted glass. In 1923 he joined the faculty, which already included Paul Klee, Wassily Kandinsky, and László Moholy-Nagy, and taught several design courses. Later he became assistant director and head of the furniture and wallpaper workshops. Among his many accomplishments in different media, he designed functional but elegant stacking tables; bent, laminated wood chairs; and glassware with bent metal. When the Nazis closed the Bauhaus in 1933, Albers came to the progressive, experimental Black Mountain College in North Carolina, where he taught for sixteen years. From 1936 to 1941 he also lectured on modern art and design principles at the Graduate School of Design at Harvard University. For nearly a decade, 1950–58, he was associated with Yale University, first as a visiting critic and later as head of the Department of Design.

With the strictest economy of form, Albers has maximized the psychological effects of color in *Study for Homage to the Square: Grisaille and Amber*. The work parallels his *Variants on a Theme* series (rectangular shapes of colors) and his *Structural Constellation* series (linear compositions executed in black and white) in its exploration of spatial and perceptual illusion. An overall tension arises from the push-pull effect created as the inner square recedes and the outer square appears to advance toward the viewer.

Over a twenty-five-year period, beginning around 1950, Albers completed nearly a thousand paintings and drawings with this simple format, consisting of only three or four squares within squares of color. As he described in his definitive book on color theory, *Interactions of Color* (1963), the square is a perfect form for investigating the aesthetic experience of color because it minimizes intrusive associative and descriptive elements. "Color, in my opinion," he wrote, "behaves like a man—in two distinct ways: first in self-realization and then in the realization of relationships with others. In my paintings I have tried to make the two polarities meet—independence and interdependence."

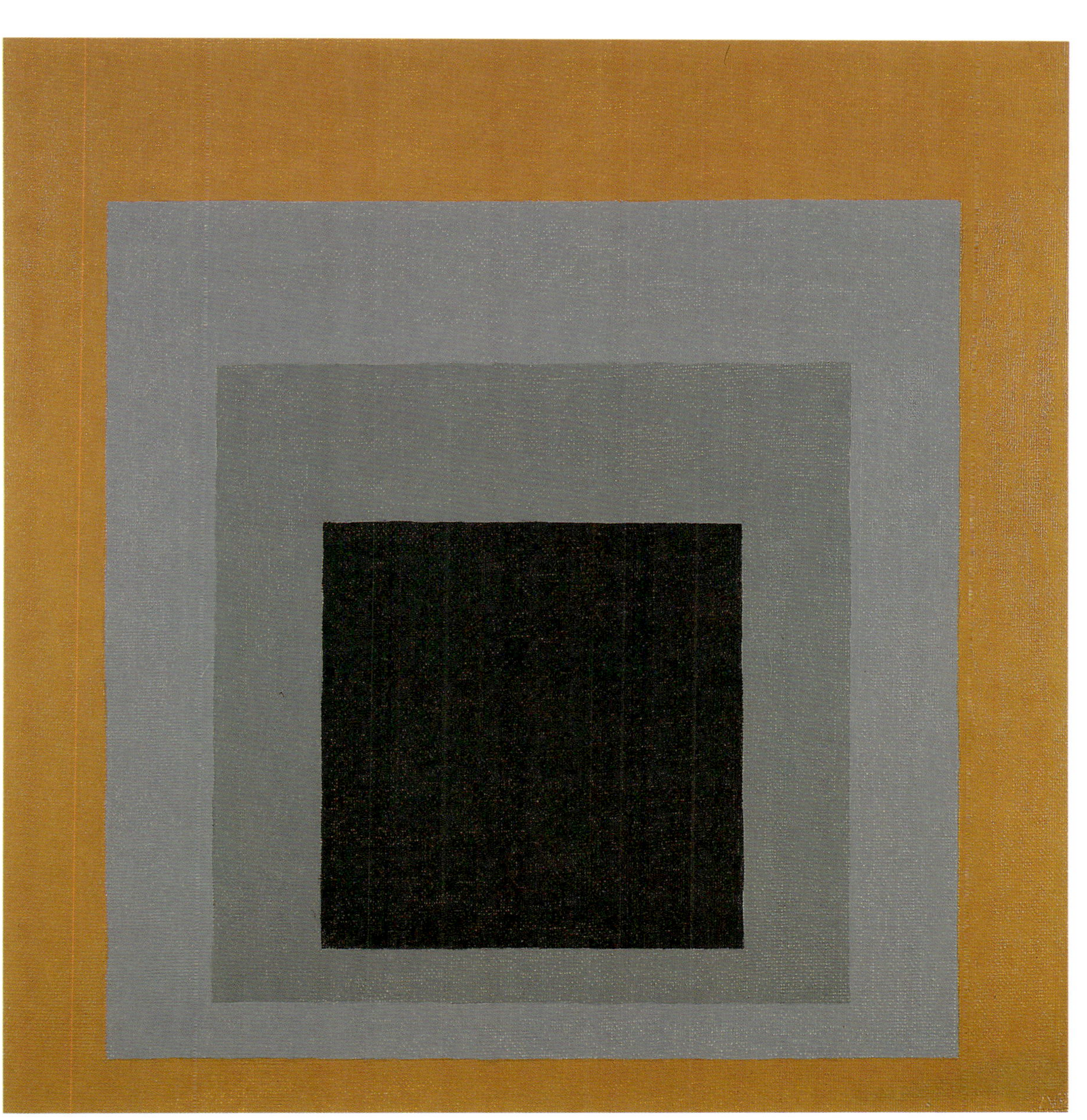

Dollar Bill
1962
pencil
30 x 40 inches
United Missouri Bank

312

The importance of the art of the enigmatic Andy Warhol has always been overshadowed by his status as an international celebrity. He was obsessed with fame, wealth, and glamour, and some critics consider the attainment of these obsessions his greatest work of art. Ironically, the image of the silver-wigged, pale Warhol and his sound-bite pronouncements ("In the future, everybody will be famous for fifteen minutes") are as much a part of the public consciousness as his paintings of Campbell's Soup cans and Marilyn Monroe. He became an American icon. But, with his background as a successful commercial artist (illustrations for *Glamour*, *Vogue*, and *Harper's Bazaar*; newspaper ads for I. Magnin; and window displays for Bonwit Teller), filmmaker (*The Chelsea Girls*, *Sleep*, and *Eat*), promoter of the rock group Velvet Underground, and publisher of the gossip magazine *Interview*, Warhol dissolved the distinctions between high and low art and forever changed notions about art and being an artist.

Although the pencil drawing *Dollar Bill* is an early work, it is pivotal for understanding Warhol's direction and influence as a pop artist. It is only appropriate that Warhol chose to depict a banknote as a reflector and, perhaps, reinforcer of the values of our market-driven, consumer culture. A dollar bill was also one of the first images he reproduced in serial format (*Eighty Two-Dollar Bills, Front and Rear*, 1962), using handcut screens to print the image on canvas. Given the legal restrictions on reproductions of money, Warhol eliminated or altered the lettering or changed the president's face in all his banknote images. He soon had his assistants in his famous studio, The Factory, use the faster commercial method of photo-silkscreening to mass produce press-agency photographs of disasters, electric chairs, and movie stars—a clear comment on the continuous bombardment of images through the mass media.

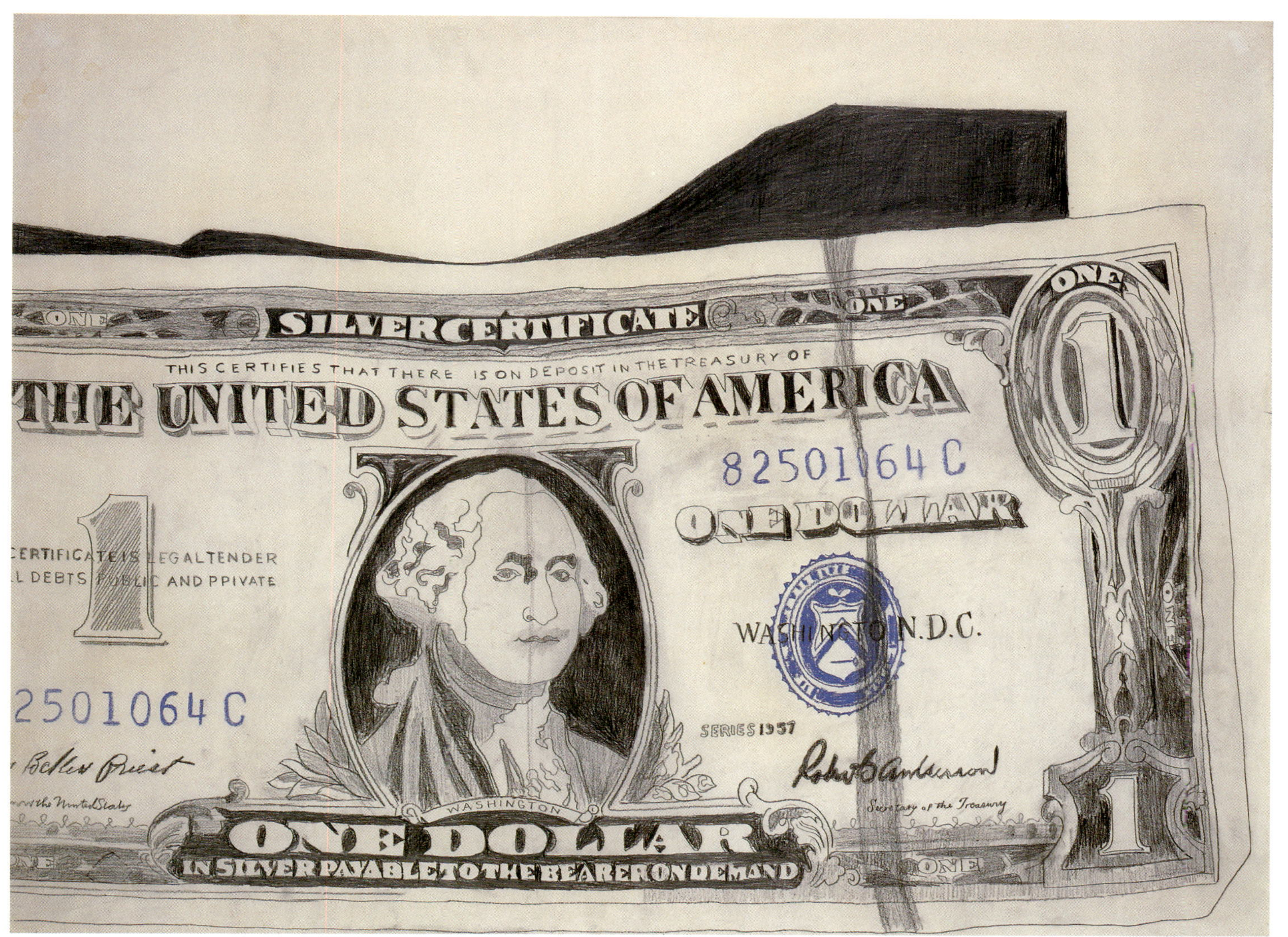
SILVER CERTIFICATE
ONE
ONE
THIS CERTIFIES THAT THERE IS ON DEPOSIT IN THE TREASURY OF
THE UNITED STATES OF AMERICA
1
82501064C
ONE DOLLAR
CERTIFICATE IS LEGAL TENDER
L DEBTS PUBLIC AND PRIVATE
WASHINGTON N.D.C.
2501064C
SERIES 1957
WASHINGTON
ONE DOLLAR
IN SILVER PAYABLE TO THE BEARER ON DEMAND
ONE
ONE
1

Allan D'Arcangelo
b. 1930

June Moon
1963
oil on canvas
48 x 48 inches
Mr. and Mrs.
Richard W. Moncrief

The great American highway—the open road—provides both the iconography and subject matter for the flat, hard-edged paintings by Allan D'Arcangelo. According to Lawrence Alloway, the art critic who coined the term "pop art," D'Arcangelo is a "man at the wheel" recording the signs and symbols of a "highway culture." During the 1950s, the same decade when Jack Kerouac (1922-69), the leader of the Beat movement, poet, and author of the highway classic *On the Road* (1957), roamed America and Mexico, D'Arcangelo was on the move. He hitchhiked across the United States, traveled to Guadalajara, Mexico, and lived for eighteen months in Cuahimalpa, near Mexico City. During this time D'Arcangelo also received a bachelor's degree in history and government from the University of Buffalo (1953), studied in New York City at City College and the New School for Social Research (1953-54), and took lessons from Boris Lurie in New York and John Golding at Mexico City College. He began painting on his own in 1955 and had his first exhibition of paintings at the Galeria Genova, Mexico City, in 1958.

June Moon captures the feeling, the beat, of traveling on endless blacktop, passing countless highway and gas station signs. D'Arcangelo has transformed the Gulf Oil sign into a full moon, perhaps commenting ironically on the man-made highway cutting through nature. By simplifying and equalizing all forms, by making them flat while at the same time creating an illusion of depth with an aggressive one-point perspective, D'Arcangelo introduces a tension and uneasiness into this image of the highway. Without sentimentality or nostalgia, he renders, in his words, "a simple fact of memory."

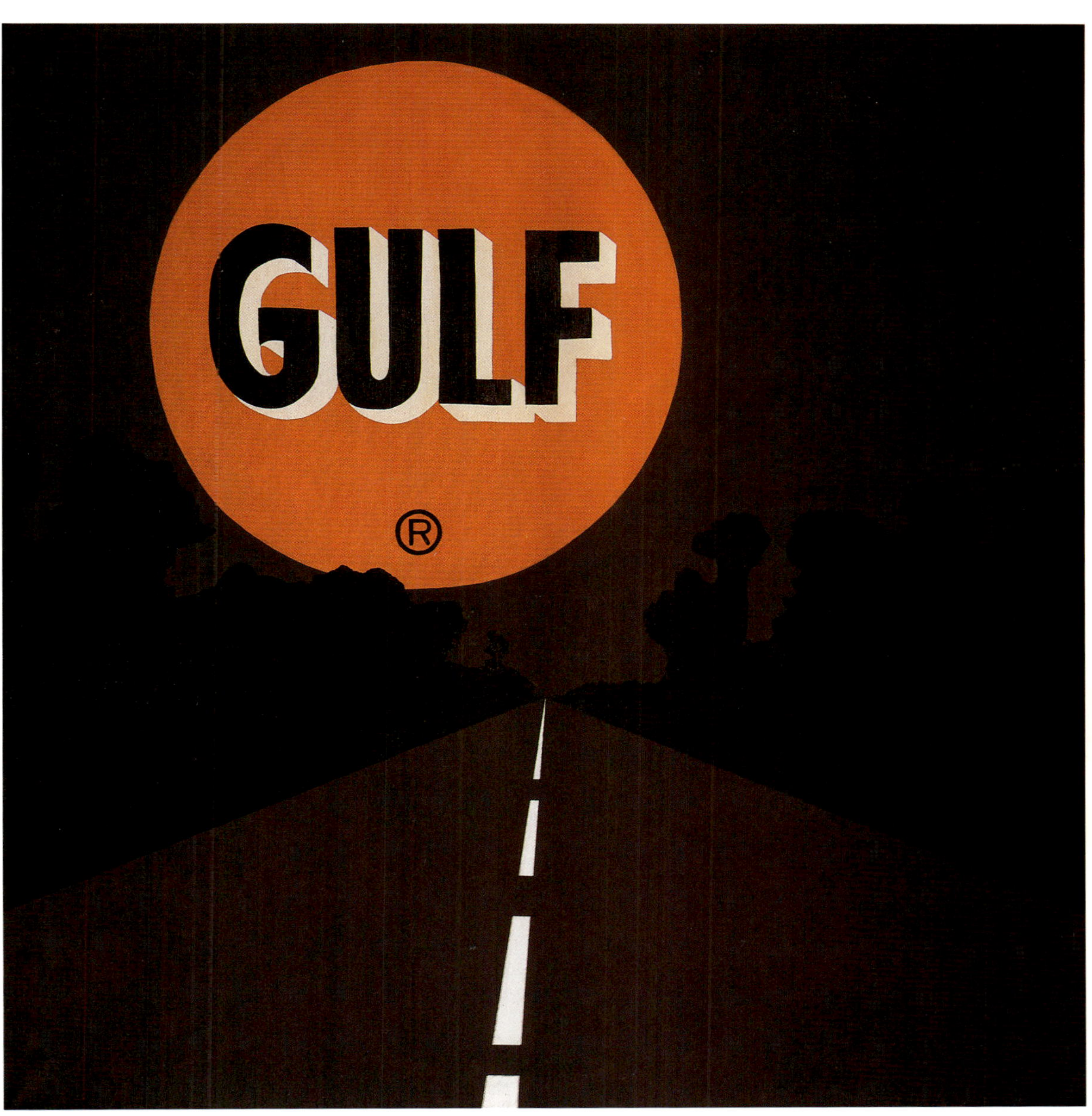

GULF
®

pls.
pump up intensity
needs to
hold the
BOB

Willem de Kooning
b. 1904

Untitled
c. 1965
gouache on paper
mounted on board
26 x 10 3/8 inches
signed lr: de Kooning
Weil Brothers

In his art the pioneering abstract expressionist Willem de Kooning combines an innovative, restless spirit with an unwavering respect for tradition. He was born in Rotterdam, the Netherlands, and apprenticed at the age of twelve with a commercial art and decorating firm. That same year he began attending evening classes at the Academie voor Beeldende Kunsten en Technische Wetenschappen Rotterdam, which was known for retaining the craft traditions of the old guilds. In 1926 he succeeded in his third attempt to migrate to the United States, arriving as a stowaway aboard a ship. He worked for a year as a housepainter in Hoboken, New Jersey, before moving to New York City, where he earned his living painting signs, creating department store displays, and painting nightclub murals. He was finally able to concentrate full time on painting when he joined the Federal Art Project of the Works Progress Administration. In 1943 he married artist and critic Elaine Fried. In 1946 he, Franz Kline, and Jack Tworkov rented a place at 39 East 8th Street for the purpose of meetings, panel discussions, and parties. For ten years the Eighth Street Club, in which de Kooning was one of the most influential artists, was the focal point of the New York art world. De Kooning moved permanently to East Hampton, Long Island, in 1963, the year after he became a United States citizen.

The lithe, soft, and sensuous woman in this painting contrasts quite strongly with the violent, demonic creatures in de Kooning's first series of women, executed in 1950–55. He creates a gentle tension by having the woman swell gracefully in and out of an ambiguous, shifting space. With its swirling red lines, smears of green paint, and rich, varied surface textures, this gouache demonstrates de Kooning's rare ability to combine control and spontaneity, draftsmanship and intuition. Throughout three prolific decades in which he oscillated between two major subjects—figurative and abstracted landscapes—de Kooning explored the measurement and determination of space. He greatly admired the intellectual approach of the Renaissance artists and their ability to get "inside" the painting. In a 1951 essay, "Renaissance and Order," he wrote: "(The artist) became . . . the idea, the center, and the vanishing point himself. . . . He shifted, pushed, and arranged things in accordance with the way he felt about them. . . . He could both invent the phenomena and inspect them critically at the same time. Michelangelo invented Adam that way, and even God."

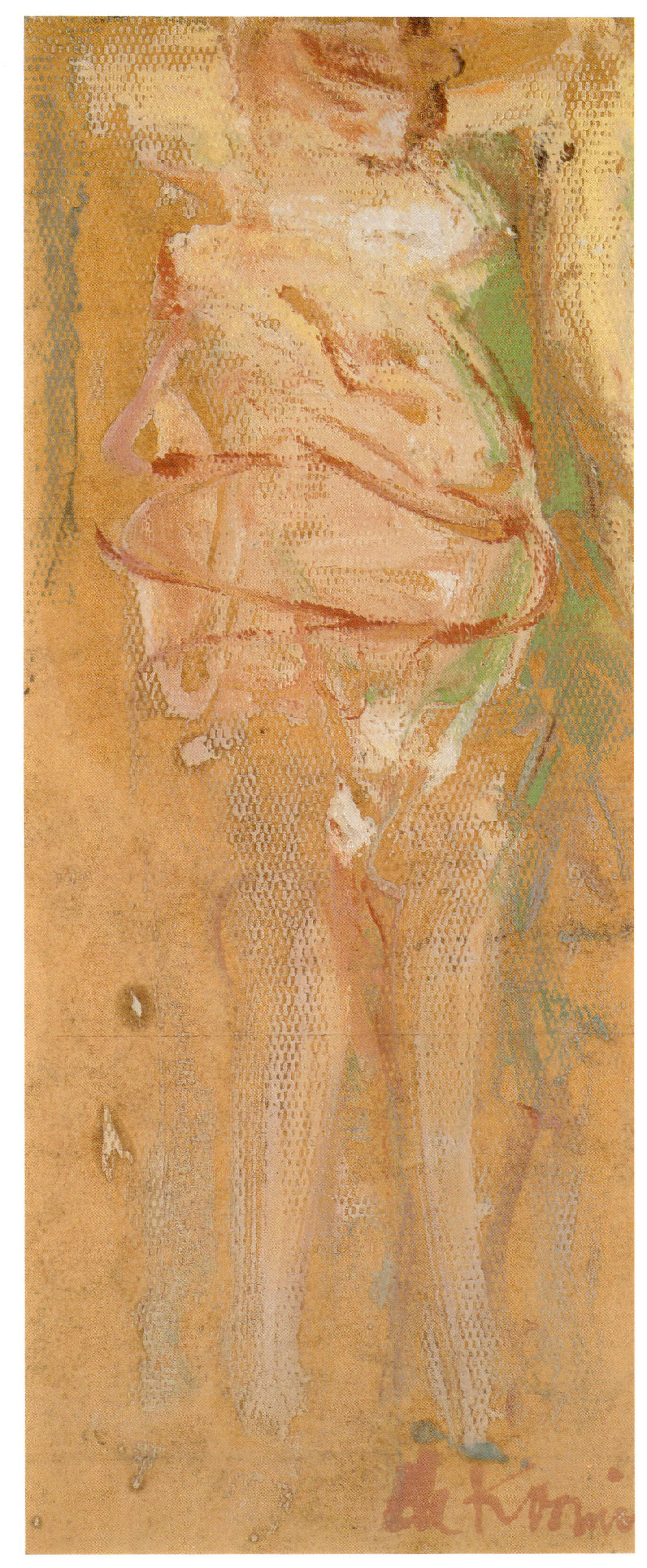

Adolph Gottlieb
1903-1974

Red, Blue and Yellow
1966
oil on canvas
84 x 90 inches
Collection of
Mr. and Mrs. Graham Gund

318

Adolph Gottlieb was one the most influential painters of the New York School, later known as the first generation of abstract expressionists. He left high school in 1920 to study at the Art Students League with John Sloan and Robert Henri; the following year he lived in Paris for six months and attended sketching classes at the Académie de la Grande Chaumière. In the mid-thirties Gottlieb cofounded and exhibited regularly with The Ten, a group of artists who worked in an expressionist style that countered the predominant social realism and regionalism. As an easel painter for the Federal Art Project of the Works Progress Administration, he spent a year creating works for public buildings such as hospitals and schools. He then moved to the desert near Tucson, Arizona. There he began adding Native American art objects to his collection of primitive and tribal art and painted still lifes of dried cactus and gourds that resembled the flattened, abstracted, and animate forms found in the work of Salvador Dali. Often politically involved, Gottlieb was president in 1944-45 of the Federation of Modern Painters and Sculptors and in 1950 joined The Irascibles in their protest of the policies of the Metropolitan Museum of Art.

In *Red, Blue and Yellow* defined circles of intense color hover near loose, thick calligraphic lines. With his understanding of the emotional power of certain colors and his technique of shadowing and splattering paint, Gottlieb has created an image that evokes a series of dualities: control and openness, tension and calmness, rationality and spontaneity. This singular image composed of opposing forces relates to his Imaginary Landscapes (1951-57) and Bursts (1957-74). In his earlier Pictographs (1941-51) Gottlieb, inspired by his reading of Carl Jung's theory of archetypes and the collective unconscious, randomly placed within a grid images drawn from Native American and ancient Greek art plus abstracted images of parts of the human body. He created a playful tension as he compartmentalized these symbolic images. In his Imaginary Landscapes, celestial shapes seem to be pulling against the gravity of the "earth" below, a chaotic land mass of familiar pictographs. In the Bursts, a luminous disc is suspended above a turbulent, exploding ground mass. For Gottlieb, a whole image, like human life itself, is the result of a dynamic balance of opposites.

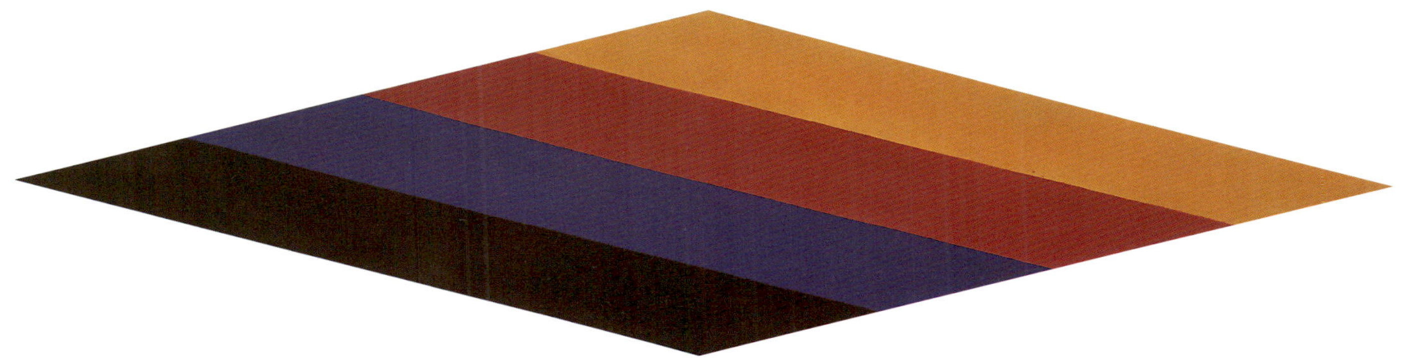

With his clean, cropped, larger-than-life portraits of his wife Ada, son Vincent, and circle of famous friends, Alex Katz became the recognizable leader of the New Realism that emerged in the 1960s. Although inspired by movies and billboard advertising, Katz's depictions of people at the beach or at a cocktail party are not related to pop art's critique of the superficiality of our culture; instead, they are investigations of the formal values of painting. Influenced by Henri Matisse, Edouard Manet, and Fernand Léger, Katz simplifies and generalizes his portraits to depict a convincing likeness of the subject without sentimentality. His explorations of abstraction and representation took a playful turn in his collaboration with Paul Taylor on nine dances beginning in 1960 and his sets (life-size wood cutouts) for Kenneth Koch's off-Broadway production *George Washington Crossing the Delaware* in 1962.

Upon graduation from Cooper Union in New York City in 1949, Katz received a fellowship to The Skowhegan School of Painting and Sculpture in Maine, where he began not only a lifetime commitment to the school, but also a love affair with the state. In Maine Katz, who has always been interested in impressions of light, began to paint outdoors, directly from nature.

Sunny IV, the fourth version of a portrait of his dog, is set on the rocky coast of Maine and is imbued with exhilarating light. Typical of Katz, the images in the background are considerably smaller than the image in the foreground, thereby causing an engaging play between flatness and depth, pictorial reality and the real world.

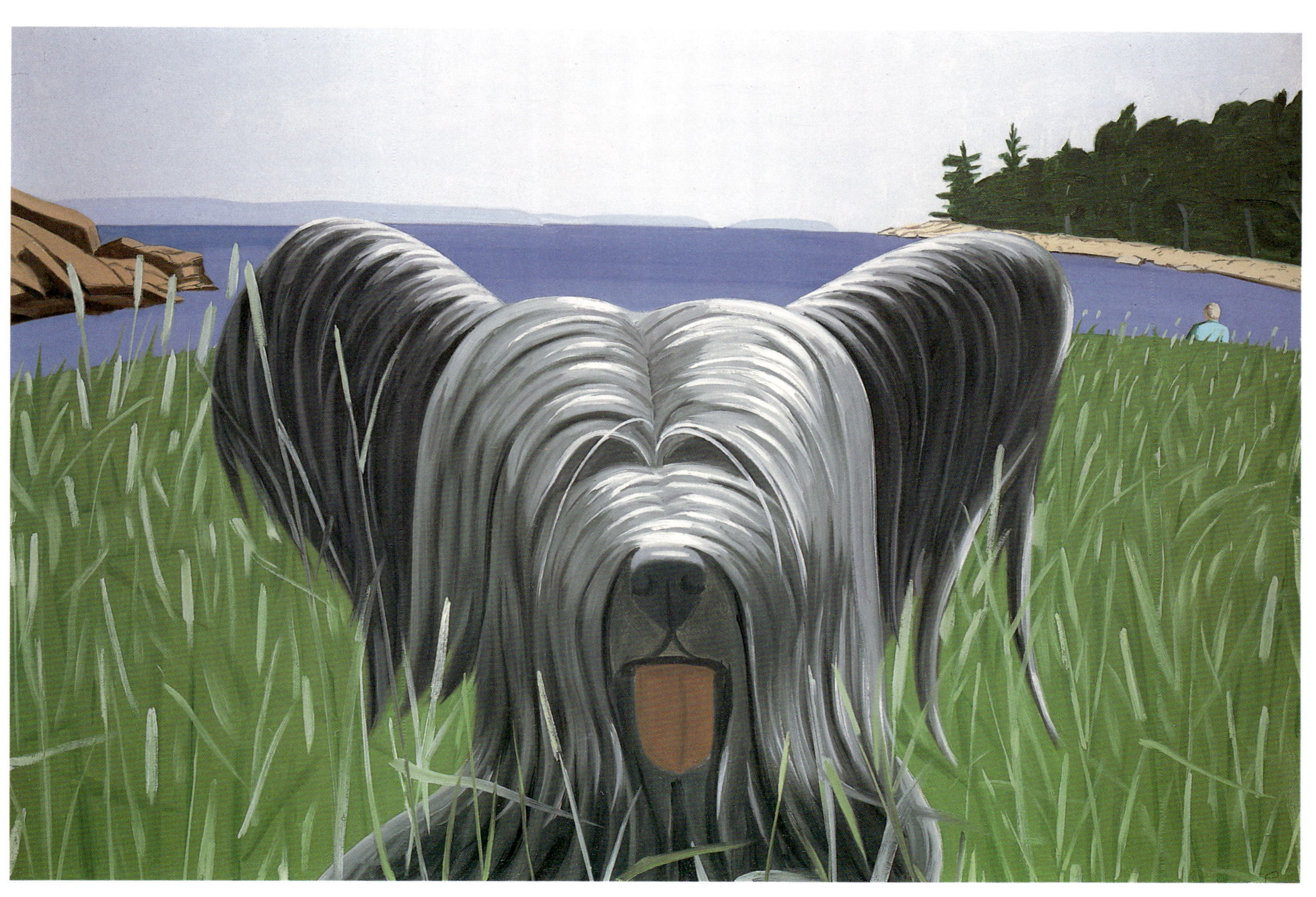

Nefer
c. 1971
oil on canvas
64 x 80 inches
United Missouri Bank

Nancy Graves began her art career as a painter, receiving a combined BFA/MFA from the Yale University School of Art and Architecture in 1964. However, her first artistic triumph came from a trio of life-size camels, inspired by casts of human and animal forms she had seen in the Museum of Natural History in Florence, that she exhibited at The Whitney Museum of American Art in 1969. In the interrelated sculptures, films, drawings, and paintings that followed, Graves joined art and science and evoked the spiritual, ritualistic, and magical qualities of both. Her camel bones ("fossils," she says), hanging, propped, or scattered as if choreographed gestures, and her films of camels, two of which were shot on location in the Sahara (*Goulimine*, 1970, and *Izy Boukir*, 1970), were influenced by her studies in archaeology and paleontology as well as by Eadweard Muybridge's recording of motion with a camera in the 1880s. Throughout the 1980s Graves continued to push the physical properties of sculpture, creating brightly painted cast and welded assemblages of exotic plants, sea animals, household objects, and industrial debris that lyrically defy gravity.

During the 1970s, however, Graves largely abandoned sculpture for paintings that were based on the science of cartography. Like her "fossils," which are visual impressions of the past, maps are important to Graves as two-dimensional representations of three-dimensional experience—movement, space, and time. Graves even used for her paintings satellite photographs of the moon and Mars and scientific data gathered by the Mariner 9 satellite.

With *Nefer* Graves has created a cosmic world in which the head of Nefertiti takes the form of a red constellation of stars. The atmospheric colors, with layers of yellow and orange calligraphic lines, light-filled dots, and thick streaks of white, produce a galaxy of infinite, luminous depth. *Nefer* was inspired by Graves's studies of topographic maps of the moon, Mars, and the earth's ocean floor.

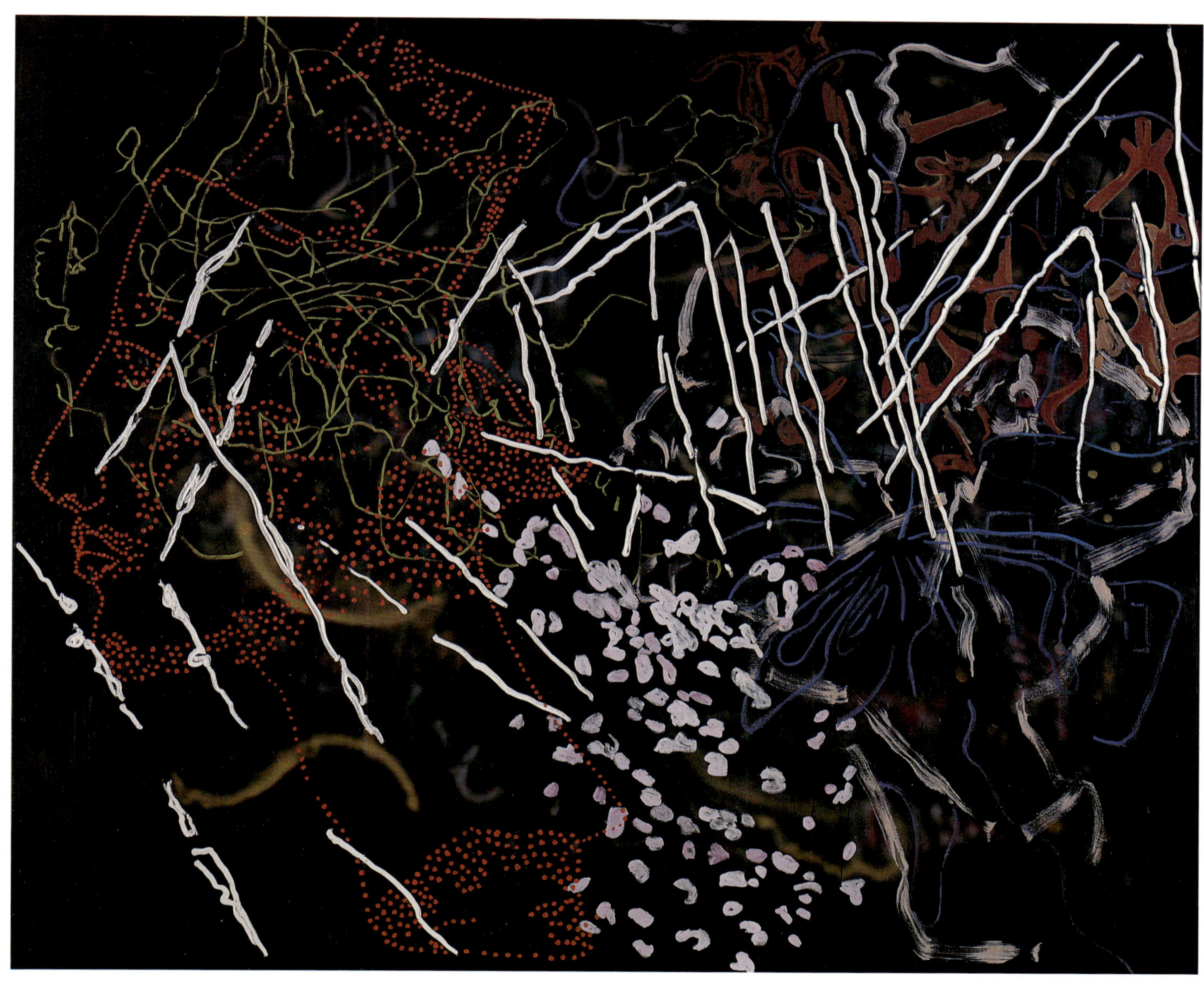

Alexander Calder
1898-1976

Untitled
1972
painted sheet metal
and wire
9 x 14 x 7 inches
signed and dated: CA72
Mr. and Mrs.
W. A. Moncrief, Jr.

Alexander Calder's large, lyrical mobiles have added the playful beauty of nature to public spaces throughout the United States and have made him into the nation's preeminent sculptor. Calder was born in Lawton, Pennsylvania, into a family of artists: his grandfather and father were sculptors, and his mother was a professional portrait painter. He studied mechanical engineering at the Stevens Institute of Technology in Hoboken, New Jersey. After a succession of jobs, he enrolled in the Art Students League in New York City in 1923, where he studied under Thomas Hart Benton and Ash Can School painters George Luks and John Sloan. In these years he was also a free-lance cartoonist for the *National Police Gazette*, which gave him press credentials that led to two influential weeks sketching the Ringling Brothers and Barnum and Bailey Circus in 1925. In 1926 he moved to Paris, where he made a series of wire sculptures (the best known is of cabaret dancer Josephine Baker) and his famous *Circus*. These are based on the single-line principle he had perfected while working for the *Gazette*. He created this miniature circus of acrobats and animals from bits of wire, string, cloth, yarn, and wood. Though he hoped to market it through a toy manufacturer, he earned money instead by giving many "performances," accompanied by recorded music, in his apartment. Calder's *Circus* brought him critical acclaim from the Parisian circle of intellectuals and artists.

In this playful and poetic combination of a mobile and stabile, lightly moving white discs and a larger yellow disc create a metaphor for a solar system quietly orbiting in infinite space. Calder produced his first mobile, which was so named by Marcel Duchamp, after he visited Piet Mondrian's studio in 1930. Calder "wanted to make Mondrian's colored rectangles oscillate" and soon produced his first abstract, geometrical constructions that could be operated by electric motors or hand cranks. Calder shared Mondrian's preference for using primary colors set in opposition to black and white because "secondary colors and intermediate shades serve only to confuse and muddle the distinctness and clarity." He soon became dissatisfied with the predictability of motorized motion and turned to balanced structures propelled by air. In 1932 he began creating stationary sculptures that imply movement, which his friend and fellow sculptor Jean Arp called stabiles. Whichever form Calder chose or combined, he was motivated by the idea of a universal form, the idea of the Universe, itself a moving system. "When I have used spheres and discs," he said, "I have intended that they should represent more than what they are. More or less as the earth is a sphere, but also has miles of gas about it, volcanoes upon it, and the moon making circles around it."

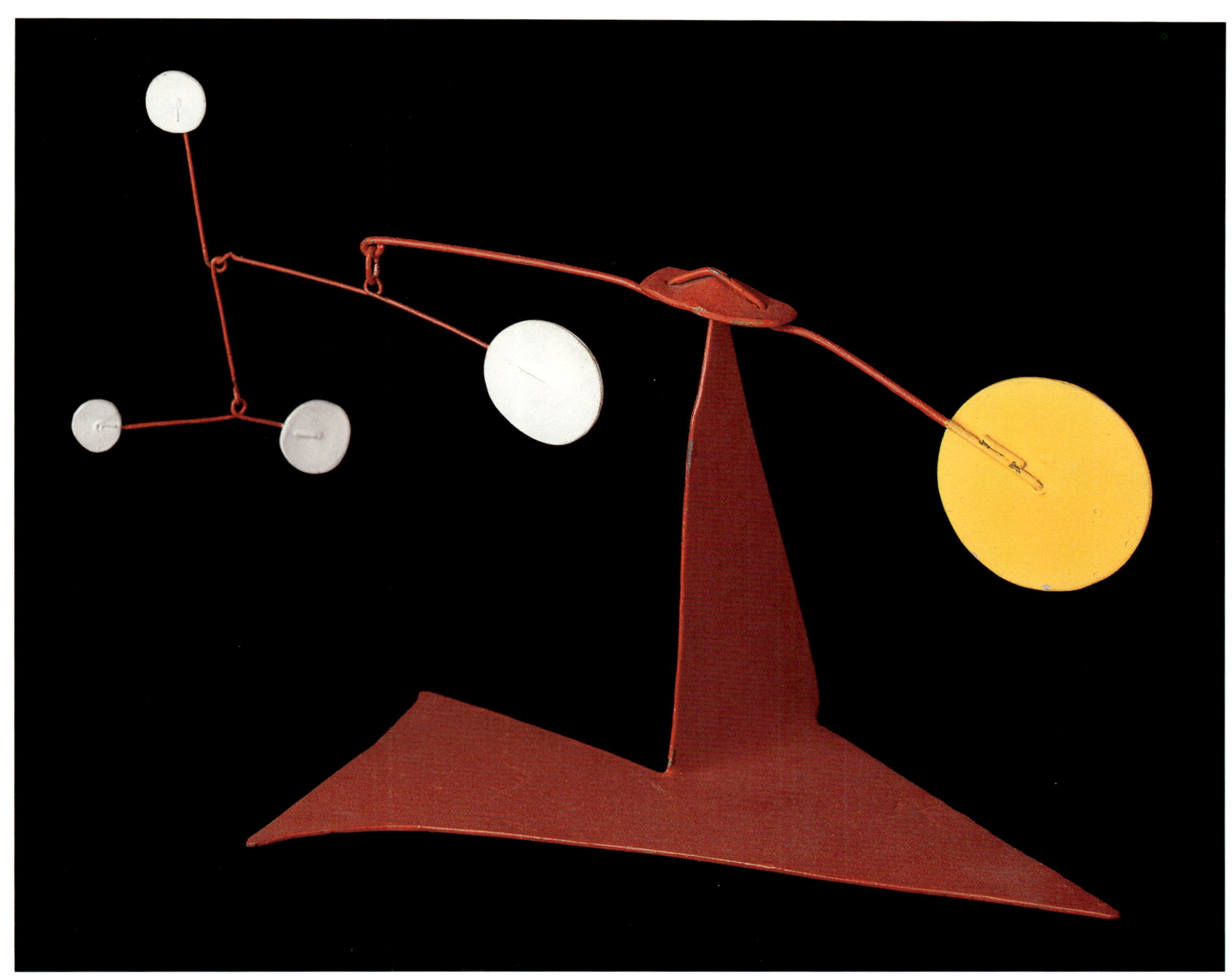

Joseph Raffael
b. 1933

Fish in Spring Water
1978
oil on canvas
30 x 42 inches
Collection of Mr. and Mrs.
Frederic D. Wolfe

Joseph Raffael is best known for his lyrical paintings of glistening, sparkling water—shallow streams with swirling trout or calm pools with Japanese carp, dotted with lily pads and blossoms. Like the artist Janet Fish, Raffael has investigated the dynamic relationship of light with specific objects. However, he is more concerned with the meditative and contemplative qualities of light in nature. His exploration of natural phenomena through painting has been inspired by the poetry of Wallace Stevens and several years of practicing the Taoist meditative concept of *ch'i*. A native New Yorker, Raffael studied art at Cooper Union and then under Josef Albers at Yale University School of Fine Arts (BFA 1956). He rounded out his studies during the year (1958–59) he spent in Europe on a Fulbright Fellowship.

In *Fish in Spring Water* Raffael has applied thinned, luminous colors that seem to be as translucent, wet, and fluid as the clear water. In essence, he has unified his medium and subject, heightening and transcending the beauty of this close-up view of nature. The allover design and jewel-like patterning were inspired by his work as a free-lance fabric designer for a textile studio in the mid-1950s.

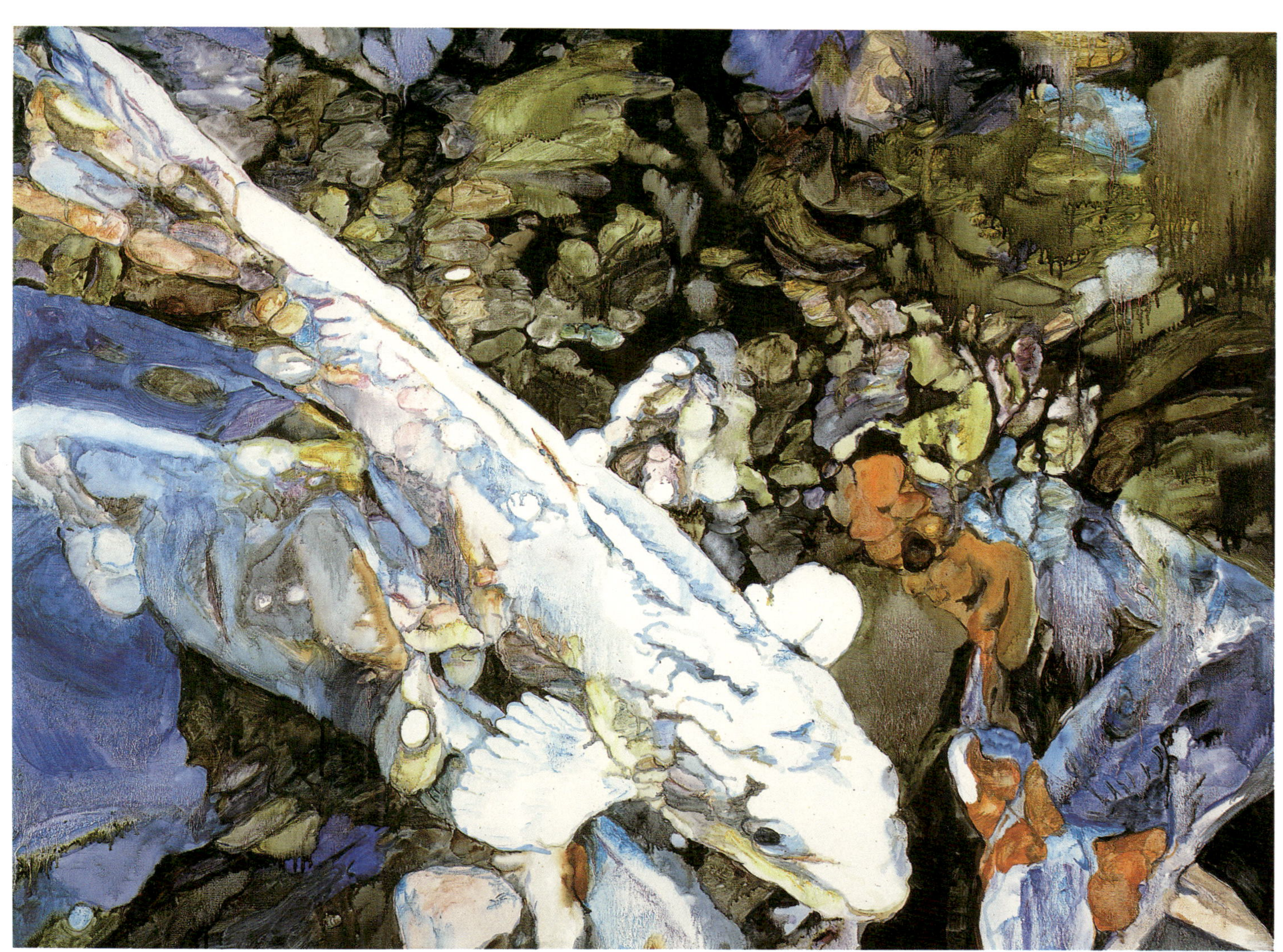

Louise Nevelson
1899-1988

Cosmos X
1979
mixed media
32 x 42 inches
Collection of Mr. and Mrs.
Frederic D. Wolfe

Louise Nevelson's majestic "walls," made from found wood and painted entirely in either black, white, or gold, have become contemporary altars, containing icons of urbanity. Born Louise Berliawsky in Kiev, Russia, Nevelson emigrated with her family to Rockland, Maine, where her father established a lumber business in 1905. She married Charles Nevelson in 1920 and they divorced shortly after the birth of their son in 1922. During the next decade she studied under Kenneth Hayes Miller, Hans Hofmann, and George Grosz at the Art Students League; took classes in voice, modern dance, and drama; and even briefly worked as a film extra in Berlin and Vienna. In 1932 Nevelson assisted the Mexican artist Diego Rivera on a mural for the New Workers' School in New York. Her own work at this time featured small, abstracted human and animal forms in marble, stone, terra cotta, and "tatti-stone," a self-hardening stone. They reveal her interest in African and Pre-Columbian sculpture and early American farm tools, which she collected along with Native American pottery and Puerto Rican *santos.*

In the early 1940s Nevelson began working primarily with wood she collected in the streets and loading docks near her New York studio. She assembled rough pieces of wood, abandoned packing crates, fragments of furniture, and architectural ornamentation into three basic forms: "reliefs," "boxes," and "columns." The "reliefs," which are fastened to a wall, evolved from a flattening of her table-top arrangements, or "landscapes," of found objects in the 1940s. The "boxes" are crates that are either hinged to open at the top or front, or perforated at the sides, and hold groups of salvaged objects. The "columns," which evoke towers, spires, and tree trunks, are derived from the small anthropomorphic sculptures on pedestals that she made in the mid-1950s. Perhaps inspired by the MesoAmerican art and artifacts she saw on two trips to Mexico, in the 1950s Nevelson began to create a series of thematic environmental or "architectural" exhibitions of "walls," a combination of her "boxes" and "columns."

As in the "reliefs," the rough pieces of wood and collaged elements in *Cosmos X* form a three-dimensional picture plane. The concentration of subdued, dark tones produces a subtle play of shadows across the surface, creating a moment of mystery. With its intuitive combination of decaying wood and collaged fragments of newspapers, *Cosmos X* recalls the Merz-pictures and collages of the German artist Kurt Schwitters. Like Schwitters, Nevelson discovered the expressive, poetic potential of fragments from our daily lives.

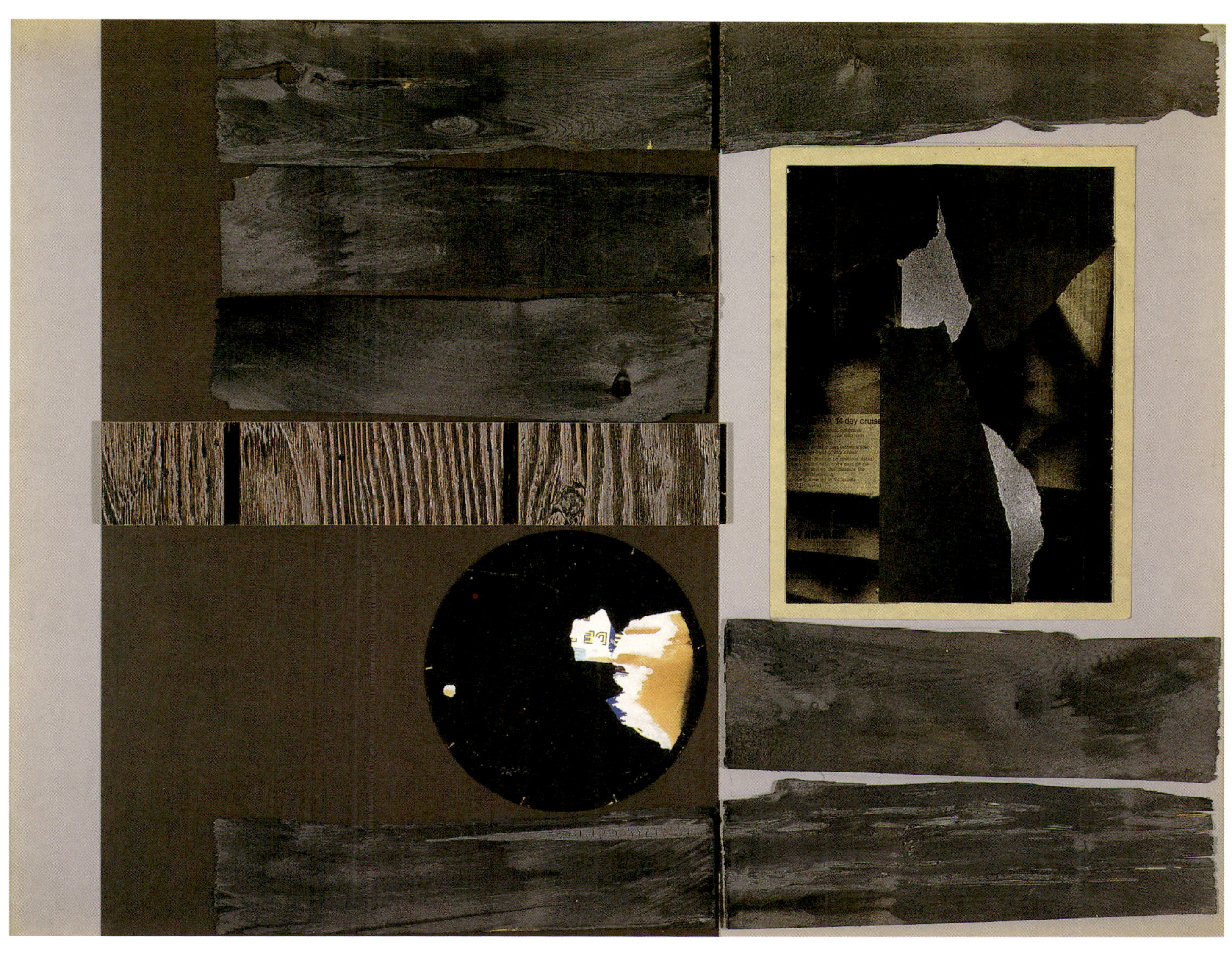

Ed Ruscha
b. 1937

Horses
1981
oil on canvas
60 x 48 inches
Mr. and Mrs.
Charles B. Moncrief

332

With his paintings of words, trademarks, and logos drawn from the commercialism of our popular culture, specifically the cinematic world of Southern California, Ed Ruscha is often considered the West Coast Andy Warhol. An early aspiration to be a commercial artist prompted Ruscha to move from Oklahoma City to Los Angeles in 1956 to study graphic and industrial design at the Chouinard Art Institute, at that time considered a training school for Disney illustrators. He became a successful commercial artist and sign painter, and did layouts for *Artforum* under the name Eddie Russia. Within a short time, especially after seeing Jasper Johns's flags and targets, he wanted to become an artist. In 1963, the same year he had his first solo exhibition at The Ferus Gallery, he published *Twentysix Gasoline Stations*, a thin volume of black-and-white photographs of gas stations on Route 66 between California and Oklahoma. It was the first of fifteen books—or collections of what he calls "facts"—containing images of parking lots, palm trees, real estate opportunities, and buildings on Sunset Strip. One of the most versatile contemporary artists, Ruscha has also produced two films: *Premium* (1970) and *Miracle* (1975).

In *Horses* Ruscha has detached the word "horses" from its normal linguistic function as a noun specifying objects. With the deadpan humor of Belgian artist René Magritte, Ruscha has floated the word in a surrealistic space. Horizontal bands of graduated colors, creating an illusion of depth, seem to represent the expansive western sky and landscape at sunset. Ruscha's background in commercial art and his interest in typography are evident also in the composition and layout of *Horses*. Like his late-1960s paintings of liquid words embedded with cherries, beans, and crawling insects, here the visual and expressive qualities of a word have become the subject.

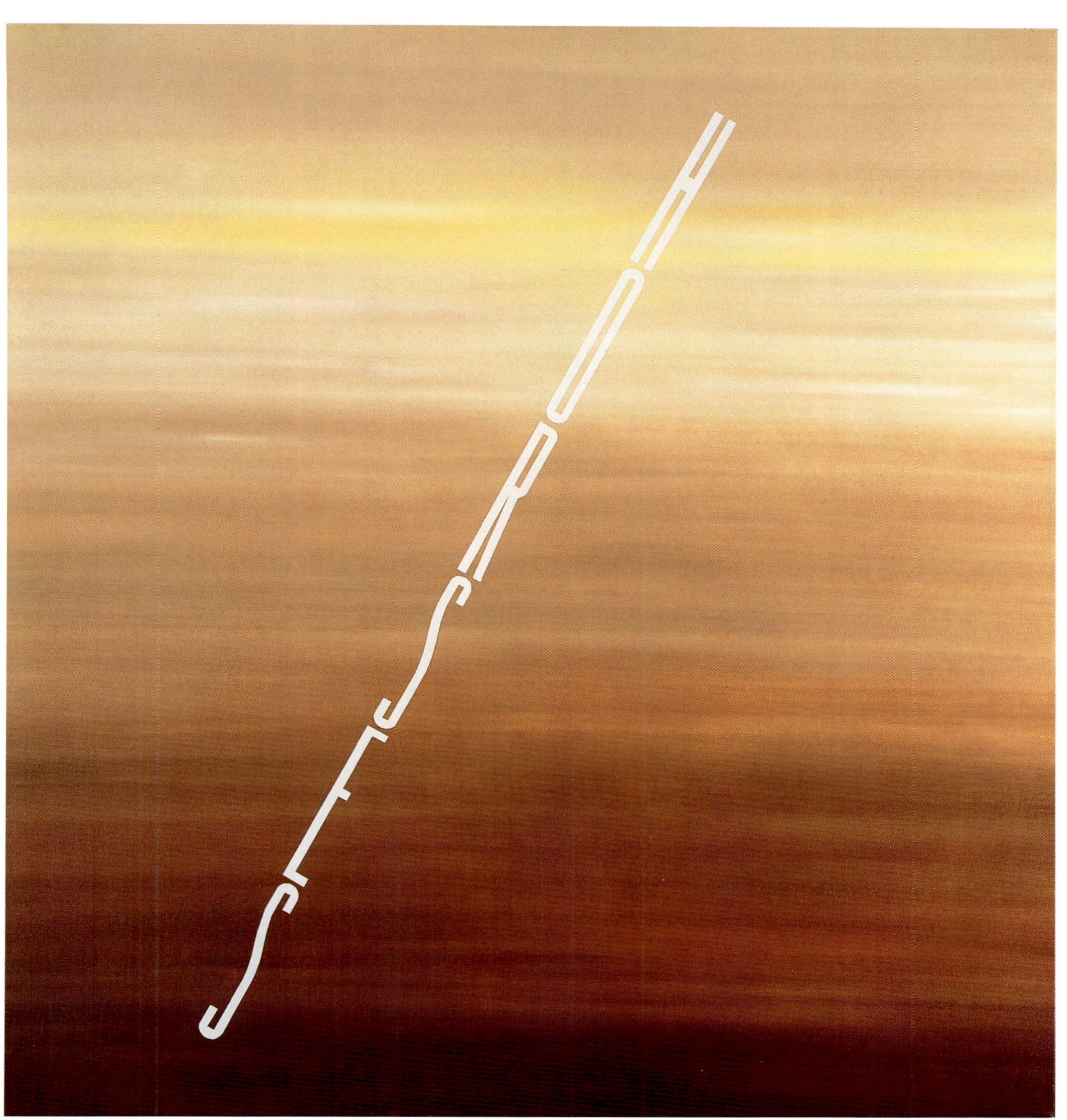

Robert Cottingham
b. 1935

Wichita
1985
acrylic on board
29 1/2 x 39 1/4 inches
signed and dated lr:
Cottingham 1985
Spring Creek Art
Foundation, Inc.

Robert Cottingham is a seminal figure in the photorealist movement. His depictions of the urban landscape, including fragments of neon signs, storefronts, and theater marquees, are unsentimental observations of the daily activities that define our culture. Like Allan D'Arcangelo, who paints icons of the American highway, Cottingham paints the icons of consumerism. Usually sharp-angled, as if viewed looking up from the streets, these icons are edited not only to focus on the dynamics of design, color, and typography, but also to discover visual puns. Cottingham studied advertising and graphic design at the Pratt Institute in Brooklyn and was the art director for the advertising agency Young and Rubicam in New York City from 1959 to 1964. In 1968, four years after being transferred to Los Angeles, he had his first solo exhibition, which consisted of paintings of Los Angeles landmarks, at the Molly Barnes Gallery. He is a prolific printmaker and was among the group of photorealists who worked with Shorewood Press in New York to produce lithographs for *Documenta 5* in Kassel, Germany, in 1972.

Wichita depicts the tower at the Wichita airport in its pristine condition of the 1950s. Stripped to the bare essentials, *Wichita* is a brilliance of blues—tiles, tower, and sky. Although hard-edged and hyperreal, this painting is unlike other photorealist works in that it is hand painted and not airbrushed. Cottingham also departs from his colleagues by using his camera as a tool for exploring formal possibilities and not to capture and then reproduce a photographic reality. He constantly adjusts and analyzes color and composition through a long process that begins with his photographing of street scenes using both 35-mm and 2 1/4-inch transparency film. He then selects an image and completes studies in ink, acrylic, watercolor, and gouache to discover basic abstract patterns. *Wichita* was completed after his solo exhibition at the Wichita Art Museum in 1984.

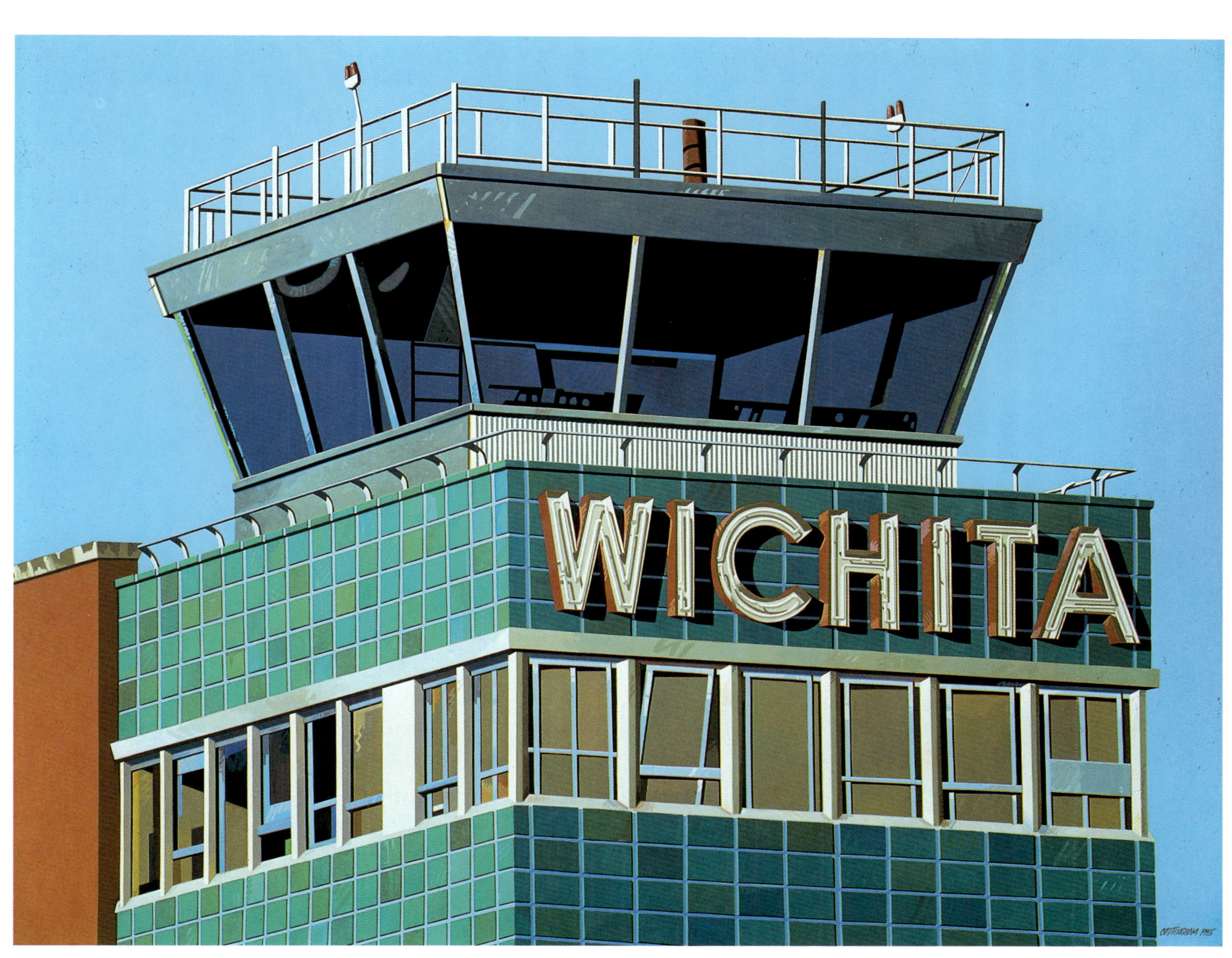
WICHITA

Janet Fish
b. 1938

Waiting for Will
1986
oil on canvas
70 x 60 inches
signed and dated lr:
Janet Fish 86
United Missouri Bank

336

Janet Fish's mesmerizing paintings of glasses from the 1970s and her still lifes with flowers, fruit, and glassware from the 1980s have as their subject the relationship of light to all things in life. Rather than depictions of discrete objects, her still lifes are "situations," she says, in which the complex interactions of light and color create sensuous moments, "things at their most exciting." Fish uses multiple photographs of the subject as a compositional tool, arranging them as preliminary drawings, and works on paintings at various times throughout the day, producing a composite of the conditions. Fish's use of light is reminiscent of seventeenth-century Baroque artists such as Georges de La Tour (French, 1582-1647) and Francisco de Zurbarán (Spanish, 1598-1664), both artists she admires. For her, light is energy, and the movement of light structures the painting. Her interest in light and painting outdoors began when she was quite young; she recalls that when she was twelve and living in Bermuda, she painted outdoors at different times of the day. It also shows the influence of Alex Katz, her first-year painting teacher at Yale University School of Art and Architecture, where she received a BFA/MFA in 1963.

Tactile and lush, *Waiting for Will* exhibits what Fish calls "painterly realism," a "realism that comes out of abstraction." Although the canvas includes a figure, the artist considers it part of the still life. Fish began adding figures to her works in the 1980s, often painting her friends in Vermont, where she spends half the year. In this painting, her close friend Lauren McConnell is waiting for her husband, Will. Movement of light across the surface integrates the painting. There is a lively play between surface and depth, interior and exterior, as the table is tilted toward the viewer and the storm in the Vermont mountains, seen through the window, is far away. With patterns of contrasting colors and subtle variations of brushwork, Fish forces the eye not to linger upon intriguing details such as the photograph or the roll of stamps. Here Fish has not told a story, but has created a psychologically charged moment that recalls the work of Edward Hopper

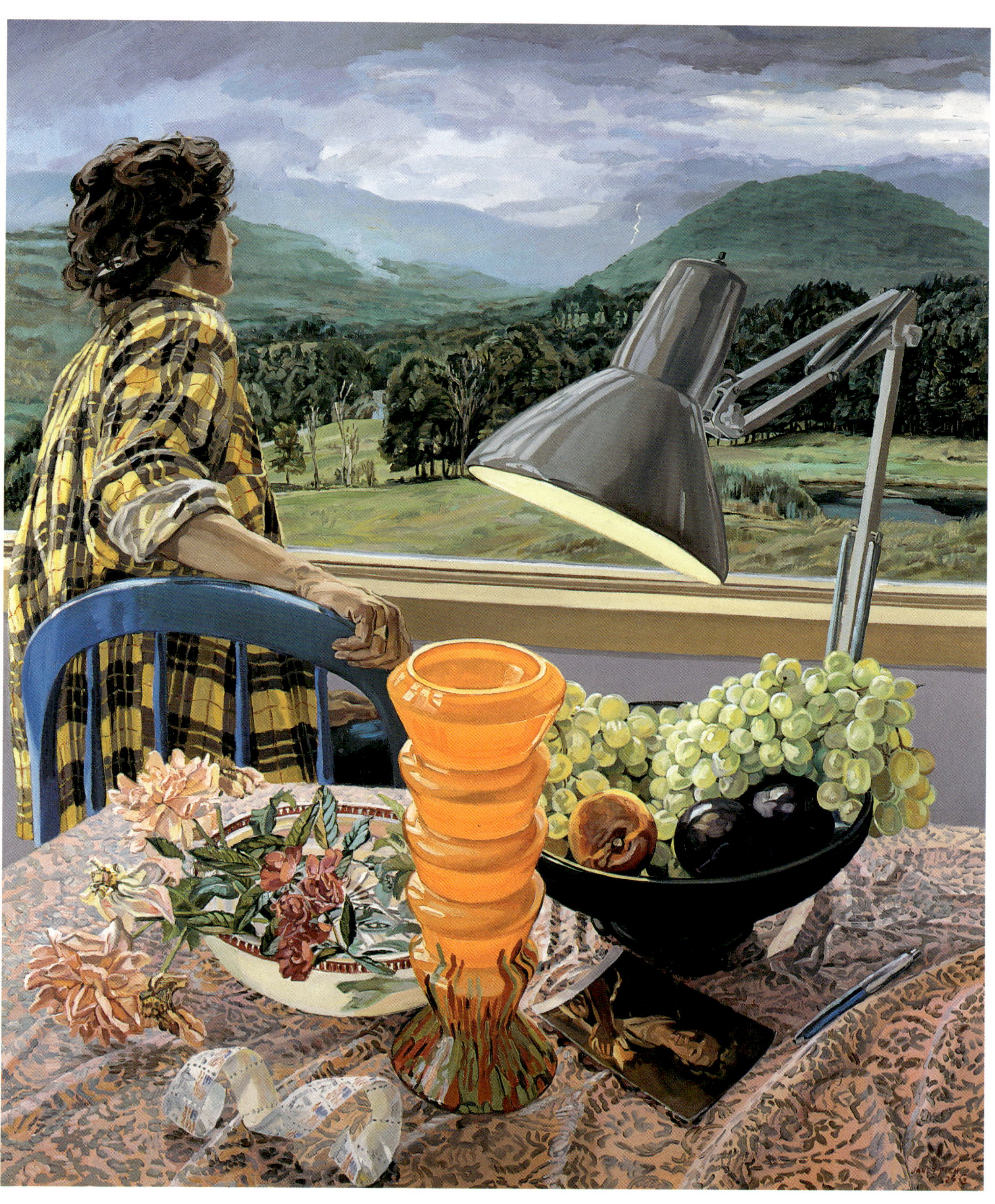

Gladiolas
1987
chalk and tar on vinyl
composite
96 x 96 inches
Private Collection,
Mexico

Donald Sultan's bold, dark, and provocative paintings of still lifes (lemons, single or stacked, have become his trademark) and cityscapes are both elegant and rough. His use of such industrial materials as linoleum tiles, tar, latex paint, and butyl rubber has familial roots. His paternal grandfather emigrated from Russia to Detroit, via New York, to work in the automobile factories. His father, who always wanted to be a painter (the basement was lined with photographs of Jackson Pollock's paintings), had to open a tire business to support the family. At first Sultan wanted to be in theater and entered the University of North Carolina at Chapel Hill as a dramatic arts major; he did set designs for children's plays and worked in summer stock on Cape Cod. He changed to painting, receiving his BFA at Chapel Hill and then MFA at the Art Institute of Chicago School of Art. While in Chicago he helped organize the N.A.M.E. Gallery, an artists' cooperative.

By setting delicate, white gladiolas in a clear, glass vase cut out of thick tiles of black tar, Sultan plays with our perceptions of the beautiful. The tiles create a visible grid that recalls the work of Carl Andre and other minimalist artists, who eliminated representation in favor of repeated forms made from manufactured, industrial materials. Like Sultan's "debris paintings" (small objects embedded into thick layers of acrylic) and "puzzle paintings" (pieces cut out and then reglued in different arrangements on tiles covered with rubber) of the 1970s, *Gladiolas* addresses changes in perception and the contradictions inherent in any classifications.

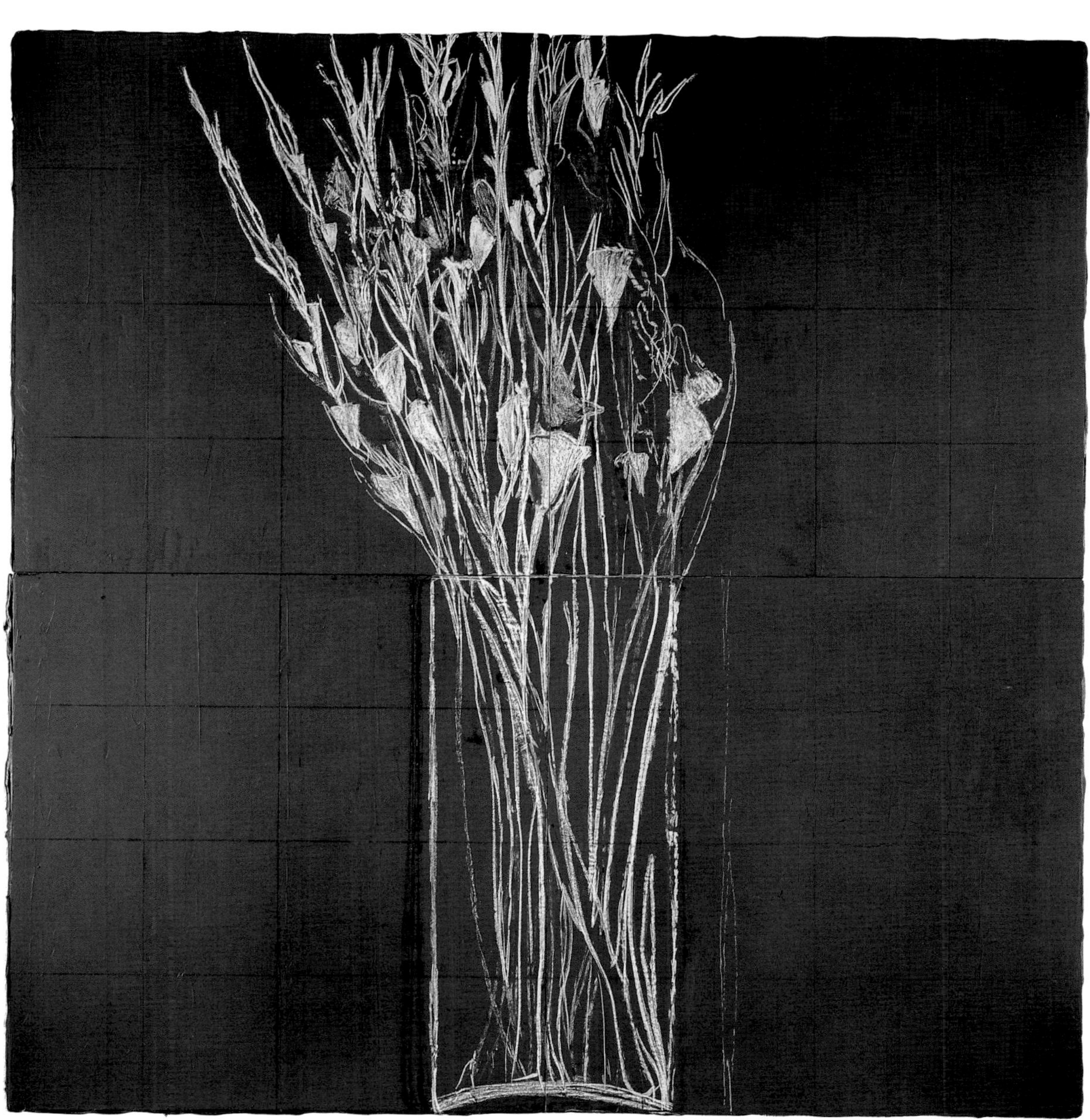

Roy De Forest
b. 1930

Mutley and the Woodsprite
1987-88
polymer vinyl,
acrylic on linen
74 x 84 inches
Collection of
Paul and Fredrica Cassiday

Roy De Forest's paintings and mixed-media constructions of cartoonish dogs, bizarre humanoid figures, and animated plants in carnival colors are a Lewis Carroll world of magic and fantasy. These whimsical works of the 1960s and 1970s linked him to a loosely defined group of Bay-area artists, including Robert Arneson, William T. Wiley, Bruce Conner, and Joan Brown, who made "funk," "dirty," or "bad" art. Their manipulation of found objects and nontraditional materials, often rough and poorly crafted, appeared to satirize the consciously serious art being made in New York. De Forest has been living in Northern California since the early 1950s, when he attended the California School of Fine Arts (now the San Francisco Art Institute) and studied with Elmer Bischoff, Hassel Smith, and David Park. After receiving his BA from San Francisco State College in 1953 (MFA 1958), he served in the army for two years and began exhibiting his works. From 1965 to 1982 he was a professor of painting and drawing at the University of California at Davis, where Wiley, Arneson, and Wayne Thiebaud also taught. De Forest now lives near Berkeley, sharing his house with a number of dogs, including the domesticated dingoes that have appeared in his works.

In *Mutley and the Woodsprite*, a dog that, with its glowing eyes, is both funny and frightening is surrounded by what De Forest calls "a phantasmagoric microworld"— here a crazy-quilt of grotesque anthropomorphic creatures and animated plants. Dabs and dashes of bold colors throughout the canvas and on the frame intensify this fragment of a story, perhaps an epic tale, in which humans, animals, and plants represent a different social and political order. Decorative and demented, engaging and menacing, *Mutley and the Woodsprite* exemplifies and celebrates the magical power of art to transport the viewer to another reality.

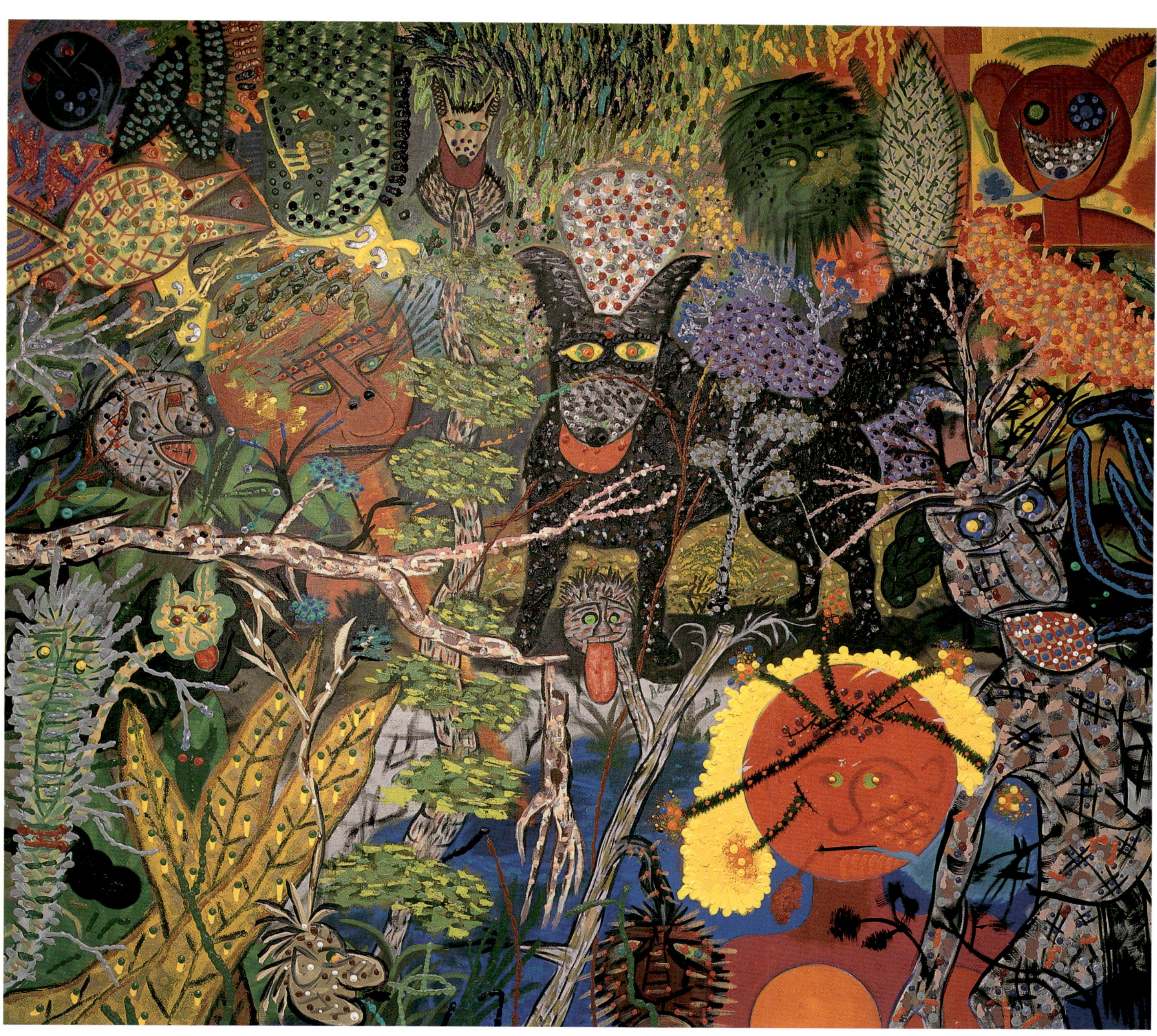

Jennifer Bartlett
b. 1941

In the Garden II, #3
1981
oil on canvas; oil pastel
on paper under Plexiglas
48 x 72 inches installed
Collection of Mr. and Mrs.
Frederic D. Wolfe

Jennifer Bartlett's large-scale works in serial format combine imagery and a painterly sensuality with the cool, detached conceptual approach of minimalism. She was educated at Mills College and Yale University School of Art and Architecture (BFA 1964; MFA 1965), where her teachers were Jack Tworkov, James Rosenquist, Jim Dine, and Al Held. In 1976 she first exhibited what became one of her most famous works, the monumental *Rhapsody*, which consists of nearly one thousand one-foot-square painted steel plates on a grid. The plates, rendered in a variety of styles and in both pastels and vibrant hues, have three main groups. Some contain archetypal images of a house, ocean, tree, and mountain; others are painted simply with lines or with squares, circles, or triangles, either done freely or ruled; and the last 126 plates, evoking ocean waters, are painted in fifty-four shades of blue. In the 1980s Bartlett began creating whole environments by incorporating sculptural elements such as folding screens, boats, houses, and fences. Recently, she completed her most ambitious commission, the ceiling of the Homanji Temple, which belongs to the Jodo Shinshu (True Pure Land) Buddhist sect, in Choshi-shi, Japan. The ceiling is comprised of 316 works on handmade paper, which have images of everyday things such as tableware and kimono patterns painted in traditional Japanese paints and techniques. Since 1971 Bartlett has published poems, stories, and extracts of her diaries. In 1986 she published her autobiographical *History of the Universe: A Novel*, illustrated with several of her own photomontages.

In the Garden II, #3 juxtaposes two views of the same scene. The image on the left panel is rendered in short brush strokes and patterns of light and shadow that recall the impressionist paintings of Claude Monet and Georges Seurat. The image on the right panel is rendered with an uninterrupted line and vibrant color reminiscent of Henri Matisse's work. There is a play of perspectives as the pool in both presses or tilts forward but retains a hint of vanishing one-point perspective, a method brought to prominence by Renaissance painters. The grid in both recalls the method, also begun in the Renaissance, of transferring a cartoon, a preliminary drawing of an image, to another surface. *In the Garden II, #3* is one of eight works based on one drawing in Bartlett's *In the Garden* series, two hundred sketches that, like the works Monet painted of his garden at Giverny, depict the same subject—here a garden with a pool, cherub, and row of cypresses—in different kinds of light. Bartlett began the sketches, which range from abstract to naturalistic and are in various media, in 1979 while spending the winter at a villa near Nice.

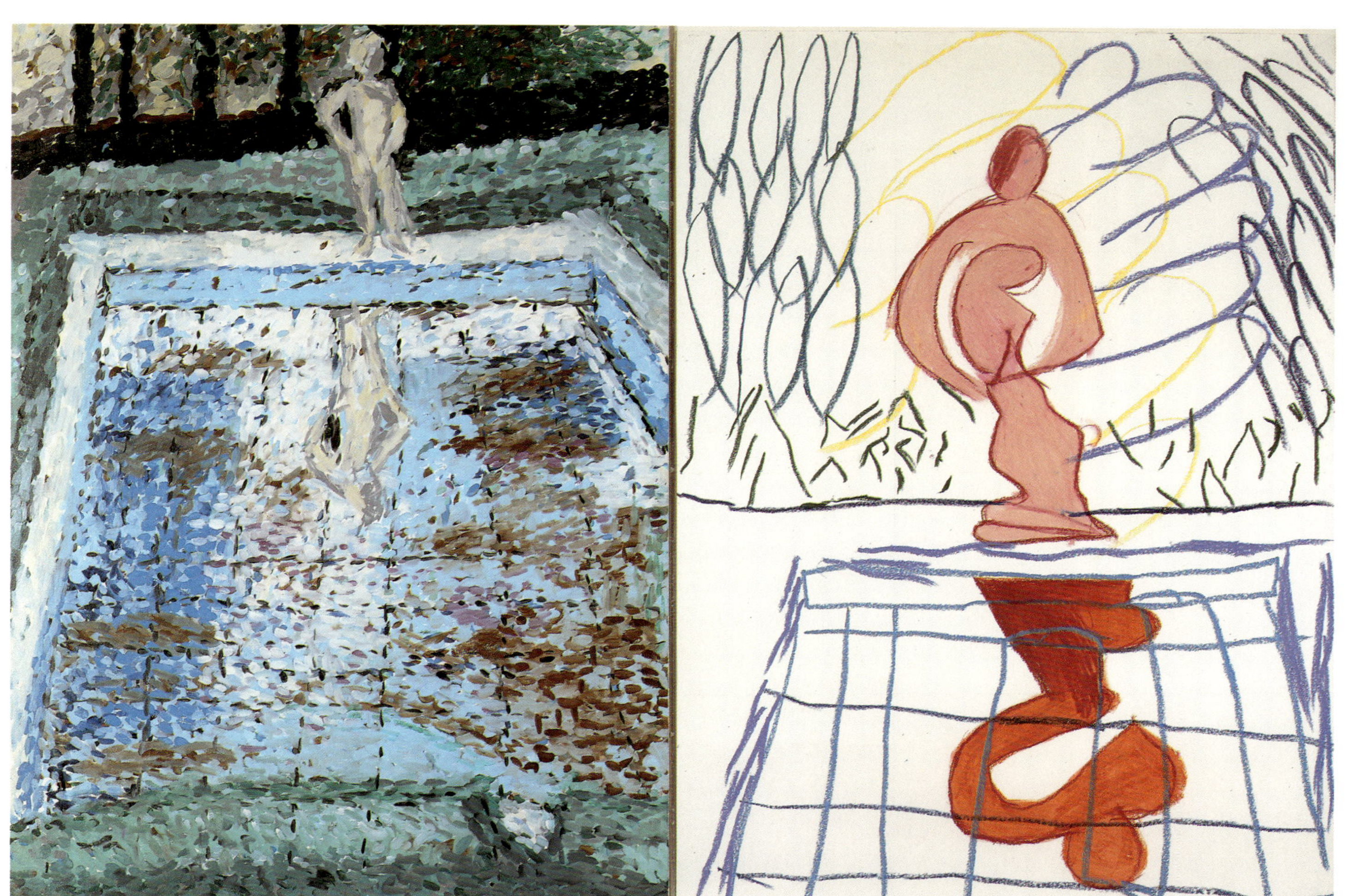

Lynda Benglis
b. 1941

Torso
1992
ceramic and paint
14 x 28 inches
Collection of Mr. and Mrs.
Frederic D. Wolfe

344

Organic, sensuous, and even at times erotic, the sculptural work of Lynda Benglis is about sensory pleasure and knowledge derived from materials and form. Benglis, who trained as a painter at Sophie Newcomb College in New Orleans (BFA 1964), considers her works three-dimensional paintings. Beginning with her "fallen paintings" (pools of poured pigmented latex rubber) and her "frozen gestures" (poured polyurethane foam, either in oozing mounds on the floor or theatrical armatures coming off the wall), Benglis has explored the dynamic and dialectical relationship between herself and her medium. This process is exemplified by the work of Jackson Pollock, whom she admires. In the 1980s she pushed the possibilities of her medium further with billowing metallized reliefs, which were made by spraying fine layers of molten metal over fine wire mesh. Like her wax lozenges, embellished knots, and gold-leaf torsos, these reliefs are paradoxical: they are both beautiful and vulgar, fluid and solid. In all of Benglis's sculptural work there is an underlying critique of the cultural signs of femininity. It is a more subtle comment on sexual stereotyping or issues of gender differences than her earlier photographic advertisements and her provocative videos of the 1970s.

Torso is a fragment of a shiny, flowing garment that seductively swells and seems suspended in its movement. Pinched, twisted, and crinkled, *Torso* is both flamboyantly decorative and luxuriantly sensual. It differs from her linear, bulbous "torsos" of the late 1970s (gold leaf over plaster and chicken wire), which referred to vessels and urns, symbols for the womb and fertility, in that it is a metaphor for the transformation of the female body through adornment.

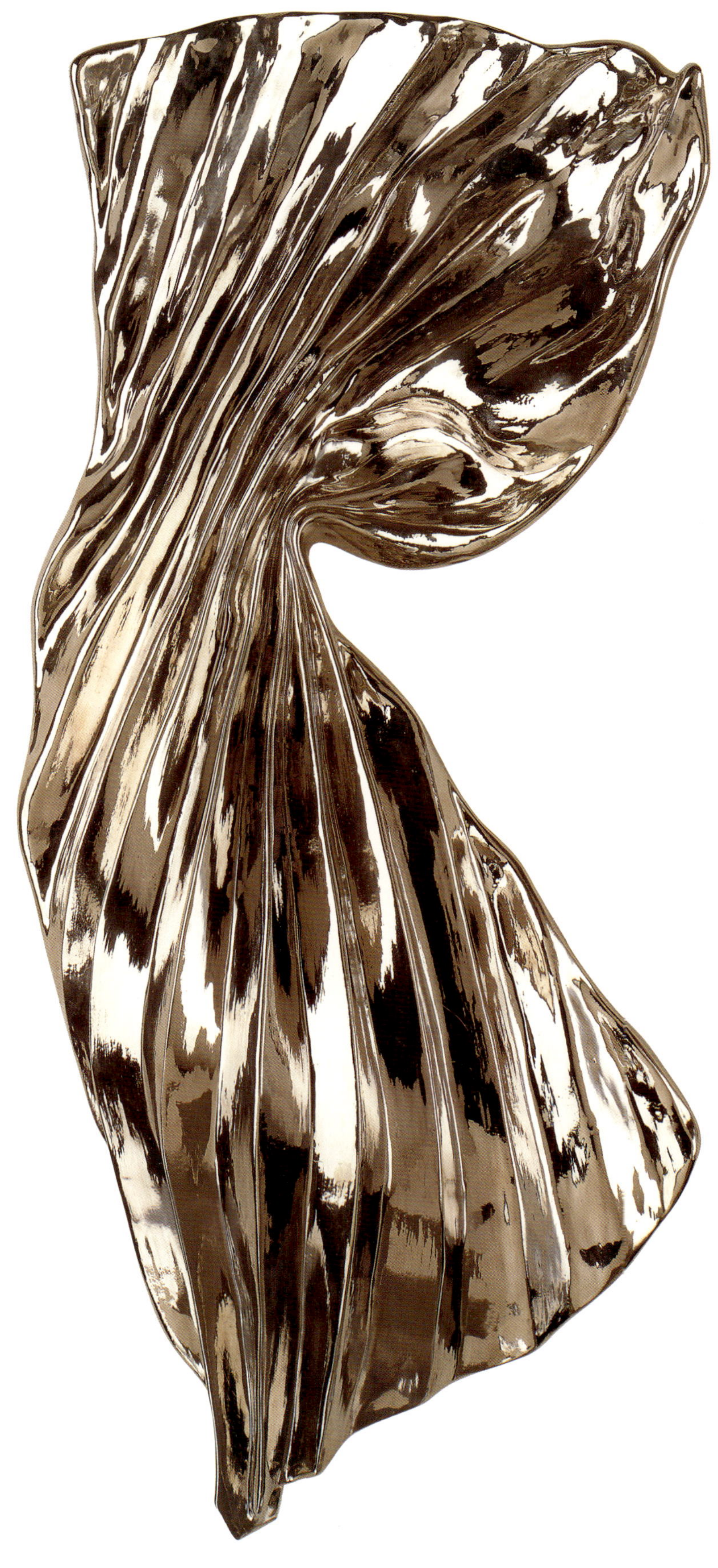

Larry Rivers
b. 1923

Art and the Artist: Picasso
1992
oil on canvas mounted
on sculpted foamboard
63 x 56 x 6 1/2 inches
signed and dated lr:
Larry Rivers '92
Collection of Mr. and Mrs.
Frederic D. Wolfe

Larry Rivers was born Yitzroch Loiza Grossberg, the only son of a Russian-Polish immigrant couple. Before studying painting with Hans Hofmann at his schools in New York and Provincetown in 1947-48, he was a professional jazz musician. A nightclub comedian had changed his name. Within a short time, Rivers, who continued to support himself for several years by playing saxophone at night, acquired a reputation as an iconoclast and provocateur and a celebrity status that would be surpassed only by Andy Warhol. Like Warhol, Rivers worked in multiple fields: he performed in Kenneth Koch's *The Tinguely Machine* and *Pull My Daisy,* based on a play by Jack Kerouac; he designed sets for two off-Broadway plays by LeRoi Jones (later Imamu Baraka) and sets and costumes for Stravinsky's *Oedipus Rex*, conducted by Lukas Foss at Lincoln Center; and with filmmaker Pierre-Dominique Gaisseau he made a television travelogue, *Africa and I*, that was broadcast in 1968 on the National Broadcasting Company's *Experiments in Television*. While working on the film, he and Gaisseau barely escaped execution as white mercenaries in Nigeria.

Although Rivers is considered a leading second-generation abstract expressionist, his work is often controversial, difficult to classify, and ambiguous in its satire. For example, his painting *Washington Crossing the Delaware*, 1953, a reworking of the popular nineteenth-century image by Emanual Leutze, appears to satirize the seriousness of abstract expressionism and to anticipate the use of ready-made images by pop artists. His nudes of the 1950s and 1960s—such as poet Frank O'Hara with his socks on; his mother-in-law Berdie with her aging, corpulent body; and "Vocabulary Lessons" (drawings and paintings of nudes whose body parts are identified with large stenciled lettering)—seem to be parodies of academic studies. His interest in art history extends as well to more complex appropriations. His painting *Dutch Masters and Cigars* (1963) is derived from Rembrandt's *Syndics of the Cloth Drapers' Guild* (1662) and his very humorous *The Greatest Homosexual* (1964) is derived from Jacques-Louis David's full-length portrait of Napolean.

Art and the Artist: Picasso is one of a series of portraits of modern masters. Here an older, arrogant Picasso stands among images from his painting *The Women of Algiers* (1955), which is a reconstruction of Eugène Delacroix's painting of the same name. Layers of sculptured foamboard, carved and lavishly painted with the same colors of the appropriated painting, jut out into the viewer's space. Rivers also executed portraits of Henri Matisse and Fernand Léger amid images from their famous works.

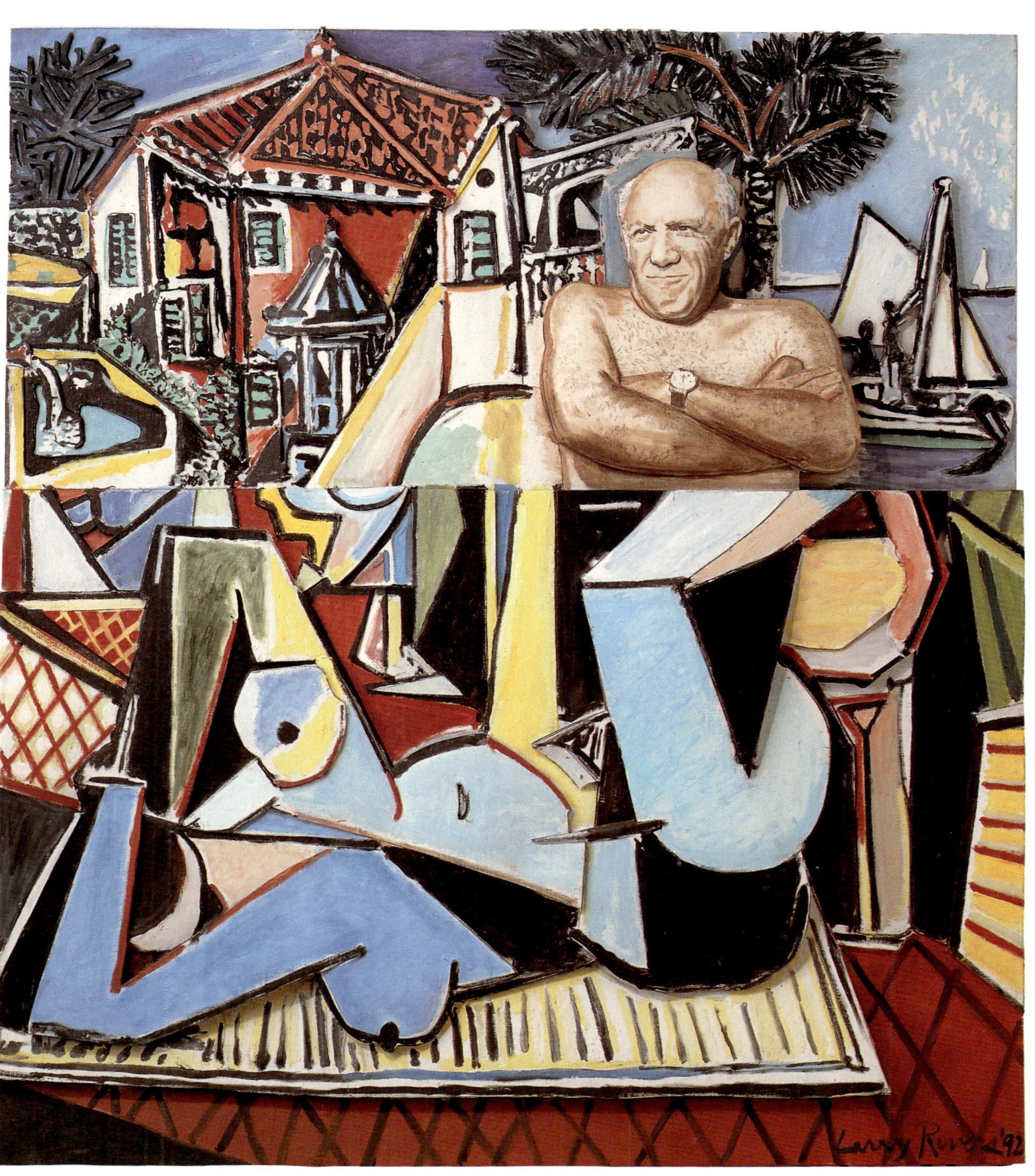

One of the most satisfying aspects of completing this ambitious project is having the opportunity to thank the many people who have made *American Traditions* tangible. Realization of the exhibition and catalogue marking the centennial of the Culver Academies has been a collaborative effort that has called upon the talents and goodwill of several individuals and institutions.

At the Indianapolis Museum of Art, numerous members of the curatorial division have participated in the organization of the exhibition and its accompanying publication. Chief curator Ellen W. Lee oversaw this work and, more than any other museum staff member, deserves credit for pulling together the entire project. Her professionalism, dedication, sound judgment, and sensitivity to others have never been more evident than in this enterprise. Together, she and curatorial associate Harriet G. Warkel served as curators for the IMA portion of the exhibition trilogy, which encompasses American paintings from 1825 to 1945. Working from the leads provided by the Culver Art Committee, they have scouted alumni collections from coast to coast in order to assemble an exhibition that documents American tastes and traditions. Harriet Warkel is also the author of the catalogue texts for this segment of the show. With her prodigious research skills, good judgment, and awesome organizational abilities, Harriet was the ideal person for this complex project. Holliday T. Day, curator of contemporary art, and Suzanne Weaver, curatorial associate in the contemporary department, have curated the exhibition of American contemporary art presented at the Indianapolis Museum of Art-Columbus Gallery. Making numerous trips and tough curatorial decisions, they have shaped a show that reflects many of the important trends of the last forty years. To Suzanne goes enormous credit for researching, synthesizing, and writing the catalogue entries for paintings and sculpture embodying such a wide range of aesthetic expression.

Stewarding the creation of any exhibition catalogue is a serious undertaking, but when the finished product is a publication that represents three different shows and several authors, the task borders on the heroic. With grace, wisdom, and a firm grip on the timetable, IMA production manager Jane Graham has coordinated and guided every element of this book. Working with Jane were two of the most skilled professionals in museum publications today. The book's design was entrusted to Richard Poulin of Richard Poulin Design Group Inc., New York. Richard's enthusiasm and his dedication to crafting a book that also reflects Culver traditions have enhanced the entire endeavor. Debra Edelstein of Medford, Massachusetts, has edited this complicated volume with her customary eye for detail and her uncanny capacity to grasp the effect of the whole. The IMA's photography department, headed by photographer John Geiser and managed by Ruth Roberts, provided ongoing consultation and assistance with the catalogue reproductions.

American Traditions has also benefited from the experience and resourcefulness of IMA registrar Vanessa Burkhart, who, with Beth James of the Eiteljorg Museum, organized the logistics for the shipping and handling of our trilogy. Gayle Lewis, assistant to the registrar, was responsible for keeping track of all details relating to the loan agreements. To museum designers Laura M. Jennings and Sherman W. O'Hara go our thanks for the sensitivity and elegance they brought to the installation of the exhibitions. With its three-museum presentation, *American Traditions* created an even greater demand for the communication and organizational skills of Sue Ellen Paxson, exhibition coordinator and liaison with the IMA-Columbus Gallery. Deborah N. Lorenzen, curatorial secretary, also contributed to virtually every phase of preparing the exhibition and catalogue.

There is one person, not officially on the staff of any of the organizing institutions, who has earned the gratitude and friendship of his colleagues in all the participating museums. To Charles Hilburn, curator of the Warner Collection, Tuscaloosa, Alabama, go our warm thanks and appreciation for his collaboration, not just on the Warner Collection loans, but on numerous other aspects of the project.

Bret Waller
Director
Indianapolis Museum of Art

American Traditions has been a cooperative project involving several distinctly different institutions. As with any collaborative effort, it has presented many challenges and even greater rewards. Bringing to the Eiteljorg Museum some of the best works of Native American and Western artists has truly been a labor of love. Numerous staff members of the Eiteljorg Museum assisted in making this project a reality.

For the project's success we owe considerable gratitude to two individuals whose organizational skills and tenacity kept it on track and on schedule. Joyce Helvie, executive assistant, provided structure and organization during the crucial early stages of development. Beth James, registrar, performed a myriad of important tasks, including working closely with the lenders, processing mounds of complex paperwork, organizing shipping arrangements, managing photographic needs, and coordinating the efforts of the curatorial staff.

Marla K. Dankert, senior curator for art history, deserves particular recognition for her authorship of the majority of catalogue texts, her patient and exhaustive research, and her expertise in integrating and refining the entries for the Eiteljorg Museum portion of the catalogue.

The concerted efforts of Robert B. Tucker, curator of collections; Victoria J. Copenhaver, associate curator for ethnology; Jennifer L. Complo, associate curator of exhibitions; and Mike Leslie, former chief curator, have enriched both the catalogue and the exhibition. They merit special praise for their assistance in researching and writing text for the entries on Western and Native American art. Thanks are also extended to interns Erin McDonald and Heather Stewart for their research contributions.

American Traditions: Art from the Collections of Culver Alumni

With his customary artistic talents Larry Samuels, head of exh:bition and 351
graphic design, created a striking gallery setting for the display of the Western works of art.

Such a complex exhibition and catalogue cannot be completed without the help of people outside the museum. I especially wish to thank Jack Morris of Altermann & Morris Galleries, Houston, for his assistance in coordinating the photography of Bud Adams's collection.

Michael W. Duty
Executive Director
Eiteljorg Museum of American Indian and Western Art